CAT

Level B

Paper B2

Cost Accounting Systems

Textbook

5545/J02

British Library Cataloguing-in-Publication Data

A catalogue record for this book is available from the British Library.

Published by Foulks Lynch Ltd
Number 4
The Griffin Centre
Staines Road
Feltham
Middlesex
TW14 0HS

ISBN 0 7483 5554 5

© Foulks Lynch Ltd, 2002

Printed and bound in Great Britain

Acknowledgements

We are grateful to the Association of Chartered Certified Accountants, the Chartered Institute of Management Accountants and the Institute of Chartered Accountants in England and Wales for permission to reproduce past examination questions. The answers have been prepared by Foulks Lynch Ltd.

CONTENTS

PREFACE

This new edition of the CAT Textbook for Paper B2, Cost Accounting Systems, is up-to-date with the syllabus and has been prepared specifically for the CAT examination

DETAILED COVERAGE OF THE OFFICIAL TEACHING GUIDE

The Textbook covers the syllabus in great detail and, where appropriate, incorporates the syllabus revisions effective from June 2002. In addition, however, we have endeavoured to ensure that it provides very precise and thorough coverage of the Teaching Guide, which has been prepared and revised by the ACCA and is the primary source of guidance to this subject. Therefore, this Textbook is not limited to general syllabus coverage, but focuses precisely on the Official Teaching Guide, so that, where appropriate, the chapters follow closely the order of topics in it.

It is this very focused coverage of the Teaching Guide that sets Foulks Lynchs' textbooks apart.

LEADERS IN THE ART OF COMMUNICATION

Our books are not dense, complex, reference style textbooks, but rather books with specific features designed to help you, the student, learn more easily.

- **Pathfinder introduction.** Each chapter starts with the relevant part of the Teaching Guide that the chapter specifically addresses. You are then shown how the chapter coverage builds on the content of earlier chapters if appropriate, followed by the structure of the chapter and what key learning areas are covered.

- **Definitions.** The text clearly defines key words or concepts. The purpose of including these definitions is not that you should learn them - rote learning is not required and can be positively harmful. The definitions are included to focus your attention on the point being covered.

- **Brick-building approach.** Each topic is developed slowly and carefully, with clear explanations and illustrations to build your understanding of each technique.

- **Activities.** This text involves you in the learning process with a series of activities designed to arrest your attention and make you concentrate and respond.

- **Conclusions.** Where helpful, the text includes conclusions that summarise important points as you read through the chapter, rather than leaving the conclusion to the chapter end. The purpose of this is to summarise concisely the key material that has just been covered so that you can constantly monitor your understanding of the material as you read it.

- **Self test questions.** At the end of each chapter there is a series of self test questions. The purpose of these is to help you revise some of the key elements of the chapter. The answer to each is a paragraph reference, encouraging you to go back and re-read and revise that point.

- **End of chapter questions.** At the end of each chapter we include practice questions. These will give you a very good idea of the sort of thing the examiner will ask and will test your understanding of what has been covered.

Complementary Examination Kits

A revised edition, fully up to date as at 1 December 2002 and including the most recent exams, will be available in early 2003.

SYLLABUS

Content

(a)   Cost accounting; role and purpose, nature of internal reporting function, comparison with external financial reporting.

(b)   Cost and revenue classification; nature and purpose of classification, different costs for different purposes.

(c)   Cost behaviour; fixed, variable and semi-variable costs, charting cost behaviour.

(d)   Cost bookkeeping systems; links to financial accounts, recording cost transaction entries (ledger and journal), manufacturing and trading accounts.

(e)   Materials; types of, purchasing procedures and documentation, receipt, storing and issuing, standard and actual cost, procedure for establishing a standard, use of technical and purchasing information, methods of materials pricing (LIFO, FIFO, AVCO).

(f)   Stock control and stock valuation; max/min stock levels, re-ordering procedures, control procedures, relationship to material costing system, product and period costs.

(g)   Payment methods and procedures; labour cost computations, remuneration systems, establishing standard labour costs.

(h)   Expenses types; direct and indirect, depreciation charges, allocation procedure and control documentation, establishing standard expense costs.

(i)   Indirect costs; apportionment methods, calculation of absorption rates, treatment of capacity variations, reciprocal services, full absorption and marginal costing compared, activity based methods (outline only).

(j)   Costing systems for production processes; the operation of systems and the calculation of cost under job, batch, contract and process costing methods.

(k)   Service costing; application of costing methods to service based industries.

(l)   Standard costing: objectives, establishing standards, presentation of standard cost based management reports.

(m)   Variance calculation; materials variances (usage and price), labour variances (rate and utilisation), expense variances (usage and price), indirect cost variances (capacity, price and usage), sales variances (quantity, price and mix).

(n)   Data collection and analysis; for divisions, services, departments, functions, facilities, products and processes using time series analysis, index numbers, moving averages, seasonal trends, adjustment for changing price levels, performance indicators (for productivity, cost per unit, resource utilisation, profitability), ratios (gross profit margin, net profit margin, return on capital employed).

(o)   Data presentation; graphical and diagrammatic, tables.

Content

Session 10
Cost bookkeeping
Syllabus reference d

- describe and illustrate an interlocking (memorandum) cost accounting system using both absorption and marginal costing procedures
- record transactions in an interlocking cost accounting system

- describe the advantages and limitations of using interlocking and integrated cost accounting systems.

Session 11
Job, batch and contract costing
Syllabus reference j

- describe situations where the use of job, batch and contract costing are appropriate

- calculate product costs in a job and batch costing system using absorption and marginal costing

- describe the practical problems relating to cost control in a contract accounting system

- complete cost records and accounts in job, batch and contract costing systems.

Note: Contract costing questions will be confined to contracts completed within one year. Candidates will not be required to calculate the profit allowable on incomplete contracts

Session 12
Process costing 1
Syllabus reference j

- describe situations where the use of process costing is appropriate

- calculate the cost per unit of process outputs when there may or may not be losses in process as well as closing work in progress in the same process

- distinguish between by-products and joint products

- treatment of by-products and joint products at the point of separation

- evaluate and advise on the benefit (or otherwise) of further processing to enhance a product or products.

Content

Session 16
Material and labour variances
Syllabus reference m

- prepare and evaluate material (price and usage) and labour (rate and efficiency) variances

- explain potential causes of material and labour variances

- explain inter-relationships between material and labour variances.

Note: Idle time variances and material mix variances will not be examined

Session 17
Overhead variances
Syllabus reference m

- prepare and evaluate variable production overhead expenditure (sometimes called rate) and efficiency variances

- prepare and evaluate fixed production overhead expenditure and volume variances

- awareness of the sub-analysis of the fixed production overhead volume variance

- explain the significance of overhead variances for control purposes

- explain potential causes of overhead variances

- explain the inter-relationships between material, labour and overhead variances.

Session 18
Sales volume and price variances
Syllabus reference m

- prepare sales price and volume variances in marginal and absorption costing systems

- explain potential causes of sales variances

- explain the inter-relationship between sales and cost variances

Content

Session 19
Reconciliation
Syllabus reference l

- produce statements reconciling budgeted and actual profit in absorption and marginal costing systems

- produce reports explaining the key features of variances and making recommendations for management action.

Session 20
Data collection and interpretation
Syllabus reference n, o

- describe quantitative and qualitative data and information

- describe internal and external sources of data

- describe the relevance and limitations of data sources and collection techniques

- extract and interpret key information from tables and charts.

Session 21
Data presentation
Syllabus reference o

- present and evaluate the use of charts and graphs

- present data in diagrammatic form, simple bar charts and graphs.

Note: the following methods of data presentation are not examinable: histograms, frequency curves, ogives, Lorenz curves and pie charts.

Session 22
Index numbers
Syllabus reference n

- define the nature of an index number

- calculate simple price and quantity indices for a single product

- describe the nature of a weighted index and the limitations of their use

- use price indices for adjusting for changing price levels

- use indices for comparing performance between cost units and cost/profit centres.

Content

THE OFFICIAL CAT TEACHING GUIDE
(including format of the examination)

Aim of paper B2

To develop knowledge and understanding of the operation and maintenance of accounting systems for the capture, measurement and reporting of cost based information.

On completion of this module candidates should be able to:

•   Describe costs by classification and purpose

•   Undertake accounting transactions for material costs

•   Undertake accounting transactions for labour costs

•   Undertake accounting transactions for expenses

•   Calculate the costs of products and services using full cost absorption, marginal and activity based methods

•   Use tools and techniques for the analysis and presentation of data

•   Prepare and present standard cost reports.

Assessment methods and format of the paper

Questions based on demonstrating that the candidates have acquired the above skills with all questions to be answered.

	Number of marks
20 multi-choice questions	40
4 traditional questions	60

* The paper can also be taken as a 2 hour computer-based examination.

Prerequisite knowledge

Understanding of the accounting principles from Level A and a basic competence in numeracy

Development of Paper B2

Students need a sound understanding of the techniques covered in Paper B2 for the more advanced papers C2 and C5 (optional).

COMPUTER-BASED EXAMINATIONS

ACCA was the first professional body to introduce computer-based examinations (CBEs) in 1998, and now offers CBEs for CAT levels A and B. An online demonstration of the CBE format is available on the ACCA website www.accaglobal.com.

Apart from the benefits to students inherent in making an alternative form of assessment available – some assessment methods suit some students better than others – CBE has the added benefit of enabling assessment to be offered virtually 'on demand', rather than at fixed six-monthly intervals.

Students also benefit from the facility of CBE to provide instant on-screen feedback on their performance. That is, they know how well they performed as soon as they complete the CBE.

CBE IN PRACTICE

Students have two hours to complete each CBE. Questions are displayed on the screen and answers are entered using keyboard and mouse. At the end of the examination, the student is given a certificate showing the result achieved. The student's answers are stored on a disk that is then sent to ACCA by the examination centre where the CBE was taken. ACCA uses the disk to confirm the student's result when the student applies for recognition of the CBE result.

Each CBE at Levels A and B is worth 100 marks. In the case of Level A, there are 50 questions in the form of traditional multiple choice, where students select one answer from (typically) four on offer. The Level A CBEs are broadly similar to the Level A paper-based examinations.

In addition to the traditional multiple choice question type, the Level B CBEs also contain other types of questions, such as number entry questions, formula entry questions, and stem questions with multiple parts. There are also questions that carry several marks. Examples of the various question types can be seen on the sample CBEs provided by ACCA.

Students do not need to have registered with ACCA before sitting the Level A CBEs, but they must be registered and have their registration number and photocard with them when sitting the Level B CBEs.

APPROACHING REVISION FOR CBEs

It is important that students realise that the approach to learning the syllabus should be the same, irrespective of the nature of the assessment. The key difference in approach arises at the point when the material has been learnt. In fact, many tutors would argue that there really ought to be very little difference in the way a student prepares for CBEs compared to the way in which he or she prepares for paper-based examinations. However, this is really dependent upon how thoroughly the student has revised the material and upon how experienced the student is in being assessed under the form of assessment selected.

Thoroughness of revision

If a student knows the material well, understands it, and knows how to apply it, there really ought not to be a significant difference in performance in CBEs and paper-based examinations. If a student knows the material well enough to pass a paper-based examination, the same student should also be able to pass a CBE.

Experience of the form of assessment

No one does as well as they should in an examination that adopts a format they have never previously experienced. If an examination comprises of short answer questions of the type typically found in accounting examinations (e.g. short essay questions, preparation of statements like profit and loss accounts, calculations such as gross profit and net profit) students need to be sure they know how to do questions of this type before they sit the examination.

For example, students sitting an examination where they are going to be asked to write short descriptions and explanations of terms and definitions, should know that they need to read the questions carefully, identify precisely what is being asked, and provide an answer that is both detailed enough and focused enough to ensure that they gain a good mark.

The only way to learn how to do this is through experience of answering similar questions and then comparing answers to the ones provided. Where the examination is going to include questions on preparing financial statements or performing calculations, practising similar questions beforehand is, once more, the key to obtaining a good mark. As with essay questions, it is essential that questions are read carefully, that what is being asked is identified, and that the answer is both detailed enough and focused enough to ensure that a good mark is achieved.

For paper-based examinations, practice of similar questions is essential. Without practice, even though a student knows the material well, so much time may be wasted that it proves impossible for the student to write enough relevant material to pass the examination.

Computer-based examinations also require practice. No longer is there such a need to learn format and layout – students cannot, for example, be asked to produce a profit and loss account (though they could be asked to indicate in which order certain items appear in one). However, there is a need to know how to approach answering a maximum of 50 questions in two hours. Once more, the key is practice, and there is ideal practice available for the Level A CBEs – the Level A paper-based examinations! Students should practice the sample examination papers and past examination papers against a strict time limit to the point where a two-hour time limit is not a concern.

For Level B, there is also a similar source of practice material, albeit much less of it. However, for both Levels A and B there are many other sources of multiple choice questions that can be used, such as textbooks, examination kits, and computer-based instructional materials.

What is less available is the most relevant source of practice material – practice versions of CBEs that use the same software and work in exactly the same way as the CBEs. The ACCA sample material is the most obvious source. However, the most useful source will be the CBEs themselves. Sitting Paper A1 is excellent preparation for sitting Paper A2 and sitting Paper B1 is excellent preparation for sitting Papers B2 and B3. Unfortunately, the first experience of sitting a paper at Level A and the first experience of sitting a paper at Level B will always be harder than sitting the rest of the papers at these levels because students have never done so before.

HOW TO APPROACH EACH CBE

The following list of points to remember should help greatly in ensuring that students maximise their performance.

Before going to sit a CBE

- Do not attempt a CBE until you have completed all the study material relating to it.

- Do not skip any of the material in the syllabus – CBEs allow examiners to cover far more of the syllabus than they can cover in a paper-based examination.

- Objective test questions can ask for numerical answers but often they give a phrase and ask for the word it defines, or give a word and ask which of a list of phrases defines or explains the word. Others ask you to select what someone did from a list of things or mention something and ask which of the following people did that. Others ask what a particular rule or law means, and so on. All these questions require that students have *memorised* definitions, *remembered* names and what they were connected with, and *remembered* the names of rules and what they mean.

- Study the papers one at a time (you are not restricted by having only two opportunities a year to sit the CBEs).

- Do not start studying a paper until you have passed the previous one.

- Study each paper in the sequence in which it is presented (they are in a sequence for a reason!).

- Plan ahead. If you fail a CBE, retake it as quickly as possible, and as often as necessary until you pass it. Set aside sufficient free time after each CBE to enable you to revise for and then retake any CBE you fail.

Chapter 1

COST ACCOUNTING: ROLE AND PURPOSE

PATHFINDER INTRODUCTION

This chapter covers the following elements of the CAT Official Teaching Guide. At the end of this chapter you should have learned these teaching guide elements thoroughly.

Session 1
Cost accounting: role and purpose
Syllabus reference a

- Compare cost accounting with external financial reporting
- Describe the accounting technician's role in a cost accounting system
- Explain and illustrate the concept of cost units, cost centres and profit centres

Putting the chapter in context

Running a business means making decisions. Which products to produce, how and in what quantities, should components or services be made or purchased from outside suppliers, are costs as expected, what will happen to costs in the future as activity levels change? The cost accounting system produces and presents information so that such questions can be answered. This syllabus is all about how it does this. The first 15 chapters explain how costs are recorded and analysed to identify cost per product or cost for a part of the business. The final 5 chapters explain how information is collected and presented to management.

This first chapter provides background knowledge about a cost accounting system and how it differs from a financial accounting system.

1 COST ACCOUNTING AND FINANCIAL REPORTING

1.1 Financial reporting

The financial accounts record transactions between the business and its customers, suppliers, employees and owners, eg, shareholders. The managers of the business must account for the way in which funds entrusted to them have been used and, therefore, records of assets and liabilities are required as well as a statement of any increase in the total wealth of the business. This is done by presenting a balance sheet and a profit and loss account at least once a year.

1.2 Cost accounting

In performing their task, managers will need to know a great deal about the detailed workings of the business. This knowledge must embrace production methods and the cost of processes, products etc.

Cost accounting involves the application of a comprehensive set of principles, methods and techniques to the determination and appropriate analysis of costs to suit the various parts of the organisation structure within a business.

1.3 Management accounting

Management accounting is a wider concept involving professional knowledge and skill in the preparation and particularly the presentation of information to all levels of management in the organisation structure. The source of such information is the financial and cost accounts. The information is intended to assist management in its policy and decision-making, planning and control activities.

1.4   Financial accounts and management information

It may be helpful at this stage to examine a simple profit and loss account to consider the work of the management accountant:

XYZ Company
Trading and profit and loss account for period X

	£	£
Sales		200,000
Cost of sales:		
Materials consumed	80,000	
Wages	40,000	
Production expenses	15,000	
		135,000
Gross profit		65,000
Marketing expenses	15,000	
General administrative expenses	10,000	
Financing costs	4,000	
		29,000
Net profit		36,000

This statement may be adequate to provide outsiders with a superficial picture of the trading results of the whole business, but it is obvious that managers would need much more detail to answer questions such as:

(a)   What are the major products and which are most profitable?
(b)   How much have stocks of raw materials increased?
(c)   How does labour cost per unit compare with the last period?
(d)   Are personnel department expenses more than expected?

The cost accountant will aim to maintain a system which will provide the answers to these (and many other) questions on a regular and ad hoc basis. In addition, the cost accounts will contain detailed information concerning stocks of raw materials, work in progress and finished goods as a basis for the valuation necessary to prepare final accounts.

2   ACCOUNTING TECHNICIANS AND COST ACCOUNTING

2.1   Cost accounting system

The cost accounting system is the entire system of documentation, accounting records and personnel that provide periodic cost accounts and cost information for management as part of the management accounting system.

2.2   Accounting technician's role

As part of the cost accounting team the accounting technician is likely to be involved in the determination and analysis of any of the following typical examples of costs in a manufacturing organisation:

- cost of raw materials used in product manufacture;
- cost of stocks of remaining raw materials;
- valuation of work in progress and finished goods;
- cost of labour force used in the period;
- cost of expenses used in the period;
- analysis of overhead costs for each product type;
- determination of total cost of each product type.

All these costing methods and techniques will be covered in this study text.

3   COST UNITS, COST CENTRES AND PROFIT CENTRES

3.1   Classification and analysis of costs

Classification is a means of analysing costs into logical groups so that they may be summarised into meaningful information for management use or for use in the preparation of both internal and external financial reports.

Management will require information to make decisions on a variety of issues, each of which may require different cost summaries, for example costs may be required for a particular product, or for a department or for the organisation as a whole.

3.2   Cost units

Definition   A **cost unit** is a unit of product or service in relation to which costs are ascertained, ie, it is the cost of the output or product of the business.

For a paint manufacturer, the unit would be a litre (or a thousand litres) of paint, for an accountancy firm it would be an hour of work.

The ascertainment of the cost per cost unit is important for:

(a)   making decisions about pricing
(b)   measuring changes in costs as the activity level changes
(c)   stock valuation
(d)   planning future costs
(e)   controlling costs i.e.comparing actual to budgeted.

3.3   Cost centres

Definition   A **cost centre** is a production or service location, function, activity or item of equipment for which costs can be ascertained.

A **cost centre** is a 'part of a business' to which cost can be directly allocated or apportioned.

For a paint manufacturer cost centres would include:

- mixing department
- packaging department
- stores
- administration
- selling and marketing departments.

For an accountancy firm, the cost centres would include:

- audit
- taxation
- accountancy
- word processing
- administration
- canteen
- various geographical locations eg, the London office, the Cardiff office, the Plymouth office.

The ascertainment of the cost of each cost centre is important for:

(a)   relating costs to cost units;
(b)   planning future costs;
(c)   controlling costs, i.e.comparing either actual to budgeted, or actual to cost to 'buy in'.

3.4   Profit centres

Definition   A **profit centre** is a production or service location, function or activity for which costs and revenues can be ascertained.

Thus a profit centre is similar to a cost centre, but has identifiable revenues as well as costs.

For a paint manufacturer profit centres might be wholesale division and retail division. For an accountancy firm the profit centres might be the individual locations or the type of business undertaken (audit, consultancy, accountancy etc.).

The ascertainment of the excess of revenue over cost for each profit centre is important for:

(a)   planning future profits;
(b)   controlling costs and revenues, i.e.comparing actual to budget.

Conclusion   A cost unit is a unit of the product or service of the organisation for which costs can be ascertained.

A cost centre is a part of the organisation for which costs can be ascertained such as a production department.

A profit centre is a part of the organisation for which both costs and revenues, and therefore profit, can be ascertained.

A cost centre manager is cost accountable, whereas a profit centre manager is accountable for cost, revenues and profit.

4   CHAPTER SUMMARY

In this chapter we have looked at cost accounting systems and how they differ from financial accounting systems. We also considered cost units, cost centres and profit centres as well as the vital role of the accounting technician.

5   SELF TEST QUESTIONS

5.1   Who are financial accounts prepared for? (1.1)

5.2   Who are cost accounts prepared for? (1.2)

5.3   What is management accounting? (1.3)

5.4   Give examples of information needed to manage a business that is not revealed by the financial statement. (1.4)

5.5   Give examples of costs that a cost accountant might have to determine? (2.2)

5.6   What is a cost unit? (3.2)

5.7   Distinguish between a cost centre and profit centre (3.3/3.4)

5.8   Give examples of cost centres for a manufacturing organisation? (3.3)

6   PRACTICE QUESTION

6.1   Differences

(a)   Explain clearly the differences between financial accounting information and cost accounting information.

(b)   Discuss one problem associated with production of

     (i)   financial accounting information, and
     (ii)   cost accounting information.

7   ANSWER TO PRACTICE QUESTION

7.1   Differences

(a)   Financial accounting information is generally produced for external purposes, that is for a variety of user groups external to the company. The financial data is used to draw up a set of accounts in accordance with the Companies Acts and accounting standards, specifically to be able to publish a balance sheet, profit and loss account, cash flow statement and accompanying notes.

     Although the financial accounting information is produced primarily for the shareholders, it is also targeted at a range of other user groups who have a legitimate interest in the company, namely employees, customers, suppliers, analysts, the public, debenture holders, etc.

     Cost accounting information is generally produced for internal purposes, that is for management to help them with their decision-making responsibilities. It explains what costs have been incurred in which areas (products, branches, countries, etc.) and is often summarised into a monthly set of management accounts presented to senior managers.

     Financial accounting is generally based on the historical cost convention only. In cost accounting, however, other valuation bases may be relevant, eg, current costs, opportunity costs, etc.

(b)   (i)   Financial accounting information is expensive to produce, since there are very many accounting rules to be followed; specialist expertise may have to be used in particular areas, e.g. leasing or tax complications. Many of the complicated statutory requirements seem to have been drawn up with large companies only in mind, although there are few statutory exemptions for smaller companies. There is a serious question in whether the benefits for small companies in complying with statutory accounting requirements are greater than the costs in following them all.

         (ii)   If cost accounting information is to be relevant to management decision-making, it must be recent. It is acceptable for financial accounting statements to be published months after the balance sheet date, but such a delay would make cost accounting information useless to management. A usual delay might be for management accounts to be prepared seven days after the end of each month; that way the information is still recent enough for management to be able to make useful decisions based upon it.

Chapter 2

COST CLASSIFICATION AND COST BEHAVIOUR

PATHFINDER INTRODUCTION

This chapter covers the following elements of the CAT Official Teaching Guide. At the end of this chapter you should have learned these teaching guide elements thoroughly.

Session 2
Cost classification and cost behaviour
Syllabus reference b, c

- Describe the variety of cost classifications used for different purposes in a cost accounting system including by responsibility, direct and indirect, fixed, semi-variable and variable, production and non-production.
- Explain and illustrate the nature of fixed and variable costs, including the use of graphs.
- Explain and illustrate the nature of direct and indirect costs
- Use the high-low method to split semi-variable costs.

Putting the chapter in context

This chapter explains how a cost accountant classifies and analyses costs. It provides the necessary background information for the next 7 chapters which explain each type of cost in detail. It is important you understand what happens to costs as production levels change.

1 CLASSIFICATION OF COSTS

1.1 Introduction

Similar costs are grouped together to aid managerial decision making and to produce the analysis necessary for external financial reporting. The criteria used for the classification will depend on the reason for which the information is being collected. The classification considered for this syllabus are:

- key responsibility or function
- product and period costs
- controllable and uncontrollable costs
- by behaviour
- direct and indirect costs

1.2 Functional or responsibility analysis of costs

Costs can be analysed by function. This is often called analysis by responsibility, as usually a manager will be responsible for each of these functions and their associated costs. Some possible functions within an organisation are:

(a)   manufacturing
(b)   administration
(c)   selling
(d)   distribution
(e)   research.

Clearly the exact functions depend on the type of organisation. Classification of costs by function is used by management to:

(a)   produce the financial statements;

(b)   decide which costs should or should not be included in cost unit calculations for stock valuations;

(c)   cost control. Costs of the various functions can be compared with budget or with the cost to buy in rather than produce in-house.

1.3   Production costs and non-production (period) costs

Definition   The **production cost** is the cost of making the stock item and includes: direct labour, direct material, direct expenses and production overhead. Production costs are costs included in a stock valuation. The stock valuation is used in the calculation of cost of sales and gross profit.

Definition   **Non-production**, or **period** costs are those costs charged in the profit and loss account for the period and excluded from the stock valuation and calculation of gross profit.

Examples of non-production costs are selling, marketing, administration.

This distinction between production and non-production costs is necessary to calculate stock valuations and profit figures. Many period costs are fixed costs.

1.4   Controllable and uncontrollable costs

It is to be hoped that all costs that an organisation incurs are controllable by management at some level. However if the costs allocated to a particular department or cost centre are considered then it may be that only some of those are controllable by the cost centre manager whilst others are uncontrollable as far as that manager is concerned.

For example, the costs of the manufacturing function of an organisation may include a centrally allocated rental cost representing the factory's share of the total rent for the entire building. The factory manager will probably have no control over the total amount of rent paid by the organisation and may also have little or no control over the amount of floor space allocated to the factory. In this case he would view the rental cost as an uncontrollable cost.

1.5   Cost analysis by behaviour

Definition   **Analysis of costs by behaviour** entails determining how a cost will vary if the level of activity in the organisation varies.

For example, if the level of production increased, would a particular cost increase in line with the additional output or would it remain constant and show no increase at all?

Costs can be classified by behaviour into:

- fixed costs;
- variable costs;
- semi-variable costs; and
- stepped costs.

These will be considered in more detail later in this chapter.

1.6   Direct and indirect costs

Costs can also be classified as either direct costs or indirect costs. Direct costs are those which can be directly allocated or attributed to a cost centre or cost unit. Indirect costs are those which support the production function and are usually apportioned to cost centres.

These will be considered in more detail later in this chapter.

2   FIXED AND VARIABLE COSTS

2.1   Fixed costs

Definition   **Fixed costs** are costs which are not affected in total by changes in the level of activity.

Therefore fixed costs do not change in total as the activity level of the organisation changes. For example, the rent paid on a factory is £5,000 per month whether 2 units or 200 units of output are made. This is often illustrated diagrammatically:

Fixed costs in total

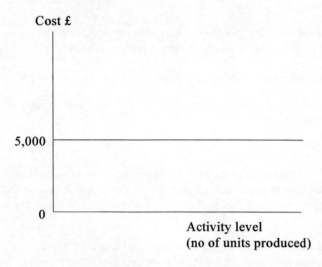

In reality, there must be a level of activity so large that more than one factory needs to be rented and rent is no longer a true fixed cost (but a stepped cost); but, as long as we are only considering a reasonable range of activity, management accountants can consider the rent to be a fixed cost.

If such costs are fixed in total, then the cost per unit must be falling as the activity level increases, illustrated below.

Fixed cost per unit

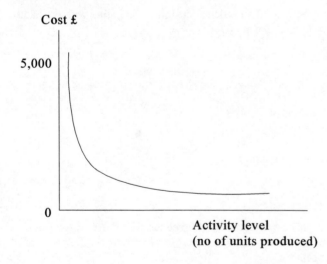

If 2 units are made the fixed cost per unit is $\dfrac{£5,000}{2}$ ie, £2,500 per unit. If 200 units are made the fixed cost per unit is $\dfrac{£5,000}{200}$ ie, £25 per unit.

2.2   Variable costs

Definition

Variable costs are costs which change in total in direct proportion to the level of activity. For example if the cost of materials for a unit of output is 2 kg at £2 per kg, this amounts to £4 per unit. So, total material cost is £4 if one is made, £8 if 2 are made and £800 if 200 are made. Again this is usually illustrated in a diagram.

Variable costs in total

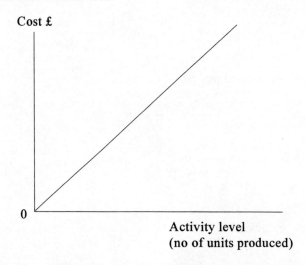

In reality as the activity level increases, there will be economies or diseconomies of scale. For example, as the organisation buys ever greater quantities of materials it can negotiate a bulk discount from its suppliers, and thus the cost per unit falls. But, as long as we are considering only a reasonable range of activity, management accountants can consider the cost of direct materials to be a variable cost. If such costs vary in direct proportion to the level of activity then the cost per unit is constant, illustrated below.

Variable cost per unit

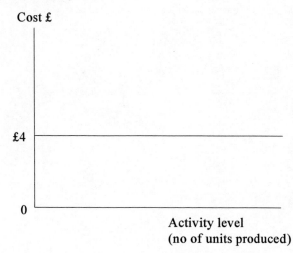

2.3   Semi-variable costs

Definition   **Semi-variable costs** are costs which have both a fixed element and a variable element. For example, telephone rental is fixed, but there is also a variable cost per call.

A semi-variable cost eg, telephone

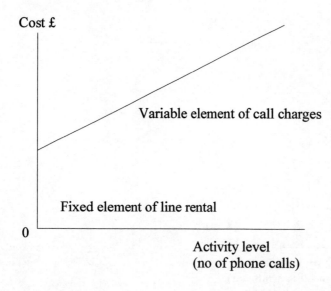

In order to predict how these costs will change in total as activity level changes, we need to be able to split them between their fixed and variable elements. We look at the 'high-low' method of splitting semi-variable cost in the next section.

2.4   Stepped costs

Definition   **Stepped costs** are costs that are constant for a range of activity levels, and then change, and are constant again for another range.

Stepped costs increase in steps as the activity level increases.

Stepped costs eg, supervisors' salaries

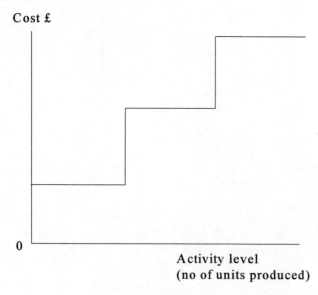

Conclusion   Managers will classify costs according to how they react to changes in the activity level when decisions concerning activity levels are being made. This is also known as analysis of costs by behaviour.

3   SPLITTING SEMI-VARIABLE COSTS

3.1   Introduction

The use of cost behaviour described in the previous sections rests on being able to predict costs associated with a given level of activity. Where a cost appears to be semi-variable, we can use historic data of total cost against activity levels to estimate the underlying fixed and variable elements. Of course, in some cases, such as telephone costs, these elements will be shown on the bill. But in other cases we have to use a technique, such as the **high-low method**, to split them out and alternative approaches must be used. In this process historical information provides valuable guidance, but it must be recognised that the environment is not static, and what was relevant in the past may not be relevant in the future.

Five main approaches may be identified:

(a)   the engineering approach;
(b)   the account analysis approach;
(c)   the high-low method;
(d)   scatter charts; and

3.2   Linearity

Whichever technique is used to split semi-variable costs, the assumption is made that the linear model of cost behaviour is valid, and therefore the relation between costs, y, and activity, x, is the form:

$y = a + bx$

where			
	y	=	total costs
	x	=	activity
	a	=	fixed costs
	b	=	unit variable (or marginal) cost

3.3   High low (or range) method

The most important approach for now is probably the high low method. This is based on an analysis of historic information on costs at different activity levels. To illustrate the method the data below will be used as an example.

3.4   Activity

Output inspection costs for the six months to 31 December 20X8 are as follows:

Month	Units produced	Cost
		£
July	340	2,260
August	300	2,160
September	380	2,320
October	420	2,400
November	400	2,300
December	360	2,266

You are required to split these costs.

3.5   Activity solution

The variable element of a cost item may be estimated by calculating the unit cost between high and low volumes during a period.

Six months to 31/12/X8		Units produced	Inspection costs
			£
Highest activity	(October)	420	2,400
Lowest activity	(August)	300	2,160
Range		120	240

The additional cost per unit between high and low is $\dfrac{£240}{120 \text{ units}} = £2$ per unit

which may be estimated as the variable content of inspection costs.

Fixed inspection costs are then deduced from using either of the two sets of data. For example, using the highest activity:

	£
Total cost	2400
Less: estimated variable element (420 x £2)	(840)
Fixed element	1560

You can check for yourself that the same result will be obtained from using the lowest activity data.

3.6   Limitations

The limitations of the high low method are:

(a)   Its reliance on historic data, assuming that (i) activity is the only factor affecting costs and (ii) historic costs reliably predict future costs.

(b)   The use of only two values, the highest and the lowest, means that the results may be distorted due to random variations in these values.

3.7   Activity

Use the high-low points method to calculate the fixed and variable elements of the following cost:

	Activity	£
January	400	1,050
February	600	1,700
March	550	1,600
April	800	2,100
May	750	2,000
June	900	2,300

3.8   Activity solution

	Activity level	£
High	900	2,300
Low	(400)	(1,050)
	500	1,250

Variable cost = £1,250/500 = £2.50/unit

Fixed cost = £1,050 − (400 × £2.50) = £50.

4   DIRECT AND INDIRECT COSTS, PRIME COST AND OVERHEADS

4.1   Direct costs and indirect costs

Definition   A direct cost is expenditure which can be directly identified with a specific cost unit or cost centre.

Direct costs normally include the material input into the product, direct materials, the cost of labour working on the product, direct labour and any expenses specifically attributable to the product, direct expenses.

Definition   Indirect costs (or overheads) are expenditure which cannot be directly identified with a specific cost unit or cost centre and must be 'shared out' on an equitable basis.

This sharing out of overheads is known is apportionment or allocation depending on the method used. This will be covered again in a later chapter.

Direct costs can be calculated per cost unit without knowing the activity level. For example, the direct labour cost per unit could be 2 hours at £10 per hour whether 10 units or 100 are made each week (ignoring any economies or diseconomies of scale). However indirect costs per cost unit can only be calculated once the activity level is known, for example the wages paid to the factory supervisor of £150 per week would be £15 per unit if 10 were made in the week but only £1.50 per unit if 100 were made.

4.2   Prime cost, production (total) cost

Definition   Prime cost is the total of direct material, direct labour and direct expenses of a unit of output.

The **production (total)** cost of a cost unit is the prime cost plus its share of indirect costs or overheads, consisting of indirect materials (e.g. lubricants for machines), indirect labour (e.g. supervisors) and indirect expenses (e.g. rent).

To calculate a cost unit's share of indirect costs, such costs may first be apportioned to cost centres and then related to the cost units passing through those cost centres (this is explained fully in a later chapter).

Conclusion

direct materials		
direct labour	} Prime cost	
direct expenses		
	+ = }	= Production cost
Indirect materials	} Overhead	

5   CHAPTER SUMMARY

In this chapter we looked at the cost classification and analysis – be sure you fully understand these areas before moving onto the following chapters.

6   SELF TEST QUESTIONS

6.1   Give examples of analysis of costs by responsibility of function (1.2)

6.2   What is the importance of the distinction between production costs and non-production costs? (1.3)

6.3   Why might a cost be classified as uncontrollable? (1.4)

6.4   What is a fixed cost? (2.1)

6.5   What is the effect upon fixed cost per unit if production levels increase? (2.1)

6.6   What is a variable cost? (2.2)

6.7   What is the effect upon total variable cost if production levels increase? (2.2)

6.8   What is the effect upon variable cost per unit if production levels increase? (2.2)

6.9   What is a semi-variable cost? (2.3)

6.10   What is the difference between direct costs and indirect costs? (4.1)

7   MULTIPLE CHOICE QUESTIONS

Each question is worth 2 marks.

7.1

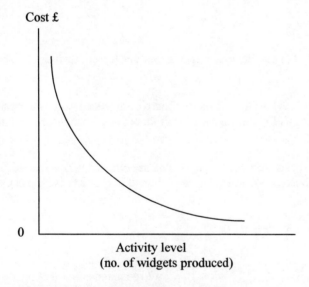

Which of the following descriptions best suits the graph?

A   Total fixed costs
B   Total variable costs
C   Variable cost per unit
D   Fixed cost per unit

7.2   Which of the following costs are fixed?

A   Telephone costs
B   Property rental cost
C   Direct material
D   Supervisory cost

8   PRACTICE QUESTIONS

8.1   Cost graphs

Prepare a report for the Managing Director of your company explaining how costs may be classified by their behaviour, with particular reference to the effects both on total and on unit costs.

Your report should

(a)   say why it is necessary to classify costs by their behaviour;
(b)   be illustrated by sketch graphs within the body of the report.

(15 marks)

8.2   Classify

A company manufactures and retails clothing.

Group the costs which are listed as (1) - (10) below into the following classifications (each cost is intended to belong to only one classification):
(i)   direct materials;
(ii)   direct labour;
(iii)   direct expenses;
(iv)   indirect production costs;
(v)   research and development costs;
(vi)   selling and distribution costs;
(vii)   administration costs; and
(viii)   finance costs.

(1)   lubricant for sewing machines;
(2)   floppy disks for general office computer;
(3)   wages of operatives in the cutting department;
(4)   telephone rental plus metered calls;
(5)   interest on bank overdraft;
(6)   performing Rights Society charge for music broadcast throughout the factory;
(7)   market research undertaken prior to a new product launch;
(8)   wages of security guards for factory;
(9)   carriage on purchases of basic raw material;
(10)   royalty payable on number of units of product XY produced.

(Total: 10 marks)

9   ANSWERS TO MULTIPLE CHOICE QUESTIONS

9.1   D

9.2   B

10   ANSWERS TO PRACTICE QUESTIONS

10.1   Cost graphs

REPORT

To: The managing director
From: The management accountant
Date: X-X-20XX
Subject: Cost behaviour

Costs can be classified in many different ways. They can be classified according to their function e.g. selling costs or production costs. They can be classified as to whether or not they directly relate to units or output or they can be classified according to their behaviour.

For budgetary control purposes it is important to classify costs according to their behaviour as it is necessary to be aware of which costs will vary with a change in production levels and which will remain substantially the same. Also if the organisation uses marginal costing techniques then it is necessary to be able to recognise the different types of cost behaviour in order to be able to value stocks accordingly.

Some costs are said to be fixed costs. These are costs that remain constant regardless of the level of activity of the organisation. These might include building rentals, business rates and basic salaries.

A sketch graph of a fixed cost would look like this.

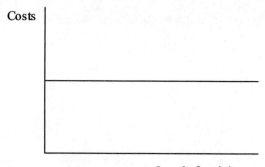

Variable costs in contrast are costs that will increase as the volume of activity of the organisation increases. Variable costs might include overtime payments, direct materials and sales commissions.

Variable costs could be illustrated as follows:

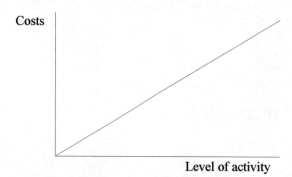

Step costs are costs that are fixed within a certain range of activity, known as the relevant range, but increase if the activity of the organisation strays outside that range. For example warehousing space may be fixed costs until production exceeds a certain amount at which point additional warehousing space must be rented.

Step costs could be represented graphically as follows:

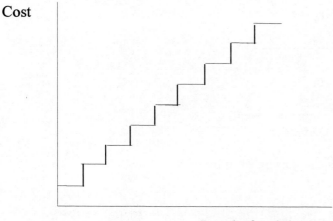

Cost

Level of activity

Finally some costs are known as semi-variable or semi-fixed costs. These are cost items that have both a fixed and a variable element, such as the telephone bill with its standing charge and charge for calls made.

The graph of a semi-variable cost would be as follows:

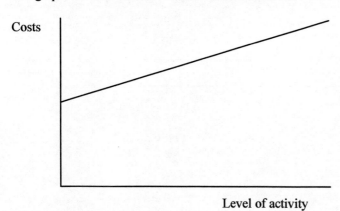

Costs

Level of activity

The graphs above have illustrated how the total cost of each type varies with output. If we consider the cost per unit then as volume increases the fixed costs will be absorbed by a greater number of units and therefore the cost will decrease per unit as illustrated below.

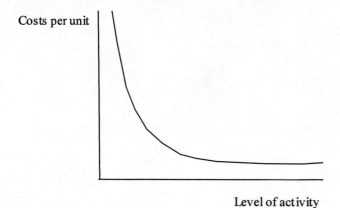

Costs per unit

Level of activity

However variable costs per unit will remain constant whatever the level of output as illustrated below.

Cost per unit

```
|
|
|
|
|_____
|
|
|_____
```

Level of activity

If you require any further information on this area please let me know.

10.2   Classify

Cost number	Classification number
1	iv
2	vii
3	ii
4	vii
5	viii
6	iv
7	vi
8	iv
9	i or iv
10	iii

Chapter 3

MATERIAL COSTS

PATHFINDER INTRODUCTION

This chapter covers the following elements of the CAT Official Teaching Guide. At the end of this chapter you should have learned these teaching guide elements thoroughly.

Session 3
Material costs
Syllabus reference e

- Identify the main types of material classification
- Describe the operation of an efficient store
- Describe the material control cycle and the documentation necessary to order, receive and issue materials from stock
- Explain the procedures required to ensure the correct coding, analysis and recording of direct and indirect material costs
- Explain and illustrate the methods for producing standard material costs
- Explain, illustrate and evaluate methods used to price raw material stock issued (LIFO, FIFO, AVCO, Standard cost)

Putting the chapter in context

The next 6 chapters explain how a cost accountant calculates what it costs to make a unit of a product, or to run part of the organisation ie, how much material, labour and expenses are incurred.

This chapter explains how material costs are controlled, recorded and calculated.

1 MATERIALS COST CLASSIFICATION

1.1 Introduction

The main classification for materials used by the cost accountant are direct materials and indirect materials.

1.2 Direct materials

Definition   **Direct materials** are the materials that can be directly attributed to a unit of production.

The direct materials are therefore the raw materials that are directly input into the products that an organisation makes. For example the many different components which make up a motor vehicle are direct materials.

1.3 Indirect materials

Definition   **Indirect materials** are other materials used in the production process that cannot be directly attributed to a unit of production.

An example of indirect materials might be the oil used for the lubrication of the production machinery. This is a material that is used in the production process but it cannot be directly attributed to each unit of finished product.

2   STORES DEPARTMENT

2.1   Function of the stores department

The stores or stock department is responsible for the receipt, storage, issue and recording of the raw materials used in the production process. To carry out these functions the stores department must be efficient.

2.2   Receipt of goods

When raw materials are received from suppliers they will normally be delivered to the stores department. The stores personnel must check that the goods delivered are the ones that have been ordered, in the correct quantity, of the correct quality and in good condition. (Details of this procedure are covered later in this chapter).

2.3   Storage of materials

Once the materials have been received they must be stored until required by the production departments.

Storage of materials must be appropriate to their type. For example food stuffs must be stored at the correct temperature and wood must be stored in dry conditions. Storage should also be laid out in the most efficient manner possible for retrieval of the materials. This will require an amount of careful planning to ensure that shelving, racks, pallets etc. are laid out in such a manner that the correct materials can be accessed easily either manually or by machinery.

2.4   Issue of materials

When the production departments require raw materials for production it is essential that the stores department can provide the correct quantity and quality of materials at the time they are required. In particular this will require careful attention to stock control policies to ensure that the most efficient levels of stocks of raw materials are kept. (This is covered in more detail in the following chapter).

2.5   Recording of receipts and issues

In many organisations the stores department is also responsible for the recording of the quantities of raw materials that are received from suppliers and issued to the production departments. This normally takes place on the bin cards or stores ledger cards (this is considered in more detail later in this chapter).

3   MATERIALS CONTROL CYCLE

3.1   Introduction

Materials can often form the largest single item of cost for a business so it is essential that the material purchased is the most suitable for the intended purpose.

3.2   Control of purchasing

When goods are purchased they must be ordered, received by the stores department, recorded, issued to the manufacturing department that requires them and eventually paid for. This process will entail a great deal of paper work and strict internal controls.

The key elements of this internal control are full documentation and appropriate authorisation of all transactions in and movements of materials and of all requisitions, orders, receipts and payments.

If control is to be maintained over the purchasing of materials it is necessary to ensure the following:

- only necessary items are purchased;

- orders are placed with the most appropriate supplier after considering price and delivery details;

- the goods that are actually received are the goods that were ordered and in the correct quantity;

- the price paid for the goods is that which was agreed when the order was placed.

To ensure that all of this takes place requires a lot of documentation and a system of checking and control.

3.3   Overview of procedures

It is useful to have an overview of the departments concerned in the purchasing process.

Production department - (the user of the goods)	Orders from the stores department using a goods requisition note
Stores department	Requisitions goods from the purchasing department using a purchase requisition
Purchasing department	Orders goods from external supplier using a purchase order
External supplier	Delivers goods to stores department, with a delivery note. A purchase invoice will be sent to the accounts dept
Stores department	Raises goods received note (GRN) and issues goods to production department.

There are many variations of the above system in practice, but it is a fairly typical system and does provide good control over the purchasing and issuing process.

3.4   Purchase requisition

It is important that an organisation controls the goods that are ordered from suppliers. Only goods that are genuinely necessary should be ordered. Therefore, before any order for goods is placed a purchase requisition must be completed.

It is important that each purchase requisition is authorised by the appropriate person. This will usually be the storekeeper or store manager.

When the purchase requisition has been completed it is sent to the purchasing department so that the purchase order is prepared.

3.5   Purchase order

Purchase orders will be placed with suppliers by the purchasing department. The choice of supplier will depend upon the price, delivery promise, quality of goods and past performance.

The person placing the order must first check that the purchase requisition has been authorised by the appropriate person in the organisation.

Once the supplier of the goods has been chosen the purchase price of the goods must be determined. This will either be from the price list of the supplier or from a special quotation of the price by that supplier. The price agreed will be entered on the purchase order together with details of the goods being ordered.

The purchase order must then be authorised by the appropriate person in the organisation before being despatched to the supplier.

A copy of the purchase order is sent to the goods receiving department or stores department as confirmation of expected delivery. The goods receiving department therefore know that goods are due and can alert appropriate management if they are not received. A copy is also sent to the accounts department to be matched to the supplier's invoice.

3.6   Delivery note

A delivery note is sent by the supplier with the goods being delivered. This must include full details of the goods being delivered. The delivery note is signed by the person receiving the goods as evidence that the goods arrived.

3.7   Goods received note (GRN)

When goods are received by the organisation they will usually be taken to a central goods receiving department or stores department rather than being delivered directly to the part of the organisation that will use the goods. This is because it enables the receipt of goods to be controlled.

The goods receiving department has copies of all purchase orders. It is important that the goods that arrive actually agree in all detail to those ordered before they are accepted.

When the goods are received the goods receiving department will firstly check what the goods are. They will be identified and counted and the supplier and purchase order to which they relate will be identified.

The details of the delivery note are checked to the actual goods and to the purchase order.

Finally when the goods received department are satisfied with all of the details of the delivery the details are recorded on a goods received note. (GRN)

The GRN is evidence that the goods that were ordered have been received and therefore should be, and can be, paid for. The GRN will, therefore, be sent to the accounts department to be matched with the supplier's invoice.

As evidence of the actual receipt of the goods the GRN is also used as the base document for entering receipts of materials in the stores records (see later in this chapter).

3.8   Purchase invoice

The purchase invoice for goods details the amount that the receiver of the goods must pay for them and the date that payment is due. The purchase invoice might be included when the goods themselves are delivered or might be sent after delivery.

The person responsible for payment must check that the details of the purchase invoice agree to the goods received note, the delivery note and the purchase order to ensure that what was ordered was received and what was received is what is being paid for and the price charged is that agreed.

Once it is certain that the purchase invoice agrees with the goods that were actually received then the invoice can be authorised for payment by the appropriate person in the organisation.

3.9   Bin cards

As was noted earlier in this section the goods received note is the source document used to write up the receipts of goods in the stores records.

Obviously the storekeeper must know at any time how much of any item he has in stock. This is done by use of a bin card.

Definition   A **bin card** is a simple record of receipts, issues and balances of stock in hand kept by storekeepers, recorded in quantities of materials stock.

The bin card is a duplication of the quantity information recorded in the stores ledger (see later in this chapter) but storekeepers frequently find that such a ready record is a very useful aid in carrying out their duties.

An example of a bin card for an item of stock is given below.

BIN CARD

Description ....Chipboard.......... Location ....Stores.......... Code ....D35..........

Maximum ....3,000m..........Minimum ....1,000m..........Reorder level ....1,400m..........Reorder quantity ....200m..........

Receipts			Issues			Current stock level	On order		
Date	GRN Ref	Quantity	Date	Issue Ref	Quantity		Date	Ref	Quantity
30/7/X9	8737	200m							

The bin card does not carry value columns.

3.10   Goods requisition note

Materials issued to production departments from the stores department are controlled by a goods requisition note (also referred to as a stores requisition). This document authorises the storekeeper to release the goods.

3.11   Goods returned note

When unused materials are returned from user departments to the stores the transaction will be recorded on a document similar to the materials requisition but usually printed in a different colour. This will be a goods returned note. It will be completed by the user department that is returning the goods and signed by the storekeeper as evidence that the goods were returned to stores.

These returns must also be recorded in the bin card and stock ledger account.

When the goods are returned the details on the goods returned note must be checked to the actual goods themselves.

Conclusion

Purchase requisition

- filled out by stores;
- authorised;
- sent to purchasing department.

Purchase order

- filled out by purchasing department;
- supplier chosen by purchasing department;
- price of goods calculated from price list;
- authorised;
- sent to supplier.

Delivery note

- provided by supplier with delivery;
- received together with goods by stores department;
- compared to actual goods;
- goods checked and counted;
- delivery note and goods checked to purchase order.

Goods received note

- a document provided by stores department for their own use;
- goods checked and counted;
- written up and signed;
- matched with delivery note and purchase order;
- sent to accounts to await purchase invoice.

Purchase invoice

- received from supplier;
- checked to purchase order, delivery note and goods received note authorised for payment;
- authorised for payment;
- payment made.

Stores requisition note

- filled out by user department;
- authorised;
- sent to stores.

Goods returned note

- filled out by returning department;
- actual goods checked against goods returned note by stores;
- signed as evidence of receipt.

Bin card

- maintained by stores department
- written up from goods received note, goods requisition note and goods returned note
- shows quantity of goods held in stores.

Stock ledger account

- maintained by accounts department
- written up from goods requisition note and goods returned note
- shows quantity of goods held in stores.

4   CODING, ANALYSIS AND RECORDING OF MATERIALS COSTS

4.1   Introduction

In earlier chapters of this text the classification of costs was discussed. It is possible to classify costs according to their function eg, materials or wages, their behaviour eg, fixed or variable or their relationship to the product being produced eg, direct or indirect.

Each type of classification is useful for different purposes. The main aim of the cost accountant however is to determine the cost of each of the organisation's products. To do this, expenses must be capable of being handled in some manageable form. In practice this is often done by classifying each expense according to its cost centre and type of expense. A cost code is then allocated to the expense to represent this classification.

4.2   Cost codes

Definition   A **code** is a system of symbols designed to be applied to a classified set of items, to give a brief accurate reference, facilitating entry to the records, collation and analysis.

A **cost code** is a code used in a costing system.

4.3   Cost centre code

The first step will be to determine the cost centre to which the cost relates and then to allocate the correct cost centre code.

For example if a cost relates to Machine Group 7 the cost centre code might be 07.

4.4   Generic or functional code

Once a cost has been allocated its correct cost centre code then it may also be useful to know the particular type of cost involved. Therefore possibly another two digits might be added to the cost centre code to represent the precise type of cost.

For example if an expense for Machine Group 7 is for oil then its code might be 07 (for its cost centre) followed by 23 to represent indirect materials.

4.5   Specific code

Finally it may be necessary for cost allocation, decision making or accounting purposes to allocate a code which specifically identifies the item of cost.

For example the oil for Machine Group 7 might eventually be coded as:

072304

This represents Machine Group 7 (07) indirect use (23) of oil (04).

4.6   Activity

The following is a short extract from an organisation's code structure.

Cost centres

	Code
Factory	
Machine shop A	301
Machine shop B	302
Boiler house	303
etc.	
Administration	
Accounts department	401
Secretary	402
Security officers	403
etc.	
Selling	
South area	501
North area	502
East area	503
etc.	

Type of expense

Materials	
Machine lubricants	001
Cleaning supplies	002
Stationery	003
Direct materials	004
	etc.
Wages	
Supervisor's salary	051
Cleaning wages	052
etc.	
Expenses	
Depreciation of machinery	071
Insurance of machinery	072
etc.	

How would the following items be likely to be coded?

(a)   A stores requisition for an issue of machine lubricant to machine shop B.
(b)   An issue of direct materials to machine shop A.

4.7   Activity solution

(a)   302001
(b)   301004

Conclusion   A cost code is designed to analyse and classify the costs of an organisation in the most appropriate manner for that organisation. Therefore there are no set methods of designing a cost code and the cost code of a particular organisation will be that which best suits the operations and costs of that business.

5   STANDARD MATERIALS COSTS

5.1   Standard costs

Standard costs are the budgeted or expected cost of producing a product. Standard costs are often produced on a cost unit basis. Therefore the standard or expected cost of producing one unit of a product is determined. This will consist of the standard or expected cost for each of the following items:

- direct materials cost;
- direct labour cost;
- direct expenses cost;
- indirect expenses or overhead cost.

5.2   Standard direct materials cost

The standard direct materials cost is the expected cost of the materials to be input into one unit of the product. This expected cost will consist of the expected quantity of the material to be used in each unit of the product and the expected price paid for that particular raw material.

5.3   Standard direct material quantity

The standard or expected quantity of each material used in a unit of a product will normally be determined from the original technical specification for the product. However as materials and technology change it is possible that this original quantity be updated to reflect such changes.

5.4   Standard direct material price

The standard or expected price paid for a raw material is either the current price of the material or the best estimate of the price to be paid taking into account specific and general changes in prices.

5.5   Activity

The technical specification for a product indicates that each unit is made up of 2kgs of raw material X and 5kgs of raw material Y. The most recent purchase price for material X is £12 per kg and for material Y £7 per kg.

What is the standard direct material cost for this product?

5.6   Activity solution

	£
Material X (2 kgs @ £12)	24
Material Y (5 kgs @ £7)	35
	59

Conclusion   The standard or expected direct materials cost for a cost unit is the quantity of material expected to be used in product multiplied by the price expected to be paid for that material.

◇ FOULKS*lynch*

6   STOCK LEDGER ACCOUNT

6.1   Introduction

As seen in an earlier paragraph, the bin card gives information to the storekeeper about the amount of each type of material that there is in the stores and on order.

The accounting function of the organisation will also require this information and this is given by the stock ledger account (also referred to as a stores ledger account or a stores record card). The stock ledger account is, therefore, very similar to the bin card although values are included as well as quantities. The difference is that the bin card is kept by the storekeeper and the stock ledger account by the accounts department.

Definition   A **stock ledger account** records the quantity and value of receipts, issues and the current balance of each item of stock.

6.2   Activity

A company has received 200 metres of chipboard quality D35 on 30 July 20X9. The purchase invoice shows that the price for the goods was £4.35 per metre.

The GRN number is 8737.

Enter this receipt in the chipboard D35 stock ledger account.

6.3   Activity solution

STOCK LEDGER ACCOUNT

Material: Chipboard .... Maximum Quantity: ....

Code: .... D35 .... Minimum Quantity: ....

	Receipts					Issues				Stock		
Date	GRN No	Quantity	Unit Price £	Amount £	Date	Stores Req. No.	Quantity	Unit Price £	Amount £	Quantity	Unit Price £	Amount £
30.7.X9	8737	200m	4.35	870.00								

The recording of issues and the subsequent stock balance will be dealt with in the following paragraph.

7   PRICING OF MATERIALS ISSUED

7.1   Introduction

If materials were purchased exactly as required for production, the cost of a particular consignment could be immediately attributed to a specific job or production order. Frequently, however, materials are purchased in large quantities at different prices and issued to production in smaller lots.

When materials are issued from stores to manufacturing or production departments, to determine the cost of these materials a number of questions must be answered. Which materials were these? What was their original cost?

It is often impossible to answer these questions exactly, and assumptions must be made in order to estimate the original cost of the materials.

7.2   Illustration

The stock ledger of a business shows that at 31 January there are 100 kg of material GHJ available. 60 kg are issued from stores to the factory on 1 February.

The 100 kg in stores were purchased as follows:

        4 January   50 kg @   £10 per kg
        20 January   50 kg @   £12 per kg

What is the cost of the 60kg issued to the factory?

Should they be priced at £10 per kg or £12 per kg or a mixture of the two? This depends entirely on the method of pricing issues that the organisation uses.

The obvious alternatives are:

(a)   price 50 kg at £10 and 10 kg at £12 = £620 which assumes that the first material to come in is the first to go out; or

(b)   price 50 kg at £12 and 10 kg at £10 = £700 which assumes that the last material to come in is the first to go out.

Other possibilities would be to use the weighted average cost (100 kg cost £1,100, so average cost is £11 per kg), or a standard cost.

7.3   Activity

Crescent Chemicals market agricultural products.

In November 1,000 tonnes of 'GX3' were purchased in three lots:

        3 November   400 tonnes at £60 per tonne
        11 November   300 tonnes at £70 per tonne
        21 November   300 tonnes at £80 per tonne

during the same period four materials requisitions were completed for 200 tonnes each, on 5, 14, 22 and 27 November.

To calculate the actual material cost of each requisition the cost accountant needs to identify from which consignment(s) each issued batch of 200 tonnes was drawn. Such precision is uneconomic as well as impractical, so a conventional method of pricing materials is adopted.

◈ **FOULKS**lynch

The possible methods that will be examined are:

(a)   first-in-first-out (FIFO) price
(b)   last-in-first-out (LIFO) price
(c)   weighted average price
(d)   standard cost

7.4   Activity solution

First-in-first-out (FIFO) price

Definition   The pricing of the issues are based on the earliest purchases of stock items.

Each issue is valued at the price paid for the material first taken into the stocks from which the issue could have been drawn.

The stock ledger account (in abbreviated form) would appear as below:

STORES LEDGER ACCOUNT

Material: ....'GX3'...................................   Maximum Quantity: ....

Code: ....   Minimum Quantity: ....

	Receipts				Issues					Stock		
Date	GRN No	Quantity	Unit price £	Amount £	Date	Stores Req. No.	Quantity	Unit price £	Amount	Quantity	Unit price £	Amount
3 Nov		400	60	24,000						400	60	24,000
					5 Nov		200	60	12,000	200	60	12,000
11 Nov		300	70	21,000						500		33,000
					14 Nov		200	60	12,000	300		21,000
21 Nov		300	80	24,000						600		45,000
					22 Nov		200	70	14,000	400		31,000
					27 Nov		200	75	15,000	200		16,000
30 Nov bal										200	80	16,000

5 November issue - priced at £60, which is the price of the purchase on 3 November.

14 November issue - priced at £60, which is the price of the remaining purchases from 3 November.

22 November issue - priced at £70, which is the purchase price for the 11 November purchase.

27 November issue - 100 tonnes of the 11 November purchase remain, priced at £70, and the final 100 tonnes comes from the 21 November purchase at £80.

7.5   Activity solution

Last-in-first-out (LIFO) price

Definition   The pricing of the issues are based on the most recent purchases of stock items.

Each issue is valued at the price paid for the material last taken into the stock from which the issue could have been drawn.

STORES LEDGER ACCOUNT

Material: .... 'GX3' ....   Maximum Quantity: ....

Code: ....   Minimum Quantity: ....

Receipts					Issues					Stock		
Date	GRN No	Quantity	Unit price £	Amount £	Date	Stores Req. No.	Quantity	Unit price £	Amount	Quantity	Unit price £	Amount
3 Nov		400	60	24,000						400	60	24,000
					5 Nov		200	60	12,000	200	60	12,000
11 Nov		300	70	21,000						500		33,000
					14 Nov		200	70	14,000	300		19,000
21 Nov		300	80	24,000						600		43,000
					22 Nov		200	80	16,000	400		27,000
					27 Nov		200	75	15,000	200	60	12,000
30 Nov bal										200	60	12,000

5 November issue - priced at £60, the price of the previous purchase on 3 November.

14 November issue - priced at £70, the price of the previous purchase on 11 November.

22 November issue - priced at £80, the price of the previous purchase on 21 November.

27 November issue - 100 tonnes can be priced at £80, the amount remaining of the 21 November purchase. The balance of 100 tonnes is priced at £70, the purchase on 11 November.

7.6   Solution - Weighted average price (AVCO)

Definition   The materials issued are priced at a weighted average price of the items in stock at that time.

Each time a consignment is received a weighted average price is calculated as:

$$\frac{\text{Stock value} + \text{Receipt value}}{\text{Quantity in stock} + \text{Quantity received}}$$

The price so calculated is used to value subsequent issues until the next consignment is received.

STORES LEDGER ACCOUNT

Material: .... 'GX3' ....   Maximum Quantity: ....

Code: ....   Minimum Quantity: ....

Receipts					Issues					Stock		
Date	GRN No	Quantity	Unit price £	Amount £	Date	Stores Req. No.	Quantity	Unit price £	Amount	Quantity	Unit price £	Amount
3 Nov		400	60	24,000						400	60	24,000
					5 Nov		200	60	12,000	200	60	12,000
11 Nov		300	70	21,000						500	66	33,000
					14 Nov		200	66	13,200	300	66	19,800
21 Nov		300	80	24,000						600	73	43,800
					22 Nov		200	73	14,600	400	73	29,200
					27 Nov		200	73	14,600	200	73	14,600
30 Nov bal										200	73	14,600

5 November issue - priced at £60, the price of the only purchase to date.

14 November issue - priced at weighted average price at that date.

$$\frac{£33,000}{500} = £66 \text{ per tonne}$$

22 and 27 November issues - priced at weighted average price on both those dates.

$$\frac{£43,800}{600} = £73 \text{ per tonne}$$

7.7   Standard cost price

Definition   Issues to production and stock balances are valued at their standard price. The standard price is an estimate of the price to be paid for the goods.

The method avoids the fluctuations in issue prices caused by timing and provides the considerable benefit of avoiding the need to maintain value records in the stores ledger.

Suppose a standard cost of £70 per unit.

			£
Cost of receipts:			
3 November	400 @ £60		24,000
11 November	300 @ £70		21,000
21 November	300 @ £80		24,000
			69,000
Value of issues	800 @ £70		56,000

Conclusion   Under the FIFO method of issue pricing the earliest price of materials held in stock is used. If prices are rising then this may be a fairly low price compared to the current price.

Under the LIFO method of issue pricing the most recent price of materials held in stock is used. If prices are rising then this will be a higher, more up to date, price than the FIFO price.

Under the weighted average method of issue pricing the price used will be somewhere between the extremes of the FIFO and LIFO prices.

Under the standard cost method the price used should be a reasonable estimate of the current price for the item.

8   VALUATION OF CLOSING STOCK

8.1   Introduction

Closing stock is the amount of physical stock that a business has at the end of an accounting period. This must be valued in some way. SSAP 9 states that stocks should be valued at the lower of cost or net realisable value.

The method of pricing of issues also affects the value that is put on this closing stock.

8.2   First-in-First-out method

Under the FIFO method of pricing materials issued, each issue is charged at the cost of the earliest purchase. Therefore, any stock remaining at the end of the period must be priced at the most recent purchase price.

8.3   Last-in-First-out method

Under the LIFO method of pricing issues, each issue is charged at the most recent purchase price. This means that any remaining stock must be valued at the earliest purchase prices.

8.4   Weighted average method

Under the AVCO method of pricing issues, all issues are priced at the weighted average price at the date of issue. Similarly the stock at the end of the period is priced at the weighted average at that date.

8.5   Standard cost method

Under the standard cost system all issues and all closing stocks are valued at the standard cost for the period.

8.6   Activity

Continuing with the information from the example of 'GX3':

Calculate the value of closing stock under the four pricing methods considered in the example.

8.7   Activity solution

First-in-first-out (FIFO)

Definition   Closing stock is valued at the price of the most recent purchase.

The closing stock of 200 tonnes is therefore valued at £80 per tonne, £16,000, the price of the 21 November purchase.

8.8   Activity solution

Last-in-first-out (LIFO)

Definition   The closing stock is valued at the earliest purchase price.

The closing stock of 200 tonnes is therefore valued at £60 per tonne, £12,000, the price of the earliest purchase on 3 November.

8.9   Solution - Weighted average (AVCO)

Definition   The closing stock is valued at the weighted average price at the end of the period.

The closing stock of 200 tonnes is valued at the weighted average price at the end of November, £73 per tonne, £14,600.

8.10   Solution - Standard cost

Definition   The closing stock is valued at the standard cost for the period.

The closing stock of 200 tonnes is valued at £70 per tonne, £14,000, which is the standard cost for the period.

Conclusion   Under the FIFO method the closing stock is valued at the most recent purchase price. If prices are rising then the stock will have a relatively high value.

Under the LIFO method the closing stock is valued at the earliest price of materials in stock. If prices are rising then the stock will have a lower value than using the FIFO method.

Under the weighted average method the closing stock is valued at the current weighted average price which will be somewhere between the two extremes of the FIFO and LIFO prices.

Under the standard cost method the closing stock is value at the standard price which should be a reasonable estimate of the current price of the item.

9   CHAPTER SUMMARY

In this chapter we started to look at material costs and techniques used to value materials. We also looked at the procedures concerned with ordering, receiving, storing and issuing materials. We shall continue to look at material costs in the next chapter.

10   SELF TEST QUESTIONS

10.1   What document is used to request the purchase of an item of raw materials? (3.4)

10.2   When goods are received into the stores department from a supplier which document is filled out by the stores department as evidence that the correct quantity of the correct material in the correct condition has been received? (3.7)

10.3   What information is recorded on a bin card? (3.9)

10.4   What is a goods requisition note? (3.10)

10.5   How is the standard raw material cost for a product be determined? (5.4)

10.6   Distinguish between a stock ledger account and a bin card. (6.1)

10.7   What is meant by a FIFO method of stock issue pricing? (7.4)

10.8   How does an AVCO method of stock issue pricing work? (7.6)

10.9   How is closing stock valued under the LIFO method of stock issue pricing? (8.3)

11   MULTIPLE CHOICE QUESTIONS

Each question is worth 2 marks.

11.1   Aberdeen Ltd holds stocks of ratchets which it uses in production. Over the last month receipts and issues were as follows:

	Receipts	Issues	
Opening balance	200 @ £5		
5th	300 @ £4.50	7th	400
12th	100 @ £6		
22nd	400 @ £5.50	23rd	400
29th	200 @ £7	30th	200

If a FIFO stock valuation method were used, the value of stocks at the month end would be

A   £1,000   B   £1,100   C   £1,200   D   £1,400

11.2   M Ltd uses a raw material, T. Movements in T for the month of August are set out below.

	Goods received			Issues to production	
Date	kgs	Price £/kg		Date	kgs
12 August	4,000	5.00		15 August	3,900
19 August	1,200	6.00		21 August	1,100
24 August	2,800	7.50			

There were no stocks of T held at 1 August.

What would be the closing stock valuation at 31 August 20X2 on a weighted average cost basis, to the nearest £?

A	£18,075	B	£18,500	C	£22,185	D	£22,046

11.3   Waugh Ltd has closing stock at 31 July of 400 units valued, using LIFO, at £10,000. Stock movements in July were:

5 July	300 units bought for £25/unit
10 July	500 units issued
15 July	400 units bought for £22/unit
20 July	200 units issued

What was the value of the company's opening stock?

A   £11,200
B   £10,000
C   £9,400
D   Cannot be found

11.4   A firm has a high level of stock turnover and uses the FIFO (first in first out) issue pricing system. In a period of rising purchase prices, the closing stock valuation is:

A   close to current purchase prices
B   based on the prices of the first items received
C   much lower than current purchase prices
D   the average of all goods purchased in the period

12   PRACTICE QUESTIONS

12.1   Stock records

A and B are in business, buying and selling goods for resale. Neither of them are accountants but A has read a book on stock control whereas B has purchased a software package for daily stock records. During September 20X9 the following transactions occurred:

September	1	Balance brought forward	NIL
September	3	Bought 200 units @ £1.00 each	
September	7	Sold 180 units	
September	8	Bought 240 units @ £1.50 each	
September	14	Sold 170 units	
September	15	Bought 230 units @ £2.00 each	
September	21	Sold 150 units	

A prepares the stores ledger card using the LIFO method and B uses the same data to test the software package which uses the weighted average method of pricing.

You are required:

(a)   to show the stock ledger cards as they would appear for **each** method (calculations should be made to two decimal places of £1.00);   **(10 marks)**

(b)   to comment on the effect on profits of using **each** method of valuing stock.   **(5 marks)**

(Total: 15 marks)

12.2   Source and purpose

The following tasks relate to a material control system. Explain the source and purpose of the under mentioned documents

(i)   Goods received note
(ii)   Materials transfer note
(iii)   Purchase requisition
(iv)   Materials returned note

13   ANSWERS TO MULTIPLE CHOICE QUESTIONS

13.1 $200 \times 7 = £1,400$

Therefore **D.**

13.2

			£/Kg	
Received	4,000	@	5	20,000
Issued	3,900	@	5	19,500
	100			500
Received	1,200	@	6	7,200
	1,300	@	5.923	7,700
Issued	1,100			6,515
	200			1,185
Received	2,800	@	7.50	21,000
	3,000			22,185

Therefore **C.**

13.3   Closing stock = 200 of the units bought on 15th July (at £22) and 200 units of the opening stock (at £25).
Value $(200 \times £22) + (200 \times £25) = £9,400$

13.4   **A**

FIFO means that the value of closing stock reflects the most recent prices paid.

14   ANSWERS TO PRACTICE QUESTIONS

14.1   Stock records

(a)   **LIFO**

Date	Receipts	Issues	Balance	
			No.	*£*
1 September 20X9				Nil
3 September 20X9	200 × £1.00		200	200.00
7 September 20X9		180 × £1.00	20	20.00
8 September 20X9	240 × £1.50		260	380.00
14 September 20X9		170 × £1.50	90	125.00
15 September 20X9	230 × £2.00		320	585.00
21 September 20X9		150 × £2.00	170	285.00

Weighted average

Date	Receipts	Issues	Balance		Average cost
			No.	*£*	*£*
1 September 20X9				Nil	
3 September 20X9	200 × £1.00		200	200.00	
7 September 20X9		180 × £1.00	20	20.00	
8 September 20X9	240 × £1.50		260	380.00	1.462
14 September 20X9		170 × £1.46	90	131.58	1.462
15 September 20X9	230 × £2.00		320	591.58	1.849
21 September 20X9		150 × £1.85	170	314.33	1.849

(b)   In times of rising prices the use of the LIFO method will give lower profits than the use of the weighted average method. This is because the latest prices will be charged to cost units and thus to cost of sales, whereas with the weighted average method the price changes are smoothed out over a period of time.

14.2   Source and purpose

(i)   **Goods received note**

This is a document recording details which relate to the receipt of materials into stores from an external supplier. The document will be generated by the goods inwards department as soon as materials are received, the purpose being to establish proof of receipt which is then used to verify that the related purchase order has been properly executed. The goods received note may also be compared with details shown on the supplier's invoice, so that authorisation for payment may be given.

(ii)   **Materials transfer note**

Whenever material is transferred out of stores, or between cost centres, details of the stock movement should be recorded on a materials transfer note. The document should be raised by the issuing department and signed by the receiving department. The purpose of the document is to ensure that a proper charge is made to each cost centre for the use of materials.

(iii)   **Purchase requisition**

This is a formal authorisation document giving instructions to the buying department to make a specified purchase of goods. An authorised official such as the stores controller should issue the requisition and this should be countersigned by the purchasing officer. When duly signed and authorised the document provides a proper instruction to the buying department to place an order with a materials supplier.

(iv)   **Materials returned note**

This document records the return of unused or unwanted material back into the stores, and would be completed by a cost centre which is returning materials. This would enable a credit to be made against the cost centre, cancelling in whole or in part the earlier charge relating to the purchase requisition raised at the time when materials were first issued.

Chapter 4

MATERIAL STOCK CONTROL

PATHFINDER INTRODUCTION

This chapter covers the following elements of the CAT Official Teaching Guide. At the end of this chapter you should have learned these teaching guide elements thoroughly.

Session 4
Material stock control
Syllabus reference f

- Explain and illustrate the costs of stock holding
- Describe the procedures required to monitor stock and minimise stock losses
- Explain, illustrate and evaluate stock control levels to minimise stockholding costs, including reorder levels, reorder quantity
- Recognise the significance of economic order quantity and be able to apply the EOQ formula.

Putting the chapter in context

This chapter, like the last, is concerned with material costs. It explains stock control, and how the management accountant calculates how much stock should be held and how much should be ordered.

1 MONITORING OF STOCK AND STOCK LOSSES

1.1 Stock taking

The procedures for the recording of stocks were considered in the previous chapter.

The bin card for each line of stock will provide information to the stock keeper about the amount of that item that is meant to be in stock at any one time.

The only way to check whether this is the amount actually in stock is to count the number of items of that particular type of stock. This is known as a physical stock take.

Definition   A **stock take** is the counting and recording of the physical quantities of each item of stock.

Stock takes will take place at varying intervals usually on a rotational basis so that not all stock items have to be counted at the same time.

1.2 Monitoring of stock levels

When the stock items are actually counted the quantity counted is compared with the balance shown on the bin card. If all receipts and issues of stocks have been correctly accounted for on the bin card the actual quantity of stock should agree with the balance shown on the bin card.

If there is a difference between the amount of the item shown on the bin card and the actual amount held in stores then the reasons for this difference must be investigated.

1.3   Possible reasons for differences

There are a number of possible explanations for differences between the bin card balance and the actual stock level:

- errors may have been made in entering items on the bin card or calculating the balance shown;
- goods received or issues made may have been omitted from the bin card;
- items of stock may have been stored in the wrong position in stores and were, therefore, not counted;
- items of stock may have been stolen.

1.4   Action to be taken

Once the reasons for the difference have been identified then the appropriate action must be taken.

- if errors have been made when writing up the bin card or items omitted then the bin card must be corrected;
- if items of stock were stored in the wrong place then they must be moved and a new total of actual stock calculated;
- if items have been stolen then security arrangements must be reviewed and the cost of the items stolen accounted for as an expense of the business.

2   COSTS OF STOCK HOLDING

2.1   Introduction

Most organisations need to hold some stocks of materials used in the organisation.

The problem that the organisation faces is how much stock of each type of material is required.

Organisations will recognise that apart from the cost of the stock item itself (ie, the purchase price) there are costs of holding stock and costs of ordering stock. The organisations will usually seek to minimise the total of all these costs.

2.2   Holding costs

Definition   **Holding costs** are the costs incurred in holding and storing stock.

The costs of holding stock are such costs as insurance, heating and lighting the warehouse, warehouse person's wages etc. These costs can be attributed to individual units so that it is possible to quote these costs as an average cost per unit stored.

2.3   Activity

A company holds on average 5,000 electric toasters in stock at any time throughout the year. Each toaster costs the company £20 to buy, and costs the company £0.50 pa to store - the cost being the apportioned cost of insurance, heating etc. In addition, the company borrows money at 10% pa.

What is the total annual holding cost and the average holding cost per unit?

2.4   Activity solution

			£
Cost of storage	$5,000 \times £0.50$	=	2,500
Interest costs	$5,000 \times £20 \times 10\%$	=	10,000

(Note that purchase price itself is not a holding cost)

Total holding cost per annum		12,500

Average holding cost per unit	=	$\dfrac{£12,500}{5,000 \text{ units}}$
	=	£2.50 per unit

2.5   Ordering costs

Definition   **Ordering costs** are costs involved in ordering, receiving and paying for stock.

Placing an order for stock costs money. Filling in the paperwork, receiving the goods into stock, checking quantities, paying invoices etc., all cost a certain amount of money per order.

These costs may be expressed as a total cost per order placed.

2.6   Minimising the total costs of holding and ordering stock

If a company sells 50,000 items a year, it has a choice of ordering a large number at a time placing only a few orders a year, or ordering a small amount at a time but placing many orders a year. Clearly there is a trade-off between annual holding costs and annual order costs.

Conclusion   Apart from purchase price the two main costs of holding stock are the holding costs and the ordering costs. As the number of orders per year increases, annual holding costs fall but annual order costs rise. We return to the problem of minimising these costs later, where we shall consider the theoretical Economic Order Quantity (EOQ) model.

2.7   Stock Levels

In addition to the consideration of the costs associated with the frequency and size of orders to meet expected demand levels businesses must also take into account the general levels of stock to be held throughout the year. Enough stock must be held to meet the requirements of sales or production departments whilst minimising the amount of working capital tied up in the stock.

If insufficient stock levels are maintained then the business runs the risk of not being able to provide customers with finished goods, or manufacturing departments with the materials they require, when they require them.

On the other hand if too high levels of stock are held then this will be expensive to the business in terms of the amounts of money tied up in the stock.

The business must develop a system of stock control to ensure, where possible, demand can be met whilst still keeping costs down.

2.8   Stock control systems

There are various approaches that an organisation can take to stock control. The stock levels can either be reviewed at set intervals of time and a suitable order then placed or alternatively each time the stock holding falls to a particular level then an order will be placed for new stocks.

These two approaches to stock control are known as a periodic review system and a re-order level system respectively. The detailed operation of these systems is considered in the following paragraphs.

3   PERIODIC REVIEW SYSTEM

3.1   Introduction

Definition   In a **periodic review** system of stock control the stock levels are reviewed at fixed time intervals eg, every four weeks.

At each review the amount of stock ordered is that required to bring the stock levels up to a predetermined level.

3.2   Activity

A company reviews the level of one line of stock every four weeks. An order is placed at each review and the new stock is received almost immediately. The company policy is that the amount ordered is the number of units required to bring the total stock holding to 40 units.

At the last review there were four units of the item in stock. How many units would the replacement order be for?

3.3   Activity solution

40 − 4 units = 36 units

3.4   Stock-outs

Definition   A **stock-out** is a situation where goods are required from stock but there are not enough of those items in stock at the time.

A periodic review system runs the risk of stock-out if more than the expected number of units of the item are required in the period between reviews.

In the previous activity at each review the stock level is brought up almost immediately to 40 units. Therefore, if only 38 units are required in the next four week period there will be enough stock to satisfy that demand.

However, if 45 units of that item are in fact required during the next four weeks then the stores will not be able to provide five of those units as they are not in stock.

There will therefore be a stockout of five units.

3.5   Buffer stock

The risk of stock-outs can be reduced by the holding of buffer stock.

Definition   **Buffer stock** is an additional amount of stock held with the intention of reducing or eliminating the risk of stock-outs.

Continuing the situation being used, suppose that the expected usage of that particular item in a week is 10 units, which will total 40 units in the four week review period. The stock level is brought up to 40 units every four weeks when the replacement order is made. Then, if the actual usage is the same as that expected, 40 units, the amount of stock remaining at the end of the four week period will be zero.

However, if the actual usage is more than 10 units per week there will be stock-outs.

This could be prevented by holding say five units of buffer stock. In this case each time an order is placed it will be for an amount which will bring the total number of units of that item up to 45 units.

3.6   Activity

If the buffer stock in the earlier activity is to be five units and the number of units of the item remaining at the last review was seven how many units would have been ordered?

3.7   Activity solution

45 – 7 units = 38 units

Conclusion   A periodic review system of stock control requires the stock level to be reviewed at fixed time intervals. An order is then placed for enough items to return the stock level to a pre-determined amount. If no buffer stock is kept then the organisation runs the risk of stock outs under such a system.

3.8   Re-order period

The re-order period or review period will depend upon the expected usage of the item, the maximum amount of the item that the organisation wishes to hold and any buffer stock that is required.

3.9   Activity

A business expects to use 100 units of an item each week and does not hold any buffer stock. The maximum number of units of this item that the business wishes to keep in stock is 500. What is the periodic review period for this item of stock?

What would be the review period if the business wishes to hold a buffer stock of 100 units?

3.10   Activity solution

If the stock level is brought up to 500 units when each order is placed and no buffer stock is to be kept then the stock level will be reviewed when it is expected to be zero. This will take place every five weeks (500 units/100 units).

Alternatively, the business may keep a buffer stock of 100 units. In this case the review would take place when it was expected that there would be 100 units left in stock, the buffer stock. This would take place after 400 units (500 units – 100 units) had been expected to be used. If 100 units are expected to be used each week then the stock level will be reviewed every 4 weeks (400 units/100 units).

3.11   Re-order quantity

Definition   The re-order quantity is the number of units of stock ordered.

In all of the examples used so far it has been assumed that when an order is placed the items of stock are received virtually immediately. Therefore, the re-order quantity is simply the amount necessary to take the stock levels from their level at the review date to the required level for the business.

It is often based on the EOQ, economic order quantity.

3.12   Lead time

In practice, there will be a delay between the placing of the order and the receipt of the goods. This is known as the lead time.

Definition   The lead time is the interval of time between the placing of a replenishment order and the receipt of the goods.

The expected lead time and the expected usage of materials in that period must also therefore be considered when determining the re-order quantity.

3.13   Activity

A car manufacturing company reviews its stock levels every four weeks and then places an order for enough tyres to bring the stock level up to 1,000 tyres. The company expects to use 200 tyres each week.

If the stock level at the last review was 250 tyres what would be the re-order quantity:

(a)   If the new order of tyres is expected to be received immediately after the order is placed?
(b)   If the new order of tyres is expected to take one week to arrive after the order is placed?

3.14   Activity solution

(a)   Re-order quantity

1,000 units – 250 units = 750 units

(b)   In this example not only are 750 tyres required to take the current stock level to 1,000 tyres but during the week that it will take to receive the tyres a further 200 are expected to be used.

If the stock level is to be 1,000 when the new order is received then the re-order quantity must be

750 units + 200 units = 950 units

Conclusion   The re-order quantity in a periodic review stock control system must take into account the expected usage of stock during the expected lead time.

4   FIXED RE-ORDER LEVEL SYSTEM

4.1   Introduction

In a periodic review system of stock control the orders were placed at particular fixed time intervals. Under a fixed re-order level system orders are placed whenever stocks fall to a particular level (ie, at irregular intervals).

The fixed re-order level system may be operated using either:

(a)   the visual control method (or two-bin system); or
(b)   calculated control levels.

4.2   Two-bin systems

Under this system the existence of two bins is assumed, say A and B. Stock is taken from A until A is empty. A new order is then made to replenish bin A. During the lead time stock is used from B. The standard stock for B is the expected demand in the lead time, plus any buffer stock. When the new order arrives, B is filled up to its standard stock and the rest placed in A. Stock is then drawn as required from A, and the process repeated.

The same sort of approach is adopted by some firms for a single bin. In such cases a red line is painted round the inside of the bin, such that when sufficient stock is removed to expose the red line, this indicates the need to re-order. The stock in the bin up to the red line therefore represents bin B, that above the red line bin A.

4.3   Re-order level

Definition   The **re-order level** is the level of stockholding at which a replenishment order is placed.

If it is assumed that no stock-outs are allowed then the re-order level (ROL) is

Maximum demand in the maximum lead time.

If the maximum lead times likely to occur and the maximum rate of stock usage can be predicted then it is possible to calculate a ROL which will avoid stock-outs giving a minimum stock level of zero.

4.4   Activity

A company operates a fixed re-order level of stock control and wishes to set the re-order level for a new material, JK6. It is company policy to ensure that they do not run out of any required materials.

It is estimated that 100 tonnes of JK6 will be the maximum amount used in a day in manufacturing and that the maximum delay between placing an order and receiving the materials will be three working days.

What is the re-order level for JK6?

4.5   Activity solution

Re-order level = 100 tonnes × 3 days = 300 tonnes

Conclusion   If no stockouts are to be allowed then the re-order level is set at the maximum expected usage in the maximum expected lead time.

4.6   Re-order quantity

Definition   The **re-order quantity** is the quantity of stock ordered each time the re-order level is reached.

Under the periodic review system the level of stock when the order was placed would be likely to be different at each review date and therefore so would the re-order quantity.

However, under a re-order level system orders are always placed when stock is at the same level therefore the re-order quantity will be the same amount each time an order is placed.

4.7   Activity

An item of stock in a business is always re-ordered when stock levels fall to 30 units. The amount of stock that the company wishes to hold immediately after the delivery is 250 units. If the lead time is estimated to be one week and the usage of these items is 25 units each week what is the re-order quantity?

4.8   Activity solution

	Units
Maximum stock	250
Current stock	30
	220
Usage in lead time	25
Re-order quantity	245

4.9   Other control levels for stock management

In addition to the basic re-order level, businesses may define other stock quantity levels at which action should be taken – the minimum and maximum stock levels. These are explained in the following paragraphs.

4.10   The minimum stock level

Definition   Minimum stock level is the level below which stocks would not normally be expected to fall without the fact being noted and possible action considered e.g. emergency replenishment. It may be calculated as:

Re-order level – (Average usage per day x Average lead time (days))

Minimum stock level basically corresponds with buffer stock.

4.11   Activity

Calculate the minimum stock level from the following data:

Re-order level	3,600 units
Average lead time	5 days
Minimum usage	300 units per day
Maximum usage	500 units per day

4.12   Activity solution

On an average basis:

$$3,600 - = \left(\frac{500+300}{2} \text{ x } 5 \right) = 1,600 \text{ units}$$

4.13   Maximum stock level

Definition   The maximum stock level is the level above which stock should not normally rise. It is given by:

Re-order level + Re-order quantity – (Minimum usage per day x Minimum lead time (days))

Maximum level of stock would represent the peak holding ie, buffer stocks plus the re-order quantity.

4.14 Activity

Z Limited places an order of 500 units, to replenish its stock of a particular component whenever the stock balance is reduced to 300 units. The order takes at least four days to be delivered and Z Limited uses at least 50 components each day. What is the maximum stock level?

4.15 Activity solution

The maximum level:

$300 + 500 - (50 \times 4) = 600$ units.

5 ECONOMIC ORDER QUANTITY (EOQ)

5.1 Costs of stock holding

Remember the costs associated with stock are:

- the holding costs; and
- the ordering costs.

Organisations will wish to minimise the overall annual total of these two individual costs.

Here we consider a theoretical approach to this problem, under certain (quite restrictive) assumptions about stock level movements and associated cost behaviour.

5.2 Economic order quantity (EOQ)

Definition   The **economic order quantity (EOQ)** is the order quantity which minimises the annual sum of stock ordering costs and holding costs.

If the EOQ can be determined it is the order quantity for an organisation that minimises its overall stock inventory costs.

To be able to determine the economic order quantity we must assume that lead time is zero (or known and constant) and that demand is constant. If such assumptions are made, stock will be received just as the last one is sold.

The stock level situation can be represented graphically as follows:

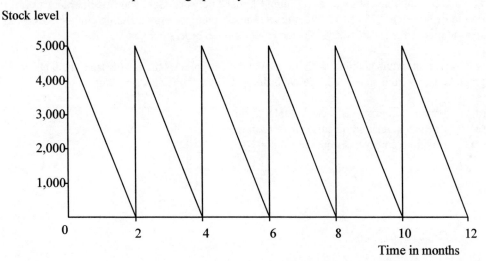

Here the company orders 5,000 units at a time which are used from stock at a constant rate.

5.3   Activity

Watallington is a retailer or beer barrels, selling 30,000 each year. The basic barrels are bought for £12 each and sold, after polishing etc. for £25 each. Supplies can be obtained immediately. Order costs are £200 per order and the annual cost of holding one barrel in stock is 10% of its cost ie, £1.20.

Calculate the total annual inventory cost of 4, 6, 8, 10 and 15 orders per year and determine the economic order quantity.

5.4   Activity solution

If the company makes 6 orders each year, it will order 30,000 ÷ 6 ie, 5,000 each time.

Every two months stock is zero and a new order is made. The average stock level is $\dfrac{5,000}{2}$ barrels, ie, half the replenishment level.

The current total annual inventory costs with an order quantity of 5,000 units are made up as follows:

			£
Ordering costs	$\dfrac{30,000}{5,000}$	× £200	1,200
Cost of holding stock	$\dfrac{5,000}{2}$	× £1.20	3,000
Total inventory costs			4,200

Compare these costs with those of ordering four, eight, ten and fifteen times a year.

A	B	C	D	E	F
No of orders per year	Annual ordering costs £(A × 200)	Order quantity 30,000 ÷ A	Average stock C ÷ 2	Stockholding costs per annum £(D × £1.20)	Total inventory cost £(B + E)
	£	barrels	barrels	£	£
4	800	7,500	3,750	4,500	5,300
6	1,200	5,000	2,500	3,000	4,200
8	1,600	3,750	1,875	2,250	3,850
10	2,000	3,000	1,500	1,800	3,800
15	3,000	2,000	1,000	1,200	4,200

To minimise total inventory costs (column F), make between eight and fifteen orders a year, ie, order quantity should be between 3,750 and 2,000 units a time. A more accurate solution could be achieved by calculating costs at nine, ten, eleven, twelve, thirteen and fourteen orders per year.

However, rather than continue with the trial and error process, the results from the table could be shown graphically, plotting actual cost against order quantity. Three curves result:

(a)   annual ordering costs curve (column B);
(b)   annual stockholding costs curve (column E);
(c)   total inventory costs curve (column F).

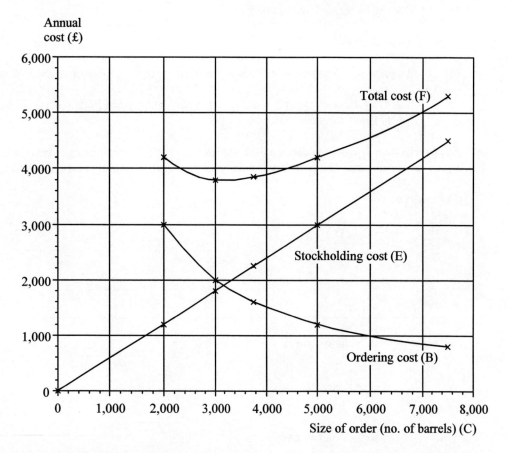

From the graph the order quantity which gives the lowest total cost is somewhere between 3,000 and 3,200 barrels. It is difficult to be much more accurate than this by reading the graph, however there is a mathematical model which provides more accurate figures which we shall now look at.

5.5 Economic order quantity model

We have already defined the EOQ earlier in the chapter, but it is worth repeating here to focus attention on what it is.

Definition   The **economic order quantity** is the most economic stock replenishment order size which minimises the sum of stock ordering costs and stockholding costs.

In the mathematical model for the EOQ the following notation will be used:

x = economic order quantity

C_O = costs of placing one order

D = expected annual sales volume (ie, demand)

C_h = annual cost of holding one item in stock.

The assumptions used in the model are as follows.

(a)   Demand is certain, constant and continuous over time.

(b)   No stock-outs.

(c)   All prices are constant and certain ie, there are no bulk order discounts.

(d)   Supply of the stock items is received all in one delivery and instantaneously after ordering or the supply lead time is constant and certain.

Since there are no stock-out costs, no buffer stocks and no bulk purchase discounts the only items of cost which vary on an annual basis with the order quantity are stock holding costs and ordering costs.

The model is:

$$x = EOQ = \sqrt{\frac{2 \times Co \times D}{Ch}}$$

5.6   Activity

Using the previous activity where:

Co   =   £200
D   =   30,000
Ch   =   £1.20

What is the economic order quantity?

5.7   Activity solution

$$x = EOQ \quad = \quad \sqrt{\frac{2 \times £200 \times 30,000}{£1.20}}$$

$$= \quad 3,162 \text{ units}$$

This would suggest that approximately 10 orders should be placed per annum, or 3,000 units per order this is, total annual demand 30,000/3,162 units per batch = 9.488, which rounded up equals 10.

5.8   Large order discounts

Frequently, discounts will be offered for ordering in large quantities. The problem is: if the order quantity to obtain discount is above what would otherwise be the EOQ, is the discount still worth taking? The problem may be solved by the following procedure:

Step 1   Calculate the EOQ ignoring discounts.

Step 2   If this is below the level for discounts, calculate total annual stock costs.

Step 3   Recalculate total annual stock costs using the order size required to just obtain the discount.

Step 4   Compare the cost of steps 2 and 3 with saving from the discount, and select the minimum cost alternative.

Step 5   Repeat for all discount levels.

5.9   Example

In the Watallington illustration, suppose additionally that a 2% discount is available on orders of at least 5,000 barrels and that a 2.5% discount is available if the order quantity is 7,500 barrels or above. With this information, would the economic order quantity still be 3,000?

			£	
Step 1 and Step 2	have already been carried out, and it is known that total annual cost at EOQ =		3,795	(ie, total inventory cost of 3,162 units)

Step 3

At order quantity 5,000, total cost

$$= \frac{xC_H}{2} + \frac{C_0D}{x}$$

$$\frac{5,000 \times 12 \times 0.98 \times 0.1}{2} + \frac{30,000 \times £200}{5,000} = \quad 4,140$$

	£
Extra costs of ordering in batches of 5,000	(345)
Less: Savings on discount 2% × £12 × 30,000	7,200

Step 4   Net cost saving   6,855

Hence batches of 5,000 are worthwhile.

Similarly purchasing in batches of 7,500 results in:

	£
Total costs	5,187.5
Costs at 5,000	4,125
Extra costs	1,062.5
Savings on extra discount (2½ – 2)% × £12 × 30,000	1,800
Net cost saving	737.5

It is concluded that a further saving can be made by ordering in batches of 7,500.

6   CHAPTER SUMMARY

In this chapter we have looked at the control of inventory costs including the use of the EOQ model.

7   SELF TEST QUESTIONS

7.1   What possible reasons might there be for a difference between a bin card balance for the quantity of an item of stock and the actual quantity of that item? (1.3)

7.2   What are the two types of cost involved in stock control calculations? (2.2 and 2.5)

7.3   What is meant by a periodic review system of stock control? (3.1)

7.4   What is a stock out? (3.4)

7.5   How is the re-order period determined in a periodic review system? (3.8)

◆ FOULKS*lynch*

7.6 Describe a two-bin system of stock control. (4.2)

7.7 In a fixed re-order level stock control system what is the re-order level if no stock outs are allowed? (4.3)

7.8 What is the mathematical model for the economic order quantity? (5.5)

8 MULTIPLE CHOICE QUESTIONS

8.1 What is the name given to a system of stocktaking, whereby a stock count is made each day of a number of items in store, and the count is checked against stock records, so that every item in store is checked at least once a year?

A continuous stocktaking
B perpetual inventory
C ABC inventory analysis
D annual stock accounting

8.2 A large retailer with multiple outlets maintains a central warehouse from which the outlets are supplied. The following information is available for Part Number SF525.

Average usage	350 per day
Minimum usage	180 per day
Maximum usage	420 per day
Lead time for replenishment	11 – 15 days
Re-order quantity	6,500 units
Re-order level	6,300

Based on the data above, what is the maximum level of stock?

A 5,250
B 6,500
C 10,820
D 12,800

8.3 Based on the data above, what is the approximate number of Part Number SF525 carried as buffer stock?

A 200
B 720
C 1,680
D 1,750

8.4 A national chain of tyre fitters stocks a popular tyre for which the following information is available:

Average usage	140 tyres per day
Minimum usage	90 tyres per day
Maximum usage	175 tyres per day
Lead time	10 to 16 days
Re-order quantity	3,000 tyres

Based on the data above, at what level of stocks should a replenishment order be issued to avoid the possibility of a stock-out?

A 2,240
B 2,800
C 3,000
D 5,740

8.5   Based on the data above, what is the maximum level of stocks possible?

   A   2,800
   B   3,000
   C   4,900
   D   5,800

9   PRACTICE QUESTIONS

9.1   Computer bureau order quantity

It has been estimated that a computer bureau will need 1,000 boxes of line printer paper next year. The purchasing officer of the bureau plans to arrange regular deliveries from a supplier, who charges £15 per delivery.

The bureau's accountant advises the purchasing officer that the cost of storing a box of line printer paper for a year is £2.70. Over a year, the average number of boxes in storage is half the order quantity (that is the number of boxes per delivery).

The ordering cost is defined as the delivery cost plus the storage cost, where the annual costs for an order quantity of x boxes will be:

Delivery cost:

$$\text{Number of deliveries} \times \text{Cost per delivery} = £\frac{100}{x} \times 15$$

Storage stock:

$$\text{Average stock level} \times \text{Storage cost per box} = £\frac{x}{2} \times 2.70$$

You are required:

(a)   to calculate the delivery cost, storage cost and ordering cost for order quantities of 50, 100, 150, 200 and 250 boxes;

(b)   to sketch these values for delivery cost, storage cost and ordering cost on the same graph; and

(c)   to estimate the order quantity which will minimise cost.

9.2   Raw material

The following data relates to an item of raw material:

Cost of the raw material	£10 per unit
Usage per day	100 units
Minimum lead time	20 days
Maximum lead time	30 days
Cost of ordering material	£400 per order
Stock holding cost	10% pa

Working weeks per annum 48, × 5 days/week.

Calculate:

(i)   the re-order level; and
(ii)   the re-order quantity based on EOQ.

10   ANSWERS TO MULTIPLE QUESTIONS

10.1   Continuous stocktaking is defined in the question. Perpetual inventory is a stock recording system whereby each movement in or out of stock is recorded as it occurs, and so stock records for *every* item are always up-to-date. ABC inventory analysis is a stock control system which categorises stock items into three categories, according to the proportion and value of total stock usage of the item. The stock items in category A which represent the largest proportion of stock usage by value (but the smallest number of items) merit the greatest amount of stock control effort. Low-value or small usage items in category C merit the least amount of stock control.

Therefore **A.**

10.2   C

Maximum stock   =   Re-order level + Re-order quantity -
                                                (Minimum usage/day × Minimum lead time)

                                 =   6,300 + 6,500 − (180 × 11)

                                 =   10,820 units

10.3   D

Average buffer stock   =   Re-order level - (Average usage/day × Average lead time)

                                 =   6,300 − (350 × 13)

                                 =   1,750 units

10.4   B

Reorder when level is maximum usage in maximum lead time, i.e.

Maximum usage: 175 per day
Maximum lead time: 16 days

⇒ 175 × 16 = 2,800

10.5   C

	Tyres
Number in stock when order placed	2,800
Received in minimum lead time	3,000
Minimum usage in minimum lead time (90 × 10)	(900)
	4,900

11   ANSWERS TO PRACTICE QUESTIONS

11.1   Computer bureau order quantity

(a)   **Calculation of cost associated with particular order quantities**

Order Quantity	Delivery cost $\dfrac{1,000}{x} \times 15$	Storage cost $\dfrac{x}{2} \times 2.70$	Ordering cost Delivery cost + Storage cost
	£	£	£
50	$\dfrac{1,000}{50} \times 15 = 300$	$\dfrac{50}{2} \times 2.70 = 67.50$	367.50
100	$\dfrac{1,000}{100} \times 15 = 150$	$\dfrac{100}{2} \times 2.70 = 135.00$	285.00
150	$\dfrac{1,000}{150} \times 15 = 100$	$\dfrac{150}{2} \times 2.70 = 202.50$	302.50
200	$\dfrac{1,000}{200} \times 15 = 75$	$\dfrac{200}{2} \times 2.70 = 270.00$	345.00
250	$\dfrac{1,000}{250} \times 15 = 60$	$\dfrac{250}{2} \times 2.70 = 337.50$	397.50

(b)   For graph see below.

(c)   From the graph, the optimum order quantity is approximately **106 units**.

           (ie, the graph enables us to obtain a more accurate solution.)

           Note: from the figures calculated in (a) we can see that the order quantity of 100 units results in the lowest cost.

           This would be the answer to give if we had not been required to prepare a graph.

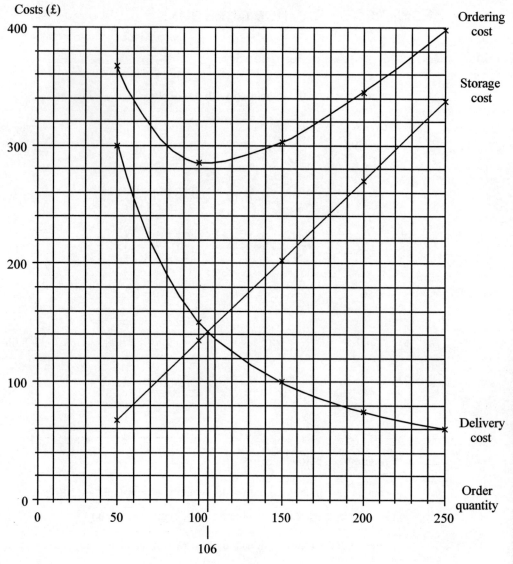

11.2   Raw material

(i)   Re-order level   = usage in maximum lead time
                            = 30 days × 100 units   = 3,000 units

(ii)   Re-order quantity $= \sqrt{\dfrac{2 \times C_0 \times D}{C_h}}$

where C_0 = order cost per order
            D = annual demand
            C_h = holding cost per item per annum

$$= \sqrt{\frac{2 \times 400 \times (100 \times 48 \times 5)}{10\% \times 10}} = \sqrt{\frac{19,200,000}{1}} = 4,382 \text{ units}$$

Chapter 5

LABOUR COSTS

PATHFINDER INTRODUCTION

This chapter covers the following elements of the CAT Official Teaching Guide. At the end of this chapter you should have learned these teaching guide elements thoroughly.

Session 5
Labour costs
Syllabus reference g

- Describe procedures for recording labour costs and associated documentation
- Explain the procedures required to ensure the correct coding, analysis and recording of direct and indirect labour costs
- Explain, illustrate and evaluate remuneration methods (candidates will not be expected to remember the names of traditionally used bonus schemes)
- Explain and illustrate the methods for producing standard labour costs
- Explain and evaluate the costs and causes of labour turnover
- Describe and illustrate measures of labour efficiency and utilisation, including idle time, overtime levels, absenteeism and sickness rates

Putting the chapter in context

To calculate the cost of a product, the cost accountant needs to identify the cost of all inputs. The previous two chapters looked at materials. This chapter explains how labour is recorded and rewarded.

1 DOCUMENTATION AND PROCEDURES TO RECORD LABOUR COSTS

1.1 Employee personnel records

When an employee joins an organisation it must record details of the employee and their job and pay. This is done by the personnel department in the individual employee's personnel record.

Details that might be kept about an employee are as follows:

- full name, address and date of birth;
- personal details such as marital status and emergency contact name and address;
- National Insurance number;
- previous employment history;
- educational details;
- professional qualifications;
- date of joining organisation;
- employee number or code;
- clock number issued;
- job title and department;
- rate of pay agreed;
- holiday details agreed;
- bank details if salary is to be paid directly into bank account;
- amendments to any of the details above (such as increases in agreed rates of pay);
- date of termination of employment (when this takes place) and reasons for leaving.

1.2   Employee record of attendance

On any particular day an employee may be at work, on holiday, absent due to sickness or absent for some other reason. A record must be kept of these details for each day.

1.3   Holiday

Employees have an agreed number of days holiday per year. This will usually be paid holiday for salaried employees but may well be unpaid for employees paid by results or on time rates. (see later in this chapter)

It is important for the employer to keep a record of the days of holiday taken by the employee to ensure that the agreed number of days per year are not exceeded.

1.4   Sickness

The organisation will have its own policies regarding payment for sick leave as well as legal requirements for statutory sick pay. Therefore, it is necessary to keep a record of the number of days of sick leave each year for each employee.

1.5   Other periods of absence

A record needs to be kept of any other periods of absence by an employee. These might be perfectly genuine such as jury service or training courses or alternatively unexplained periods of absence that must be investigated. (Absenteeism is covered in more detail later in this chapter).

1.6   Source of information

This information about an employee's attendance will come from various sources such as clock cards, time sheets job sheets and job cards.

1.7   Clock cards

Definition   A **clock card** is a document which records the starting and finishing time of an employee.

There is usually some form of electronic or computerised recording system, so that when the employee's clock card is entered into the machine the time is recorded. This will give the starting and finishing time for the day and also in some systems break times taken as well.

Clock cards are used as a source document in the calculation of the employee's earnings.

1.8   Time sheets

Definition   A **time sheet** is a record of how a person's time at work has been spent.

The total hours that an employee has worked in a day or week are known from the employee's clock card but a breakdown of how those hours were spent is shown on the time sheet.
Each employee fills out a time sheet on a daily, weekly or monthly basis depending upon the policies of the organisation.

The employee enters their name, clock number and department at the top of the time sheet together with details of the work engaged on in the period and the hours spent on that work.

This enables the cost of each employee's labour hour to be correctly charged to the correct function. This may be to a particular job or batch if the hours were direct labour hours or to a particular cost centre if the hours are classified as indirect labour hours. (This classification and distinction will be covered later in this chapter.)

1.9 Job sheets

Definition   A **job sheet** records the number of each type of product that an employee has produced in the period.

Time sheets are prepared by employees who are paid for the number of hours that they work. However it is also possible to pay employees on the basis of the number of units of a product they produce, known as a results or piece rate basis. (This will be considered in more detail later in this chapter.)

For an employee paid on the basis of the number of products produced a time sheet is of little use. Instead such an employee would complete some form of job sheet, which is used to calculate their pay.

Payment to the employee will then be based upon the information on this job sheet.

1.10 Job cost cards

Definition   A **job cost card** is a card that records the costs involved in a particular job.

Some organisations produce individual products for each customer. This is often the case in the engineering business or some form of tailor-made manufacturing business, or service businesses such as accountancy.

In such organisations it is necessary to know precisely how many hours each employee has spent on precisely which jobs so that his time can be specifically charged to the correct job. This is done by recording of the labour hours on a job card.

Instead of a record being kept of each employee's work a record is kept of the work performed on each job. This must of course be reconciled to the total amount of work recorded by the employee on his time sheet or clock card.

Conclusion   In order to correctly account for labour costs and pay the correct amount to employees. It is vital that the labour cost documentation is accurately completed.

2 CODING AND ANALYSIS OF DIRECT AND INDIRECT LABOUR COSTS

2.1 Introduction

Labour is a cost of producing the products of the organisation. Just as it is necessary to know the cost of the materials input into each product it is also necessary to know the amount or cost of the labour.

2.2 Direct labour costs

Definition   **Direct labour costs** are the labour hours worked by employees directly producing the product.

For example the employee who works on the production line each day is working directly on the products that pass along the production line. The packer of a product into boxes is working directly on that product. The roof tiler in a construction business is working directly on each house.

2.3 Indirect labour costs

Definition   **Indirect labour costs** are the cost of hours worked by employees in support of the labour working directly on the product, e.g. supervisory labour, stores personnel and maintenance labour.

There are many functions in an organisation that do not work directly on the products of the business. For example the maintenance engineer works on the machines that make the products but not on the products themselves. The canteen workers do not work on the products themselves but are necessary to feed those who do work on the products. The accountant does not work on the products directly but is a necessary part of any organisation producing products.

2.4   Coding of labour hours

When the labour hours worked or units produced by employees are initially recorded on clock cards, timesheets, job sheets or job cards then they must be adequately described and/or coded to ensure that the direct and indirect labour hours worked an be clearly distinguished.

Conclusion   For costing purposes a distinction is required between direct and indirect labour costs. This distinction comes from adequate coding/description of labour hours on the initial labour documentation.

3   REMUNERATION METHODS - TIME RELATED PAY

3.1   Introduction

There are two main methods of calculating the pay or remuneration of employees. These are to pay employees either for the time spent at work, (time related pay,) or for the work actually produced, (output related pay).

3.2   Time related pay

Employees paid under a time related pay method are paid for the hours that they spend at work regardless of the amount of production or output that they achieve in that time. Time related pay employees can be split into two types, salaried employees and hourly rate employees.

3.3   Salaried employees

Definition   A **salaried employee** is one whose pay is agreed at a fixed amount for a period of time whatever hours that employee works in that period.

This might be expressed as an annual salary such as £18,000 per year or as a weekly rate such as £269.50 per week.

Each organisation will have a set number of hours that are expected to be worked each week, for example a standard working week of 38 hours, and salaried employees will be expected to work for at least this number of hours each week.

However if the salaried employee works for more than the standard number of hours for the week then the employment agreement may specify that overtime payments are to be made for the additional hours (see later in this section).

3.4   Hourly rate employees

Definition   An **hourly rate employee** is one who is paid a set hourly rate for each hour that he works.

These employees are paid for the actual number of hours of attendance in a period, usually a week. A rate of pay will be set for each hour of attendance.

3.5   Overtime

Definition   **Overtime** is the number of hours worked by an employee which is greater than the number of hours set by the organisation as the working week.

It is common that employees that work overtime are paid an additional amount per hour for those extra hours.

3.6   Overtime premium

Definition   **Overtime premium** is the amount over and above the normal hourly rate that employees are paid for overtime hours.

3.7   Activity

An employee's basic week is 40 hours at a rate of pay of £6 per hour. Overtime is paid at 'time and a half'.

The employee works a 45 hour week.

What is the total wage cost for this employee for the week?

Distinguish between the overtime payment and overtime premium for the week?

3.8   Activity solution

	£
Basic pay (40 hours × £6)	240.00
Overtime hours (5 hours × (£6 × 1.5))	45.00
Weekly wage cost	285.00

Alternatively this could be shown as:

	£
Basic pay (45 hours × £6)	270.00
Overtime premium (5 hours × (£6 × 0.5))	15.00
Weekly wage cost	285.00

The overtime payment for the week is £45 and the overtime premium is £15.

Conclusion   The overtime premium is the additional over the basic rate of pay that is paid for the overtime hours rather than the total payment made for the overtime hours.

4   REMUNERATION METHODS - OUTPUT RELATED PAY

4.1   Introduction

Output related pay is also known as payment by results or piecework. This is a direct alternative to time related pay.

Definition   **Payment by results** or **piecework** is where a fixed amount is paid per unit of output achieved irrespective of the time spent.

4.2   Activity

If the amount paid to an employee is £3 per unit produced and that employee produces 80 units in a week how much should be paid in wages?

4.3   Activity solution

$$80 \text{ units} \times £3 = £240$$

4.4   Advantages of payment by results

As far as an employee is concerned, payment by results means that they can earn whatever they wish within certain parameters. The harder they work and the more units they produce the higher the wage.

From the employer's point of view higher production or output can also be encouraged with a system of differential piecework (this will be considered later in the chapter).

4.5   Problems with payment by results

There are two main problems associated with payment by results. One is the problem of accurate recording of the actual output produced. The amount claimed to be produced determines the amount of pay and, therefore, is potentially open to abuse unless it can be adequately supervised. A system of job sheet and checking of job sheets needs to be in place.

The second problem is that of the maintenance of the quality of the work. If the employee is paid by the amount that is produced then the temptation might be to produce more units but of a lower quality.

For these reasons basic piecework systems are rare in practice and there are two main variations of the remuneration method.

4.6   Piece rate with guarantee

A piece rate with guarantee gives the employee some security if the employer does not provide enough work in a particular period. The way that the system works is that if an employee's earnings for the amount of units produced in the period are lower than the guaranteed amount then the guaranteed amount is paid instead.

4.7   Activity

Jones is paid £4.00 for every unit that he produces but he has a guaranteed wage of £40.00 per eight hour day. In a particular week he produces the following number of units:

Monday	12 units
Tuesday	14 units
Wednesday	9 units
Thursday	14 units
Friday	8 units

Calculate Jones's wage for this week.

4.8   Solution

Total weekly wage

	£
Monday (12 × £4)	48
Tuesday (14 × £4)	56
Wednesday (guarantee)	40
Thursday (14 × £4)	56
Friday (guarantee)	40
	240

Conclusion   The payment of a guaranteed amount is not a bonus for good work but simply an additional payment required if the amount of production is below a certain level.

4.9   Differential piece-work

Definition   A **differential piece-work system** is where the piece rate increases as successive targets for a period are achieved and exceeded.

This will tend to encourage higher levels of production and acts as a form of bonus payment for employees who produce more units than the standard level.

4.10   Activity

Payment by results rates for an organisation are as follows:

Up to 99 units per week   £1.75 per unit
100 to 119 units per week   £2.00 per unit
120 or more units per week   £2.25 per unit

If an employee produces 102 units in a week how much will he be paid?

4.11   Activity solution

The amount the employee will be paid will depend upon the exact wording of the agreement. Production of 102 units has taken the employee out of the lowest band (up to 99 units) and into the middle band (100 – 119 units). The question now is whether **all** his units are paid for at the middle rate (£1.50), or only the units produced in excess of 99. The two possibilities are as follows:

(a) $102 \times £2.00 = £204$

(b) $(99 \times £1.75) + (3 \times £2.00) = £179.25$

Most organisations' agreements would apply method (b).

Conclusion   Output related pay is often known as piecework. Organisations paying employees in this manner normally operate a piecework with guarantee system or differential piecework systems.

5   REMUNERATION METHODS - BONUS SCHEMES

5.1   Introduction

Bonuses may be paid to employees for a variety of reasons. An individual employee, a department, a division or indeed the entire organisation may have performed particularly well and it is felt by the management that a bonus is due to some or all of the employees.

5.2   Basic principle of bonuses

The basic principle of a bonus payment is that the employee is rewarded for any additional income or savings in cost to the organisation. This may be for example because the employee has managed to save a certain amount of time on the production of a product or a number of products. This time saving will save the organisation money and the amount saved will tend to be split between the organisation and the employee on some agreed basis. The amount paid to the employee/employees is known as the bonus.

5.3   Type of employee

The typical bonus payable will often depend on the method of payment of the employee. The calculation and payment of bonuses will differ for salaried employees, employees paid by results and employees paid on a time rate basis.

6   SALARIED EMPLOYEES - BONUSES

6.1   Introduction

Salaried employees are paid a predetermined salary or wage every week or every month. It may also be the organisation's policy to pay employees a bonus each month, quarter or annually.

6.2   Calculation of bonus

The calculation of the amount of bonus to be paid to each individual will depend upon the policy of the organisation. The policy may be to assign the same amount of bonus to each employee or alternatively to base the amount of each individual employee's bonus on the amount of their salary.

6.3   Flat rate bonus

Definition   A **flat rate bonus** is where all employees are paid the same amount of bonus each regardless of their individual salary.

The principle behind such a payment is that all of the employees have contributed the same amount to earning the bonus no matter what their position in the organisation or their salary level.

6.4   Activity

Suppose that a small business made a profit of £100,000 in the previous quarter and the managing director decided to pay out £20,000 of this as a flat rate bonus to each employee. The business has 50 employees in total including the managing director earning a salary of £48,000 per annum and Chris Roberts his secretary who earns £18,000 per annum.

How much would the managing director and Chris Roberts each receive as bonus for the quarter?

6.5   Activity solution

Total bonus	£20,000
Split between 50 employees (£20,000/50) =	£400 per employee
Managing director's bonus	£400
Chris Roberts's bonus	£400

6.6   Percentage bonus

The alternative method of calculating the bonus due to each employee is to base it upon the annual salary of each employee.

Definition   A **percentage bonus** is where the amount paid to each employee as bonus is a set percentage of that employee's annual salary.

The principle behind this method of calculating the bonus payable is to give a larger bonus to those with higher salaries in recognition that they have contributed more to the earning of the bonus than those with a lower salary.

6.7 Activity

Using the earlier example again, a small business made a profit of £100,000 in the previous quarter and the managing director decided to pay out £20,000 of this as a bonus to each employee. The business has 50 employees in total including the managing director earning a salary of £48,000 per annum and Chris Roberts his secretary who earns £18,000 per annum.

The bonus for each employee is to be calculated as 1.6% of each employee's annual salary.

How much would the managing director and Chris Roberts each receive as bonus for the quarter?

6.8 Activity solution

Managing director's bonus
$$(£48,000 \times 0.016) = £768$$

Chris Roberts's bonus
$$(£18,000 \times 0.016) = £288$$

Conclusion   A bonus for a salaried employee will normally be related to the overall profit levels of the organisation. The total bonus is split either equally amongst all of the employees or on the basis of a percentage of salary.

7 TIME RATE EMPLOYEES - BONUSES

7.1 Introduction

Employees paid on a time rate basis are paid a certain amount per hour regardless of the amount produced in that hour. Therefore, industrious and lazy employees are remunerated equally.

The principle of a bonus or incentive scheme for time rate remunerated employees is to encourage them to achieve additional output in the time they work.

7.2 Basis of bonus schemes

The basis of bonus schemes in these instances is to set a predetermined standard time (or target time) for performance of a job or production of a given amount of output. If the job is completed in less than the standard time or more than the given output is achieved in the standard time then this will mean additional profit to the employer.

Definition   **Individual bonus schemes** are those that benefit individual workers according to their own results.

This additional profit earned by the individual employee will then be split between the employer and the employee in some agreed manner.

7.3   Activity

It is expected that it will take 90 minutes for an employee to make a product. If the employee makes the product in 60 minutes what is the saving to the employer if the employee's wage rate is £6.00 per hour?

7.4   Activity solution

Time saving = 30 minutes

At a wage rate of £6.00 per hour the cost saving is £3.00.

Conclusion   This employee's efficient work has saved the organisation £2.00. The basis of a bonus scheme for time rate workers is that a proportion of this £2.00 should be paid to the employee as a bonus. The manner in which the proportion is calculated must now be considered.

7.5   Payment to employee under a bonus scheme

There are many methods of splitting the time saved between the employer and employee in order to calculate the employee's bonus and two popular schemes are the Halsey scheme and the Rowan scheme. These differ only in the proportion of the time savings that are attributed to the employee as his bonus.

7.6   Halsey scheme

Under a Halsey bonus scheme the employee and the employer split the benefit of the time saving equally between themselves.

The formula that is used to calculate this is:

$$\text{Bonus} = \frac{(\text{Time allowed} - \text{Time taken}) \times \text{Rate paid}}{2}$$

7.7   Activity

Employee's basic rate   £6.00 per hour
Allowed time for job A   1 hour
Time taken for job A   36 minutes

What is the total amount that the employee will earn for job A?

7.8   Activity solution

		£
Basic rate	$\dfrac{36}{60} \times £6.00$	3.60
Bonus	$\dfrac{60-36}{2} \times \dfrac{£6.00}{60}$	1.20
Total payment for job A		4.80

7.9 Rowan scheme

Under a Rowan scheme the proportion of the time saving paid to the employee is based on the ratio of time taken to time allowed.

The formula to calculate this is:

$$\text{Bonus} = \frac{\text{Time taken}}{\text{Time allowed}} \times \text{time saved} \times \text{rate paid}$$

7.10 Activity

Employee's basic rate	£6.00 per hour
Allowed time for job A	1 hour
Time taken for job A	36 minutes

What is the total amount that the employee will earn for job A if the bonus is calculated based upon a Rowan scheme?

7.11 Activity solution

		£
Basic rate	$\frac{36}{60} \times £6.00$	3.60
Bonus	$\frac{36}{60} \times (60 - 36) \times \frac{£6.00}{60}$	1.44
Total payment for job A		5.04

Conclusion   The Halsey and Rowan schemes are examples of how time saving bonuses can be calculated. However, it is not necessary to use one or other of these schemes and you are not expected to remember them by name. An organisation can determine its own method of splitting the time saving between the employee and employer.

8 GROUP BONUS SCHEMES

8.1 Introduction

Definition   A **group bonus scheme** is where the bonus is based upon the output of the workforce as a whole or a particular group of the workforce. The bonus is then shared between the individual members of the group on some pre-agreed basis.

8.2 Advantages of a group scheme

A group scheme has a number of advantages over individual schemes:

- 'group loyalty' may result in less absenteeism and lateness;

- it is not necessary to record the output of each individual worker, therefore it is an easier system to operate and control;

- in a production line situation where the speed of the output is determined by the speed of the production line then a group scheme is more appropriate than an individual scheme.

8.3   Activity

Ten employees work as a group. The standard output for the group is 200 units per hour and when this is exceeded each employee in the group is paid a bonus in addition to the hourly wage.

The bonus percentage is calculated as follows:

$$50\% \times \frac{\text{Excess units}}{\text{Standard units}}$$

Each employee in the group is then paid as a bonus this percentage of an hourly wage rate of £5.20 no matter what the individual's hourly wage rate is.

The following is one week's record of production by the group:

	Hours worked	Production Units
Monday	90	24,500
Tuesday	88	20,600
Wednesday	90	24,200
Thursday	84	20,100
Friday	88	20,400
Saturday	40	10,200
	480	120,000

(a)   What is the rate of the bonus per hour and what is the total bonus to be split between group members?

(b)   If Jones worked for 42 hours and was paid £5.00 per hour as a basic rate what would be his total pay for this week?

8.4   Activity solution

(a)   Actual production for the week   120,000 units

Standard production for the week
480 hours × 200 units   96,000 units

Excess production   24,000 units

$$\text{Bonus percentage} = \frac{24,000}{96,000} \times 50\%$$

$$= 12.5\%$$

$$\text{Bonus rate} = 12.5\% \times £5.20$$

$$= £0.65 \text{ per hour}$$

The total bonus to split between the group is therefore
480 hours × £0.65 = £312

(b)   Total pay for Jones

		£
Basic pay 42 hours × £5.00		210.00
Bonus 42 hours × £0.65		27.30
		237.30

Conclusion   A group bonus scheme is a method of rewarding a group of employees or department for efficient work on a group.

9   STANDARD LABOUR COSTS

9.1   Introduction

In a previous chapter the standard cost of materials was introduced and explained as being the expected cost of the materials to be input into a unit of a product. In just the same way a standard labour cost can be determined.

Definition   The **standard labour** cost for a unit of a product is the predetermined cost of the standard (expected) labour hours spent on the unit.

Therefore in order to determine the standard labour cost the expected number of hours of labour must be determined as well as the expected labour rate.

9.2   Standard hours

The standard labour hours to be spent on a product can be determined either using historical data or starting afresh with a work study. Production can be expressed in standard hours. For example, one unit of 'Chemit' takes 1.5 standard hours, therefore 1,000 units would equal 1,500 standard hours produced.

9.3   Historical data

One way of determining a standard time for the production of an item is to take an average of the times taken in the past. This is historical data. This method is widely used in practice.

There is little additional expense involved in this method and as the employees do not know that they are being timed then there is unlikely to be any distortion due to employees working faster or slower than usual.

9.4   Work study

A more technical and theoretically sounder method of determining standard times is to use work study methods.

Definition   The function of **work study** is to analyse, measure and value operations and processes.

Work study results can be used in a number of different ways by organisations and just one of these is in setting standard times for the operation of processes or the production of products.

9.5   Elements of work study

There are three main elements of work study:

- Method study - observation and analysis of existing and suggested methods of operation to find the most efficient ways.

- Motion study - development or improvement in work by reducing effort and fatigue, and by relating human effort to the availability and use of mechanical data.

- Time study - using the results of method and motion study to determine a standard time for each operation.

9.6   Standard rate

As well as the standard hours for each grade of labour involved in a product it is also necessary to determine the standard rate for the grades of labour.

The standard rate for labour will generally be the current pay rates for the grades of labour that are working on that particular product. These pay rates can be advised by the personnel department who will generally have set them.

9.7   Activity

The standard labour hours for making one unit of output of 'Chemit' is two hours of Grade II labour and 3.5 hours of Grade IV labour.

The personnel department have provided the following list of current pay rates for the grades of labour employed.

Grade	£
I	4.60 per hour
II	5.30 per hour
III	6.00 per hour
IV	7.50 per hour

The company works a 35 hour week and a 52 week year.

What are the standard rates of labour for the labour used in the production of a unit of output?

9.8   Activity solution

Grade II labour	£5.30 per hour
Grade IV labour	£7.50 per hour

9.9   Standard labour cost

Definition   The **standard cost of labour** is the standard hours allowed for each grade multiplied by the standard rate of pay for each grade.

9.10   Activity

Continuing with the previous example, what is the standard cost of the labour for a unit of 'Chemit'?

9.11   Activity solution

		£
Grade II		
(2 hours × £5.30 per hour)		10.60
Grade IV		
(3.5 hours × £7.50 per hour)		26.25
Standard cost of labour		36.85

Conclusion   The standard cost of labour is the standard usage of each grade of labour multiplied by the standard rate for each grade.

10   LABOUR TURNOVER

10.1   Introduction

One of the main objectives of a personnel department is to minimise turnover of labour, i.e. the speed at which the labour force leaves.

Definition   **Labour turnover** is a measure of the speed at which employees leave an organisation and are replaced.

Labour turnover is often calculated as: $\dfrac{\text{Average annual number of leavers who are replaced}}{\text{Average number of employees}} \times 100\%$

10.2   Activity

On average a company employees 7,000 workers but during the last year 200 of these workers have resigned and have had to be replaced.

What is the labour turnover for the year?

10.3   Activity solution

Labour turnover $=$ $\dfrac{200}{7,000} \times 100\%$ $=$ 2.86%

10.4   Costs of labour turnover

The cost of replacing employees who have left is not just the obvious cost of advertising, interviewing, choosing and taking on the new employee. There are also a number of other less obvious costs such as:

- additional training of new employee;
- loss of efficiency of production due to new employees;
- general administration costs of new employee;
- effect on morale of the existing work force leading to loss of efficiency.

10.5   Causes of labour turnover

The employee records should show as clearly as possible the reasons for each employee leaving. If a particular cause is **recurrent** this should be investigated. However, often employees leaving do not give the full story of why they are leaving, therefore, any statistics gathered from this source should be treated with caution.

Conclusion   High labour turnover has a high cost to a business that is not necessarily always obvious. Labour turnover should be closely monitored and reduced if possible.

11   IDLE TIME, OVERTIME AND ABSENTEEISM

11.1   Idle time

Definition   **Idle time** or **down time** is time paid for that is non-productive.

Idle time will exist in most organisations. What is important is that the amount of idle time and the reasons for it are accurately assessed, reported to management for corrective action if necessary and treated correctly in terms of allocation to cost of products.

11.2   Classification of idle time

Idle time can be classified as avoidable (or controllable) and unavoidable (or uncontrollable). Such classification is often a matter for discretionary judgement. For example, are the idle time effects of a power cut avoidable? In most situations the answer is probably no but if a standby generator was available but unused then the idle time would be classified as avoidable.

11.3   Avoidable idle time

Definition   **Avoidable idle time** is non-productive time that could have been avoided by appropriate management action.

The main causes of avoidable idle time are:

(a)   Production disruption: this could be due to machine breakdown, shortage of materials, inefficient scheduling, poor supervision of labour etc.

(b)   Policy decisions: examples of this might include run-down of stocks, changes in product specification, retraining schemes etc.

11.4   Avoidable idle time costs

The costs of paying for avoidable idle time are costs that simply should not have been incurred. Therefore if such costs were included in the cost of products each unit of the product would be overpriced.

Avoidable costs should, therefore, be written off to the profit and loss account and monitored closely so that corrective action can be taken to prevent a recurrence.

11.5   Activity

On a particular day in a factory one of the machines was out of order for 2.5 hours. It was possible to reschedule the work of most of the employees but three employees had no work for two hours each. These employees were paid on an hourly basis for the hours spent at work at the rate of £6.00 per hour.

What is the cost of this machine breakdown in terms of wages and how should it be treated?

11.6   Activity solution

Cost of machine breakdown
$(3 \times 2 \text{ hours} \times £6.00)$ £36

This would be written off to the profit and loss account as an idle time cost that is not part of normal product costs.

11.7   Unavoidable idle time

Definition   **Unavoidable idle time** is idle time that cannot be helped, an uncontrollable or necessary cost of the business.

This might include payments for tea breaks or rest periods as well as idle time due to outside influences such as a sudden and unexpected fall in demand for a product or a strike at a supplier affecting vital supplies.

11.8   Unavoidable idle time costs

An unavoidable idle time cost is a realistic cost of a unit of a product. As such it should therefore be included as part of the cost of the product.

Not only that, but the future standard cost of the units of the product concerned should be modified to include such idle time costs.

11.9   Activity

The 30 employees that work in a factory work on a shift basis from 12.00 noon to 7.00 pm and they are paid £5.50 per hour for each of those seven hours.

However, in total the tea and rest breaks for each employee within that seven hour period total 1 hour and 15 minutes.

What is the cost of a day's work for those 30 employees to the organisation and how should this be treated?

11.10   Activity solution

The cost to the employer is the full seven hours per day at £5.50 per hour, £38.50 per employee.

As the tea and rest breaks are a necessary cost of production and are therefore described as unavoidable idle time they should be included as part of the cost of the products on which the employees work.

11.11   Overtime

Earlier the calculation of overtime and overtime premiums was discussed.

Definition   **Overtime** is time that is paid for, usually at a premium, over and above the basic hours for the period.

Overtime might be incurred for two reasons - either to make up for lost time earlier in the production process or in order to produce more of the product than was originally anticipated.

Whatever the reason for the overtime being worked the effect will be that more units of a product are produced. However, if the overtime is being worked to make up for lost production earlier in the process then the units produced in the overtime may simply be enough to bring production back up to its anticipated level.

11.12 Avoidable and unavoidable overtime

Definition   Overtime that is being worked in order to make up for unnecessarily lost production time is **avoidable** and should not have occurred.

Definition   Overtime that is necessary in order to fulfil customer orders is **unavoidable** overtime.

The rationale for the treatment of overtime costs is similar to that expressed for idle time costs. Avoidable overtime costs should be charged to the profit and loss account for the period. Unavoidable or necessary overtime costs are valid costs of the units of production and as such should be charged in full to those units.

11.13 Overtime premium

Where avoidable overtime is to be charged to the profit and loss account rather than to the cost of the products then it is clearly only the additional cost of the overtime premium that is charged to the profit and loss account.

If additional hours are spent making products then the cost of the labour for those hours is the basic hourly rate. Only the overtime premium is the additional unnecessary cost and only that should be written off to the profit and loss account.

11.14 Activity

During a particular month the workers in a factory worked on production for 2,500 hours. Of these 200 hours were hours of overtime of which 50 hours were to cover lost production and 150 were spent on an urgent job.

The basic wage rate was £6.00 per hour and overtime was paid at the rate of time and a third.

Calculate the total wage cost for the month and show any amounts to be written off to the profit and loss account.

11.15 Activity solution

Total wage cost
(2,300 hours × £6) + (200 hours × £8)   £15,400

This can be broken down as follows:

	£
Normal production costs 2,300 hours × £6	13,800
Additional production to cover lost time 50 hours × £6	300
Special overtime for special order 150 hours × £8	1,200
Overtime premium written off to the profit and loss account in relation to avoidable production losses 50 hours × (£8 − £6)	100
	15,400

11.16 Absenteeism

An employee can be absent from work for a variety of reasons. These might include holiday, sickness, maternity leave, training or simply unexplained absence.

11.17 Holiday

In most organisations employees are given a certain number of paid days of holiday a year. The wage cost of the employee for the year is, therefore, the cost for the entire year and not just the weeks that he works.

11.18 Sickness

When an employee is absent from work due to ill health then in most circumstances the organisation must pay him something. There are statutory levels of sick pay that the employer must pay and over and above that some employers choose to pay more.

Conclusion   When an employee is off work due to holiday or sickness he is being paid at some level by the organisation although this may not be at his normal rate, but he is not producing any goods.

11.19 Unexplained absence

If an employee is absent but it is not part of their holiday, they cannot produce a certificate from their doctor to indicate ill health and are not on maternity leave or a training course, then their absence will be unexplained.

Such absence from work will not only require investigation and possibly disciplinary action but it will also mean that the employee is not paid for the period of absence.

12   LABOUR EFFICIENCY AND UTILISATION

12.1 Efficient labour

Definition   The labour force of an organisation is described as **efficient** if it produces more than the standard amount of goods in a set period of time.

If the labour force is efficient then it is working faster than anticipated or producing more goods than anticipated in a set period of time.

This might be because the employees are of a higher grade than anticipated or are more experienced or motivated or simply better at their job than the average employee.

Alternatively, it might be due to a better grade of material being used that is easier to work with or an improved design specification that requires fewer labour hours.

12.2 Inefficient labour

Definition   The labour force of an organisation is described as **inefficient** if it produces less than the standard amount of goods in a set period of time.

If the labour force is working more slowly than anticipated or producing less units in a set period of time than anticipated then the employees will be said to be inefficient.

This inefficiency might be because of poor morale within the workforce, use of inexperienced or below par employees or workers having an 'off day'.

It could also be due to the use of cheaper or lower grade materials that require more work or a change in the design specification that requires more hours.

12.3   Activity

A group of 10 employees work a 35 hour week each. In the 350 total hours for the week it is expected that the workforce will produce 175 units. This means that the standard utilisation for labour is two hours per unit.

Suppose that the workforce only produce 165 units in the week. What would you say about the efficiency of the workforce?

12.4   Activity solution

It appears that the workforce had been inefficient as they had only produced 165 units instead of 175 units in the 350 hour week. This means a labour utilisation rate of 2.12 hours per unit (350 hours/165 units) rather than two hours per unit.

12.5   Activity

Suppose, however, that in the same example although 350 hours had been paid for in the week only 330 hours had been worked due to 20 hours of idle time.

What is the efficiency of the workforce now?

12.6   Activity solution

If only 330 hours were worked to produce 165 units then the utilisation of labour is still at the standard rate of two hours per unit (330 hours/165 units). The employees are working at standard efficiency.

Conclusion   The efficiency of labour is determined by comparing the hours worked to the output achieved in those hours. The output achieved being expressed in standard hours.

12.7   Labour productivity

In the previous paragraphs the efficiency of the workforce has been considered. The following paragraphs take this a little further and investigate the effectiveness of the workforce.

An effective workforce is one that meets its set production targets. An efficient workforce is one that minimises labour use and cost for any level of output.

Definition   The link that ensures that a workforce is effective whilst also being efficient is **productivity**.

Productivity is often analysed using three control ratios. These are the production/volume ratio, the capacity ratio and the efficiency ratio.

12.8   Standard hour

Before these ratios can be calculated it is important that the concept of the standard hour is understood.

Definition   A **standard hour** is the output expected in one hour of production at normal efficiency.

12.9 Activity

Suppose that the budgeted output for a period is 2,000 units and the budgeted time for the production of these units is 200 hours. Calculate the standard hour per unit.

12.10 Activity solution

Standard hours per unit

$$\frac{200 \text{ hours}}{2,000 \text{ units}} = 0.10 \text{ Std hours per unit.}$$

Conclusion   A standard hour is a measure of production rather than a measure of time.

12.11 Production/volume ratio or activity ratio

Definition   The **production/volume ratio** assesses how the overall production level compares to planned levels.

Over 100% indicates that overall production is above planned levels and below 100% indicates a shortfall compared to plans.

The production/volume ratio is calculated as:

$$\frac{\text{Actual output measured in standard hours}}{\text{Budgeted production hours}} \times 100$$

12.12 Capacity ratio

Definition   The **capacity ratio** provides indications for worker capacity in terms of the hours of working time that have been possible in a period.

The capacity ratio is calculated as follows:

$$\text{Capacity ratio} = \frac{\text{Actual hours worked}}{\text{Budgeted hours}} \times 100$$

12.13 Efficiency ratio

Definition   The **efficiency ratio** is a useful indicator of productivity with the benchmark again being 100%.

The efficiency ratio is calculated as follows:

$$\frac{\text{Actual output measured in standard hours}}{\text{Actual production hours}}$$

The efficiency ratio is often referred to as the productivity ratio.

12.14 Activity

The budgeted output for a period is 2,000 units and the budgeted time for the production of these units is 200 hours.

The actual output in the period is 2,300 units and the actual time worked by the labour force is 180 hours.

Calculate the three ratios.

12.15   Activity solution - production/volume ratio; activity ratio

$$\text{Standard hours per unit} \quad = \quad \frac{200 \text{ hours}}{2,000 \text{ units}}$$

$$= \quad 0.10/\text{std hr}$$

Actual output measured in standard hours
or standard hours produced $\quad = \quad 2,300 \times 0.10 \text{ std hrs}$

$$= \quad 230 \text{ standard hours}$$

$$\text{Production/volume ratio} - \text{activity ratio} \quad = \quad \frac{230}{200}$$

$$= \quad 115\%$$

This shows that production is 15% up on planned production levels.

12.16   Solution - capacity ratio

$$\text{Capacity ratio} = \frac{180 \text{ hours}}{200 \text{ hours}} = 90\%$$

Therefore this organisation had only 90% of the production hours anticipated available for production.

12.17   Solution - efficiency ratio

$$\text{Efficiency ratio} \quad = \quad \frac{230}{180} \times 100\%$$

$$= \quad 127.78\%$$

This can be proved. The workers were expected to produce 10 units per hour. Therefore, in the 180 hours worked it would be expected that 1,800 units would be produced. In fact 2,300 units were produced. This is 27.78% more than anticipated (500/1,800).

12.18   Ratio relationships

The three ratios calculated above can be summarised diagrammatically as follows:

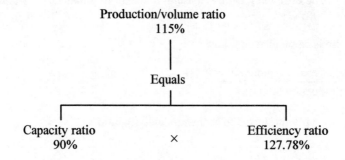

Conclusion   Capacity ratio   –   a measure of utilisation
Efficiency ratio   –   a measure of productivity
Activity ratio   –   a measure of production volume

You are recommended to read an article on 'Control Ratios' by Dr Philip E. Dunn on www.accountingweb.co.uk/dunn/index.html.

13   CHAPTER SUMMARY

This chapter has explained the methods of recording and analysing labour times, and those methods for calculating their cost so they may be attributed to work done.

14   SELF TEST QUESTIONS

14.1   What is a job card? (1.10)

14.2   What is an overtime premium? (3.6)

14.3   What is piece work with guarantee? (4.6)

14.4   What is differential piecework? (4.9)

14.5   What are the advantages of a group bonus scheme? (8.2)

14.6   How is the standard cost of labour calculated? (9.9)

14.7   How are unavoidable idle time costs treated? (11.8)

14.8   What is meant by efficient labour? (12.1)

14.9   How is the labour efficiency ratio calculated? (12.13)

15   MULTIPLE CHOICE QUESTIONS

15.1   A manufacturing firm is very busy and overtime is being worked.

The amount of overtime premium contained in direct wages would normally be classed as:

A   part of prime cost
B   factory overheads
C   direct labour costs
D   administrative overheads

15.2   A contract cleaning firm estimates that it will take 2,520 actual cleaning hours to clean an office block. Unavoidable interruptions and lost time are estimated to take 10% of the operatives' time. If the wage rate is £4 per hour, what is the budgeted labour cost?

A   £10,080
B   £11,088
C   £11,200
D   £12,197

15.3   Which of the following would be classed as indirect labour?

A   assembly workers in a company manufacturing televisions
B   a stores assistant in a factory store
C   plasterers in a construction company
D   an audit clerk in a firm of auditors

15.4   Gross wages incurred in Department 1 in June were £135,000. The wages analysis shows the following summary breakdown of the gross pay

	Paid to direct labour £	Paid to indirect labour £
Ordinary time	62,965	29,750
Overtime		
Basic pay	13,600	8,750
Premium	3,400	2,190
Shift allowance	6,750	3,495
Sick pay	3,450	650
	£90,165	£44,835

What is the direct wages cost for Department 1 in June?

A   £62,965   B   £76,565   C   £86,715   D   £90,165

16   PRACTICE QUESTIONS

16.1   Components A, B and C

A factory manufactures three components A, B and C.

During Week 26, the following was recorded:

Labour grade	Number of employees	Rate per hour £	Individual hours worked
I	6	6.00	40
II	18	5.00	42
III	4	4.50	40
IV	1	4.00	44

Output and standard times during the same week were:

Component	Output	Standard minutes (each)
A	444	30
B	900	54
C	480	66

The normal working week is 38 hours, overtime is paid at a premium of 50% of the normal hourly rate.

A group incentive scheme is in operation. The time saved is expressed as a percentage of hours worked and is shared between the group as a proportion of the hours worked by each grade.

The rate paid is 75% of the normal hourly rate.

You are required:

(a)   to calculate the total payroll showing the basic pay, overtime premium and bonus pay as separate totals for each grade of labour.

(b)   to summarise two advantages and two disadvantages of group incentive schemes.

16.2 FG Toyles Ltd

(a) Nessa Trandheim works in the production area of FG Toyles Ltd. Her clock card number is NT 641. She is paid an hourly rate of £4.80 for the work that she performs and she must record this work on a weekly time sheet. She works on one of three products J, K and L.

The standard working week for the company is 38 hours and any overtime is paid at twice the normal hourly rate.

During the week commencing 4 June 20X7 Nessa worked the following hours:

Monday 4/6	9.00 am - 12.00 pm	Product J
	1.00 pm - 7.00 pm	Product L
Tuesday 5/6	8.00 am - 12.00 pm	Product L
	1.00 pm - 6.00 pm	Product K
Wednesday 6/6	9.00 am - 12.00 pm	Product K
	1.00 pm - 5.00 pm	Product K
Thursday 7/6	8.00 am - 1.00 pm	Product K
	2.00 pm - 5.00 pm	Product K
Friday 8/6	8.00 am - 11.00 am	Product L
	12.30 pm - 5.30 pm	Product J

Draft a time sheet for Nessa for the week commencing 4 June 20X7.

(b) A group of six employees work on a particular batch of a product on a production line. In one particular day they work on two batches. One batch, number 239457, requires in total 25 hours of their labour at an average cost of £6.50 per hour and the second batch, number 239458, requires only 23 hours at an average cost of £6.50 per hour. Both batches also require the labour of additional employees who are paid by results. Their agreed payment is £2.50 per unit produced. Batch 239457 totals 27 units and batch 239458 totals 24 units.

Record these details on cost cards for each batch number.

17 ANSWERS TO MULTIPLE CHOICE QUESTIONS

17.1 **B** Unless the overtime can be traced to a specific product or job, it will be treated as an indirect production cost, i.e. factory overhead.

17.2 **C**

$$\text{Actual expected total time} = \frac{2{,}520}{0.9} = 2{,}800 \text{ hours}$$

∴ Budgeted labour cost = 2,800 × £4 = £11,200.

17.3 **B**

The stores function in a factory is an indirect activity. Any costs of the stores function are therefore classified as indirect.

17.4 62,965 + 13,600 = £76,565. The only direct costs are the wages paid to direct workers for ordinary time, plus the basic pay for overtime. Overtime premium and shift allowances are usually treated as overheads. However, if and when overtime and shiftwork are incurred specifically for a particular cost unit, they are classified as direct costs of that cost unit. Sick pay is treated as an overhead and is therefore classified as an indirect cost.

Therefore **B.**

18   ANSWERS TO PRACTICE QUESTIONS

18.1   Components A, B and C

(a)   **Calculation of total payroll cost**

		I £	II £	III £	IV £	Total £
Basic pay:						
I	$6 \times £6.00 \times 40$	1,440.00				
II	$18 \times £5.00 \times 42$		3,600.00			
III	$4 \times £4.50 \times 40$			720.00		
IV	$1 \times £4.00 \times 44$				160.00	
		1,440.00	3,600.00	720.00	160.00	5,920.00

		I £	II £	III £	IV £	Total £
Overtime premium:						
I	$6 \times £3.00 \times (40 - 38)$	36.00				
II	$18 \times £2.50 \times (42 - 38)$		180.00			
III	$4 \times £2.25 \times (40 - 38)$			18.00		
IV	$1 \times £2.00 \times (44 - 38)$				12.00	
		360.00	180.00	18.00	12.00	246.00

Bonus payable (see working):

		I £	II £	III £	IV £	Total £
			Grade of Labour			
I	$\dfrac{240}{1,200} \times 360 \times (75\% \times £6)$	324.00				
II	$\dfrac{756}{1,200} \times 360 \times (75\% \times £5)$		850.50			
III	$\dfrac{160}{1,200} \times 360 \times (75\% \times £4.50)$			162.00		
IV	$\dfrac{44}{1,200} \times 360 \times (75\% \times £4)$				39.60	
		324.00	850.50	162.00	39.60	1,376.10
Total (gross) pay		1,800.00	4,630.50	900.00	211.60	7,542.10

WORKING

Standard time for actual output:

Component		Std hrs
A	$444 \times 0.5 =$	222
B	$900 \times 0.9 =$	810
C	$480 \times 1.1 =$	528
Total standard hours		1,560

Actual time:

Grade		
I	6×40	240
II	18×42	756
III	4×40	160
IV	1×44	44
Total standard hours		1,200
Total hours saved		360

(b)   Advantages of a group incentive scheme:

   (i)   Emphasises the need for worker co-operation to achieve required targets for the company.

   (ii)   Applicable when a production line exists or when operatives work in crews or gangs.

   Disadvantages of a group incentive scheme:

   (i)   The more conscientious members of the group create the benefit that has to be shared with the less efficient members of the group. This can have a demotivational effect on the former.

   (iii)   Where there are different degrees of skill required by members of the group it may be difficult to recognise this easily and objectively in allocating the bonus between the group members.

18.2   FG Toyles Ltd

(a)

TIME SHEET					
Name: Nessa Trandheim				**Clock Number:** NT641	
Department: Factory					
Week commencing: 4 June 20X7					
To be completed by employee				For office use	
Day	*Start*	*Finish*	*Job*	*Code*	*Hours*
Monday	9.00	12.00	Product J		
	1.00	7.00	Product L		
Tuesday	8.00	12.00	Product L		
	1.00	6.00	Product K		
Wednesday	9.00	12.00	Product K		
	1.00	5.00	Product K		
Thursday	8.00	1.00	Product K		
	2.00	5.00	Product K		
Friday	8.00	11.00	Product L		
	12.30	5.30	Product J		
Basic pay					
Overtime premium					_____
Gross wages					_____
Foreman's signature:					
Date:					

(b)

COST CARD - BATCH 239457	
	£
Materials cost	X
Labour cost	
(25 hours × £6.50)	162.50
(27 units × £2.50)	67.50

COST CARD - BATCH 239458	
	£
Materials cost	X
Labour cost	
(23 hours × £6.50)	149.50
(24 units × £2.50)	60.00

Chapter 6

EXPENSES

PATHFINDER INTRODUCTION

This chapter covers the following elements of the CAT Official Teaching Guide. At the end of this chapter you should have learned these teaching guide elements thoroughly.

Session 6
Expenses
Syllabus reference h

- Explain the procedures required to ensure the correct coding, analysis and recording of direct and indirect expenses
- Describe capital and revenue expenditure and the relevant accounting treatment
- Calculate and explain depreciation charges using suitable methods (straight line and reducing balance)

Putting the chapter in context

Once the cost account has identified the material and labour costs of each product or part of the business, they must calculate a fair share of expenses. The next four chapters explain how this is done. This chapter explains what expenses are and how they are recorded.

1 CODING, ANALYSIS AND RECORDING OF DIRECT AND INDIRECT EXPENSES

1.1 Introduction

To a cost accountant there are three types of business expenditure: materials, labour and expenses.

Definition   **Expenses** are all revenue expenditures that are not classified as materials or labour costs.

1.2 Types of expenses

An organisation will incur many different types of expenses. There may be expenses associated with the manufacturing process or the factory, the selling process, general administration or day to day running of the business and the financing of the business.

1.3 Manufacturing expenses - examples

Examples of expenses incurred during the manufacturing process are:

- the power for the machinery;
- the lighting and heating of the factory;
- general running costs of the machinery such as oil;
- insurance of the machinery;
- cleaning of the factory and machines;
- costs of protective clothing.

1.4   Selling expenses - examples

When selling goods to customers the expenses that might be incurred are:

- advertising costs;
- packaging costs;
- costs of delivering the goods to the customer;
- commission paid to salesmen;
- costs of after sales care;
- warehouse rental for storage of goods.

1.5   Administration expenses - examples

The everyday running of the organisation will involve many different expenses including the following:

- rent of buildings;
- business rates on buildings;
- insurance of the buildings;
- telephone bills;
- postage and fax costs;
- computer costs;
- stationery;
- costs of providing a canteen for the employees;
- auditor's fees.

1.6   Finance expenses - examples

The costs of financing an organisation might include the following:

- loan interest;
- lease charges if any equipment or buildings are leased rather than purchased.

1.7   Analysis of expenses

All expenses of a business can be analysed as either direct expenses or indirect expenses.

1.8   Direct expenses

Definition   **Direct expenses** are expenses that can be attributed to a particular product or cost unit. Examples might include the following:

- running costs of a machine used for only one product line;
- packaging costs for a product.

There are generally only a very few direct expenses for most businesses

1.9   Indirect expenses

Definition   **Indirect expenses** are expenses that cannot be attributed to a particular product or cost unit but are expenses that relate to a number of different products or cost units. Examples might include the following:

- lighting and heating for the factory;
- cleaning of the factory;
- cost of running a fleet of vans or lorries for distribution;
- telephone bills;
- loan interest.

Conclusion   The majority of materials and labour costs will be direct costs as they can be specifically attributed to cost units. The majority of expenses, however, will tend to be indirect costs as they will be items of expenditure that relate to a number of different products or cost units.

1.10   Coding of expenses

The simplest way of recording expenses as either direct or indirect is to allocate some type of code when the expense is incurred or authorised. In this way the expense will then be correctly treated when it is eventually recorded in the cost accounts.

1.11   Recording of direct expenses

The direct expenses incurred are part of the cost of the cost units that the business produces and as such will be recorded in the work in progress control account together with direct materials and direct labour costs. (This will be dealt with in more detail at the end of this chapter.)

1.12   Recording of indirect expenses

Indirect expenses are part of the overheads of a business. The other elements of the overheads are indirect materials and indirect labour.

All production overheads must be attributed to cost centres. The overheads gathered together in the cost centres are then eventually included as a part of the cost of the cost units. This process is fairly complex and is dealt with in detail in the next two chapters.

Conclusion   The aim of cost accounting is to provide a total cost figure for each product. The direct cost of a product will include any direct expenses. Indirect costs or overheads, largely made up of indirect expenses, are attributed to cost centres and finally to cost units.

2   CAPITAL AND REVENUE EXPENDITURE

2.1   Introduction

When a business spends money on an item it must be classified as either capital expenditure or revenue expenditure. The importance of the distinction between these two types of expenditure is in their accounting treatments which are completely different.

2.2   Capital expenditure

Definition   **Capital expenditure** is money spent by a business on fixed assets.

Definition   **Fixed assets** are assets of the business that are for long term use in the business.

Therefore when a business buys items of machinery, cars, computers, office furniture or a building these will all be classified as capital expenditure.

2.3   Revenue expenditure

Definition   Revenue expenditure is all expenditure other than capital expenditure.

Revenue expenditure will therefore include expenditure on materials, wages, power costs, lighting and heating bills, telephone bills, rent, to name but a few.

2.4   Accounting treatment of capital expenditure

The accounting treatment of capital expenditure is that the cost of the fixed asset is included as a fixed asset in the balance sheet of the business rather than being part of the expenses of the business in the profit and loss account.

2.5   Accounting treatment of revenue expenditure

The accounting treatment of revenue expenditure is that it is treated as an expense in the profit and loss account in the period in which the expense was incurred.

Conclusion   The importance of the distinction between capital and revenue expenditure is in its accounting treatment. The cost of fixed assets, capital expenditure, is taken straight to the balance sheet of the business. The cost of all other items of expenditure, revenue expenditure, is taken to the profit and loss account as an expense for the period.

3   DEPRECIATION

3.1   Introduction

Definition   **Depreciation** is the measure of the wearing out, consumption or other reduction in the useful economic life of a fixed asset.

Depreciation is a way of reflecting that when an asset is owned and used in a business there will be a cost to the business of using this asset. This will not just be the cost of running and maintaining the asset but also a cost in terms of using up some of the working life of the fixed asset.

Remember that when a fixed asset is purchased its cost is taken straight to the balance sheet. Depreciation is a method of charging some of the initial cost of a fixed asset to the accounts in each period that the asset is used. The reason for doing this is that the asset is being used to benefit the business by making goods or earning revenues, therefore a proportion of the asset's cost should be charged to the business as an expense in order to match with these revenues.

3.2   Methods of depreciation

The simplest method of calculating depreciation is to take the cost of the fixed asset less expected resale value and simply divide by the number of years of the life of the asset. This method of calculating depreciation is known as the **straight line method** and is one that is commonly used in practice.

There are many other methods of calculating annual depreciation charges but only two others are likely to be relevant to this syllabus. These are the reducing balance method and the machine hours method.

3.3   Straight line depreciation

This is a method of charging the same amount of depreciation each year of the asset's life.

3.4   Accounting - straight line method of depreciation

Suppose that a car is purchased for £15,000 and is expected to have a resale value of £5,140 in three years time when the organisation disposes of it.

Calculate the annual depreciation charge for the car on a straight line basis.

3.5   Solution

	£
Cost	15,000
Loan: Estimated residual value	5,140
Amount by which car is to be depreciated over its 3 year life	9,860

Annual depreciation charge $= \dfrac{9,860}{3} = £3,287$

3.6   Reducing balance method of depreciation

Definition   The **reducing balance** method of depreciation applies the percentage depreciation rate to the net book value of the asset to calculate the annual depreciation charge.

3.7   Activity - reducing balance method

Using the same information as before suppose that a car is purchased for £15,000 and is expected to have a resale value of £5,140 in three years time when the organisation will dispose of it.

Calculate the depreciation charge for each of the three years if a rate of 30% is applied using the reducing balance method.

3.8   Activity solution

	£
Cost	15,000
Year 1 depreciation charge (£15,000 × 30%)	4,500
Net book value	10,500
Year 2 depreciation charge (£10,500 × 30%)	3,150
Net book value	7,350
Year 3 depreciation charge (£7,350 × 30%)	2,205
Net book value	5,145

3.9   Machine hours method of depreciation

The machine hours method of calculating depreciation is based upon the actual usage of the asset rather than the passage of time. As such it is often more appropriate for cost accounting purposes than other methods.

3.10   Activity - machine hours

A machine has been purchased for £10,000 and has an estimated residual value after the five years that it will be used by the organisation of zero. During those five years it is estimated that the machine will be operational for 15,000 hours. In the first year of operations the machine was used for 2,000 hours.

Using the machine hours method of calculating depreciation what is the depreciation charge for the first year?

3.11   Activity solution

$$\text{Depreciation charge} \quad = \quad \frac{2,000 \text{ hours}}{15,000 \text{ hours}} \times £10,000$$

$$= \qquad £1,333$$

Conclusion   Whatever the method of calculating depreciation it is an expense of the business that should appear in the financial accounting profit and loss account. The treatment of the expense of depreciation for cost accounting purposes will be as for any other expense incurred by the business.

4   JOURNAL AND LEDGER ENTRIES FOR EXPENSES

4.1   Introduction

It has already been seen in this chapter that expenses will be categorised as direct or indirect. The initial recording of the expenses in the ledger accounts will depend upon this categorisation.

4.2   Direct expenses

Direct expenses are a direct cost of making the cost units and therefore are recorded in the work in progress control account. The journal entry for the initial recording of direct expenses is therefore:

DR   Work in progress control account
CR   Cash/creditors account

4.3   Indirect expenses

Indirect expenses are overheads and as such will be initially recorded in the overhead control accounts.

The precise accounts to be used will depend upon the nature of the indirect expenses:

- production overheads will be charged to the production overhead control account;

- selling and distribution overheads will be charged to the selling and distribution overhead control account;

- administration overheads will be charged to the administration overhead control account; and finance expenses will be charged to the financial overhead control account.

The journal entry for the production overheads will be:

DR   Production overhead control account
CR   Cash/creditors account

Conclusion   Direct production expenses are charged to the work in progress account. Indirect production expenses are charged to the production overhead control account.

5 CHAPTER SUMMARY

In this chapter we have looked at expenses, the different types and how they are incurred, before looking at their treatment in the journal and ledger.

6 SELF TEST QUESTIONS

6.1 Give some examples of manufacturing expenses. (1.3)

6.2 What are direct expenses? (1.8)

6.3 What are indirect expenses? (1.9)

6.4 What is capital expenditure? (2.2)

6.5 What is the accounting treatment of capital expenditure? (2.4)

6.6 What is the accounting treatment for revenue expenditure? (2.5)

6.7 Define depreciation (3.1)

6.8 How is the reducing balance method of depreciation applied? (3.5)

6.9 What is the machine hour method of depreciation? (3.9)

6.10 In which ledger accounts are indirect production expenses recorded? (4.3)

7 PRACTICE QUESTIONS

7.1 Cost collection techniques

Cost collection techniques are fundamental to the operation of an effective cost accounting system.

Explain clearly the procedures used to collect

(a) material costs;
(b) labour costs; and
(c) other expenses.

(You should make reference to cost centre structures and documentation to be used.)

7.2 Interior Ltd

(a) Traditional Interior Ltd produces furniture items.

Consider whether the following are direct or indirect (overhead) materials

	Direct	Indirect
Wood used as raw material		
Glue and varnish		
Stationery used by secretarial staff		
Oil used to lubricate turning machines		
Hinges for doors		

Door handles

(b)   Explain whether you agree with each of the following statements:

(i)   'All direct costs are variable'
(ii)   'Variable costs are controllable and fixed costs are not'.

8   ANSWERS TO PRACTICE QUESTIONS

8.1   Cost collection techniques

Cost collection is needed to identify all costs incurred by an organisation. Only when this is known will an organisation be able to plan and control its cost structure. Normally costs are related to the cost unit for control purposes.

An effective system of classifying costs must be in operation. Costs may be classified as direct and indirect, fixed and variable, by function and by whether they are material, labour or overheads. Once the classification system is in place the costs are coded with the appropriate classification. It must be noted that even the most developed systems will require a degree of judgement in the coding of some costs.

(a)   **Materials**

Material costs normally make up a high percentage of a manufacturing organisation's costs. The costs are identified on receipt of materials from suppliers. The valuation of stock will include carriage inward and bulk discounts but not cash discounts or VAT (which can be reclaimed). Material is normally held as stock before it is used and a record is kept of all receipts and issues. The records in common usage are either stores ledger record cards or bin cards.

A stock valuation method such as first in first out (FIFO) must be used to relate the value of the receipts to the value of issues.

Documentation commonly used will include:

Goods received note: indicating that the material has been received into stock
Materials requisition note: a requirement for stock from the production or sales department.

(b)   **Labour**

Labour costs are of importance to all organisations but particularly to service organisations where they can easily be a majority of total costs.

Most remuneration systems are time based hence a record is needed of how many hours an employee has worked each day. The most common form of attendance record is the clock card. The employees are required to record their time of arrival and departure. With increasing use of flexible working hours more sophisticated recording systems may be used identifying comings and goings during the day.

A more detailed record is normally held of where the employee has worked during the day; this is called a timesheet. Timesheets record how many hours have been worked on a specific cost unit or within a cost centre in order that the costs can be identified with specific operations or departments. The timesheet should reconcile with the attendance record; idle time cards completed by managers may be required for this to be possible.

(c)   **Other expenses**

Expenses may be direct but are usually indirect with regard to the cost unit. As such cost collection will concentrate on identifying expenses to cost centres. Some expenses however only apply to the business as a whole for example, rates. More so than either material or labour costs, expenses include many different cost elements, each of which will be recorded and collected individually.

In summary, the cost accounting system requires accurate collection of costs in order to provide information for control purposes and for use in financial statements.

8.2   Interior Ltd

(a)   Wood   -   direct
       Glue and varnish   -   direct
       Stationery   -   indirect
       Oil   -   indirect
       Hinges   -   direct
       Door handles   -   direct

(b)   (i)   **All direct costs are variable**

This is not necessarily true. A direct cost is a cost which can be directly attributable to a unit of production or a cost centre. Where costs are attributed to a unit of production they will be variable, although discounts for volume will perhaps affect the linearity of this relationship. Where costs are attributable to cost centres, there will be direct costs which are not variable. For instance, where process costing is used, the process manager's wages will be a direct cost of the process, but will be a fixed cost. A similar case can be made for depreciation of process plant.

(ii)   **Variable costs are controllable and fixed costs are not**

This is not always so. While it is probably true that most variable costs are controllable and many fixed are not, there is no direct relationship between the two classifications. Costs may be classified into fixed and variable, depending on their behaviour when output levels fluctuate. Costs may also be classified into controllable and uncontrollable, depending on the circumstances, the authority of the individual and the time span being considered e.g. depreciation can be treated as a fixed cost or a variable cost. It is usually charged on a time basis and treated as fixed, but it can be charged on a usage basis and treated as variable. Depreciation will be uncontrollable to the process supervisor, but may be regarded as controllable in the long-term by the process manager who authorises capital expenditure, but once purchased, is uncontrollable by him in the short-term.

Chapter 7

OVERHEAD ALLOCATION AND APPORTIONMENT

PATHFINDER INTRODUCTION

This chapter covers the following elements of the CAT Official Teaching Guide. At the end of this chapter you should have learned these teaching guide elements thoroughly.

Session 7
Overhead allocation and apportionment
Syllabus reference i

- Describe the nature of overheads by function
- Describe and justify the process of allocating and apportioning manufacturing overhead costs
- Explain and illustrate the allocation of overheads in a responsibility accounting structure
- Explain and illustrate the apportionment of overheads using appropriate bases
- Explain and illustrate the reapportionment of service department overheads using the repeated distribution method

Putting the chapter in context

Indirect expenses cannot be separately identified with each product or part of the business, but must be shared out over products. This chapter explains how such expenses are allocated or apportioned between cost centres. This is the first stage in the calculation of cost per product which continues in the next chapter.

1 NATURE OF OVERHEADS

1.1 Introduction

In an earlier chapter a distinction has been drawn between direct costs and indirect costs.

Direct costs of a business are recorded in the cost accounting records of cost units. These direct costs will be made up of direct materials, direct labour costs and where applicable direct expenses.

Indirect costs or overheads of the organisation cannot by definition be costed directly to units of production. They must therefore be dealt with separately. These indirect costs or overheads will be made up of indirect materials, indirect labour costs and indirect expenses.

1.2 Treatment of indirect costs

Indirect costs or overheads are treated in one of two ways for cost accounting purposes. Overheads related to the production of cost units are treated as production overheads. Other overheads are treated as non-production overheads. This is analysis of overheads by their function within the businesses.

1.3 Production overheads

Definition   **Production overheads** are those indirect costs that are directly related to the production of the products of the business. They are part of the cost of those products. These might include overheads such as the power necessary to run the machinery, the rent of the factory and the costs involved in providing a canteen for the production workers. Production overheads are also referred to as **manufacturing overheads**.

1.4   Production overhead cost centres

Production overheads can be incurred by a variety of different cost centres. The typical cost centres that incur production overheads are the factory itself which may be split into a number of different departments or cost centres, the stores function, the maintenance function, the canteen and the warehouse.

1.5   Non-production overheads

Definition   **Non-production overheads** are necessary expenses of the organisation that are not directly related to the production of the cost units or products.

These overheads are classified as selling and distribution overheads, administration overheads and finance overheads.

Conclusion   In this syllabus we are primarily concerned with the treatment of production overheads and how they are allocated as costs to a cost unit.

2   PROCESS OF ALLOCATING AND APPORTIONING MANUFACTURING OVERHEAD

2.1   Introduction

To calculate the full cost of producing a unit it is necessary to identify not only the direct cost of the product, but also the indirect costs that are relevant to the production of the product.

2.2   Allocation and apportionment

The first task is to identify production overheads with cost centres. Those relating solely to a single production department, such as a specific part of the factory, are **allocated** directly to that production department.

Those overheads that relate to a number of different areas of the business, or cost centres, must be shared between them. This is done by **apportioning** any joint overheads amongst all of the cost centres that share in incurring that overhead.

Definition   **Apportioning overheads** in a method of splitting any joint overheads amongst the cost centres that incur them.

2.3   Overheads to be apportioned

The overheads apportioned to cost centres can be either fixed costs or variable costs.

If expenses such as rent or rates of premises are to be apportioned then this will be the apportionment of a fixed cost. Equally variable costs can also need to be apportioned between cost centres.

For example the total electricity cost of a building may need to be apportioned between the various cost centres that use electricity in the building such as the factory, the offices and the warehouse.

Conclusion   The apportionment or splitting up, of overheads to the relevant cost centres can involve both fixed and variable overheads.

3   ALLOCATION OF OVERHEADS IN A RESPONSIBILITY ACCOUNTING STRUCTURE

3.1   Introduction

The syllabus refers to the allocation of overheads in a responsibility accounting structure. This refers to allocating overheads to the appropriate responsibility centre.

Definition   A **responsibility centre** is an area of the business that is the responsibility of a particular manager of the business.

A responsibility centre is likely also to be a **cost centre**, as previously discussed. For the purposes of overhead allocation, we may distinguish between production and service cost centres.

3.2   Production cost centres

Definition   A production cost centre is a cost centre which actually produces cost units.

For example the various departments or divisions of a factory will all be production cost centres.

3.3   Service cost centres

Definition   A service cost centre is a cost centre that does not actually produce any cost units but it is a necessary support or service provided for the production cost centred.

Examples of service cost centres are stores and maintenance departments.

Conclusion   Responsibility centres are usually cost centres. These can be either production or service cost centres and overhead must be allocated or apportioned to them.

4   APPORTIONMENT OF OVERHEADS

4.1   Introduction

The basis to be used for apportioning or splitting up overhead to cost centres depends upon the reason for the overhead being incurred. Some of the most common overheads that will require apportionment are considered in the sub-paragraphs below.

For the purposes of this examination paper the examiner will give the basis of apportionment to use but it is important to understand the reasons for the basis given.

4.2   Rent

If an organisation rents its premises, it will pay rent for all the floor area that it occupied. This total floor area might be shared by the factory, stores, maintenance, warehouse, canteen, personnel, accounts, marketing and selling functions.

The fairest method of apportioning the total rent to each of these cost centres is on the basis of the amount of floor area that each function occupies. Therefore the rent apportioned to each cost centre will depend upon the proportion of the total space that the cost centre uses.

4.3   Rates

The business rates of an organisation are similar to the rent of premises. Both are costs of occupying premises. As such it is usual also to apportion the rates to cost centres on the basis of the floor area occupied by each cost centre.

4.4   Insurance

Insurance costs might be for buildings, machinery or vehicles.

The buildings insurance is most commonly apportioned on the basis of the floor area occupied by each cost centre.

The insurance of machinery could be apportioned either on the basis of the number of machines used by each cost centre, the value of the machines in each cost centre or possibly by the machine time used by each cost centre.

The insurance of vehicles could be apportioned on the basis of usage of the actual vehicles by each cost centre.

4.5   Choice of bases

The examples above show there is no 'right' basis for the apportionment of costs. The basis that is chosen is dependent upon the nature of the organisation itself and the policies that it chooses to follow. The basis given will normally be a common service basis related to the underlying course of that particular overhead.

4.6   Activity

The total rental cost for an organisation is £20,000. The total floor area of the buildings is 100,000 square feet. The assembly department takes up 6,000 square feet and the stores department 10,000 square feet.

How much of the total rent cost should be apportioned to the assembly department and the stores department?

4.7   Activity solution

Assembly department:

		£
$\dfrac{6,000}{100,000} \times £20,000$		1,200

Stores department:

$\dfrac{10,000}{100,000} \times £20,000$	2,000

Conclusion   Overhead costs are apportioned to cost centres on the most appropriate basis for that organisation. This will generally be based around the reasons or physical cause of the overhead such as the amount of floor space occupied or the number of employees in each cost centre. Students will be given the basis of apportionment to use in the exam.

5   ALLOCATION AND APPORTIONMENT OF OVERHEADS TO PRODUCTION COST CENTRES

5.1   Introduction

The purpose of the apportionment of joint overheads to cost centres is to eventually gather together the total of **all** production overheads into the production cost centres.

It was noted earlier in this chapter that there are a number of overheads that are incurred by non-production cost centres. These are costs of production as they are necessary costs involved in the production of the cost units. However they are costs incurred by **service** cost centres rather than **production** cost centres. Examples of service cost centres are stores, maintenance, warehouse and the canteen.

The process must, therefore, recognise that costs that have been initially allocated/apportioned to a service cost centre will eventually need to be attributed to production cost centres.

5.2   The process of apportioning overheads

Step 1   Allocate any costs that are specific to an individual cost centre to that cost centre.

Step 2   Apportion any overheads that relate to a number of different cost centres between all of the relevant cost centres.

Step 3   Apportion service cost centre costs to the production cost centres on some appropriate basis.

By the end of step 3 all of the production overheads of the organisation will be allocated to production cost centres.

5.3   Activity

An organisation has two production departments, A and B, and two service departments, stores and the canteen.

The overhead costs for the organisation in total are as follows:

	£
Rent	32,000
Rates	5,000
Machinery insurance	2,400
Machinery depreciation	11,000
Machinery running expenses	6,000
Power	7,000

There are also specific costs that have already been allocated to each cost centre as follows:

	£
Department A	5,000
Department B	4,000
Stores	1,000
Canteen	2,000

The following information about the various cost centres is also available:

	Total	Dept A	Dept B	Stores	Canteen
Floor space (sq ft)	30,000	15,000	8,000	5,000	2,000
Power usage	100%	45%	40%	5%	10%
Value of machinery (£'000)	250	140	110	-	-
Machinery hours ('000)	80	50	30		

Allocate and apportion the costs on the following bases the four departments:

- Rent and rates - Floor space
- Machinery insurance and machinery deprecation - machine value
- Machinery running expenses - machinery hours
- Power - power usage.

5.4   Activity solution

OVERHEAD ANALYSIS SHEET	TOTAL	PRODUCTION		SERVICE	
		Dept A	Dept B	Stores	Canteen
	£	£	£	£	£
Overheads allocated directly to cost centres	12,000	5,000	4,000	1,000	2,000
Overheads to be apportioned					
Rent Basis: floor space	32,000				
15/30 × £32,000		16,000			
8/30 × £32,000			8,534		
5/30 × £32,000				5,333	
2/30 × £32,000					2,133
Rates Basis: floor space	5,000				
15/30 × £5,000		2,500			
8/30 × £5,000			1,333		
5/30 × £5,000				834	
2/30 × £5,000					333
Machinery insurance Basis: machine value	2,400				
140/250 × £2,400		1,344			
110/250 × £2,400			1,056	-	-
Machinery depreciation Basis: machine value	11,000				
140/250 × £11,000		6,160			
110/250 × £11,000			4,840	-	-

Machinery running expenses	6,000			
Basis: machine hours				
50/80 × £6,000		3,750		
30/80 × £6,000			2,250	-	-
Power	7,000			
Basis: power usage percentages				
£7,000 × 45%		3,150		
£7,000 × 40%			2,800	
£7,000 × 5%				350
£7,000 × 10%					700
	75,400	37,904	24,813	7,517	5,166

6   REAPPORTIONMENT OF SERVICE DEPARTMENT OVERHEADS

6.1   Introduction

In the previous section the allocation of overheads that are specific to a single cost centre (step 1) and the apportionment of all of the joint overheads to the relevant cost centres (step 2) were considered.

The object of this exercise is to find the total overhead cost for each cost centre.

At this stage it is necessary to apportion the service cost centre costs to the production cost centres on some equitable basis (step 3).

6.2   Service centre costs

The costs or overheads of the service cost centres must now be apportioned to the production cost centres. This will be done according to the most appropriate basis given the circumstances of the organisation. Again for this syllabus the basis of apportionment will be given.

6.3   Activity

Assume that we have already allocated and apportioned the overhead costs in the activity in the previous paragraph.

OVERHEAD ANALYSIS SHEET				PERIOD ENDING.................	
	TOTAL	PRODUCTION		SERVICE	
		Dept A	Dept B	Stores	Canteen
	£	£	£	£	£
Total overhead	75,400	37,904	24,813	7,517	5,166

You are required to apportion the service department costs to the production departments.

The apportionment of the stores department costs should be done on the basis of the value of requisitions by each production department. Apportionment of the canteen costs should be on the basis of the number of employees in departments A and B.

	Total	Dept A	Dept B	Stores	Canteen
Number of employees	40	20	15	3	2
Value of stores requisitions (£'000)	150	100	50	-	-

6.4 Activity solution

OVERHEAD ANALYSIS SHEET   PERIOD ENDING...........................

	TOTAL	PRODUCTION		SERVICE	
	£	Dept A £	Dept B £	Stores £	Canteen £
Total overhead	75,400	37,904	24,813	7,517	5,166
Apportion stores Basis: requisitions 100/150 × £7,517 50/150 × £7,517		5,011	2,506	(7,517)	
Apportion canteen Basis: number of employees 20/35 × £5,166 15/35 × £5,166		2,952	2,214	–	(5,166)
Total overhead		45,867	29,533	–	–

Conclusion   This is the simplest situation where the service cost centres are isolated from each other. The assumption is implicit that the stores personnel do not use the canteen and that the canteen does not use the stores function. This is a situation where service centres do not service each other.

6.5 Service departments servicing each other

A slightly more complex example is where one of the service departments provides its service to another service department. This means that part of the providers costs must be apportioned to the receiving service department

6.6   Activity

The ABC Washing Machine Co produces a standard washing machine in three production departments (Machining, Assembling and Finishing) and two service departments (Materials handling and Production control).

Costs for last year, when 2,000 machines were produced, were as follows:

Indirect materials:

Materials handling	£4,000

Indirect wages:

Materials handling	£8,000
Production control	£11,200

Other indirect expenses:

Machine shop	£41,920
Assembly	£12,960
Finishing	£7,920
Materials handling	£8,000
Production control	£2,400

It is estimated that the benefit derived from the service departments is as follows:

Materials handling:

Machine shop	60%
Assembly	30%
Finishing	10%

Production control:

Machine shop	40%
Assembly	30%
Finishing	20%
Materials handling	10%

Prepare a statement showing the overhead allocated and apportioned to each of the production departments;

6.7   Activity solution

Overhead allocation and apportionment

	Total £	Machining £	Assembly £	Finishing £	Production control £	Materials handling £
Indirect materials	4,000	-	-	-	-	4,000
Indirect wages	19,200	-	-	-	11,200	8,000
Other	73,200	41,920	12,960	7,920	2,400	8,000
	96,400	41,920	12,960	7,920	13,600	20,000
Production control	-	5,440	4,080	2,720	(13,600)	1,360
Materials handling	-	12,816	6,408	2,136	-	(21,360)
	96,400	60,176	23,448	12,776	-	-

Service department costs have been apportioned to production departments using the percentage benefit shown in the question. As 10% of the production control overhead is to be charged to materials handling, production control must be apportioned before material handling.

6.8   Reciprocal costs between service centres

The most complex situation arises when service centres provide reciprocal services to each other, e.g.:

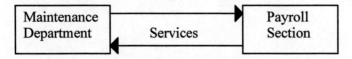

In this situation, a secondary allocation of costs arise. There are a number of methods of dealing with this. The only method required for this syllabus is the repeated distribution method.

6.9   Repeated distribution method

This method takes each service department in turn and reallocates its costs to all departments which benefit. The reallocation continues until the numbers being dealt with become very small.

6.10   Activity

Department	Production			Service	
	A	B	C	P	Q
Costs	£3,000	£4,000	£2,000	£2,500	£2,700
% of service P used	20	30	25	-	25
% of service Q used	25	25	30	20	-

6.11   Activity solution

Department	Production			Service	
	A £	B £	C £	P £	Q £
Costs	3,000	4,000	2,000	2,500	2,700
Reapportion P (20 : 30 : 25 : 25)	500	750	625	(2,500)	625
				Nil	3,325
Reapportion Q (25 : 25 : 30 : 20)	831	831	998	665	(3,325)
				665	Nil
Reapportion P (20 : 30 : 25 : 25)	133	200	166	(665)	166
				Nil	166
Reapportion Q (25 : 25 : 30 : 20)	42	41	50	33	(166)
				33	Nil

Reapportion P (20 : 30 : 25 : 25)	7	10	8	(33)	8
				Nil	8
Reapportion Q (25 : 25 : 30 : 20)	2	2	2	2	
				2	Nil
Reapportion P (20 : 30 : 25 : 25)	-	1	1	(2)	-
Total allocated to production centres	4,515	5,835	3,850	-	-

Conclusion By using the repeated distribution method the complex situation of reciprocal servicing can be dealt with. The result is that all of the overheads are apportioned to the production cost centres.

6.12 Algebraic approach to re-apportionment of overheads

There is an alternative method of arriving at the apportionment of overheads in the previous activity using simultaneous equations. This method is not compulsory for this syllabus but it is sometimes quicker than the repeated distribution method.

6.13 Activity

The algebraic approach to the previous activity is illustrated below.

6.14 Activity solution

Let P = total costs of department P
Let Q = total costs of department Q

P = £2,500 + 0.20Q   (equation 1)
Q = £2,700 + 0.25P   (equation 2)

These two equations can be solved simultaneously in a variety of ways. One of the simplest is to substitute equation (2) into equation (1) as follows:

P = £2,500 + 0.20(£2,700 + 0.25P)

Expanding, this equation becomes:

P = £2,500 + 540 + 0.05P
P = £3,040 + 0.05P

Rearranging this becomes:

0.95P = £3,040

$$P = \frac{£3,040}{0.95}$$

P = £3,200

Substituting back into equation (2):

$$Q = £2,700 + 0.25 \times £3,200$$

$$Q = £3,500$$

Reapportionment of the service departments overheads can now be carried out as follows:

	Production			Service	
	A £	B £	C £	P £	Q £
	3,000	4,000	2,000	2,500	2,700
Reapportion P £3,200 (20:30:25:25)	640	960	800	(3,200)	800
Reapportion Q £3,500 (25:25:30:20)	875	875	1,050	700	(3,500)
Total cost allocated to production departments	4,515	5,835	3,850	-	-

Conclusion   The algebraic approach to reapportioning service department costs in a reciprocal servicing situation will always give the same total of overhead costs in the production departments as the repeated distribution method. The algebraic approach will not be compulsory in the examination although some students may find it quicker than the repeated distribution method. It is important that students understand and can apply the repeated distribution method.

7   CHAPTER SUMMARY

In the examples given in this chapter the process of dealing with overheads has been carried out as follows:

Step 1   Determine the production cost centres of the organisation, for example machining and assembly departments;

Step 2   Determine the service cost centres of the organisation, for example the canteen and the maintenance departments;

Step 3   Allocate and apportion the overheads to each of the cost centres using appropriate bases of apportionment;

Step 4   Reapportion the service cost centre costs to the production cost centres using appropriate bases of apportionment.

In this manner all of the production overheads are allocated and apportioned to the production cost centres. In the following chapter we will then see how these production overheads are included in the cost of the units of production.

This process is the traditional overhead apportionment process.

There is an alternative approach to overhead apportionment known as activity based costing (ABC), which you will study in later papers.

8   SELF TEST QUESTIONS

8.1   Define production overheads. (1.3)

8.2   Give examples of classifications of non-production overheads. (1.5)

8.3   What is meant by overhead allocation? (2.2)

8.4   What is meant by overhead apportionment? (2.3)

8.5   What is a production cost centre? (3.3)

8.6   What is a service cost centre? (3.4)

8.7   How are bases of apportionment of overheads chosen? (4.5)

8.8   What is the term for the situation where service cost centres provide their service to other service cost centres? (6.8)

8.9   What is meant by the repeated distribution method of overhead apportionment? (6.9)

8.10   When is the repeated distribution method of overhead apportionment required? (6.9)

9   MULTIPLE CHOICE QUESTIONS

9.1   The process of cost apportionment is carried out so that:

A   costs may be controlled.
B   cost units gather overheads as they pass through cost centres.
C   whole items of cost can be charged to cost centres.
D   common costs are shared among cost centres.

9.2   What is cost apportionment?

A   The charging of discrete identifiable items of cost to cost centres or cost units

B   The collection of costs attributable to cost centres and cost units using the costing methods, principles and techniques prescribed for a particular business entity

C   The process of establishing the costs of cost centres or cost units
D   The division of costs amongst two or more cost centres in proportion to the estimated benefit received, using a proxy e.g. square feet.

10   PRACTICE QUESTIONS

10.1   Direct and indirect costs

(a)   **You are required** to distinguish between, and give examples of, direct costs and indirect costs.

(b)   The valuation of finished goods stocks and work-in-progress in a company manufacturing a range of products requires costs to be collected and classified according to the functions of the organisation.

You are required:

(i)   to describe the procedures necessary to collect the indirect costs of a manufacturing company;

(ii)   to explain the procedures used to ascertain the cost of stocks and work-in-progress in such organisations.

10.2   Fibrex Ltd

Shown below are next year's budgeted operating costs for Fibrex Ltd, a company with three production and two service departments.

	Weaving dept £'000	Proofing dept £'000	Finishing dept £'000	Personnel services £'000	Equipment maintenance £'000	Total £'000
	Production departments			*Service departments*		*Total*
Direct materials	7,000	2,000	1,500	-	-	10,500
Direct wages	2,500	5,500	2,000	-	-	10,000
Indirect materials and wages	1,100	900	300	1,500	3,800	7,600
Power	5,200	1,000	200	100	800	7,300
Rent and rates						8,000
Factory admin- istration and supervision						10,000
Machine insurance						2,400

Additional data extracted from next year's budget is shown below

	Weaving dept	Proofing dept	Finishing dept	Personnel services	Equipment maintenance	Total
Floor area (square metres)	12,000	27,000	6,000	12,000	3,000	60,000
Machine hours	1,600,000	400,000	400,000	-	-	2,400,000
Direct labour hours	1,200,000	1,800,000	600,000	-	-	3,600,000
Number of employees	600	1,000	400	100	400	2,500
Gross book value of equipment	£4.0 mill	£1.0 mill	£1.0 mill	-	-	£6.0 mill

Show how the overheads would be allocated to each production department. You can assume that the Equipment maintenance department does not work for the Personnel services department.

11   ANSWERS TO MULTIPLE CHOICE QUESTIONS

11.1   Distractor A is incorrect because it refers to controllability. Distractor B is incorrect because it is describing absorption of costs. Distractor C is incorrect because it is describing allocation of costs. Only answer D refers to the sharing of common costs.

The correct answer is **D.**

11.2   **D**

12   ANSWERS TO PRACTICE QUESTIONS

12.1   Direct and indirect costs

(a)   A direct cost is expenditure which can be economically identified with and specifically measured in respect to a relevant cost object.

An example of direct costs are materials that are directly used in the manufacture of a product.

An indirect cost (or overhead) is expenditure on labour, materials or services which cannot be economically identified with a specific saleable cost unit.

An example of an indirect cost is the cost of a supervisor's wages. The supervisor may be in charge of a number of workers who are working on different products.

(b)   (i)   Indirect costs will generally include indirect materials, indirect labour and indirect expenses.

Indirect materials should be charged at their cost to the various user departments as they are used.

Indirect labour time should be recorded on labour time sheets with enough information to ascertain which user departments have benefited from the indirect labour.

Indirect expenses will generally tend to be controlled centrally and then apportioned to user departments in an equitable fashion.

All of the indirect costs, be they materials, labour or expenses, will be allocated to the user departments in an equitable manner and then absorbed into the total costs of the product or process on an appropriate basis such as time or machine usage.

(ii)   The cost of raw materials stocks in a manufacturing organisation should usually be ascertained from the purchase invoice.

The cost of work-in-progress will include both direct costs and a proportion of indirect costs. The direct materials costs should be available from the original invoice or the requisition details. The direct labour costs should be collected from the labour time recording system. This should give the hours worked and this will be multiplied by the hourly rate of pay. The indirect costs will be apportioned to the work-in-progress on some equitable basis.

12.2   Fibrex Ltd

	Production departments			Service departments		Total
	Weaving dept £'000	Proofing dept £'000	Finishing dept £'000	Personnel services £'000	Equipment maintenance £'000	£'000
Overhead costs already (seemingly) allocated (ignore direct costs as these are not overhead)	6,300	1,900	500	1,600	4,600	14,900
Apportioned costs						
Rent and rates (apportioned using floor area [12:27:6:12:3])	1,600	3,600	800	1,600	400	8,000
Factory admin and supervision (apportioned using personnel numbers [600: 1,000: 400: 100: 400])	2,400	4,000	1,600	400	1,600	10,000

Machine insurance (gross value of equipment)	1,600	400	400	-	-	2,400
Totals	11,900	9,900	3,300	3,600	6,600	35,300

Reapportionment of service costs

Personnel (employee numbers, as a basis) [600:1,000:400:400]	900	1,500	600	(3,600)	600	-
Equipment maintenance (machine hours as a basis [1,600:400:400:0])	4,800	1,200	1,200	-	(7,200)	-
Total budgeted OHD	17,600	12,600	5,100			35,300

Chapter 8

OVERHEAD ABSORPTION

PATHFINDER INTRODUCTION

This chapter covers the following elements of the CAT Official Teaching Guide. At the end of this chapter you should have learned these teaching guide elements thoroughly.

Session 8
Overhead absorption
Syllabus reference i

- Calculate and apply overhead absorption rates using different methods e.g. labour hours, machine hours
- Describe and justify the use of alternative activity measures for calculating absorption rates
- Explain the advantages and limitations of using blanket, departmental, actual and predetermined absorption rates
- Describe methods of attributing non-production overheads to cost units

Putting the chapter in context

Having shared out indirect overheads to cost centres as described in the last chapter, the cost accountant must decide on a method (called absorption) to split such overheads between products. This chapter explains how this is done so that the total cost of making a product can be calculated.

1   WHAT IS ABSORPTION OF OVERHEADS?

1.1   Allocation and apportionment to cost centres

In the previous chapter some production overheads were specifically allocated to cost centres and others were apportioned between a number of different cost centres on an appropriate basis.

The costs of service cost centres were then apportioned to production cost centres on an appropriate basis. Thus all production overheads were split between the production cost centres.

1.2   Treatment of overhead costs

The overheads incurred or apportioned to a production cost centre are the overheads incurred in producing the products that are made in that production department. The overheads are a valid part of the product cost just like direct materials, direct labour and direct expenses. So, production cost centres' overhead costs must be apportioned to each individual product or cost unit in some way, this is called absorption.

1.3   Absorption of overhead costs

Definition   **Absorption of overhead costs** is a method of including a fair proportion of the total overhead costs as part of the cost of each cost unit.

Overheads are absorbed into cost units by sharing out overhead costs of a production department for the period amongst the products (or cost units) actually produced in the period.

There are many different possible methods of doing this absorption of costs. The most common methods will be considered later in this chapter.

1.4 Absorption on the basis of units produced

The simplest method of estimating the amount of overhead to be included in the cost of each unit of production is to take the total estimated production overhead and divide it by the number of units expected to be produced in the period.

1.5 Activity

The total standard production overhead for the next month for an organisation is estimated to be £40,000. In that month it is estimated that 80,000 products will be produced. What is the overhead absorption rate based upon the standard number of units to be produced?

1.6 Activity solution

$$\text{Overhead absorption rate} = \frac{£40,000}{80,000 \text{ units}}$$

$$= £0.50 \text{ per unit.}$$

Each unit produced absorbs £0.50 of indirect expense or overhead.

This is a simple and acceptable method of absorbing overheads as long as the cost units are identical, or similar. But if a range of products is made it is unequitable for small or relatively inexpensive products to absorb the same share of overheads as larger or more expensive products.

Conclusion   If an organisation produces a single product then the units produced method of **absorbing overheads** is acceptable.

2 ABSORPTION OF OVERHEADS ON A TIME BASIS

2.1 Nature of overheads

Most overheads however are not dependent upon the number of units produced. In fact most overheads are probably more dependent upon the amount of time that elapses or the amount of time that is worked in a particular department. For example rent paid is based on the amount of time that the premises are occupied, heating and lighting bills depend on the amount that the facilities are used and power for machinery depends on the amount of time that the machines are used.

Therefore some measure of time is often a better method of absorbing overheads into product costs rather than simply the number of units produced.

2.2 Problem with number of units method

The problem with the units of production approach to overhead absorption can be illustrated using the following example.

Suppose that the total production overheads of an organisation are again £40,000 and that the number of products produced is 80,000. These 80,000 products are made up of 40,000 units of product A and 40,000 units of product B.
Absorbing the production overhead on the basis of the number of units produced would lead to £0.50 per unit of overhead being included in the cost of units of both A and B.

Suppose however that product A requires 1 hour in the production departments whereas product B requires 20 hours.

In such a situation it would appear to be right that product B absorbs more of the production overhead per unit than product A. Product B spends 20 times longer in production than product A and there ought to be some reflection of this in the sharing out of the production overhead between the products.

2.3   Time basis for overhead absorption

If overheads are thought to be incurred on a time basis rather than a per unit basis then it is more appropriate to absorb overheads on the basis of the amount of time that they spend in each production department. The two main measures of time in a production department are labour hours and machine hours.

2.4   Labour hours basis for overhead absorption

One measure of the amount of time that a product spends in a production department is the standard labour hours due to be spent on that product in that department. In a labour intensive production environment the standard labour hours for a product might be the most appropriate method of absorbing the production overheads.

2.5   Activity

An organisation has a single production department which incurs expected overheads of £20,000 per annum. The estimated number of labour hours worked in the department are 80,000.

What is the overhead absorption rate per labour hour?

If a single unit of product J spends two hours in the production department what is the amount of overhead to be included in the cost of one unit of product J?

2.6   Activity solution

Overhead absorption rate	=	$\dfrac{£20,000}{80,000 \text{ hours}}$
	=	£0.25 per hour

Overhead to be included in
cost of product J
2 hours × £0.25   =   £0.50

2.7   Complications

Students may not be given the information in such a straightforward manner. The total number of labour hours in each production department may need to be calculated.

2.8   Activity

An organisation has one production department with anticipated overheads for the next quarter of £6,300. Three products are produced in that department and information regarding those products is given below.

	Number of labour hours per unit expected to be produced	Number of units expected to be produced
Product A	3	300
Product B	2	400
Product C	1	400

What is the overhead absorption rate per labour hour?

What is the amount of overhead to be included in the cost of each of the three products?

2.9 Activity solution

Total number of anticipated labour hours

		Hours
Product A	3 hours × 300 units	900
Product B	2 hours × 400 units	800
Product C	1 hour × 400 units	400
		2,100

The total standard labour hours are therefore 2,100.

$$\text{Overhead absorption rate} = \frac{£6,300}{2,100 \text{ hours}}$$

$$= £3 \text{ per labour hour}$$

Overhead included in product costs

		£
Product A	3 hours × £3 per hour	9.00
Product B	2 hours × £3 per hour	6.00
Product C	1 hour × £3 per hour	3.00

Conclusion   Absorption of overheads on the basis of labour hours is appropriate in production departments that are labour intensive.

2.10 Machine hours

An alternative measure of the time spent in a department by a product is the number of machine hours spent.

In a machine-based or automated production environment the amount of machine time spent on a product is the best basis for absorbing the production overheads into each unit of production.

2.11 Activity

An organisation has two production departments, machine shop A and machine shop B. In those departments it produces two different products, F and G.

F requires 3 hours in machine shop A and 4.5 hours in machine shop B. G requires 1.5 hours in machine shop A and 0.5 hours in machine shop B.

It is anticipated that 2,000 units of F and 5,000 units of G will be produced in the next accounting period and that the overheads for machine shop A will total £12,000 and machine shop B will total £15,000.

What is the overhead absorption rate per machine hour?

What is the total amount of overhead to be absorbed into each of the two products?

2.12 Activity solution

	Hours Machine shop A	Hours Machine shop B
Machine hours for product F		
3 hours × 2,000 units	6,000	
4.5 hours × 2,000 units		9,000
Machine hours for product G		
1.5 hours × 5,000 units	7,500	
0.5 hours × 5,000 units		2,500
	13,500	11,500
Total overheads	£12,000	£15,000

Overhead absorption rate

$$\frac{£12,000}{13,500 \text{ hours}} \qquad £0.89$$

$$\frac{£15,000}{11,500 \text{ hours}} \qquad £1.30$$

Overhead included in the cost of each product

£

Product F
3 hours × £0.89 — 2.67
4.5 hours × £1.30 — 5.85

8.52

Product G
1.5 hours × £0.89 — 1.34
0.5 hours × £1.30 — 0.65

1.99

Conclusion An appropriate basis for absorbing the overheads of machine based production departments will often be to use the standard number of machine hours as the absorption basis.

3 ALTERNATIVE ACTIVITY MEASURES FOR CALCULATING ABSORPTION RATES

3.1 Introduction

In the previous paragraphs the most common methods of absorbing overheads into the cost of cost units have been considered. These are:

- units produced method;
- labour hours method;
- machine hours method.

Now a number of alternative, although less frequently used, measures for calculating absorption rates will be considered:

- material cost;
- labour cost;
- prime cost;

3.2   Materials cost

In some situations the amount of overhead incurred by different products depends more upon the amount or cost of the materials that are input into the product than any other factor such as time.

For example if the majority of the overheads of a production department are an apportionment of the stores and materials handling cost centres then the amount of material in each product measured by its cost might be the most appropriate way of absorbing the overhead.

Alternatively perhaps in some hi-tech industries the amount of time spent on products by either machines or employees is very small, but the amount and value of materials differs widely from product to product. In such circumstances the most appropriate method of absorbing overheads into each product is on the basis of the value of those materials.

3.3   Activity

The total production overhead for a cost centre is expected to be £120,000 and the total direct materials cost of the units produced in that cost centre during the period is expected to be £300,000. Production overhead is to be absorbed on the basis of direct material cost.

What is the overhead absorption rate for the cost centre?

If each unit of Product A requires 4 kg of material input costing £16 what is the amount of production overhead to be absorbed into each unit of product A?

3.4   Activity solution

Overhead absorption rate:

$$= \quad \frac{£120,000}{£300,000} \quad = \quad £0.40 \text{ per £1 of direct material cost}$$

Overhead to be absorbed into one unit of product A

$$= \quad £16 \times 0.40 \quad = \quad £6.40$$

Conclusion   Absorption of overheads on the basis of direct materials cost is an equitable method of absorption if the materials cost is the major cause of the overheads. But, material cost is not a particularly common absorption method.

3.5   Labour cost

In a similar manner to the materials cost method it is also possible to absorb overheads on the basis of the cost of the standard labour hours involved in a product.

The circumstances where such a choice of absorption basis is appropriate might include any of, or a combination of the following:

(a)   products which have relatively small materials input costs but require large amounts of labour;

(b)   products that require a number of different grades of labour all paid different rates. In these circumstances labour hours alone would not perhaps be appropriate;

(c)   production departments whose overheads are largely due to labour based costs.

3.6   Calculation

The calculation of the overhead absorption rate per £1 labour cost would be the same as in the previous activity for materials.

Conclusion   Absorption of overheads on the basis of standard direct labour cost is a recognised method of absorption but not a particularly common method.

3.7   Prime cost

The final generally recognised method of absorbing overheads into units of production is to do this on the basis of the total standard prime cost of the products.

Definition   **Standard prime cost** is the total of the standard direct materials cost, direct labour cost and any direct expense cost.

3.8   Calculations

The calculations involved in finding the absorption rate on this basis are precisely the same as the calculations seen in the materials cost activity, but using the total of all direct production costs.

Conclusion   This method of overhead absorption is rarely seen in practice.

4   METHODS OF OVERHEAD ABSORPTION

4.1   Introduction

In the earlier part of this chapter the basic calculations of overhead absorption and a variety of different methods of determining absorption rates have been considered.

In this paragraph methods of overhead absorption will be summarised and evaluated.

4.2   Blanket overhead absorption

Definition   In **blanket overhead absorption** the total production overheads of the organisation are absorbed on a single absorption basis.

This is by far the simplest method of overhead absorption as it does not require any allocation or apportionment of overheads to cost centres nor the choice of any activity measure as the number of units to be produced is used.

However, as was seen in an earlier illustration this method will only give a fair representation of the amount of overhead incurred by products if the organisation produces a single product. If more than one product is produced then a more involved approach to overhead absorption is required.

4.3   Departmental overhead absorption

Definition   **Departmental overhead absorption** is where the total production overhead for each
                     department is determined using allocation and apportionment of overheads. Each
                     departments overhead is then absorbed into the products worked on in that department
                     using the most appropriate basis.

The main advantage of this approach is that the production overhead for each department can be absorbed
using the most appropriate basis for that department. For example a labour intensive department might use
labour hours as the basis of absorption and an automated department might use machine hours as the basis of
absorption.

The main disadvantage of the method is the volume of calculations required to allocate, apportion and then
finally absorb the overheads.

4.4   Actual and predetermined overhead absorption rates

The purpose of absorbing production overheads into the cost of each cost unit of an organisation is so that the
full cost of that product is known. If actual production overheads and actual levels of activity for a period were
used to produce the absorption rates then these calculations could not take place until after the end of the
period when the actual costs and production details were known.

However it would be more useful to know the amount of overhead likely to be included in the cost of each
product at the start of the period rather than at the end.

For that reason predetermined or budgeted figures are normally used to calculate absorption rates.

4.5   Budgeting process

Before the start of each accounting period the budgets for that period are set. This will include the budgeted or
standard amount of production overhead for the period and the budgeted or standard level of production for the
period.

The budgeted figures for each of the expense items such as rent and rates, electricity, insurance and
depreciation are allocated or apportioned to each cost centre. The budgeted service cost centre costs are
apportioned to production cost centres to give the estimated or budgeted overhead cost for each production
cost centre.

4.6   Predetermined overhead absorption rate

The budgeted production overhead for each cost centre is then divided by the budgeted level of activity for
each cost centre, i.e. budgeted number of units to be produced or labour hours to be worked or machine hours
to be incurred, to give the budgeted or predetermined overhead absorption rate.

(Tutorial note: this is the process that has been covered in this and the previous chapter although students may
not have been aware of using budgeted or standard costs and activity levels.*)*

The advantage of this method of using predetermined rather than actual absorption rates is that the amount of
overhead expected to be incurred by each product is known at the start of the production period rather than
after the event at the end of the period.

Conclusion   The apportionment of overheads is normally done as part of the budgeting process and as
                     such is based upon budgeted or standard costs for each type of overhead expense. The
                     setting of the overhead absorption rate is also normally done as part of the budgeting
                     process and is based upon the budgeted or standard production overhead and the budgeted
                     or standard level of activity. If a blanket rate of overhead absorption is to be used then this
                     level of activity could be an overall budgeted number of units of production for the
                     organisation. If departmental overhead absorption rates are to be calculated then separate
                     measures of budgeted production activity for the period, e.g. labour hours or machine hours
                     will be used for each department.

5   PROBLEMS WITH TRADITIONAL OVERHEAD ABSORPTION

5.1   Introduction

In this chapter the methods of absorbing overheads into products were discussed. The most common methods used are either labour hours or machine hours.

The assumption that underlies both of these methods is that the overheads are directly related to either the number of hours worked or the number of machine hours used. In some limited cases this will be true. The wage paid to the factory supervisor will probably be directly related to the number of hours worked by the factory employees. The amount of power necessary to drive the machines will no doubt be related to the number of hours that the machinery is worked.

However in the vast majority of cases the total overheads will not be directly related to any one of the overhead absorption bases. The total overhead will probably be related to a number of different causes and this problem is now addressed.

5.2   Example

The overhead cost for a department comprises the cost of insurance of its high value machinery, the costs of storing its large high value stock items and the large labour costs associated with its operation.

The overhead absorption rate for this production department has been decided as £1 per labour hour. Product A requires 2 hours of labour and product B requires 10 hours of labour. The overhead included in the cost of A will therefore be £2 and that included in the cost of B will be £10.

Has product B really incurred 5 times as much overhead as product A simply because of the additional time spent in the department? In most cases the answer will be no.

Suppose product A uses a larger quantity of the high value stock and/or makes greater use of the machinery - shouldn't this greater use of the resources to which the overheads relate be reflected in the absorption rate?

In fact, in exactly the same way that the different costs were **apportioned** to the department (the **cost centre**) using different bases (number of employees for the canteen cost, value of stock for the stores cost etc.), should not the different costs be **absorbed** into the cost **units** using different bases?

5.3   Alternative method of allocating overheads to products

As an alternative to the largely arbitrary method of apportioning overheads to products a totally different approach was advocated by Professor Kaplan, known as Activity Based Costing (ABC).

The main difference between activity based costing and cost centre absorption methods is that activity based costing recognises that costs are caused by many different measures of activity and attributes costs to cost units accordingly.

Cost centre absorption rates use a single measure of activity to attribute production overhead costs to cost units.

The perceived benefit of introducing an activity based costing system is that the unit costs should more accurately reflect the usage of resources, though it is questionable whether the cost of the system can be justified.

Conclusion   For the purposes of this syllabus students require only an awareness of the problems of the traditional methods of absorbing overheads, and that alternative methods do exist. ABC will be studied in other papers.

6   NON-PRODUCTION OVERHEADS

6.1   Introduction

Overheads normally absorbed into the cost of products are production overheads. These are the overheads that have been dealt with so far in this chapter. However, there also other types of overhead, in particular:

- selling and distribution overheads;
- administration overheads; and
- finance overheads.

It is also possible to include some or all of these overheads as part of the cost of the product or cost unit if the organisation wishes to determine the full cost of each cost unit.

6.2   Absorption of non-production overheads

If these non-production overheads are to be included in the cost of the cost units then they must be absorbed into the cost in a similar manner to the production overheads by using some suitable absorption basis such as a per unit basis or perhaps as a percentage of the production cost of the product.

Conclusion   It is perfectly possible to absorb non-production overheads into the cost of cost units. However this is not a particularly common practice. The more normally treatment for non-production overheads is to write them off as an expense in the profit and loss account for the period.

7   CHAPTER SUMMARY

In this chapter we have continued our look at overheads by considering how they can be apportioned between products.

8   SELF TEST QUESTIONS

8.1   What is meant by absorption of overhead costs? (1.3)

8.2   What are the two most common measures of absorbing overheads on a time basis? (2.3)

8.3   In what circumstances might absorption of overheads on a materials cost basis be appropriate? (3.2)

8.4   What is meant by blanket overhead absorption? (4.2)

8.5   When might blanket overhead absorption be appropriate? (4.2)

8.6   Why do predetermined overhead absorption rates tend to be used rather than actual overhead absorption rates? (4.6)

8.7   How is a predetermined overhead absorption rate calculated? (4.6)

8.8   What is the basic distinction between traditional methods of overhead absorption and activity based costing methods? (5.3)

8.9   What are the main categories of non-production overhead? (6.1)

9 MULTIPLE CHOICE QUESTIONS

9.1 A company absorbs overheads on machine hours which were budgeted at 11,250 with overheads of £258,750. Actual results were 10,980 hours with overheads of £254,692.

Overheads were:

A   under-absorbed by £2,152.
B   over-absorbed by £4,058.
C   under-absorbed by £4,058.
D   over-absorbed by £2,152.

9.2 The following budgeted and actual data relate to production activity and overhead costs in Winnie Ltd.

	Budget	Actual
Production overhead		
Fixed	£94,000	£102,600
Variable	£57,500	£62,000
Direct labour hours	25,000	26,500

The company uses an absorption costing system and production overheads are absorbed on a direct labour hour basis.

Production overhead during the period was:

A   under-absorbed by £4,010
B   over-absorbed by £4,010
C   under-absorbed by £9,876
D   over-absorbed by £9,876

9.3 An overhead absorption rate is used to:

A   share out common costs over benefiting cost centres
B   find the total overheads for a cost centre
C   charge overheads to products
D   control overheads

9.4 Floaters plc has the following production and fixed overhead budgets for the coming year:

Production department	1	2
Fixed overhead	£2,400,000	£4,000,000
Total production hours	240,000	200,000
Total materials cost	£200,000	£400,000

Department 1 labour is paid £5 per hour and department 2 labour £4 per hour. The variable production cost of an IC is as follows:

		£
Labour		
Department 1 3 hours		15
Department 2 2 hours		8
Materials		
Department 1 1kg	@ £4 per kg	4
Department 2 2 kgs	@ £5 per kg	10
Variable overheads		7
		——
		£44
		——

If fixed overheads are absorbed on the basis of labour cost, the fixed overhead cost per unit of IC is:

A   £70   B   £72.72   C   £102.67   D   £148

9.5 A company has four production departments. Fixed costs have been apportioned between them as follows:

Department	K	L	M	N
Fixed costs	£10,000	£5,000	£4,000	£6,000

The time taken in each department to manufacture the company's only product, X, is 5 hours, 5 hours, 4 hours and 3 hours respectively.

If the company recovers overheads on the basis of labour hours and plans to produce 2,000 units, then the fixed cost per unit is:

A	£3.00	B	£12.00	C	£12.50	D	£17.00

9.6 A firm absorbs overheads on labour hours. In one period 11,500 hours were worked, actual overheads were £138,000 and there was £23,000 over-absorption. The overhead absorption rate per hour was:

A   £10
B   £12
C   £13
D   £14

10   PRACTICE QUESTIONS

10.1   PTS Ltd

PTS Ltd is a manufacturing company which uses three production departments to make its product. It has the following factory costs which are expected to be incurred in the year to 31 December 20X2:

		£
Direct wages	Machining	234,980
	Assembly	345,900
	Finishing	134,525

		£
Indirect wages and salaries	Machining	120,354
	Assembly	238,970
	Finishing	89,700

	£
Factory rent	12,685,500
Business rates	3,450,900
Heat and lighting	985,350
Machinery power	2,890,600
Depreciation	600,000
Canteen subsidy	256,000

Other information is available as follows:

	Machining	Assembly	Finishing
Number of employees	50	60	18
Floor space occupied (m²)	1,800	1,400	800
Horse power of machinery	13,000	500	6,500
Value of machinery (£'000)	250	30	120
Number of labour hours	100,000	140,000	35,000

Number of machine hours	200,000	36,000	90,000

You are required:

(a)   to prepare the company's overhead analysis sheet for 20X2;

(b)   to calculate appropriate overhead absorption rates (to two decimal places) for each department.

10.2   Assembly and finishing

Two products A and B are produced in two production departments, assembly and finishing. The products require only small amounts of material input but large amounts of skilled labour of various grades. The organisation's policy is to absorb the production department overhead into products on the basis of total labour cost.

Details of the two production departments' activities are as follows:

	Assembly	*Finishing*
Total grade A labour hours		
Product A	1,000	200
Product B	200	100
Total grade D labour hours		
Product A	900	400
Product B	1,500	600
Total grade F labour hours		
Product A	-	100
Product B	400	400
Total standard production overhead	£40,000	£34,000

The hourly rates paid to each of these grades of labour are:

	£
Grade A	6.40
Grade D	10.80
Grade F	16.00

Required:

Calculate:

(a)   the overhead absorption rate on the basis of total standard direct labour cost, showing how the total overhead for each department is to be split between each product; and

(b)   the amount of overhead to be absorbed into each unit of each product on the assumption that 200 units of product A and 400 units of product B are produced.

10.3   ABC (1) Ltd

ABC Ltd is preparing its departmental budgets and product cost estimates for the year ending 31 December 20X5. The company has three manufacturing departments - Machining, Assembly and Finishing - together with a production maintenance department.

The following costs and related data have been estimated for the year to 31 December 20X5:

Costs:	Machining £'000	Assembly £'000	Finishing £'000	Maintenance £'000	Total £'000
Direct wages	60	32	72	-	164
Indirect wages	10	6	8	30	54
Direct materials	80	10	4	-	92
Indirect materials	15	4	8	20	47
Power					102
Light and heat					10
Depreciation					7
Rent and rates					25
Personnel					63

Other data:

	Machining	Assembly	Finishing	Maintenance	Total
Direct labour hours	12,000	8,000	16,000	6,000	42,000
Machine hours	40,000	5,000	6,000	-	51,000
Employees	6	4	8	3	21
Floor area (m²)	1,000	400	300	300	2,000
Net book value of fixed assets	20,000	8,000	3,000	4,000	35,000

The maintenance department is expected to spend 60% of its time working for the machining department, with the remainder of its time being shared equally between assembly and finishing.

You are required:

(a)   to prepare an overhead analysis sheet for ABC Ltd for its year ending 31 December 20X5;

(b)   to calculate appropriate overhead absorption rates for the machining, assembly and finishing departments;

(c)   to prepare a cost estimate, based on the following data, for a product which is to be manufactured in January 20X5:

	Machining	Assembly	Finishing
Direct materials (£)	2,500	400	200
Direct labour hours	800	350	140
Machine hours	1,400	100	80

(d)   to prepare the fixed production overhead control account for the machining department, assuming that:

(i)   all the overhead costs budgeted are fixed costs;
(ii)   the actual fixed overhead costs incurred amounted to £128,000;
(iii)   the actual direct labour and machine hours were 10,500 and 39,000 respectively;

11   ANSWERS TO MULTIPLE CHOICE QUESTIONS

11.1   A   The overhead absorption rate is based on budgeted figures:

$$\frac{£258,750}{11,250} = £23 \text{ per hour}$$

Since actual hours were 10,980, this means that overheads absorbed were $10,980 \times £23 = £252,540$. Actual overheads were £254,692, which means that overheads were under-absorbed by £2,152.

11.2   £

Budgeted absorption rate per hour
   Fixed   94,000 ÷ 25,000   3.76
    Variable57,500 ÷ 25,000   2.30
                                  ————

Total   6.06
                                  ————

                                  £

Overheads absorbed 26,500 hours × 6.06 per hour   160,590
Overheads incurred 102,600 fixed + 62,000 variable   164,600
                                  ————

Under-absorbed overhead   4,010
                                  ————

Therefore **A.**

11.3 **C**

A relates to allocation and apportionment, B is addition, and absorption does not control overheads thus D is not correct.

11.4 Department 1 recovery rate = 2,400,000 ÷ 240,000 = £10 per hour
Department 2 recovery rate = 4,000,000 ÷ 200,000 = £20 per hour
Cost per IC = 3 × 10 + 2 × 20 = £70.

Therefore **A.**

11.5 Fixed cost/unit (10,000 + 5,000 + 4,000 + 6,000) ÷ 2,000 = £12.50.

Therefore **C.**

11.6 **D**

                                  Absorbed
                                  £

Actual overhead   138,000
Add: Over absorbed   23,000
                                  ————

Absorbed overhead   161,000
                                  ————

Hours worked = 11,500

Absorption rate per hour   = £161,000/11,500
                         = £14

12   ANSWERS TO PRACTICE QUESTIONS

12.1   PTS Ltd

(a)   **Overhead analysis sheet for 20X2**

Expense	Basis of alloc'n	Machining £	Assembly £	Finishing £	Total £
Indirect wages	allocated	120,354	238,970	89,700	449,024
Factory rent	floor space	5,708,475	4,439,925	2,537,100	12,685,500
Rates	floor space	1,552,905	1,207,815	690,180	3,450,900
Heat/light	floor space	443,408	344,872	197,070	985,350
Machine power	horse power	1,878,890	72,265	939,445	2,890,600
Plant dep'n	machine value	375,000	45,000	180,000	600,000
Canteen sub'y	no of employees	100,000	120,000	36,000	256,000
		10,179,032	6,468,847	4,669,495	21,317,374

(b)   **Overhead absorption rates**

Machining $\dfrac{£10,179,032}{200,000}$ =   £50.90 per machine hour

Assembly $\dfrac{£6,468,847}{140,000}$ =   £46.21 per direct labour

Finishing $\dfrac{£4,669,495}{90,000}$ =   £51.88 per machine hour

12.2   Assembly and finishing

(a)   Total labour cost

		Assembly £	Finishing £
Grade A:			
Product A	1,000 hours × £6.40	6,400	
	200 hours × £6.40		1,280
Product B	200 hours × £6.40	1,280	
	100 hours × £6.40		640
Grade D:			
Product A	900 hours × £10.80	9,720	
	400 hours × £10.80		4,320
Product B	1,500 hours × £10.80	16,200	
	600 hours × £10.80		6,480
Grade F:			
Product A	100 hours × £16.00	-	1,600
Product B	400 hours × £16.00	6,400	6,400
		£40,000	£20,720

Overhead absorption rate

Assembly	$\dfrac{£40,000}{£40,000}$	£1.00 per £ of standard direct labour cost
Finishing	$\dfrac{£34,000}{£20,720}$	£1.64 per £ of standard direct labour cost

Total overhead included in each product:

	£
Assembly department	
Product A $((6,400 + 9,720) \times £1.00)$	16,120
Product B $((1,280 + 16,200 + 6,400) \times £1.00)$	23,880
	40,000
Finishing department	
Product A $((1,280 + 4,320 + 1,600) \times £1.64)$	11,808
Product B $((640 + 6,480 + 6,400) \times £1.64)$	22,173
	33,981
Add: Rounding	19
	34,000

(b)   Overhead absorbed per unit of each product:

£

Product A

Assembly

Product A labour cost per unit

$$\dfrac{£6,400 + £9,720}{200 \text{ units}}$$
$= 80.6 \times £1.00$ 80.60

Finishing

Product A labour cost per unit

$$\dfrac{£1,280 + £4,320 + £1,600}{200 \text{ units}}$$

$= 36 \times £1.64$ 59.04

139.64

Product B

Assembly

Product B labour cost per unit

$$\dfrac{£1,280 + £16,200 + £6,400}{400 \text{ units}}$$

$= 59.7 \times £1.00$ 59.70

Finishing

Product B labour cost per unit

$$\frac{£640 \ + \ £6,480 \ + \ £6,400}{400 \text{ units}}$$

$= 33.8 \times £1.64$ 55.43

                                             115.13

12.3 ABC (1) Ltd

(a)

Item	Basis	Machining £'000	Assembly £'000	Finishing £'000	M'tnce £'000	Total £'000
Indirect Wages	Allocated	10	6	7	30	54
Indirect Materials	Allocated	15	4	8	20	47
Power	M/c hours	80	10	12	-	102
Light & heat	Floor area	5	2	1.5	1.5	10
Depreciation	NBV of assets	4	1.6	0.6	0.8	7
Rent & rates	Floor area	12.5	5	3.75	3.75	25
Personnel	Employees	18	12	24	9	63
		144.5	40.6	57.85	65.05	308
Apportion maintenance (6:2:2)		39.03	13.01	13.01	(65.05)	-
		183.53	53.61	70.86	NIL	308

(b)   Comparing the labour and machine hours for each department shows that the machining department is machine intensive and the other departments are labour intensive.

Absorption rates

Machining department - rate per machine hour

$$\frac{\text{Overhead cost}}{\text{Machine hours}} = \frac{£183,530}{40,000} = £4.588/\text{machine hour (rounded)}.$$

Assembly department - rate per labour hour

$$\frac{\text{Overhead cost}}{\text{Labour hours}} = \frac{£53,610}{8,000} = £6.701/\text{labour hour (rounded)}$$

Finishing department – rate per labour hour

$$\frac{\text{Overhead cost}}{\text{Labour hours}} = \frac{£70,860}{16,000} = £4.429/\text{labour hour (rounded)}$$

(c)   Cost estimate

		Total £	Machining £	Assembly £	Finishing £
D Materials		3,100	2,500	400	200
D Wages	(W1)	6,030	4,000	1,400	630
Overhead		9,388	(W2) 6,423	(W3) 2,345	(W4) 620
		18,518	12,923	4,145	1,450

(d)   Machining department - Fixed production overhead control account

	£		£
Creditors	128,000	Work in progress	
* Profit and loss	50,942	(39,000 × £4.58825)	178,942
	178,942		178,942

* This represents an under-recovery of overhead in the period.

WORKINGS

(W1)   Direct wage rates/hour:

Machining $\frac{£60,000}{12,000}$ = £5/hour × 800 = £4,000

Assembly $\frac{£32,000}{8,000}$ = £4/hour × 350 = £1,400

Finishing $\frac{£72,000}{16,000}$ = £4.50/hour × 140 = £630

(W2)   1,400 machine hours × £4.588/hour = £6,423

(W3)   350 labour hours × £6.701/hour = £2,345

(W4)   140 labour hours × £4.429/hour = £620

Chapter 9

ABSORPTION AND MARGINAL COSTING

PATHFINDER INTRODUCTION

This chapter covers the following elements of the CAT Official Teaching Guide. At the end of this chapter you should have learned these teaching guide elements thoroughly.

Session 9
Absorption and marginal costing
Syllabus reference i

- Describe and illustrate the concept of contribution
- Explain and evaluate the impact of absorption and marginal costing on stock valuation and profit measurement
- Reconcile the profits reported by absorption and marginal costing
- Describe the arguments for and against absorption cost stock valuation
- Describe the benefits of using profit and contribution information

Putting the chapter in context

The last 7 chapters have shown how cost per unit is calculated. A major reason for doing this is so that a value can be put on stocks and cost of sales. This chapter explains the two methods used in cost accounting systems to value stock and calculate profit. You must be able to use both methods.

1 CONCEPT OF CONTRIBUTION

1.1 Fixed and variable costs

In previous chapters a distinction was drawn between fixed costs and variable costs.

If **all** costs of a business, both fixed and variable, are deducted from sales revenue, the remaining amount is known as **profit**.

1.2 Contribution

If only the variable costs of the business are deducted from sales revenue, the resulting figure is known as contribution.

Definition   **Contribution** is sales value less variable costs.

Contribution can be calculated on a per unit basis or alternatively on a total basis.

1.3 Activity

A company makes and sells a single product. Details of this product are as follows:

Per unit
Selling price	£20
Direct materials	£6
Direct labour	£3
Variable overhead	£4

Fixed overhead   £20,000 per month

The fixed overhead is absorbed on the basis of expected production of 20,000 units per month.

If actual production and sales are 20,000 in a month calculate the contribution per unit, the total contribution for the month and the total profit for the month.

1.4 Activity solution

Contribution per unit

	£	£
Selling price		20
Less: Variable costs		
Direct materials	6	
Direct labour	3	
Variable overhead	4	
		13
Contribution per unit		7

Total contribution and profit

	£	£
Sales (20,000 × £20)		400,000
Variable costs:		
Direct materials (20,000 × £6)	120,000	
Direct labour (20,000 × £3)	60,000	
Variable overhead (20,000 × £4)	80,000	
		260,000
Contribution		140,000
Fixed overheads		20,000
Profit		120,000

Conclusion   Contribution is the difference between sales value and variable costs either on an individual unit basis or in total. If selling price is constant and variable cost per unit is constant, contribution per unit is the same whatever the activity level. But remember, that fixed costs per unit fall each time an additional unit is made so profit per unit rises with every increase in activity.

2 ABSORPTION COSTING AND MARGINAL COSTING

2.1 Introduction

In earlier chapters the idea of absorbing production overheads into the cost of units of production was considered in some detail. The overheads that were included in the cost of the cost units were both variable production overheads and fixed production overheads.

2.2   Absorption costing

Definition   **Absorption costing** is a cost accounting system that charges both fixed and variable production overheads to cost units.

Under an absorption costing system each stock unit, whether it has been sold and charged as cost of sales or is unsold and included in closing stock, is valued at full production cost. This includes both fixed and variable production overheads.

2.3   Marginal costing as an alternative to absorption costing

Definition   **Marginal costing** is an accounting system in which variable costs are charged to cost units and fixed costs are not absorbed into cost units but written off in the profit and loss account of the period to which they relate

In a marginal costing system all cost units are valued at variable production cost only. Therefore when cost of sales is deducted from sales the result is contribution.

2.4   Activity

Company A produces a single product with the following budget:

Per unit
Selling price	£10
Direct materials	£3 per unit
Direct wages	£2 per unit
Variable overhead	£1 per unit
Fixed production overheads	£10,000 per month.

The fixed overhead absorption rate is based on production of 5,000 units per month.

Show the operating statement for the month, if 4,800 units were produced and sold under absorption costing principles and also under marginal costing price principles.

Assume that costs were as budget, and that there is no opening stock..

2.5   Activity solution

Absorption costing

	£
Sales (4,800 × £10)	48,000
Cost of sales (4,800 × £8) (W1)	38,400
Operating margin	9,600
Under absorbed overhead (W2)	(400)
Operating profit	9,200

WORKINGS

(W1)   Unit cost represents materials (£3) + wages (£2) + variable overhead (£1) + fixed overhead absorbed $(\frac{£10,000}{5,000})$ = £8 per unit.

		£
(W2)	Fixed overhead incurred	10,000
	Fixed overhead absorbed	9,600 (4,800 × £2)
	Under absorption to be debited to profit and loss	400

Marginal costing

	£
Sales (4,800 × £10)	48,000
Variable cost of sales (4,800 × £6) (W3)	28,800
Contribution	19,200
Fixed costs (incurred in the period)	10,000
Operating profit	9,200

(W3)   Variable cost is made up of materials (£3) + wages (E2) + variable overhead (£1) = £6 per unit.

In this example operating profit is the same under both methods. That will not be so, however, when production is more or less than sales, i.e. stocks of finished goods are maintained.

2.6   Marginal costing and stock valuation

Under marginal costing stock is valued at variable production cost. This is in contrast to absorption costing where fixed production overhead costs are also included in stock valuations using the predetermined absorption rate.

The following example illustrates the effects of the different stock valuations on profit.

2.7   Activity

Suppose that in the previous activity production was in fact 6,000 units i.e. 4,800 units sold and 1,200 units left in closing stock.

Prepare the profit statement for the month under absorption costing principles and marginal costing principles.

2.8   Activity solution

Absorption costing

	£	£
Sales (4,800 × £10)		48,000
Cost of sales:		
Production (6,000 × £8)	48,000	
Closing stock (1,200 × £8)	9,600	
		38,400

Operating margin		9,600
Over absorbed fixed overhead ((6,000 × £2) − £10,000)		2,000
Operating profit		11,600

Marginal costing

	£	£
Sales (4,800 × £10)		48,000
Variable cost of sales:		
Production costs (6,000 × £6)	36,000	
Closing stock (1,200 × £6)	7,200	
		28,800
Contribution		19,200
Fixed costs (incurred in the period)		10,000
Operating profit		9,200

Conclusion   Under an absorption costing system cost of sales is valued at full production cost including a share of the fixed production overhead. This may mean that there is an under or over absorption of production overhead.

Under a marginal costing system cost of sales is valued at variable production cost only. The fixed production costs are written off as they are incurred as a period cost in the profit and loss account. Therefore there is no absorption of fixed production overheads and consequently no under or over absorption.

If stock levels change the two methods give different operating profit.

3   RECONCILIATION OF PROFITS UNDER ABSORPTION AND MARGINAL COSTING

3.1   Introduction

As was seen quite clearly in the previous activity, if stock levels change, there will be a difference in the amount of profits reported under absorption costing and marginal costing.

3.2   Stock valuation

The only difference between absorption costing and marginal costing is the stock valuation.

Under absorption costing a share of the fixed production overhead is included in the stock valuation whereas under marginal costing only the variable production overheads are included in the stock valuation and all fixed production overhead is charged in the profit and loss account. It is this different treatment of fixed production overhead that causes the difference in reported profit between the two costing systems.

3.3   Changes in stock levels

If the stock levels of the business change in a period then there will be a difference between the profit reported under absorption costing in the period and the profit reported under marginal costing. This is due to the difference in the amount of fixed overhead included in stock under the two systems.

If stock levels are rising then the profit under absorption costing will be higher than under marginal costing. If stock levels are falling then the profit under marginal costing will be higher than under absorption costing.

3.4   Activity

In the previous activity a difference in profit between absorption costing of £11,600 and marginal costing £9,200 arose.

Reconcile this difference in profits.

3.5   Activity solution

The difference in profit is due to the fact that there has been an increase in closing stock levels of 1,200 units. Under absorption costing each one of these extra closing stock units includes £2 of fixed production overhead in its valuation. This £2,400 (1,200 units x £2) is therefore being carried forward to the next accounting period, in closing stock, in the balance sheet rather than being charged in this accounting period. This gives a profit figure which is £2,400 higher under absorption costing than under marginal costing.

Reconciliation

	£
Absorption costing profit	11,600
Increase in stock level 1,200 units × £2	2,400
Marginal costing profit	9,200

Conclusion   The difference between absorption costing profit and marginal costing profit will always be caused by changes in stock levels and the fixed overhead absorbed into those increasing or decreasing number of units. If stock levels are rising absorption costing profit will be higher and if stock levels are falling then marginal costing profit will be higher.

4   ABSORPTION COSTING V MARGINAL COSTING

4.1   Arguments for absorption costing

Absorption costing is widely used and you must understand both principles. Defenders of the absorption principle point out that:

(a)   it is necessary to include fixed overhead in stock values for financial statements; routine cost accounting using absorption costing produces stock values which include a share of fixed overhead;

(b)   for small jobbing business, overhead allotment is the only practicable way of obtaining job costs for estimating and profit analysis;

(c)   analysis of under/over absorbed overhead is useful to identify inefficient utilisation of production resources.

4.2   Arguments against absorption costing

Preparation of routine operating statements using absorption costing is considered less informative than using marginal costing because:

(a)   Profit per unit is a misleading figure: in the activity the operating margin of £2 per unit arises because fixed overhead per unit is based on 5,000 units. If another activity level were used, margin per unit would differ even though fixed overhead was the same amount in total.

(b)   Build-up or run-down of stocks of finished goods can distort comparison of period operating statements and obscure the effect of increasing or decreasing sales.

(c)   Comparison between products can be misleading because of the effect of arbitrary apportionment of fixed costs.

4.3   Activity

As this is a difficult area of the syllabus a further activity has been included here.

A company sells a product for £10, and incurs £4 of variable costs in its manufacture. The fixed costs are £900 per year and are absorbed on the basis of the normal production volume of 250 units per year. The results for the last four years, when no expenditure variances arose, were as follows:

Item	1st year units	2nd year units	3rd year units	4th year units	Total units
Opening stock	-	200	300	300	-
Production	300	250	200	200	950
	300	450	500	500	950
Closing stock	200	300	300	200	200
Sales	100	150	200	300	750
	£	£	£	£	£
Sales value	1,000	1,500	2,000	3,000	7,500

Calculate profit each year under both absorption and marginal costing.

4.4   Activity solution

Absorption costing

	Year 1 £	Year 2 £	Year 3 £	Year 4 £	Total £
Opening stock @ £7.60	-	1,520	2,280	2,280	-
Variable costs of production @ £4	1,200	1,000	800	800	3,800
Fixed costs @ $\frac{900}{250}$ = £3.60	1,080	900	720	720	3,420
	2,280	3,420	3,800	3,800	7,220
Closing stock (£4 + £3.60) £7.60	1,520	2,280	2,280	1,520	1,520
Cost of sales	(760)	(1,140)	(1,520)	(2,280)	(5,700)
(Under)/over absorption (W)	180	Nil	(180)	(180)	(180)
Net profit	420	360	300	540	1,620

WORKING

Calculation of over/under absorption

Fixed cost control account

	£		£
Incurred:		Absorbed:	
Year 1	900	300 × £3.60	1,080
Over absorption	180		
	———		———
	1,080		1,080
	———		———
Year 2	900	250 × £3.60	900
	———		———
Year 3	900	200 × £3.60	720
		Under absorption	180
	———		———
	900		900
	———		———
Year 4	900	200 × £3.60	720
		Under absorption	180
	———		———
	900		900
	———		———

Marginal costing

Item	1st year £	2nd year £	3rd year £	4th year £	Total £
Sales	1,000	1,500	2,000	3,000	7,500
Variable cost of sales (@ £4)	400	600	800	1,200	3,000
	———	———	———	———	———
Contribution	600	900	1,200	1,800	4,500
Fixed costs	900	900	900	900	3,600
	———	———	———	———	———
Net profit/(loss)	(300)	-	300	900	900
	———	———	———	———	———

The profit figures shown may be reconciled as follows:

	Year 1 £	Year 2 £	Year 3 £	Year 4 £	Total £
Profit/(loss) under marginal costing	(300)	Nil	300	900	900
Add: Distortion from stock increase (200 × £3.60)	720	(100 × £3.60) 360	-		(200 × £3.60) = 720
Less: Distortion from stock decrease			-	(100 × £3.60) 360	
	———	———		———	———
Profit per absorption	420	360	300	540	1,620
	———	———		———	———

Conclusion   The under/over absorption figures do not explain differences in the profit figures. The difference is simply due to changes in stock levels and the fixed cost included in stock valuations.

5   PROFIT AND CONTRIBUTION

5.1   Introduction

Both profit and contribution information will give the management of a business useful information. However each serves different purposes.

5.2   Profit information

A business must make a profit in order to survive. It must ensure that in the long run all of its costs are covered. Therefore information regarding the profit that a business has made will be of great importance to management.

5.3   Contribution information

Contribution is sales value less variable costs. Therefore it is effectively a fund out of which firstly fixed costs are covered and then a profit is made. It is argued that contribution provides more useful information than profit particularly for decision making purposes.

Contribution will vary directly with the level of activity as long as sales price and variable costs are constant per unit. Therefore if decisions are to be made about activity or production levels then contribution will be more relevant, because profit per unit changes every time the activity level changes.

To determine the profitability of individual products the fixed overheads of the organisation must be apportioned in some way to each product. This apportionment is arbitrary. Therefore, when comparing products it can be argued that the contribution of each product rather than the profit will give more useful information as there is no arbitrary apportionment involved.

Conclusion   Profit information is important to management as the business must in the long run be profitable. However for most management decision purposes contribution will be more useful.

6   CHAPTER SUMMARY

The key concept of contribution was looked at in this chapter. The preparation of financial statements using both marginal and absorption costing was then considered.

7   SELF TEST QUESTIONS

7.1   What is contribution? (1.2)

7.2   What is absorption costing? (2.2)

7.3   What is marginal costing? (2.3)

7.4   Explain under/over absorption? (2.5)

7.5   What elements of cost are included in cost of sales in an absorption costing system? (2.5)

7.6   How is closing stock valued in a marginal costing system? (2.6)

7.7   Why should there be a difference between the profit reported under absorption costing and the profit reported under marginal costing? (3.2)

7.8   If closing stock is greater than opening stock will absorption or marginal cost profit be higher? (3.3)

7.9   What are the main arguments for absorption costing? (4.1)

7.10   What are the main arguments against absorption costing (4.2)

8   MULTIPLE CHOICE QUESTIONS

8.1   Last year Garns Ltd started to make a single product with a unit selling price of £14. In the first year of operation standard capacity was 50,000 units, production was 50,000 units, and sales were 45,000 units. The actual costs incurred were:

	Fixed	Variable
Raw materials	-	£3.00 per unit produced
Direct labour	-	£2.00 per unit produced
Factory overhead	£200,000	£1.00 per unit produced
Selling and admin expenses	£80,000	£1.00 per unit sold

Actual variable costs did not diverge from standard. Any under- or over-applied overhead was written off directly at year end as an adjustment to the cost of goods sold.

What would be the values of net income, calculated using the different bases of variable costing and absorption costing?

	Using variable costing	Using absorption costing
A	£35,000	£55,000
B	£35,000	£62,000
C	£39,000	£55,000
D	£39,000	£62,000

8.2   A firm has commenced production of a new product with a planned selling price of £63. Production was at the planned level of 100,000 units although 20,000 of these remained unsold at the period end.

Actual costs incurred were as follows:

Direct materials	£13.50 per unit
Direct labour	£9.00 per unit
Variable production overhead	£4.50 per unit
Variable selling costs	£4.50 per unit
Fixed production overhead	£900,000 as per budget
Fixed selling costs	£360,000 as per budget

(a)   What is the closing stock valuation per unit, using absorption costing?

   A £36   B   £27   C   £31.50   D   £39.60

(b)   What net profit figure would be earned under absorption costing?

   A £1,350,000   B   £1,260,000   C   £1,440,000   D   £1,512,000

8.3   The budget for Bright's first month's trading, producing and selling boats, showed the following:

	£'000
Variable production cost of boats	45
Fixed production costs	30
Production costs of 750 boats	75

Closing stock of 250 boats	(25)
Production cost of 500 sold	50
Variable selling costs	5
Fixed selling costs	25
	80
Profit	10
Sales revenue	£90

The budget has been produced using an absorption costing system.

If a marginal costing system were used, the budgeted profit would be:

A   £22,500 lower
B   £10,000 lower
C   £10,000 higher
D   £22,500 higher

9   PRACTICE QUESTIONS

9.1   Rayners plc

Rayners plc manufactures and sells electric blankets. The selling price is £12. Each blanket has the following unit cost:

	£
Direct material	2
Direct labour	1
Variable production overhead	2
Fixed production overhead	3
	8

Administration costs are incurred at the rate of £20,000 per annum.
The company achieved the following production and sales of blankets:

Year	1	2	3
Production (000's units)	100	110	90
Sales (000's units)	90	110	95

The following information is also relevant:

(1)   The overhead costs of £2 and £3 per unit have been calculated on the basis of a budgeted production volume of 90,000 units.

(2)   There was no inflation.

(3)   There was no opening stock.

You are required:

(a)   to prepare an operating statement for each year using:

  (i)   marginal costing; and
  (ii)   absorption costing.

(10 marks)

(b)   to explain why the profit figures reported under the two techniques disagree.

(6 marks)
(Total: 16 marks)

Remember, only production overheads are absorbed into cost units, all non-production overheads (fixed or variable) are always treated as period costs.

9.2   Stock valuation - fixed overhead costs

The valuation of stocks in a manufacturing and trading company is dependent on a number of factors, not least of which is the company's policy concerning its treatment of fixed overhead costs, which is an important part of a company's cost accounting procedures.

You are required:

(a)   to discuss the principles of marginal and absorption costing, explaining clearly the difference between them;

(10 marks)

(b)   to explain the use of pre-determined rates to absorb overhead costs into product costs.

(10 marks)
(Total: 20 marks)

Use numerical examples to illustrate your answers, for which 8 of the total marks are available.

10   ANSWERS TO MULTIPLE CHOICE QUESTIONS

10.1   Variable costing
$45,000 \times (14 - 7) - 280,000 \quad = £35,000$
Absorption costing
$45,000 \times (7 - 4) - 80,000 \quad = £55,000.$

Therefore **A.**

10.2   (a)   £

Direct materials	13.50
Direct labour	9.00
Variable production overhead	4.50
Fixed production overhead	9.00
	£36.00

Absorption rate for fixed overheads per unit $= \dfrac{\text{Fixed production overhead}}{\text{Budgeted output}}$

$= \dfrac{900,000}{100,000} = £9.$

Therefore **A.**

(b)

		£	£
Sales revenue – 80,000 @ 63			5,040,000
Less: Variable selling costs – 80,000 @ 4.50			360,000
			4,680,000
Less: Cost of sales			
Direct materials – 100,000 @ 13.50		1,350,000	
Direct labour – 100,000 @ 9		900,000	
Variable production overhead – 100,000 @ 4.50		450,000	
Fixed production overhead – 100,000 @ 9		900,000	
		3,600,000	
Less: Closing stock – 200,000 @ 36		720,000	
			2,880,000
			1,800,000
Less: Fixed selling expenses			360,000
			1,440,000

Therefore **C.**

10.3 The fixed costs of the closing stock are £10,000 in an absorption costing system. In a marginal costing system, closing stock would be £10,000 lower and the cost of sales £10,000 higher.

Therefore **B.**

11 ANSWERS TO PRACTICE QUESTIONS

11.1 Rayners plc

(a) <center>**Operating statement (£000's)**</center>

	Year 1		Year 2		Year 3	
	£	£	£	£	£	£
(i) Marginal costing						
Sales		1,080		1,320		1,140
Opening stock @ £5	Nil		50		50	
Add: Production cost @ £5	500		550		450	
	500		600		500	
Less: Closing stock @ £5	50		50		25	
Cost of sales		(450)		(550)		(475)
Contribution		630		770		665
Less: Fixed costs:						
Production overhead	270		270		270	
Administration overhead	20		20		20	
		(290)		(290)		(290)

Profit		340		480		375

(ii) Absorption costing (£000's)

Sales		1,080		1,320		1,140
Opening stock @ £8	Nil		80		80	
Add: Production cost @ £8	800		880		720	
	800		960		800	
Less: Closing stock @ £8	80		80		40	
Cost of sales		(720)		(880)		(760)
		360		440		380
(Under)/over absorption (see working)		30		60		Nil
Administration overhead		(20)		(20)		(20)
Profit		370		480		360

Note: the control account below includes variable overhead for information i.e. the under/over recovery only occurs on fixed overheads.

WORKING

Production overhead control account

	£'000		£'000
Year 1 Incurred:		Absorbed to	
Fixed: 90 × £3 =	270	work-in progress:	
Variable: 100 × £2 =	200	100 × (2 + 3)	500
Over-recovery			
(90 − 100) × 3	30		
	500		500
Year 2 Incurred:		Absorbed to	
Fixed: 90 × £3	270	work-in-progress:	
Variable: 110 × 2	220	110 × 5	550
Over-recovery			
(90 − 110) × 3	60		
	550		550
Year 3 Incurred:		Absorbed to	
Fixed: 90 × £3	270	work-in-progress:	
Variable: 90 × 2	180	90 × 5	450
	450		450

(b) The difference in profit arises because of the difference in the amount of fixed overhead included in stock under the absorption costing system.

When the opening and closing stock includes the same amount of fixed overheads (i.e. here when the volume of opening and closing stock is the same, in year 2) profit is the same under both techniques.

Where volume of stock has gone up (year 1) and the amount of fixed overhead in stock has increased then profit is higher under absorption costing and *vice versa*.

This may be summarised as follows:

		Year 1 £'000	Year 2 £'000	Year 3 £'000
Profit per marginal costing		340	480	375
Add:	Increase in fixed overhead included in stock under absorption costing: 10 units @ 3	30	-	-
Less:	Decrease in fixed overhead included in stock under absorption costing: 5 units @ 3	-	-	(15)
Profit per absorption costing		370	480	360

11.2   Stock valuation - fixed overhead costs

Note: the narrative in the question refers to stock valuation. It is thus necessary to refer in the answer to the effect the methods have on the closing stock value.

(a)   Marginal and absorption costing are two different principles that can be used to determine the cost of a unit of output.

Marginal costing only includes those costs which are variable. Fixed costs are a function of time and not different levels of output and thus are treated as period costs.

Absorption costing includes all costs which are incurred in the production process. Fixed costs are 'absorbed' into units of output by collecting the costs in convenient cost centres and then absorbing them into units of output on this basis, for example by direct labour hours or machine hours.

It follows that stocks will often have a (significantly) higher value using absorption costing than marginal costing. If there is a change in the number of units in stock at the year end compared to the start, profit will also be significantly different under the two methods.

Example

A new business produces 1,500 units in the year. Sales are 1,000 units. Variable costs are 40% of the selling price which is £10 per unit. Fixed production costs are £6,000 per annum.

Under marginal costing the fixed costs are charged to the profit and loss account. Closing stocks are valued at variable cost of £4 per unit i.e. at 500 × £4 = £2,000.

So, under marginal costing

	£	£
Sales (1,000 × £10)		10,000
Less: Cost of sales		
Opening stock	-	
Production (1,500 × £4)	6,000	
Closing stock (500 × £4)	(2,000)	(4,000)
Contribution		6,000
Less: Fixed production costs		(6,000)
Profit		Nil

Under absorption costing the fixed costs are absorbed into both the units sold and the closing stock and each unit is valued at $£4 + \dfrac{£6,000}{1,500}$ i.e. £8.

Under absorption costing

		£	£
Sales (1,000 × £10)			10,000
Less:	Cost of sales		
	Opening stock		-
	Production (1,500 × (£4 + $\frac{6,000}{1,500}$))	12,000	
	Closing stock 500 × (£4 + $\frac{6,000}{1,500}$))	(4,000)	
			(8,000)
Profit			2,000

(b)   **The use of pre-determined overhead absorption rates**

A pre-determined rate is used:

(i)   to smooth out seasonal fluctuations in overhead costs;
(ii)   to enable cost to be calculated quickly.

The pre-determined rate is calculated by:

$$\frac{\text{Budgeted overheads}}{\text{Budgeted volume}}$$

The budgeted volume can be expressed using a number of different measures, the most common being:

(i)   number of units
(ii)   number of labour hours
(iii) number of machine hours.

The pre-determined rate will be applied to actual units produced (or hours worked).

The use of estimates usually means that at the end of the period there is a difference between the fixed production overhead incurred and the amount absorbed into product costs. This difference must be debited or credited to cost accounting profit and loss. The individual product costs are not altered.

Example

In the example in part (a) assume that a pre-determined absorption rate was calculated at the start of the year.

$$\frac{\text{Budgeted fixed overheads say £6,500}}{\text{Budgeted production say 1,600 units}} = £4.06 \text{ per unit}$$

Overheads absorbed would be:

	£
1,500 × £4.06 =	6,090
Actual overheads are	6,000
Over absorbed	90

The profit and loss account is:

	£
Sales	10,000
Cost of sales 1,000 × (£4 + 4.06)	(8,060)
	1,940
Over absorbed overhead	90
Profit	2,030
Closing stock 500 × (£4 + 4.06)	4,030

Chapter 10

COST BOOKKEEPING

PATHFINDER INTRODUCTION

This chapter covers the following elements of the CAT Official Teaching Guide. At the end of this chapter you should have learned these teaching guide elements thoroughly.

Session 10
Cost bookkeeping
Syllabus reference d

- Describe and illustrate an interlocking (memorandum) cost accounting system using both absorption and marginal costing procedures
- Record transactions in an interlocking cost accounting system
- Describe the advantages and limitations of using interlocking and integrated cost accounting systems

Putting the chapter in context

The previous 8 chapters have identified and discussed the costs that need to be recorded by a cost accounting system. This chapter explains how those costs are recorded.

1   INTERLOCKING COST ACCOUNTING SYSTEM

1.1   Introduction

In previous chapters the costing ledger account entries for materials, labour and overheads have been considered separately, in this chapter they will be considered together and the accounting entries taken a little further.

1.2   Cost bookkeeping systems

There are two main cost bookkeeping systems:

- interlocking accounts;
- integrated accounts.

For the purposes of this syllabus only interlocking cost accounts need to be considered in detail, although you need to be aware of the nature of the integrated system, and how the two compare.

1.3   Interlocking (memorandum) accounts

Definition   **Interlocking accounts** are a system in which the cost accounts are distinct from the financial accounts, the two sets of accounts being kept continuously in agreement by the use of control accounts or reconciled by other means.

The recording system may be arranged in two ways:

(a)   Separate book records without control account: separate costing records are derived independently from the source documents, but are reconciled periodically with the financial records.

(b)   Separate cost ledger with control account: a separate costing ledger is maintained under the control of the cost accountant, but integrated with the financial books by means of a cost ledger control account through which all cost and revenue information for re-analysis is transferred.

1.4   Reconciliation of financial and costing profit

Where the cost accounts are maintained independently in an interlocking system it is possible to reconcile the financial and costing results.

1.5   Activity

List the differences that you think there might be between the financial and costing profits under the following headings:

(a)   Appropriations of profit not dealt with in the costing system.

(b)   Income and expenditure of a purely financial nature (ie, nothing to do with manufacturing).

(c)   Items where financial and costing treatments differ.

1.6   Activity solution

(a)   **Appropriations of profit not dealt with in the costing system**

   (i)   Corporation tax;

   (ii)   transfers to reserves;

   (iii)   dividends paid and proposed;

   (iv)   amounts written off intangibles such as goodwill, discount on issue of debentures, expenses of capital issues, etc.;

   (v)   appropriations to sinking funds for the repayment of loans;

   (vi)   charitable donations where no direct benefit is derived by the employees of the company.

(b)   **Income and expenditure of a purely financial nature (ie, outside the scope of manufacture)**

   (i)   Interest and dividends received;

   (ii)   rents receivable - however, if this arises from part of rented business premises which have been sublet, only the profit element should be excluded, the proportion representing cost being deducted from rents payable to determine the net rent of premises;

   (iii)   profits and losses on the sale of fixed assets and investments;

   (iv)   interest on bank loans, mortgages and debentures;

   (v)   damages payable at law, fines and penalties.

(c)   **Items where financial and costing treatments differ**

   (i)   Differences in the valuation of stocks and work in progress. The latter may, for costing purposes, be valued at factory cost (including production overhead), whereas prime cost may be employed in the financial accounts. Likewise, stocks of materials and finished goods may be written down in the financial accounts to net realisable value.

   (ii)   Depreciation. In the financial accounts this charge is normally based solely upon the passage of time, whereas in the cost accounts it may be a variable charge based upon machine/man hours worked.

(iii)   Abnormal losses in production and storage. In the financial accounts, materials and wages will include any abnormal losses of material or time. In the cost accounts such losses may be excluded to avoid misleading comparisons.

(iv)   Interest on capital. Notional interest on capital employed in production is sometimes included in the cost accounts to reflect the nominal cost of employing the capital rather than investing it outside the business.

(v)   Charge in lieu of rent. Again a notional amount for rent may be included in costs in order to compare costs of production with costs of another business which occupies a rented or leasehold factory.

2   THE COST LEDGER IN AN INTERLOCKING SYSTEM

2.1   Cost ledger control account

In an interlocking system the cost accounts will only need to record transactions relating to operating revenue and costs; details of capital, debtors and creditors are part of the financial accounting routine. Frequently, however, such financial accounts are merged into a single account (cost ledger control) solely to maintain the double entry principle within the cost accounts.

2.2   Control accounts

The cost ledger for a manufacturing business will probably contain control accounts for:
(a)   stores;
(b)   work in progress;
(c)   finished stock;
(d)   production overhead;
(e)   general administration costs;
(f)   marketing costs.

2.3   Subsidiary ledgers

Each control account will be supported by a subsidiary ledger to provide the detail required for financial reporting and/or management information. Analysis will be by:

(a)   item of material;
(b)   job number (job costing), product (batch costing) or process (process costing);
(c)   job or production;
(d)   cost centres (there will be more than one of these).

2.4   Cost ledger accounts

In addition to the cost ledger control and the control accounts detailed above, separate accounts will be kept as required, particularly:
(a)   sales;
(b)   cost of sales;
(c)   wages;
(d)   profit and loss.

Subsidiary details in the form of a sub-ledger or analysis columns may be necessary.

2.5   Absorption costing and marginal costing

Production overhead costs are those costs incurred in the production function but which cannot be economically identified with the cost unit to which they relate.

The requirements of SSAP 9 for stock valuations used in financial accounting are that stocks should be valued at their total cost including an appropriate proportion of production overhead.

Since work-in-progress is a form of stock this valuation rule must also apply to work-in-progress.

To achieve this valuation production overhead absorption rates are used and applied to cost units as they are being completed (via the work-in-progress account). This ensures that finished units and work-in-progress at the end of a period are valued at their total cost. This is of course an application of absorption costing. It is also possible to have a marginal costing bookkeeping system where fixed overheads are written off in the profit and loss account as incurred rather than being absorbed in the work-in-progress account.

2.6   Cost ledger accounting entries

Entries to the cost ledger follow the sequence of transactions in the manufacturing business:

	Transaction	*Journal entry*	*Document*
(a)	Purchases	Dr Stores Cr Contra*	Invoice/GRN
(b)	Gross wages	Dr Wages Cr Contra*	Payroll
(c)	Expenses incurred	Dr Production overhead Dr General admin cost Dr Marketing cost Cr Contra*	Invoices/ Petty cash/ Journal
(d)	Materials issued	Dr Work in progress (direct) Dr Production overhead (indirect) Cr Stores	Requisitions
(e)	Analysed wages	Dr (as (d) above) Cr Wages	Time sheets, etc.
(f)	Overhead absorbed	Dr Work in progress Cr Production overhead	Cost journal
(g)	Completed work	Dr Finished stock Cr Work in progress	Production order
(h)	Goods sold	Dr Cost of sales/contra Cr Finished stock/sales	Delivery note/ Invoice

Notes:

(i)   (d) and (e) could affect general administration and marketing.

(ii)   Overhead absorbed (f) would be debited to finished stock if work in progress is valued at prime cost.

(iii)   In a marginal costing system entry (f) would be for variable overhead only.

* also referred to as cost ledger control.

2.7 Period end procedure

At the end of the reporting period a profit and loss account can be prepared from the cost ledger in the following format:

	£	£
Sales		X
Less: Cost of sales		(X)
Gross margin		X
Add/Less: Over/under-absorbed overhead		X/(X)
Less: General administration costs	X	
Marketing costs	X	(X)
Operating profit		X

Balances in stores, work in progress and finished stock represent stock valuations at cost. At the end of the financial year the costing profit and loss account will be closed by transfer to cost ledger contra and the balances in stock accounts carried forward with an offsetting credit in cost ledger contra.

2.8 Example

The following illustrates the double entry aspect of cost accounting. The entries relating to notional charges and absorption of non-production cost are unlikely to be encountered in practice, but will test your application of accounting procedure.

Details are given below of the operations during a period of one month of a manufacturing company which makes a single product.

You are required to show the entries in an interlocking set of cost accounts.

Data for a period of one month:

	Opening stock		Closing stock	
	Units	£	Units	£
Raw materials:				
Direct		15,000		20,000
Indirect production materials		1,700		3,000
Work in progress:				
Direct materials		3,000		3,500
Direct wages		1,000		1,200
Finished goods	7,500	9,000	10,000	12,000
Sales 150,000 units				225,000
Rent of offices				1,500
Advertising				2,000
Stationery				840
Rates on factory				2,700
Salesmen's commission and expenses				1,400
Insurance of offices				80
Depreciation of machinery				6,400
Warehouse rentals				800
Secretarial wages				3,000
Repairs to plant				1,850
Salesmen's salaries				6,000
Insurance of factory				1,100
Accounting staff wages				8,200
Delivery charges				450
Other factory expenses				7,950
Other administration expenses				2,480

Other marketing expenses	6,250
Purchase of materials:	
Direct	65,000
Indirect production	5,000
Direct wages	55,000
Factory indirect wages	15,000
Loan interest received	500
Included in factory expenses are:	
Notional charge for use of own premises	2,800
Notional interest on capital employed in the business	400

'Other marketing expenses' wrongly contains an amount of £4,500 which should be in 'Other factory expenses'.

The cost accounts are kept separately from the financial accounts. In the cost accounts the company absorbs factory overhead at 40% of prime cost of finished units produced, administration overhead at 10p per unit produced and marketing overhead at 9p per unit delivered.

2.9 Solution

The question should be tackled in logical sequence.

Step 1   Open the necessary cost accounts, which are:

Direct raw materials
Indirect production materials
Work in progress
Factory overhead
Administration overhead
Marketing overhead
Finished goods
Cost of sales
Profit and loss
Cost contra (memo to maintain double entry) ie, cost ledger control a/c.

Step 2   Record the opening balances on the stock accounts, crediting cost contra, and post purchases of materials.

Step 3   Post the issues of material.

Step 4   Charge direct wages to work in progress and indirect wages to factory overhead.

Step 5   Charge the remaining costs for the period to appropriate overhead accounts.

Step 6   Complete the work in progress account. The balance, after posting the closing stock, represents the prime cost of finished units produced.

Step 7   Debit finished goods account with factory and administration overhead at the absorption rates given.

Step 8   Complete the finished goods account. The balance, after posting the closing stock, represents cost of goods sold. The number of units produced (required for Step 7 above) represents Sales + Closing stock − Opening stock, ie, 150,000 + 10,000 − 7,500 = 152,500.

Step 9   Debit cost of sales with absorbed marketing overhead.

Step 10   Compile the profit and loss account by posting sales, cost of sales, and the balances on overhead accounts (under/over-absorption).

Solution (for guidance, the entries have been referenced to the sequence above)

(a)

Direct raw materials

	£		£
Opening stock b/d (2)	15,000	WIP - issued to production (3)	60,000
Cost contra - purchases (2)	65,000	Closing stock c/d	20,000
	80,000		80,000

Indirect production materials

	£		£
Opening stock b/d (2)	1,700	Factory overhead - issues (3)	3,700
Cost contra - purchases (2)	5,000	Closing stock c/d	3,000
	6,700		6,700

Work in progress

	£		£
Opening stock b/d (2)	4,000	Finished goods - prime cost	
Direct raw materials (3)	60,000	of finished units (6) (bal fig)	114,300
Direct wages (4)	55,000	Closing stock c/d	4,700
	119,000		119,000

Factory overhead

	£		£
Indirect materials (3)	3,700	Finished goods - absorbed	
Indirect wages (4)	15,000	overhead @ 40% of £114,300	45,720
Factory rates (5)	2,700		
Depreciation of machinery (5)	6,400		
Repairs to plant (5)	1,850		
Factory insurance (5)	1,100		
Other factory expenses (5)	7,950		
Marketing overhead (error)	4,500		
	43,200		
Profit and loss over-absorbed overhead (10)	2,520		
	45,720		45,720

Administration overhead

	£		£
Rent of offices (5)	1,500	Finished goods - absorbed	
Stationery (5)	840	overhead: 152,500 units	
Insurance of offices (5)	80	@ 10p per unit (7)	15,250
Secretarial wages (5)	3,000	Profit and loss -	
Accounting staff wages (5)	8,200	under-absorbed (10)	850
Other admin expenses (5)	2,480		
	16,100		16,100

Marketing overhead

	£		£
Advertising (5)	2,000	Factory overhead (error)	4,500
Salesmen's commission/		Cost of sales - absorbed	
expenses (5)	1,400	overhead @ 9p per unit on	
Warehouse rentals (5)	800	150,000 units delivered (a)	13,500
Salesmen's salaries (5)	6,000		
Delivery charges (5)	450		
Other expenses (5)	6,250		
Profit and loss - over-absorbed			
overhead (10)	1,100		
	——		——
	18,000		18,000

Finished goods

	Units	£		Units	£
Opening stock (2)	7,500	9,000	Cost of sales (8)		
Work in progress (6)	152,500	114,300	(bal fig)	150,000	172,270
Factory overhead (7)		45,720	Closing stock	10,000	12,000
Admin overhead (7)		15,250			
	——	——		——	——
	160,000	184,270		160,000	184,270

Cost of sales

	£		£
Finished goods (8)	172,270	Profit and loss (10)	185,770
Marketing overhead (9)	13,500		
	——		——
	185,770		185,770

Profit and loss

	£		£
Cost of sales (10)	185,770	Sales (10)	225,000
Admin overhead (10)	850	Factory overhead (10)	2,520
Balance - costing profit	42,000	Marketing overhead (10)	1,100
	——		——
	228,620		228,620

Cost contra account – cost ledger control

	£	£		£
Sales (10)		225,000	Balance b/d (2)	
Balance c/d:			(15,000 + 1,700 + 4,000	
Raw material	20,000		+ 9,000)	29,700
Indirect material	3,000		Purchases (2) (65,000 + 5,000)	70,000
Work in progress	4,700		Wages (4) (55,000 + 15,000)	70,000
Finished goods	12,000		Factory overhead (5)	20,000
	——		Admin overhead (5)	16,100
		39,700	Marketing overhead (5)	16,900
			Balance c/d	
			Costing profit (10)	42,000
		——		——
		264,700		264,700

2.10   Activity

Take the costing profit of £42,000 and prepare a pro-forma statement showing any additional items necessary in order to give the financial accounting profit.

2.11   Activity solution

	£	£	£
Profit per costing profit and loss account			42,000
Add: Loan interest received (excluded from cost accounts)		x	
Notional charges not included in financial accounts:			
Rent	x		
Interest	x		
		x	
			x
Profit per financial accounts			x

3   EXAMPLE

The following illustrates the double entry aspect of recording transactions, using an interlocking (memorandum) system.

3.1   Example

	£
Incurred direct wages	100,000
Incurred indirect production wages	41,200
Administration salaries paid	12,800
Purchased raw materials	46,500
Paid business rates	4,000
Paid creditor for materials	41,400
Paid wages	98,700
Paid PAYE creditor	40,900
Paid bank charges	420
Sales on credit	480,000
Production overhead costs (other than business rates) paid	81,400
Received from debtors	414,600

Notes:

(1)   In the cost ledgers production overhead costs are absorbed into cost units using an absorption rate of 100% of direct wage costs. Any under or over absorption is carried forward to the end of the year.

(2)   Stocks of raw material are valued using FIFO in the financial ledgers and LIFO in the cost ledgers. There was no opening stock, closing stock was valued:

        FIFO   £6,300
        LIFO   £4,800

(3)   There is no work-in-progress or stock of finished goods.

(4)   The amount payable to the PAYE creditor in respect of wages and salaries is £43,400.

(5)   Business rates are to be apportioned:

Production	80%
Administration	20%

3.2   Solution

Interlocking system

Financial ledger

Wages and salaries

	£		£
Wages control	154,000	Profit & loss	154,000

Wages control

	£		£
PAYE creditor	43,400	Wages &	
Bank	98,700	salaries	154,000

PAYE creditor

	£		£
Bank	40,900	Wages control	43,400

Raw material purchases

	£		£
Creditor	46,500	Profit & loss	46,500

Creditor - Raw materials

	£		£
Bank	41,400	Purchases	46,500

Bank

	£		£
Debtors	414,600	Wages control	98,700
		PAYE creditor	40,900
		Creditor	
		- materials	41,400
		Rates	4,000
		Bank charges	420
		Overhead costs	81,400

Rates

	£		£
Bank	4,000	Profit & loss	4,000

Bank charges

	£		£
Bank	420	Profit & loss	420

Sales

	£		£
Profit & loss	480,000	Debtors	480,000

Debtors

	£		£
Sales	480,000	Bank	414,600

Overhead costs

	£		£
Bank	81,400	Profit & loss	81,400

◆ FOULKS*lynch*

Stock

	£		£
Profit & loss	6,300		

Profit & loss

	£		£
Raw material	46,500	Sales	480,000
Wages &		Raw material	
salaries	154,000	stock	6,300
Rates	4,000		
Bank charges	420		
Overhead costs	81,400		
Net profit	199,980		
	486,300		486,300

Cost ledger

Raw material control

	£		£
CLC	46,500	WIP	41,700
		Bal c/d	4,800
	46,500		46,500

Cost ledger control (CLC)

	£		£
Sales	480,000	Raw material	46,500
		WIP	100,000
		Prod Ohd	41,200
		Admin Ohd	12,800
		Prod Ohd	3,200
		Admin Ohd	800
		Prod Ohd	81,400

Work in progress

	£		£
CLC	100,000	Cost of sales	241,700
Raw material	41,700		
Prod Ohd	100,000		
	241,700		241,700

Production overhead

	£		£
CLC	41,200	Work in	
CLC	3,200	progress	100,000
CLC	81,400	Bal c/d	25,800
	125,800		125,800

Sales

	£		£
Profit & loss	480,000	CLC	480,000

Administration overhead

	£		£
CLC	12,800	Profit & loss	13,600
CLC	800		
	13,600		13,600

Cost of sales

	£		£
WIP	241,700	Profit & loss	241,700

Profit & loss

	£		£
Cost of sales	241,700	Sales	480,000
Admin Ohd	13,600		
Net profit	224,700		
	480,000		480,000

Profit reconciliation

(Note that in the exam you will only have to produce the pro-forma for this - you will not have to make the accounting entries. However, we show you the entries here to reinforce your understanding.)

	£	£
Net profit as per financial ledgers		199,980
Adjust for item not in cost ledger:		
Bank charges		420
Differences in treatment of:		
Production overhead costs	25,800	
Closing stock valuation	(1,500)	
		24,300
Net profit as per cost ledgers		224,700

4   INTEGRATED ACCOUNTS

4.1   Introduction

Definition   **Integrated accounts** are a set of accounting records which provides both financial and cost accounts using a common input of data for all accounting purposes.

Integration means that there is just one set of accounting records which provide the necessary accounting information for both financial accounting purposes and cost accounting purposes.

4.2   Methods of integration

Various methods of integrating the financial and cost accounts exist and the system must reflect the structure of the company and the information requirements of management and outsiders, eg, shareholders and the Revenue. Some requirements will be met by a two-fold analysis of costs: by natural headings and by cost centres, products, etc.

The cost department will produce a detailed analysis of WIP and overhead accounts (and probably sales as well), and will supply details of transfers from WIP to finished goods and of overhead recovery.

4.3   Interlocking and integrated systems – a comparison

We can identify the following differences between these systems:

- Many transactions are recorded twice when an interlocking system is used, once in the cost ledger and once in the financial ledger. This is an additional administrative cost.

- Some transactions are not recorded in the cost ledger when an interlocking system is used.

- Some items (eg, stock) may be valued differently in each set of ledgers when an interlocking system is used.

- An integrated system classifies costs similarly to the classifications used in the cost ledger of an interlocking system. The integrated ledger records all transactions and shows the asset and liability accounts similarly to those in the financial ledger of an interlocking system.

In summarising the above it can be shown that the interlocking system provides more flexibility because it is not constrained (in the cost ledger) by the regulations of financial accounting. However, this flexibility has a cost:

- the administrative burden of recording many transactions twice (referred to above); and
- the need to prepare a statement reconciling the profit shown by the cost and financial ledgers.

5   CHAPTER SUMMARY

The information required in cost accounting is often somewhat different to that required in a financial accounting system. The traditional method of dealing with this is to keep two separate sets of ledgers which are not integrated with each other. This is known as an interlocking system. The alternative is to integrate the two systems and this is known as an integrated system, which is not examinable in detail in this paper. You should, however, be aware of the differences between the two systems.

6   SELF TEST QUESTIONS

6.1   What is an interlocking system of accounts? (1.1)

6.2   What are the two ways in which an interlocking system can be arranged? (1.1)

6.3   What type of appropriations of profit might there be that are not dealt with in a costing system? (1.4)

6.4   What types of items might be treated differently in financial and costing accounts? (1.4)

6.5   What is the name of the account used in the cost ledger of an interlocking system in order to maintain the double entry? (2.1)

6.6   What types of control accounts are likely to be kept in an interlocking system? (2.2)

6.7   What accounts, other than control accounts and the cost ledger contra, are likely to be kept in an interlocking system? (2.4)

7   MULTIPLE CHOICE QUESTIONS

7.1   A firm operates an integrated cost and financial accounting system.

The accounting entries for an issue of Direct Materials to Production would be:

A   DR work-in-progress control account; CR stores control account.
B   DR finished goods account; CR stores control account.
C   DR stores control account; CR work-in-progress control account.
D   DR cost of sales account; CR work-in-progress control account.

7.2   During a period £35,750 was incurred for indirect labour. In a typical cost ledger, the double entry for this is:

A   Dr Wages control   Cr Overhead control
B   Dr WIP control   Cr Wages control
C   Dr Overhead control   Cr Wages control
D   Dr Wages control   Cr WIP control

7.3   In the cost ledger the factory cost of finished production for a period was £873,190. The double entry for this is

A	Dr Cost of sales account	Cr	Finished goods control account
B	Dr Finished goods control account	Cr	Work-in-progress control account
C	Dr Costing profit and loss account	Cr	Finished goods control account
D	Dr Work-in-progress control account	Cr	Finished goods control account

7.4   In an integrated cost and financial accounting system, the accounting entries for factory overhead absorbed would be:

A	*Dr* Work-in-progress control account	*Cr*	Overhead control account
B	*Dr* Overhead control account	*Cr*	Work-in-progress control account
C	*Dr* Overhead control account	*Cr*	Cost of sales account
D	*Dr* Cost of sales account	*Cr*	Overhead control account

7.5   The book-keeping entries in a standard cost system when the actual price for raw materials is less than the standard price are:

A	DR	Raw materials control account	CR	Raw material price variance account
B	DR	WIP control account	CR	Raw materials control account
C	DR	Raw material price variance account	CR	Raw materials control account
D	DR	WIP control account	CR	Raw material price variance account

8   ANSWERS TO MULTIPLE CHOICE QUESTIONS

8.1   **A**   This transaction **increases** the asset 'work in progress', so debit work in progress; it **decreases** the asset 'materials stock', so credit stores control.

8.2   **C**   When the wages are paid they will be initially recorded in wages control (DR Wages control, CR Cash). They will then be charged out to the appropriate cost ledger account - in this case overheads, as it is indirect labour.

8.3   **B**

8.4   **A**   The others are incorrect.

8.5   **A**   Materials price variances are conventionally extracted when materials are bought (via the materials control account) rather than after having been transferred to the WIP account.

Chapter 11

JOB, BATCH AND CONTRACT COSTING

PATHFINDER INTRODUCTION

This chapter covers the following elements of the CAT Official Teaching Guide. At the end of this chapter you should have learned these teaching guide elements thoroughly.

Session 11
Job, batch and contract costing
Syllabus reference j

- Describe situations where the use of job, batch and contract costing are appropriate
- Calculate product costs in a job and batch costing system using absorption and marginal costing
- Describe the practical problems relating to cost control in a contract accounting system
- Complete cost records and accounts in job, batch and contract costing systems

(*Note:* Contract costing questions will be confined to contracts completed within one year. Candidates will not be required to calculate the profit allowable on incomplete contracts).

Putting the chapter in context

Different businesses present different problems to the cost accountant, and require different approaches to calculate and record costs. The next four chapters cover job costing, batch costing, contract costing, service costing and process costing. This chapter explains how costs are recorded in job, batch and contract costing.

1 USE OF JOB, BATCH AND CONTRACT COSTING

1.1 Introduction

The purpose of costing is to calculate the cost of each cost unit. To do this, the costs of each unit are gathered together and recorded in the costing system. This is the overall aim but the methods and system used will differ from organisation to organisation as the type of products and production methods differ between organisations.

1.2 Cost units

The cost units of different organisations will be of different types and this will tend to necessitate different costing systems. The main types of cost units are as follows:

(a) Individual products designed and produced for individual customers. Each individual product is a cost unit. The costing system used is job costing, unless the products take a long time to make, in which case contract costing is used.

(b) Groups of different products possibly in different styles, sizes or colours produced to be held in stock until sold. Each of the individual products of whatever style, size or colour is a cost unit. The costing system used is batch costing.

(c) Many units of identical products produced from a single production process. These units will be held in stock until sold. Each product from the process is a cost unit. The costing system used is process costing which is explained in a later chapter.

1.3   Jobs

Definition   A **job** is an individual contract or product produced as a single order or product.

A job will normally be requested by a customer and made to that customer's individual requirements and specifications. The organisation will estimate the costs of such a job, both direct and indirect, add on their required profit margin, and quote their price to the customer.

As each individual job will differ in some respects from other jobs there will be no set price or cost for each job.

If the customer accepts the quote the job will proceed according to the timetable agreed between customer and supplier.

1.4   Job costing

Job costing records the actual costs of each job, usually on a job cost card. These costs are then compared to the job price to determine the actual profit made.

1.5   Batch costing system

Definition   A **batch** is a group of identical but separately identifiable products that are all made together.

For example if a group of 100 identical products of a particular colour are made in a production run then this will be a batch. A second batch might be a production run of 140 of the same product but in a different colour.

A batch costing system is very similar to a job costing system as a batch is in many respects simply a job. The costs are of the batch are gathered together on some sort of a batch cost card . These costs will be the direct materials input into the batch, the labour worked on the batch, any direct expenses of the batch and the batch's share of overheads.

In order to find the cost of a cost unit from the batch, the total cost of the batch must be divided by the number of products in that batch.

1.6   Contract costing

Definition   A **contract** is a job which is due to be worked on for more than one accounting period.

Therefore a contract is a specific customer order job that is fairly long term and will be worked on for a period of time that spans more than one accounting period.

Contract costing is again very similar to job costing in that all of the costs involved in the job will be gathered together in a contract account. However the main difference is that the estimated profit on the contract is spread over more than one accounting period.

Conclusion   Job costing is used where the cost unit is a specific, individual product made to customer order.

Batch costing is used where a group of identical items are produced together in a batch.

Contract costing is used where a job is to be produced for a customer which is due to be worked on for a period which spans more than one accounting period.

2   JOB COSTING

2.1   Job cost card

All of the actual costs incurred in a job are recorded on a job cost card. A job cost card can take many forms but is likely to include the following information.

<table>
<tr><td colspan="5" align="center">JOB COST CARD</td></tr>
<tr>
<td colspan="2">Job number:
Estimate ref:
Start date:
Invoice number:</td>
<td colspan="3">Customer name:
Quoted estimate:
Delivery date:
Invoice amount:</td>
</tr>
</table>

COSTS:

Materials

Date	Code	Qty	Price	£
			———	———
			———	———

Labour

Date	Grade	Hours	Rate	£
			———	———
			———	———

Expenses

Date	Code	Description	£
		———	———
		———	———

Production overheads

Hours	OAR	£
———		———
———		———

Cost summary:

Direct materials
Direct labour
Direct expenses
Production overheads
Administration overheads
Selling and distribution overheads
Total cost
Invoice price
Profit/loss

The job cost card may travel with the particular job as it moves around the factory. However it is more likely in practice that the job cost cards will be held centrally by the accounts department and all relevant cost information for that job forwarded to the accounts department.

2.2   Direct materials

When materials are requisitioned for a job the issue of the materials will be recorded in the stock ledger account. They will also be recorded, at their issue price, on the job cost card. Materials may be issued at different dates to a particular job and each issue must be recorded on the job cost card.

2.3   Activity

The materials requisitions and issues for job number 3867 for customer OT Ltd at their issue prices are as follows:

1 June   40 kg Material code T73 @ £60 per kg
5 June   60 kg Material code R80 @ £5 per kg
9 June   280 metres Material code B45 @ £8 per metre

Record these on a job cost card for this job which is due to be delivered on 17 June.

2.4   Solution

JOB COST CARD	

Job number: 3867
Estimate ref:
Start date: 1 June
Invoice number:

Customer name: OT Ltd
Quoted estimate:
Delivery date: 17 June
Invoice amount:

COSTS:

Materials

Date	Code	Qty	Price	£
1 June	T73	40 kg	£60	2,400
5 June	R80	60 kg	£5	300
9 June	B45	280m	£8	2,240
				4,940

Labour

Date	Grade	Hours	Rate	£

Expenses

Date	Code	Description	£

Production overheads

Hours	OAR	£

Cost summary:

£

Direct materials
Direct labour
Direct expenses
Production overheads
Administration overheads
Selling and distribution overheads

Total cost
Invoice price

Profit/loss

2.5   Direct labour cost

The hours worked by each grade of labour are recorded. The card is then sent to the accounts department and the relevant hourly labour rate is applied to each grade of labour to give a cost for each grade and a total cost for the job.

2.6   Activity

The labour records show that the hours worked on job 3867 were as follows:

1 June	Grade II	43 hours
2 June	Grade II	12 hours
	Grade IV	15 hours
5 June	Grade I	25 hours
	Grade IV	13 hours
9 June	Grade I	15 hours

The hourly rates for each grade of labour are as follows:

	£
Grade I	4.70
Grade II	5.80
Grade III	6.40
Grade IV	7.50

Record the labour worked on job 3867 on the job cost card.

2.7   Activity solution

JOB COST CARD

Job number: 3867

Estimate ref:

Start date: 1 June

Invoice number:

Customer name: OT Ltd

Quoted estimate:

Delivery date: 17 June

Invoice amount:

COSTS:

Materials

Date	Code	Qty	Price	£
1 June	T73	40 kg	£60	2,400
5 June	R80	60 kg	£5	300
9 June	B45	280m	£8	2,240
				────
				4,940
				────

Labour

Date	Grade	Hours	Rate	£
1 June	II	43	5.80	249.40
2 June	II	12	5.80	69.60
	IV	15	7.50	112.50
5 June	I	25	4.70	117.50
	IV	13	7.50	97.50
9 June	I	15	4.70	70.50
				────
				717.00
				────

Expenses				Production overheads		
Date	Code	Description	£	Hours	OAR	£
			———			———
			———			———

Cost summary:

£

Direct materials
Direct labour
Direct expenses
Production overheads
Administration overheads
Selling and distribution overheads

Total cost ———
Invoice price

Profit/loss ———
———

2.8 Direct expenses

The third category of direct costs are any expenses that can be directly attributed to the job. Such expenses will be recorded by the cost accountant when incurred and coded in such a way that it is clear to which job or jobs they relate.

2.9 Activity

A specialised piece of machinery has been hired at a cost of £1,200. It is used on job numbers 3859, 3867 and 3874 and has spent approximately the same amount of time being used on each of those jobs. The accounts code for machine hire is 85.

Record any cost relevant to job 3867 on the job cost card.

2.10 Activity solution

As the machinery is used in equal proportions on three different jobs then only one third of the hire charge is to be charged to job 3867 (£1,200 × $\frac{1}{3}$ = £400).

JOB COST CARD

Job number: 3867
Estimate ref:
Start date: 1 June
Invoice number:

Customer name: OT Ltd
Quoted estimate:
Delivery date: 17 June
Invoice amount:

COSTS:

Materials

Date	Code	Qty	Price	£
1 June	T73	40 kg	£60	2,400
5 June	R80	60 kg	£5	300
9 June	B45	280m	£8	2,240
				————
				4,940
				————

Labour

Date	Grade	Hours	Rate	£
1 June	II	43	5.80	249.40
2 June	II	12	5.80	69.60
	IV	15	7.50	112.50
5 June	I	25	4.70	117.50
	IV	13	7.50	97.50
9 June	I	15	4.70	70.50
				————
				717.00
				————

Expenses

Date	Code	Description	£
1 June	85	Machine hire	400
			———
			400
			———

Production overheads

Hours	OAR	£
		———
		———

Cost summary:

	£
Direct materials	
Direct labour	
Direct expenses	
Production overheads	
Administration overheads	
Selling and distribution overheads	
	———
Total cost	
Invoice price	
	———
Profit/loss	
	———

2.11   Production overheads

In an earlier chapter the apportionment of overheads to cost units was considered and it was determined that the most common method of allocating overheads to specific cost units was on the basis of either the labour hours or machine hours worked. Thus, the production overhead will usually be absorbed into jobs on the basis of such a pre-determined overhead absorption rate.

2.12   Other overheads

In order to arrive at the total cost for a particular job any administration, selling and distribution overheads must also be included in the job's cost. Therefore when the job is completed an appropriate proportion of the total administration, selling and distribution overheads will also be included on the job cost card.

2.13   Activity

The production overhead absorption rate for this period is £4 per labour hour. The administration overhead to be charged to job 3867 totals £156 and the selling and distribution overhead for the job is £78.

The job was completed by the due date and the customer was invoiced at the agreed price of £7,800 on 17 June (invoice number 26457).

Using this information complete the job cost card for job 3867.

2.14   Activity solution

JOB COST CARD

Job number: 3867
Estimate ref:
Start date: 1 June
Invoice number: 26457

Customer name: OT Ltd
Quoted estimate:
Delivery date: 17 June
Invoice amount: £7,800

COSTS:

Materials

Date	Code	Qty	Price	£
1 June	T73	40 kg	£60	2,400
5 June	R80	60 kg	£5	300
9 June	B45	280m	£8	2,240
				4,940

Labour

Date	Grade	Hours	Rate	£
1 June	II	43	5.80	249.40
2 June	II	12	5.80	69.60
	IV	15	7.50	112.50
5 June	I	25	4.70	117.50
	IV	13	7.50	97.50
9 June	I	15	4.70	70.50
				717.00

Expenses

Date	Code	Description	£
1 June	85	Machine hire	400
			400

Production overheads

Hours	OAR	£
123	4.00	492
		492

Cost summary:

	£
Direct materials	4,940
Direct labour	717
Direct expenses	400
Production overheads	492
Administration overheads	156
Selling and distribution overheads	78
Total cost	6,783
Invoice price	7,800
Profit/loss	1,017

Conclusion   Job costing requires all of the elements of cost accounting considered so far to be applied to a single cost unit, the job.

3   BATCH COSTING

3.1   Introduction

In exactly the same way as in job costing the costs of a batch are gathered together on some sort of a batch cost card. These costs will be the materials input into the batch, the labour worked on the batch, any direct expenses of the batch and the batch's share of overheads.

The layout of the batch cost card will be similar to that of a job cost card, and will show the total cost of that particular batch of production.

3.2   Cost of a cost unit

Remember that a batch does however differ from a job in that a batch is made up of a number of identical products or cost units. To find the cost of each item or cost unit the total cost of the batch must be divided by the number of products in the batch.

3.3   Example

Batch number 0692 has the following inputs:

15 June	Material X	20 kg @ £30 per kg
		40 hours of grade II labour @ £6.00 per hour
16 June	Material Y	15 kg @ £10 per kg
		60 hours of grade III labour at £5.00 per hour

Production overhead is to be absorbed into the cost of each batch on the basis of labour hours at a rate of £0.50 per labour hour.

The number of items in batch 0692 was 100.

Calculate the cost of each item in batch 0692.

3.4   Solution

Materials cost

	£
Material X 20 kg × £30	600
Material Y 15 kg × £10	150

Labour cost

Grade II 40 hours × £6	240
Grade III 60 hours × £5	300

Production overhead

100 hours × £0.50	50
	___
	1,340
	___

Cost per cost unit or product

$$\frac{£1,340}{100 \text{ units}} = £13.40$$

Conclusion   Batch costing requires all of the costs of the batch to be accounted for on the batch cost card. Total costs are then divided by the number of cost units in the batch to determine the cost per cost unit.

4   COST CONTROL IN A CONTRACT ACCOUNTING SYSTEM

4.1   Introduction

Contract costing is used where an organisation carries out large long-term jobs for customers typically in the construction industry.

4.2   Contract accounting system

In a contract accounting system all of the costs incurred on the contract are gathered together in a contract account. This means that an account for each individual contract is set up and debited with all of the costs for that contract.

4.3   Cost control

For the contract to be properly monitored over its life and to ensure profitability, it is obviously necessary to have accurate recording and control of the costs of the contract.

The nature of contract costing means that there are specific practical problems involved in cost control.

4.4   Problems of cost control

The problems of controlling costs in a contract accounting system might include some or all of the following:

- Time scale - by definition a contract is long term and covers more than one accounting period. Therefore the costs that are accumulated on the contract are incurred over a number of years.

- Materials - materials charged to the contract may include both materials purchased specially for the contract and materials issued from the organisation's stores. The materials are then physically transferred to the site of the contract and any unused materials transferred back to stores. It is therefore important that there exist good controls over the recording of receipts and returns to and from the site and stores.

- Labour - labour costs will be made up of the cost of the hours worked by employees on the site of the contract. Again this might mean that there are physical difficulties in controlling the recording of all of the hours worked on the contract.

- Expenses - contracts will often incur significant costs other than materials and labour which again must be accurately recorded. One of the most major of these expenses is likely to be the used of plant and machinery. If the plant and machinery is hired then the hire charge must be charged to the contract. If the plant and machinery used is owned by the organisation then a share of the depreciation must be charged to the contract.

Conclusion   Contract costing introduces costs of additional problems to those normally incurred in costing, largely due to the time scale and physical nature of a long term contract.

5   COST RECORDS AND ACCOUNTS

5.1   Introduction

So far in this chapter the nature of job costing, batch costing and contract costing have been considered together with the basic costing records that are kept. In this final element of the chapter the cost records and accounts for each type of costing system will be considered a little further.

5.2   Job costing records

All of the costs incurred in a job are recorded on a job cost card so that the final total cost for the job can be compared with the price of the job to calculate a profit.

In the accounting records the same total costs of the job are recorded in a job account. There is a job account for each job that the organisation undertakes and it operates in a similar way to a work in progress account.

The job account is debited with all of the costs of the job as they are incurred. Upon completion of the job the balance of the costs on the job account is transferred to cost of sales as part of the profit and loss account.

5.3   Batch costing

Batch cost accounting works in exactly the same way as job cost accounting. The costs of the batch are gathered together on a batch cost card and are also recorded in a work in progress account for each batch under operation. Upon completion of the batch the total costs are transferred from the work in progress account to cost of sales.

5.4   Contract costing

All of the costs involved in a contract are recorded as debits in a contract account. There is one contract account for each individual contract that the organisation undertakes. However as the contract will by definition span more than one accounting period then there is a further problem with contract accounting, known as attributable profit.

5.5   Attributable profit on uncompleted contracts

Where a contract extends over a long period **SSAP 9 (Stocks and long-term contracts)** allows the contractor to take credit for part of the profit **attributable** to the contract in each year's accounts. This percentage of completion method avoids the inconsistency of having a number of years with no profit from a particular contract and then suddenly making all the profit in the year it is completed. In deciding to what extent profit can be taken on uncompleted contracts the following matters are important considerations:

(a)   the successful outcome of the contract should be certain before any interim profit is taken;

(b)   any profit should only be taken in proportion to the work completed to date on the contract; and

(c)   any anticipated overall loss on the contract should be provided for as soon as it is recognised.

However for this syllabus students are not expected to be able to calculate attributable profit nor enter it into the accounting records.

5.6   Activity

Contract No. 412 commenced during 20X1 and has a fixed contract price of £200,000. The costs incurred during the year 20X1 for materials, wages and sub-contractors' charges totalled £90,000. Plant costing £20,000 was purchased during 20X1 specifically for Contract No. 412.

At the end of 20X1:

(a)   the plant was valued at £15,000;

(b)   unused materials on the site were valued at £19,000;

You are required to prepare the entries for this year in the contract account.

5.7   Activity solution

Contract number 412

	£		£
Materials, wages and sub-contractors' costs	90,000	Materials c/d	19,000
Plant (at cost)	20,000	Plant c/d	15,000

(Tutorial note: by debiting the contract account with £20,000 the cost of the plant, and crediting it with £15,000, the value of the plant at the end of the period the contract has effectively been charged with £5,000 of depreciation of the plant.*)*

The value of the unused materials at the end of the period are also carried down in the contract account to ensure that the contract is only charged with the materials used in the period.

Conclusion   The costs incurred in a job, batch or contract must be carefully monitored and recorded. In each of the three costing systems these costs are recorded as a debit in a job, batch or contract account.

6   CHAPTER SUMMARY

In this chapter the different forms of specific order cashing, job costing, batch costing and contract costing were discussed and distinguished from each other.

7   SELF TEST QUESTIONS

7.1   What is a job? (1.3)

7.2   What is a batch? (1.6)

7.3   Distinguish between a job and a contract? (1.7)

7.4   What is the purpose of a job cost card? (2.1)

7.5   What is recorded on a job cost card? (2.1)

7.6   How would the cost of machinery used be included in the costs of a contract? (4.4)

7.7   Would a job account be debited or credited with the costs of the job? (5.2)

7.8   What is meant by attributable profit on an uncompleted contract? (5.5)

7.9   How is the cost of fixed assets purchased for use in a contract dealt with in a contract account? (5.7)

7.10   How are any unused materials at the contract site at the end of the period dealt with in the contract account ? (5.7)

8   MULTIPLE CHOICE QUESTIONS

8.1   A job requires 2,400 actual labour hours for completion and it is anticipated that there will be 20% idle time. If the wage rate is £10 per hour, what is the budgeted labour cost for the job?

A   £19,200
B   £24,000
C   £28,800
D   £30,000

8.2   The following items may be used in costing jobs in an absorption costing system:

(i)   Actual material cost
(ii)   Actual manufacturing overheads
(iii)   Absorbed manufacturing overheads
(iv)   Actual labour cost

Which of the above are contained in a typical job cost?

A   (i), (ii) and (iv) only.
B   (i) and (iv) only.
C   (i), (iii) and (iv) only.
D   All four of them.

8.3   A small management consultancy has prepared the following information:

Overhead absorption rate per consulting hour	£12.50
Salary cost per consulting hour (senior)	£20.00
Salary cost per consulting hour (junior)	£15.00

The firm adds 40% to total cost to arrive at a selling price.

Assignment number 652 took 86 hours of a senior consultant's time and 220 hours of junior time.

What price should be charged for assignment number 652?

A   £5,355
B   £7,028
C   £8,845
D   £12,383

9   PRACTICE QUESTIONS

9.1   Printing and publishing

A printing and publishing company has been asked to provide an estimate for the production of 100,000 catalogues, of 64 pages (32 sheets of paper) each, for a potential customer.

Four operations are involved in the production process; photography, set-up, printing and binding.

Each page of the catalogue requires a separate photographic session. Each session costs £150.

Set-up would require a plate to be made for each page of the catalogue. Each plate requires four hours of labour at £7 per hour and £35 of materials. Overheads are absorbed on the basis of labour hours at an hourly rate of £9.50.

In printing, paper costs £12 per thousand sheets. Material losses are expected to be 2% of input. Other printing materials will cost £7 per 500 catalogues. 1,000 catalogues are printed per hour of machine time. Labour and overhead costs incurred in printing are absorbed at a rate of £62 per machine hour.

Binding costs are recovered at a rate per machine hour. The rate is £43 per hour and 2,500 catalogues are bound per hour of machine time.

A profit margin of 10% of selling price is required.

You are required to determine the total amount that should be quoted for the catalogue job by the printing and publishing company.

9.2   Job FR73

You are given the following information about job FR73 that an organisation is producing for their customer GH Ltd.

1 May	25 kg material D issued valued at £12 per kg
	4 kg of material E issued valued at £49 per kg
	17 hours of grade A labour used at £8.50 per hour
	13 hours of grade D labour used at £5.50 per hour

| 4 May | 20 hours of grade B labour used at £7.20 per hour |
| | 3 kg of material D issued valued at £12 per kg |

| 5 May | 10 hours of grade B labour used at £7.20 per hour |
| | 30 hours of grade C labour used at £6.40 per hour |

| 6 May | 2 metres of material X issued valued at £36 per metre |
| | 4 hours of grade A labour used at £8.50 per hour |

The job was completed as agreed on 6 May and delivered to the customer together with invoice number 3956 showing the agreed price of £2,000.

The organisation's policy is to absorb production overheads on the basis of labour hours and the overhead absorption rate for this period is £2.00 per labour hour. The proportion of administration overhead to be charged to job FR73 is 2% and of selling and distribution overhead 5%. The estimated administration overhead for the month is £2,600 and selling and distribution overhead £1,900.

Using this information complete the following job cost card for job FR73.

JOB COST CARD

Job number: Customer name:
Estimate ref: Quoted estimate:
Start date: Delivery date:
Invoice No: Invoice amount:

COSTS:

Materials   **Labour**

Date   Code   Qty   Price   £   Date   Grade   Hours   Rate   £

                   ____   ____

                   ____   ____

Expenses   **Production overheads**

Date   Code   Description   £   Hours   OAR   £

                   ____   ____

                   ____   ____

Cost summary:
                                                                £

Direct materials
Direct labour
Direct expenses
Production overheads
Administration overheads
Selling and distribution overheads

                                                                ____

Total cost
Invoice price

                                                                ____

Profit/loss

                                                                ____

---

10   ANSWERS TO MULTIPLE CHOICE QUESTIONS

10.1   D $2,400 \times \dfrac{100}{80} \times £10 = £30,000$

10.2   C   Overheads are charged to jobs at predetermined absorption rate.

10.3   D

			£
Senior	86hrs @ £20		1,720
Junior	220hrs @ £15		3,300
Overheads	306hrs @ £12.50		3,825
			____
Total cost			8,845
Mark-up	(40%)		3,538
			____
Selling price			12,383

11   ANSWERS TO PRACTICE QUESTIONS

11.1   PRINTING AND PUBLISHING

(Note: this question needs careful thought. Consider what the costs relate to, e.g. per page or per hour.*)*

		£	£
Photography			
64 pages @ £150 per page			9,600
Set-up			
Labour	64 plates × 4 hours × £7	1,792	
Material	64 plates × £35	2,240	
Overheads	64 plates × 4 hours × £9.50	2,432	
		____	
			6,464
Printing			
Material - paper (see working)		39,184	
- other (£7 × 100,000/500)		1,400	
Labour and overheads	$\dfrac{100,000}{1,000}$ hours × £62	6,200	
		____	
			46,784
Binding			
Labour and overheads	$\dfrac{100,000}{2,500}$ hours × £43		1,720
			____
Total costs			64,568
			____
Selling price	£64,568 ÷ 90%		71,742
			____

WORKINGS

(W1)   Material cost

1 catalogue requires 32 sheets
Number of sheets of output required for 100,000 catalogues
$= 100,000 \times 32 = 3,200,000$ sheets

This represents 98% of **input** required (2% of input is lost).

$\therefore$ Input required $= 3,200,000 \times \dfrac{100}{98}$

$= 3,265,306$

Cost is £12 per thousand sheets

$\therefore$ Total cost of sheets

$= \dfrac{3,265,306}{1000} \times £12$

$= £39,184$

11.2   Job FR73

JOB COST CARD

Job number: FR73   Customer name: GH Ltd
Estimate ref: Quoted estimate:
Start date: 1 May   Delivery date: 6 May
Invoice No: 3956   Invoice amount: £2,000

COSTS:

Materials

Date	Code	Qty	Price	£
1 May	D	25kg	12	300
	E	4kg	49	196
4 May	D	3kg	12	36
6 May	X	2m	36	72
				___
				604

Labour

Date	Grade	Hours	Rate	£
1 May	A	17	8.50	144.50
	D	13	5.50	71.50
4 May	B	20	7.20	144.00
5 May	B	10	7.20	72.00
	C	30	6.40	192.00
6 May	A	4	8.50	34.00
				_____
				658.00

Expenses

Date	Code	Description	£
			—
			—

Production overheads

Hours	OAR	£
94	2.00	188
		___
		188

Cost summary:

	£
Direct materials	604
Direct labour	658
Direct expenses	-
Production overheads	188
Administration overheads (2% × £2,600)	52
Selling and distribution overheads (5% × £1,900)	95
	___
Total cost	1,597
Invoice price	2,000
	___
Profit/loss	403

Chapter 12

PROCESS COSTING 1

PATHFINDER INTRODUCTION

This chapter covers the following elements of the CAT Official Teaching Guide. At the end of this chapter you should have learned these teaching guide elements thoroughly.

Session 12
Process costing 1
Syllabus reference j

- Describe situations where the use of process costing is appropriate
- Calculate the cost per unit of process outputs when there may or may not be losses in process as well as closing work in progress in the same process
- Distinguish between by-products and joint products
- Treatment of by-products and joint products at the point of separation
- Evaluate and advise on the benefit (or otherwise) of further processing to enhance a product or products.

Putting the chapter in context

Having looked at job, batch and contract costing, the next two chapters cover process costing. In process costing, cost per unit is calculated by dividing expenditure by output quantity, but is complicated by joint products (explained in this chapter) and losses and work in progress (explained in the next chapter).

1 USE OF PROCESS COSTING

1.1 Comparison of a batch and a process

In the previous chapter batch costing was discussed. A batch is effectively a process that produces a number of identical cost units. However a batch has an end and only produces a set number of units. In simple terms a process is a batch that never ends.

Definition   A **process** is the production of identical units from a number of different inputs, being material, labour and overheads.

The main difference between a batch and a process is that the process is continuous whereas a batch comes to an end when, for example, that particular production run finishes.

1.2 Examples of processes

The typical examples of processes where process costing would be employed as the costing system are the following types of production:

- (a) drinks;
- (b) food;
- (c) chemicals;
- (d) soap;
- (e) paint; and
- (f) oil refining.

There are many others but this should give students an idea of the type of practical situation where process costing is used.

1.3   Process costing

The aim of process costing is to find the cost of each unit that is output from the process. This is done by totalling the process costs and dividing this total by the number of units of output.

Conclusion   Although the calculations can sometimes seem quite complicated in all cases all that is being done is to take the total process costs and divide by the number of units produced to calculate cost per unit.

2   COST PER UNIT OF PROCESS OUTPUTS

2.1   Introduction

The value of the output from any process is the cost of the process divided by the number of units produced.

2.2   Process input costs

The typical costs of a process are materials, labour and any overheads apportioned to the process. In process costing the total of the labour costs and the overhead costs tend to be known as costs of conversion.

Definition   **Costs of conversion** are the labour costs of the process plus the overheads of the process.

2.3   Activity

Suppose that the input to a particular process is 60,000 kg of materials at a cost of £2 per kg. The amount of labour spent on the process during the period was 10,000 hours at a rate of £6 per hour and the overhead absorption rate for this process is £1 per labour hour.

If 19,000 units were produced from the process what is the cost per unit?

2.4   Activity solution

The cost per unit is simply the total cost of the process divided by the number of units produced.

Total cost

	£
Materials 60,000 kg × £2	120,000
Labour 10,000 hours × £6	60,000
Overhead 10,000 × £1	10,000
	190,000

$$\text{Cost per unit} \quad = \quad \frac{\text{Total cost}}{\text{Number of process units}}$$

$$= \quad \frac{£190,000}{19,000 \text{ units}}$$

$$= \quad £10 \text{ per unit}$$

Conclusion   The basic calculation of cost per unit is

$$\frac{\text{Material cost} \; + \; \text{Conversion cost}}{\text{Number of units produced}}$$

3   JOINT PRODUCTS AND BY PRODUCTS

3.1   Introduction

In the examples of process costing that have been considered so far one simplifying assumption has been made. That is that the output from a process is just one product.

In practice however a single process might produce a number of different products or alternatively different materials that can then be further processed to produce different products. For example a chemical process might involve a number of chemical inputs which give two different chemical liquids as output as well as a gas that can be further processed to produce yet another chemical product.

3.2   Joint products

Definition   **Joint products** are separate products that emerge from a single process. Each of these products has a significant sales value to the organisation.

The key point about joint products is that they are all relatively significant to the organisation in terms of sales value.

3.3   By-products

Definition   A **by-product** is a product that is produced from a process, together with other products, that is either of insignificant quantity or insignificant sales value.

A by-product is therefore similar to a joint products in that it is one of a number of products output from a process. However whereas joint products are all saleable products with significant sales value, a by-product will usually have such a small selling price or be produced in such small quantities that its overall sales value to the organisation is insignificant.

Conclusion   Joint products and by-products are both one of a number of products produced by a process. The distinguishing feature between the two is whether or not they have a significant sales value. If the sales value of the product is significant it will be a joint product, if not it will be a by-product.

4   TREATMENT OF BY-PRODUCTS AND JOINT PRODUCTS

4.1   Introduction

Suppose that three products, A, B and C are all produced from a single process. The costs involved in the process are, say, £100,000.

Definition   **Joint costs** are the costs incurred in a process that must be split or apportioned amongst the products produced by the process.

How is this £100,000 of joint costs to be apportioned amongst the three products?

What value or cost is to be assigned to each unit of A, B and C?

4.2   Point of separation (split-off point)

The value of each of the products that are produced by a process will normally be determined at the point of separation.

Definition   The **point of separation (or split-off point)** is the point in the process when the products become separately identifiable.

This is the point where a value or cost per unit must be assigned to any joint products and by-products.

4.3   Methods of apportioning joint costs to joint products

There are two main methods of apportioning joint costs to joint products:

- split the joint costs in proportion to the physical quantity of each product produced;
- split the joint costs in proportion to their relative sales values.

4.4   Activity

A process produces the following products:

Product	Quantity in kg	Selling price per kg
X	100,000	£1
Y	20,000	£10
Z	80,000	£2.25

The costs incurred in the process prior to the separation point of these three products were £240,000.

Show how the joint costs would be apportioned to each product on the basis of physical quantity and relative sales value.

4.5   Activity solution

Physical quantity method

	kg
X	100,000
Y	20,000
Z	80,000
	200,000

Apportionment of joint costs

		£
X	£240,000 × 100,000 kg/200,000 kg	120,000
Y	£240,000 × 20,000 kg/200,000 kg	24,000
Z	£240,000 × 80,000 kg/200,000 kg	96,000
		240,000

Conclusion   This method may be appropriate in some processes but it can give peculiar results. For example product X can only be sold for £100,000 (100,000 kg × £1 per kg) and yet under this method £120,000 of costs have been allocated to it.

Total sales value

		£
X	100,000 kg × £1 per kg	100,000
Y	20,000 kg × £10 per kg	200,000
Z	80,000 kg × £2.25 per kg	180,000
		480,000

Apportionment of joint costs

X	£240,000 × 100,000/480,000	50,000
Y	£240,000 × 200,000/480,000	100,000
Z	£240,000 × 180,000/480,000	90,000
		240,000

Conclusion   This apportionment of costs gives a completely different picture to that based upon the physical quantities of the products produced.

4.6   Treatment of by-products

The usual accounting treatment for by products is as follows:
(a)   do not allocate any costs to the by products and therefore do not treat as items of stock;
(b)   treat either as miscellaneous income or as a reduction in the costs of the main process as and when the by product is sold.

Conclusion   For this level the most important thing is that students can distinguish a by product from a joint product.

5   FURTHER PROCESSING DECISIONS

5.1   Problems of common costs

Even if careful technical estimates are made of relative benefits, common costs apportionment will inevitably be an arbitrary calculation. When providing information to assist decision making, therefore, the cost accountant will emphasise cost revenue differences arising from the decision.

Examples of decisions involving joint products are:

(a)   withdrawing, or adding, a product;
(b)   special pricing;
(c)   economics of further processing.

Apportioned common costs are **not** relevant to any of the above decisions although a change in marketing strategy may affect total joint costs e.g. withdrawing a product may allow capacity of the joint process to be reduced.

In the short or medium term, it is probably impractical and/or uneconomic to alter the processing structure. The relative benefit derived by joint products is, therefore, irrelevant when considering profitability or marketing opportunities.

5.2   Benefits (or otherwise) of further processing

The joint process should, as stated above, be evaluated by looking at the **total** revenue and **total** cost for that process. However, it is important also to note that further processing may well increase profits. This further processing is only possible **if** the joint process is carried out.

It is assumed that further processing of products is independent i.e. a decision to process one joint product in no way affects the decision to process further the other joint products. It should also be noted that joint costs are not affected by whether individual products are further processed, and are therefore not relevant.

To evaluate processing of the individual products it is necessary to identify the **incremental** costs and **incremental** revenues relating to that further processing i.e. the **additional** costs and revenue brought about directly as a result of that further processing.

5.3   Example

The following data relates to products A and B produced from a joint process:

	Kgs produced	Kgs sold	Selling price at split-off point	Further processing costs	Selling price after further processing
Product A	100	80	£5	£280 + £2.00 per kg	£8.40
Product B	200	150	£2	£160 + £1.40 per kg	£4.50

Evaluation of further processing:

		Product A			Product B	
		£	£		£	£
Incremental revenue	$100 \times £(8.40 - 5.00)$		340	$200 \times £(4.50 - 2.00)$		500
Incremental cost:						
Fixed		280			160	
Variable	$100 \times £2$	200		$200 \times £1.40$	280	
		——	480		——	440
Increase/(decrease) in profit			(140)			60

On the basis of these figures the decision to recommend would be:

A   Sell at split-off point for £5.
B   Sell after further processing for £4.50.

This would result in overall profits on this **production** volume of:

	£
Common process	150
Further processing of B	60
Profit	210

Note: the timing of recognition of this profit is dependent on the basis used for valuation of stocks, as discussed above.

The recommendation to sell A at the split-off point and B after further processing is based on two assumptions:
(a)   all relevant 'effects' of the decision have been included i.e. quantified;
(b)   production volume achieved is A 100 kgs, B 200 kgs.

Before a final decision is made these assumptions must be considered:

(a)   **All effects of decision quantified**

The course of action recommended could have other effects not included above, e.g.

- Products A and B in their final state may be in some way 'complementary' i.e. it may only be possible to sell B for £4.50 if A is also available in a further processed state at a price of £8.40.

- The company may currently be carrying out further processing of A. The decision above could therefore result in having to reduce the workforce employed in this processing. The remaining workforce could, for example, go out on strike, causing a loss of production and sales of A and B. These factors should be carefully assessed before a final decision is made.

(b)   **Production volume**

By looking in more detail at the further processing of A it is possible to see that further processing of 1 kg of A results in an incremental contribution of:

	£
Incremental revenue £(8.40 − 5.00)	3.40
Incremental variable cost	2.00
Incremental contribution	1.40

It is therefore possible to identify the level of activity at which further processing of A becomes worthwhile i.e. the 'break-even volume'.

$$\text{Break-even volume} = \frac{\text{Incremental fixed costs}}{\text{Incremental contribution per kg}}$$

$$= \frac{280}{1.40}$$

$$= 200 \text{ kgs}$$

Hence, if the volume of A in the future is greater than 200 kgs, further processing becomes economically worthwhile.

6   CHAPTER SUMMARY

In this chapter we have started to look at process costing including the treatment of joint and by-products, we shall continue with this topic in chapter 13.

7   SELF TEST QUESTIONS

7.1   How is a process distinguished from a batch? (1.1)

7.2   What is the basic calculation involved in finding the cost per unit of output from a process? (2.4)

7.3   Distinguish between joint products and by-products. (3.3)

7.4   What are the two common methods of apportioning joint costs to joint products? (4.3)

7.5   How should the possibility of further processing to enhance a product be evaluated? (5.2)

8   PRACTICE QUESTION

8.1   XY Ltd

XY Ltd operates a chemical process which jointly produces four products, A, B, C and D. Product B is sold without further processing, but additional work is necessary on the other three before they can be sold. Budgeted data for the year were as follows:

	Production lb	Closing stock lb	Sales lb
Production:			
Product A	150,000	10,000	140,000
Product B	110,000	15,000	95,000
Product C	60,000	5,000	55,000
Product D	180,000	Nil	180,000

There were no opening stocks of the four products. Closing stocks were ready for sale.

	Selling prices per lb £	Cost of additional work to make product saleable per lb
Product A	0.70	0.10
Product B	0.60	-
Product C	0.60	0.20
Product D	1.35	0.35

	£
Production cost of the joint process	180,000
Other costs:	
Administration (fixed)	45,000
Selling:	
Fixed	35,000
Variable (£0.01 per lb sold)	4,700

An overseas customer has expressed interest in buying from existing production 50,000lb each in one year of any or all of Products A, C and D before they have been further processed by XY Ltd. He has offered to pay the following prices:

	Price per lb
	£
Product A	0.65
Product C	0.52
Product D	0.90

On such sales, variable selling costs would be only £0.006 per lb. Fixed administration and selling costs would remain as stated above.

The costs of the joint process are to be apportioned to individual products on the following bases:
(a)   weight of products produced;
(b)   sales value of products produced less the cost of additional work incurred to make products saleable.

You are required for each of the above bases to calculate for the year:

(a)   gross profit per product (i.e. before deducting administration and selling overhead);
(b)   total gross profit;
(c)   total net profit.

You are also required:

(d)   to state which products you would recommend XY Ltd to sell to the overseas customer before further processing at the prices quoted in order to increase net profit;

(e)   to calculate the increase in the annual net profit of XY Ltd if your advice at (d) above was followed.

9   ANSWER TO EXAMINATION TYPE QUESTION

9.1   XY Ltd

(a)   )
(b)   )   Profit statement (see below)
(c)   )

(i)   **Joint costs apportioned on weight of products**

	A 000 lb	B 000 lb	C 000 lb	D 000 lb	Total 000 lb
Sales	140	95	55	180	470
	£	£	£	£	£
Sales	98,000	57,000	33,000	243,000	431,000
Less: cost of sales	64,400	34,200	30,800	127,800	257,200
Gross profit	33,600	22,800	2,200	115,200	173,800
Less: Administration costs				45,000	
Less: Selling costs: Fixed				35,000	
Variable				4,700	
					84,700
Net profit					89,100

WORKINGS

$$\text{Joint cost per lb} = \frac{\text{Costs}}{\text{Weight produced}}$$

$$= \frac{£180,000}{500,000}$$

$$= 0.36$$

As closing stocks are **ready for sales**, cost of sales is valued at joint plus additional costs, i.e.:

Product	Joint	Cost per lb additional	Total	Sales 000 lb	Cost of sales
	£	£			£
A	0.36	0.10	0.46	140	64,400
B	0.36	-	0.36	95	34,200
C	0.36	0.20	0.56	55	30,800
D	0.36	0.35	0.71	180	127,800

(ii)   **Joint costs apportioned on net sales value of production**

	Product				Total
	A	B	C	D	
	£	£	£	£	£
Sales	98,000	57,000	33,000	243,000	431,000
Less: Cost of sales	56,000	28,500	22,000	153,000	259,500
Gross profit	42,000	28,500	11,000	90,000	171,500
Less: Administration and selling costs:					84,700
Net profit					86,800

WORKINGS

	Product				Total
	A	B	C	D	
	000 lb	000 lb	000 lb	000 lb	000 lb
Production	150	110	60	180	500
	£	£	£	£	£
Selling prices	0.70	0.60	0.60	1.35	
Sales value of production	105,000	66,000	36,000	243,000	450,000
Less: Additional costs	15,000	-	12,000	63,000	90,000
Net sales value of production	90,000	66,000	24,000	180,000	360,000
Apportioned joint cost (50%)	45,000	33,000	12,000	90,000	180,000
Additional costs	15,000	-	12,000	63,000	90,000
Production costs	60,000	33,000	24,000	153,000	270,000
Closing stock	$(\frac{10}{150})4,000$	$(\frac{15}{110})4,500$	$(\frac{5}{60})2,000$	-	10,500
Cost of sales	56,000	28,500	22,000	153,000	259,500

(d)   **Price comparison**

	Product		
	A	C	D
	£	£	£
Existing price per lb	0.70	0.60	1.35
Less: Additional costs per lb	0.10	0.20	0.35
Net revenue per lb	0.60	0.40	1.00
Overseas offer	0.65	0.52	0.90
Gain/(loss) per lb	0.05	0.12	(0.10)
Reduction in variable selling costs per lb	0.004	0.004	0.004
Net gain/(loss) per lb	0.054	0.124	(0.096)

Recommendation: sell Products A and C to the overseas customer.

(e)   **Increase in annual net profit**

	£
Additional revenue:	
Product A 50,000 lb @ £0.05	2,500
Product C 50,000 lb @ £0.12	6,000
	8,500
Add: Reduction in variable selling costs 100,000 lb @ £0.004	400
Net profit increase	8,900

Note: all other costs and revenue will be unaffected.

Chapter 13

PROCESS COSTING 2

PATHFINDER INTRODUCTION

This chapter covers the following elements of the CAT Official Teaching Guide. At the end of this chapter you should have learned these teaching guide elements thoroughly.

Session 13
Process costing 2
Syllabus reference j

- Describe the concept of equivalent units
- Allocate process costs between closing work in progress and finished output
- Complete cost records and accounts in a process costing system
- Explain and illustrate the nature of normal losses and abnormal losses/gains

(**Note:** Calculations will not incorporate opening Work in Progress)

Putting the chapter in context

We have now studied, job, batch, contract and part of process costing. This chapter explains how work in process and losses are dealt with in process costing and how process accounts record costs, losses and valuations.

1   EQUIVALENT UNITS

1.1   Introduction

A process is a continuous method of production and at any one time when measurement is taking place there are likely to be unfinished units within the process.

In practice this means that there will be unfinished units at the beginning of the measurement period awaiting completion and these are known as opening work in process. There will also be units that are incomplete at the end of the measurement period and these are known as closing work in process.

For this paper we will deal only with closing work in process.

Definition   **Closing work in process** (WIP) is part finished items of stock which remain in the process at the end of the period.

1.2   Problem with part finished closing stock

During the month of May 1,000 units of a product are introduced into a process but only 800 of them are actually completed in the month. The remaining 200 units have only had 70% of their materials input and 70% of the labour worked on them.

The total costs incurred in the process this month were £3,760.

The total costs of £3,760 must somehow be divided between the 800 completed units and the 200 units that are only 70% complete at the end of the month. If the costs were split equally amongst all 1,000 units then each unit would be valued at £3.76. This would value the two types of units as follows:

	£
Completed units (800 × £3.76)	3,008
Incomplete units (200 × £3.76)	752
	3,760

This would seem to be unfair as the incomplete units have only had 70% of both the material and labour input whereas the other units are fully complete. To value both at the same amount of £3.76 would not seem right.

1.3 Equivalent units

Definition   **Equivalent units** are the number of completed units that the incomplete units are equivalent to.

An alternative is to measure the number of completed units that the incomplete units are equivalent to. So in this example the 200 units that are 70% complete are equivalent to 140 completed units (200 × 70%).

2 ALLOCATION OF PROCESS COSTS - CLOSING WORK IN PROGRESS

2.1 Allocation of costs

Once the number of equivalent units in the closing work in progress have been determined then the costs are apportioned between the completed units and the number of equivalent units of the incomplete finished stock. Using the illustration from the previous paragraph the equivalent units calculation can be tabulated as follows:

Step 1   Calculate the total costs for the period (this has already been done)

Step 2   Calculate the equivalent units.

	Actual units	Completion	Equivalent units
Completed units	800	100%	800
Incomplete units	200	70%	140
	1,000		940

Step 3   Calculate cost per equivalent unit.

The costs are then apportioned over this total number of equivalent units.

$$\text{Cost per equivalent unit} = \frac{\text{Total costs of process}}{\text{Equivalent units}}$$

$$= \frac{£3,760}{940 \text{ units}} = £4/\text{unit}$$

Step 4   Value completed units and the closing WIP.

The two types of units can now be fairly valued as follows:

	£
Completed units (800 × £4)	3,200
Incomplete units (140 × £4)	560
	3,760

2.2   Activity

20,000 units of a product were started in a process in January. Of these, 14,000 were completed in the month and the remainder were estimated to be only 40% complete for material and labour at the end of January.

The cost of materials input into the process in the month was £26,000, the cost of labour, £15,000 and the associated overhead costs £16,400.

What is the value to be given to the goods actually completed in the month and the closing stock of work in process at the end of the month?

2.3   Activity solution

Step 1

Total cost

	£
Materials	26,000
Labour	15,000
Overheads	16,400
	57,400

Step 2

Equivalent units

	Actual units	*Completion*	*Equivalent units*
Completed units	14,000	100%	14,000
Closing stock	6,000	40%	2,400
	20,000		16,400

Step 3

Cost per unit $= \dfrac{\text{Total input cost}}{\text{Equivalent units}}$

$= \dfrac{£57,400}{16,400 \text{ units}} = £3.50 \text{ per unit}$

Step 4

Valuation

	£
Completed units (14,000 × £3.50)	49,000
Closing stock (2,400 × £3.50)	8,400
	57,400

Conclusion   When there is closing work in progress the equivalent units of the closing WIP must be determined, and the total cost for the period spread over the completed units and the equivalent units of closing WIP.

2.4   Different degrees of completion

So far, the percentage of material and labour input into the closing work in process at the end of the month was the same.

This may not always be the case. It is quite possible for a certain amount of material to have been input into the products and a different proportion of the total labour time worked on the products at the end of the month.

For example there may be 2,000 units of work in process remaining in a process for which 80% of the materials have already been input but only 30% of the total labour time required for the product has yet been worked on these units. This is probably quite a common situation as many processes are likely to input the vast majority of materials at the start of the process before much labour time is actually spent on the process.

In such a situation the equivalent units calculation will require some modification.

2.5   Activity

The number of units input into a process in a month were 10,000. Of those 7,000 were completed and 3,000 were incomplete at the end of the month.

The materials cost for the month was £11,280 and the costs of conversion (labour and overhead) £14,760.

The 3,000 units of work in process were 80% complete for material input but only 40% complete as far as labour is concerned. The overheads to be allocated to the process are based upon labour hours.

What is the value of the 7,000 completed units and the 3,000 units of closing work in process?

2.6   Activity solution

Step 1   Calculate the total costs for the period.

Total costs

	£
Materials	11,280
Costs of conversion	14,760
	26,040

Step 2   Calculate the equivalent units.

When there are different degrees of completion of the work in process then the equivalent units for closing work in process must be calculated separately for materials and costs of conversion (as the overhead is based upon the labour costs, labour and overheads can be treated as one cost in this calculation).

Equivalent units

	Actual units	Completion	Equivalent units
Completed units	7,000	100%	7,000
Closing work in process			
Materials	3,000	80%	2,400
Costs of conversion	3,000	40%	1,200

Step 3   Calculate costs per unit for materials and conversion.

The valuation of completed units and closing work in process must also be done separately for materials and costs of conversion.

Materials:

	£
Cost	£11,280
Equivalent units	
Completed units	7,000
Closing work in process	2,400
	9,400

$$\text{Cost per unit for materials} \quad = \quad \frac{£11,280}{9,400 \text{ units}} \quad = \quad £1.20$$

Costs of conversion:

	£
Cost	£14,760
Equivalent units	
Completed units	7,000
Closing work in process	1,200
	8,200

$$\text{Cost per unit for conversion costs} \quad = \quad \frac{£14,760}{8,200 \text{ units}} \quad = \quad £1.80 \text{ per unit}$$

Step 4   Value completed units and closing work in process

	£
Completed units	
Materials ($7,000 \times £1.20$)	8,400
Conversion ($7,000 \times £1.80$)	12,600
	21,000

This is the same as multiplying the 7,000 completed units by the total cost of £3 per unit (£1.20 + £1.80).

	£
Closing work in process	
Materials (2,400 equivalent units $\times$ £1.20)	2,880
Conversion (1,200 equivalent units $\times$ £1.80)	2,160
	5,040

Step 5   Reconcile the total cost to the valuations.

	£
Completed units	21,000
Closing work in process	5,040
Total cost	26,040

Conclusion   When the closing WIP has reached differing levels of completion for materials and conversion costs then separate calculation for equivalent units and cost per unit must be carried out for each element of cost.

3   NORMAL LOSS

3.1   Introduction

In many processes there is some form of loss or wastage of material.

This loss or wastage might be in the form of pieces cut off or shaved off from wood or metal, cuttings or amounts unused from fabrics or evaporation from liquids.

3.2   Normal loss

In most processes there are a certain amount of materials that are expected to be lost during the production process.

Definition   A **normal loss** is the expected or anticipated loss from a particular process which occurs under normal operating conditions.

Only in an ideal world could the production process be so good that there were no losses. In the absence of this ideal world there will usually be these expected or normal losses.

3.3   Activity

4,000 kg of material X are input into a process. The standard material content of a single product from this process is 10 kg. If the normal loss from the process is 5% then how many products are expected to be produced from this amount of input?

3.4   Activity solution

	kg
Materials input	4,000
Normal loss (5% × 4,000)	200
Expected output in kg	3,800

$$\text{Expected output in units} = \frac{3,800 \text{ kg}}{10 \text{ kg}}$$

$$= 380 \text{ units}$$

Conclusion   The normal loss is the amount of materials input that are expected to be lost during the process.

4   ABNORMAL LOSSES AND GAINS

4.1   Introduction

In the previous paragraph normal losses were considered. These are the amounts that it is estimated, usually based upon past experience, are lost in the normal production process. The amount of actual loss from a process may be equal to the expected or normal loss, may be more than the normal loss or indeed may be less than the normal loss.

4.2   Abnormal loss

Definition   An **abnormal loss** is a loss in the process that is actually greater than the expected or normal loss.

An abnormal loss might be caused by excess wastage, carelessness, accidents or poor materials. By definition an abnormal loss is a loss that is unexpected and not a normal part of the process.

4.3   Activity

A process has an input of 50,000 kg of materials and the normal loss is 10%. If the actual number of kg output from the process is 42,000 what is the amount of normal and abnormal loss?

4.4   Solution

		kg
Materials input		50,000
Normal loss (10% × 50,000)		5,000
		45,000
Abnormal loss		3,000
Actual output		42,000

Conclusion   An **abnormal loss** is any loss or waste from a process that is more than the expected loss or waste.

4.5   Abnormal gains

In some circumstances it may be that a process produces more than is expected. This is an abnormal gain.

Definition   An **abnormal gain** is the amount of production from a process that is greater than the expected amount of production.

4.6   Activity

A process has an input of 50,000 kg of materials and the normal loss is 10%. If the actual number of kg output from the process is 46,500 what is the amount of normal and abnormal loss or gain?

4.7   Activity solution

		kg
Materials input		50,000
Normal loss (10% × 50,000)		5,000
		45,000
Abnormal gain		1,500
Actual output		46,500

Conclusion   An abnormal gain is any loss or waste from a process which is less than the normal loss or waste from the process.

5   COST PER OUTPUT UNIT WITH LOSSES

5.1   Introduction

In the previous chapter, we computed the cost per unit of process outputs as

$$\frac{\text{Material cost} + \text{conversion cost} (= \text{Total costs})}{\text{Number of units produced}}$$

This needs to be adapted slightly where losses are involved.

5.2   Activity - normal losses

The following are inputs into process I on 1 May:

	£
Materials (10,000 kg @ £3 per kg)	30,000
Labour	20,000
Overheads	9,400
	59,400

During the month of May 19,800 units were produced. The normal level of losses from this process is 1% and each unit is expected to take 0.5 kg of material.

What is the cost per unit from process I for May?

5.3   Activity solution

In this case, there are normal losses. By definition these are expected or anticipated parts of the process and thus their cost should be included in the cost of the normal level of output.

	kg
Materials input	10,000
Normal loss (1% × 10,000 kg)	100
Expected output in kg	9,900
Expected output in units (9,900 kg/0.5 kg)	19,800

$$\text{Cost per unit} = \frac{\text{Total costs}}{\text{Expected level of output}}$$

$$= \frac{£59,400}{19,800}$$

$$= £3 \text{ per unit}$$

Conclusion

If a process has an expected level of losses then cost per unit $= \dfrac{\text{Total costs}}{\text{Expected level of output}}$

5.4   Activity - abnormal losses

A process has a normal loss of 6% of the materials input. The amount of materials input in June was 100,000 kg at a price of £1 per kg and from that 47,000 units are expected to be produced as each unit requires 2 kg of materials. The other process costs for the period are conversion costs of £135,000.

What is the cost per unit of production if:

(a)   47,000 units are produced;

(b)   45,000 units are produced?

5.5   Activity solution

As has been discussed above, the cost of normal loss from a process is an anticipated part of the process and as such is included as part of the cost of the actual output.

In contrast, any abnormal losses are amounts that should not have been incurred. Thus the units of abnormal loss are costed in the same way as the units of good output and then charged to the profit and loss account.

Total costs

		£
Materials (100,000 kg × £1 per kg)		100,000
Costs of conversion		135,000
		235,000

		kg
Materials input		100,000
Normal loss (6% × 100,000)		6,000
Expected output in kg		94,000

(a)	Expected output in units 94,000/2	47,000
	Actual output	47,000
	Abnormal loss/gain	-

$$\text{Cost per unit} = \frac{£235,000}{47,000 \text{ units}}$$

$$= £5 \text{ per unit}$$

(b)   The cost per unit of production is still £5 per unit (which includes the cost of the normal loss) although in this case only 45,000 units have been produced.

45,000 units will be charged to finished goods, and then cost of sales, at £5 per unit and the 2,000 units not produced, the abnormal loss, will be charged to the profit and loss account as an expense, at the same rate of £5/unit.

Conclusion   If there are abnormal losses the cost per unit calculation is exactly the same as if output were the amount expected. The abnormal loss units are valued at cost per unit and written off to the profit and loss account.

5.6   Activity - abnormal gains

A process has a normal loss of 6% of the materials input. The amount of materials input in June was 100,000 kg at a price of £1 per kg and from that 47,000 units are expected to be produced as each unit requires 2 kg of materials. The other process costs for the period are conversion costs of £135,000.

If the actual amount of production was this time 48,000 units what would be the cost per unit for the output from the process?

5.7   Activity solution

As with the situation of abnormal losses the calculation of cost per unit is always the same even if there is an abnormal gain. Whatever the amount of abnormal loss or gain the calculation of the cost per unit will always be:

$$\frac{\text{Cost of input}}{\text{Expected output from production}}$$

Therefore in this case:

	£
Materials (100,000 kg × £1 per kg)	100,000
Costs of conversion	135,000
	235,000
Cost per unit =	$\dfrac{£235,000}{47,000 \text{ units}}$
=	£5 per unit

The amount actually produced from the process was 48,000 units. Therefore £240,000 (48,000 units × £5) will be charged to finished goods and then cost of sales when sold and the abnormal gain units of 1,000 (48,000 − expected output of 47,000) at £5 per unit, £5,000, will be credited to the profit and loss account.

Conclusion   Whatever the actual amount of output from a process the calculation of the cost per unit of output is always the same:

$$\frac{\text{Cost of input}}{\text{Expected output}}$$

6   PROCESS ACCOUNTS

6.1   Introduction

So far in this chapter the costs of units produced in a process have simply been calculated. The costs also need to be recorded in process ledger accounts.

6.2   Process ledger accounts

There will be one ledger account for each process. Process ledger accounts have four columns showing both the number of units and their value.

The process account records the following information:

(a)   on the debit side all of the costs input into the process;

(b)   on the credit side the value of the output from the process (and any closing work in process) together with the number of units of normal loss;

(c)   any balancing figure will be the abnormal loss or gain.

6.3   Activity - no losses

The input to a particular process is 60,000 kg of materials at a cost of £2 per kg. The amount of labour spent on the process during the period was 10,000 hours at a rate of £6 per hour and the overhead absorption rate for this process is £1 per labour hour. There are no expected losses during the production process.

If 19,000 units were produced from the process write up the process account.

6.4   Activity solution

Total cost

	£
Materials 60,000 kg × £2	120,000
Labour 10,000 hours × £6	60,000
Overhead 10,000 × £1	10,000
	190,000

$$\text{Cost per unit} = \frac{\text{Total cost}}{\text{Number of units}}$$

$$= \frac{£190,000}{19,000 \text{ units}}$$

$$= £10 \text{ per unit}$$

Process account

	Units	£		Units	£
Materials	19,000	120,000	Process output –		
Labour	-	60,000	finished goods	19,000	190,000
Overheads	-	10,000			
	19,000	190,000		19,000	190,000

(*Tutorial notes:*

(a)   There are columns for both the number of units and the amounts. The reason for this will become clearer when accounting for losses is introduced.

(b)   The material input is deemed to be exactly the correct amount for the output of 19,000 units in this example as there are no normal or anticipated losses.

(c)   Labour and overheads by convention do not have a number of units allocated to them. The balancing of units is simply between the materials input and the process output.)

6.5   Activity - normal losses

The following costs are the amounts input into a process on 1 May:

	£
Materials (10,000 kg @ £3 per kg)	30,000
Labour	20,000
Overheads	9,400
	59,400

During the month of May all of the processing was completed and 19,800 units were produced. The anticipated level of losses from this process is 1% and each unit is expected to take 0.5 kg of material.

Write up the process account for process for May.

6.6   Activity solution

	kg
Materials input	10,000
Normal loss (1% × 10,000 kg)	100
Expected output in kg	9,900
Expected output in units (2 × 9,900 kg)	19,800

$$\text{Cost per unit} = \frac{£59,400}{19,800 \text{ units}}$$

$$= £3 \text{ per unit}$$

Process account

	Units	£		Units	£
Materials	20,000	30,000	Process output -		
Labour	-	20,000	finished goods	19,800	59,400
Overheads	-	9,400	Normal loss	200	-
	20,000	59,400		20,000	59,400

(Tutorial notes:

(a)   The amount of materials input was enough for 20,000 units (10,000 kg × 2 units per kg).

(b)   The entire cost of the process, £59,400, is allocated to the good output from the process, 19,800 units, as the normal loss is part of what is expected from the process. The cost of the process output is 19,800 units × £3 per unit = £59,400.

(c)   The normal loss shows the number of units in order to balance the output units with the materials input units. However the normal loss is allocated no part of the cost of the process as this is all borne by the good production.*)

6.7   Activity - abnormal losses

A process has a normal loss of 6% of the materials input. The amount of materials input in June was 100,000 kg at a price of £1 per kg and from that 47,000 units are expected to be produced as each unit requires 2 kg of materials. The other process costs for the period are conversion costs of £135,000.

Write up the process account if actual production is:

(a)   47,000 units;
(b)   45,000 units.

6.8   Activity solution

Total cost

	£
Materials (100,000 kg × £1 per kg)	100,000
Cost of conversion	135,000
	235,000

	kg
Materials input	100,000
Normal loss (6% × 100,000)	6,000
Expected output in kg	94,000

The normal loss in units is 3,000 units (6,000 kg/2 kg).

(a)

	£
Expected output in units 94,000/2	47,000
Actual output	47,000
Abnormal loss/gain	-

Cost per unit $= \dfrac{£235,000}{47,000\ units}$

$= $ £5 per unit

Process account

	Units	£		Units	£
Materials	50,000	100,000	Process output	47,000	235,000
Conversion	-	135,000	Normal loss	3,000	-
	50,000	235,000		50,000	235,000

(*Tutorial notes:*

(i)   As there is only a normal loss in this instance of 3,000 units then the cost of the process output equals the total costs of the process, 47,000 units × £5 = £235,000.

(ii)   No value is allocated to the normal loss; only the number of units of normal loss are shown.)

(b)

Process account

	Units	£		Units	£
Materials	50,000	100,000	Process output	45,000	225,000
Conversion	-	135,000	Normal loss	3,000	-
			Abnormal loss	2,000	10,000
	50,000	235,000		50,000	235,000

(Tutorial notes:

(i)   The value of the actual output is the number of units actually output at the cost per unit, 45,000 units × £5 per unit = £225,000.

(ii)   The normal loss is only shown in the units column as no value is allocated to it.

(iii)   The abnormal loss is valued at the cost per unit of the process as this is not an expected part of the process, 2,000 units × £5 per unit = £10,000. The other side of the double entry for this abnormal loss is to an abnormal loss account and then to the profit and loss account as a charge. This is illustrated below.

Abnormal loss

	Units	£		Units	£
Process account	2,000	10,000	P&L a/c	2,000	10,000
	2,000	10,000		2,000	10,000

6.9   Activity - abnormal gains

The information from the previous example is as follows:

A process has a normal loss of 6% of the materials input. The amount of materials input in June was 100,000 kg at a price of £1 per kg and from that 47,000 units are expected to be produced as each unit requires 2 kg of materials. The other process costs for the period are conversion costs of £135,000.

If the actual amount of production was this time 48,000 units write up the process account.

6.10   Activity solution

Process account

	Units	£		Units	£
Materials	50,000	100,000	Process output	48,000	240,000
Conversion	-	135,000	Normal loss	3,000	-
Abnormal gain	1,000	5,000			
	51,000	240,000		51,000	240,000

(*Tutorial notes:*

    (i)   The amount of actual production is valued at the cost per unit, 48,000 units × £5 = £240,000.

    (ii)   This time there is an abnormal gain as more is produced than expected. This gain is shown on the debit of the process account and in turn credited to an abnormal gains account and then to the profit and loss account as shown below. The value placed on the abnormal gain is the cost per unit of the process, 1,000 units × £5 per unit.)

Abnormal gain

	Units	£		Units	£
P&L a/c		1,000	Process a/c	1,000	5,000
5,000				1,000	5,000
	1,000	5,000			

6.11   Closing work in process

A further entry that students might be required to make in the process account is the value of any closing work in process as calculated in earlier paragraphs.

The closing work in process is a balance that is carried down at the end of the period to be an asset at the beginning of the next period. Therefore the closing work in process is shown as a carried down balance on the credit side of the process account.

6.12   Activity

The information from a previous example is reproduced below.

20,000 units of a product were started in a process in January. Of these, 14,000 were completed in the month and the remainder were estimated to be only 40% complete regarding their material and labour input at the end of January.

The cost of materials input into the process in the month was £26,000, the cost of labour, £15,000 and the associated overhead costs £16,400.

The value of completed units and closing work in process were calculated using equivalent units as follows:

	£
Completed units (14,000 × £3.50)	49,000
Closing stock (2,400 × £3.50)	8,400
	57,400

Write up the process account for this period.

6.13   Activity solution

Process account

	Units	£		Units	£
Materials	20,000	26,000	Completed output	14,000	49,000
Labour	-	15,000	Closing WIP c/d	6,000	8,400
Overheads		16,400			
	20,000	57,400		20,000	57,400

Conclusion   When writing up the process accounts remember that opening WIP, input costs, materials and conversion costs, are on the debit side, and the costs of the output, completed units, normal/abnormal loss units, closing WIP units, are all recorded on the credit side of the process account.

7   CHAPTER SUMMARY

In this chapter we concluded our look at process costing by looking at work-in-process and losses and how these are dealt with in the accounts.

8   SELF TEST QUESTIONS

8.1   Why is it necessary to calculate equivalent units when there is closing WIP? (1.2)

8.2   What are equivalent units? (1.3)

8.3   How is the value of closing WIP calculated? (2.3)

8.4   What is a normal loss? (3.2)

8.5   What is an abnormal loss? (4.2)

8.6   What is an abnormal gain? (4.5)

8.7   How is cost per unit calculated in a process that has normal losses? (5.3)

8.8   How is cost per unit calculated in a process that has abnormal losses? (5.5)

8.9   What is recorded on the debit side of a process account? (6.2)

8.10   What is the accounting entry for any balance on an abnormal gain account? (6.10)

9   MULTIPLE CHOICE QUESTIONS

9.1   Which one of the following statements is *incorrect*?

A   Job costs are collected separately, whereas process costs are averages

B   In job costing the progress of a job can be ascertained from the materials requisition notes and job tickets or time sheets

C   In process costing information is needed about work passing through a process and work remaining in each process

D   In process costing, but not job costing, the cost of normal loss will be incorporated into normal product costs

9.2   Process B had no opening stock. 13,500 units of raw material were transferred in at £4.50 per unit. Additional material at £1.25 per unit was added in process. Labour and overheads were £6.25 per completed unit and £2.50 per unit incomplete.

If 11,750 completed units were transferred out, what was the closing stock in Process B?

A   £77,625.00.   B   £14,437.50.   C   £141,000.00.   D   £21,000.00.

9.3 Glasgow Inc has started a new process assembling window frames. In the first month 2,000 frames were started and at the end of the month 1,700 had been finished. Of those not finished 50% of the materials had been incorporated and 30% of the labour and overhead needed had been incurred. Materials cost for the period were £5,550 and for labour and overhead were £4,475.

The value of the closing work in progress was:

A £675	**B** £720	**C** £825	**D** £940

9.4 In process costing an equivalent unit is:

A   a notional whole unit representing incomplete work
B   a unit made at standard performance
C   a unit being currently made which is the same as previously manufactured
D   a unit made in more than one process cost centre.

9.5 In a process account, abnormal losses are valued:

A   at their scrap value
B   the same as good production
C   at the cost of raw materials
D   at good production cost less scrap value

9.6 A chemical process has a normal wastage of 10% of input. In a period, 2,500 kgs of material were input and there was an abnormal loss of 75 kgs.

What quantity of good production was achieved?

A   2,175 kgs
B   2,250 kgs
C   2,325 kgs
D   2,475 kgs

9.7 A cleaning fluid is produced by a series of processes. The following information relates to the final process:

	Litres
Opening work in progress	2,000
Closing work in progress	1,500
Input	42,300
Transfer to finished goods stock	40,100
Normal loss	400

The abnormal loss is

A   800 litres
B   1,300 litres
C   1,800 litres
D   2,300 litres

9.8 Vare Ltd produces various inks at its Normanton factory. Production details for Process 1 are as follows:

Opening work in progress, 1 April	400 units	60% complete
Closing work in progress, 30 April	600 units	20% complete
Units started		1,000
Units finished		800

The degree of completion quoted relates to labour and overhead costs. Three-quarters of the materials are added at the start of the process and the remaining quarter added when the process is 50% complete.

The equivalent units of production for materials in the period are:

A 1,250   **B** 1,000   **C** 850   **D** 680

10   PRACTICE QUESTIONS

10.1   Equivalent units

A firm operates a process, the details of which for the period were as follows.

There was no opening work-in-progress.

During the period 8,250 units were received from the previous process at a value of £453,750, labour and overheads were £350,060 and material introduced was £24,750.

At the end of the period the closing work-in-progress was 1,600 units, which were 100% complete in respect of materials, and 60% complete in respect of labour and overheads.

The balance of units were transferred to finished goods.

You are required to

(a)   calculate the number of equivalent units produced.

(b)   calculate the cost per equivalent unit.

(c)   prepare the process account.

(d)   distinguish between joint products and by-products, and briefly explain the difference in accounting treatment between them.

10.2   Process 21 and 22

(a)   Process 21 had 150,000 units started in the month of March. The materials input totalled £194,550, the labour worked in the month on the process was £140,000 and the monthly overhead to be apportioned to the process is a total of 50% of the labour cost for the month.

At the end of the month 120,000 units had been completed and placed in finished goods stores and the remaining 30,000 units were estimated to have had 65% of their material and labour input during the month.

Determine the value of the goods in finished goods stock at the end of the month and the value of the closing work in process.

(b)   Process 22 has an input of 10,000 kg of materials priced at £20,000 and the labour and overhead costs for the process are a further £19,900. The normal loss from the process is 5%.

Write up the process account for output levels of:

(i)   9,500 kg;
(ii)   9,400 kg;
(iii)   9,700 kg.

11   ANSWERS TO MULTIPLE CHOICE QUESTIONS

11.1   Statement A is correct. Job costs are identified with a particular job, whereas process costs (of units produced and work in process) are averages, based on equivalent units of production.

Statement B is also correct. The direct cost of a job to date, excluding any direct expenses, can be ascertained from materials requisition notes and job tickets or time sheets.

Statement C is correct, because without data about units completed and units still in process, losses and equivalent units of production cannot be calculated.

Statement D is incorrect, because the cost of normal loss will usually be incorporated into job costs as well as into process costs. In process costing this is commonly done by giving normal loss no cost, leaving costs to be shared between output, closing stocks and abnormal loss/gain. In job costing it can be done by adjusting direct materials costs to allow for normal wastage, and direct labour costs for normal reworking of items or normal spoilage.

Therefore **D.**

11.2

Process B - Account

	Units	£		Units	£
Raw materials	13,500	60,750.0	Output	11,750	141,000.0
Additional materials		16,875.0	Closing WIP	1,750	14,437.5
Labour/overheads		77,812.5			
	13,500	155,437.5		13,500	155,437.5

Closing WIP units	=	Input units − output units
	=	13,500 − 11,750
	=	1,750

Each uncompleted unit is valued at:	£
Transferred materials	4.50
Additional materials	1.25
Labour/overheads	2.50
	8.25

1,750 units × £8.25 =   £14,437.50

The correct answer is **B.**

11.3 $150 \times 3 + 90 \times 2.5 = £675$

Therefore **A.**

11.4   **A**   100 units that are 60% complete are 60 equivalent units

11.5   **B**

In process costing, abnormal gains and losses are valued at the same cost per unit as normal good production output.

11.6   The correct answer is **A.**

	kg
Material input	2,500
Normal loss @ 10%	(250)
Abnormal loss	(75)
Good production achieved	2,175

11.7 $2,000 + 42,300 - (1,500 + 40,100 + 400) = 2,300$

Therefore **D.**

11.8   400 units started and finished + 600 units 75% complete = 850 units

Therefore **C.**

12   ANSWERS TO PRACTICE QUESTIONS

12.1   Equivalent units

(a)

	Previous process/ Materials		Labour/Overhead	
	%	eu	%	eu
Output (8,250 – 1,600)	100	6,650	100	6,650
Closing WIP (1,600)	100	1,600	60	960
Equivalent units produced		8,250		7,610

(b)

$$\frac{\text{Costs}}{\text{Equivalent units}} = \qquad \frac{£478,500}{8,250} = £58.00 \qquad \frac{£350,060}{7,610} = £46.00$$

(c)

Process account

	Units	£		Units	£
Previous process	8,250	453,750	Output	6,650	691,600
Materials		24,750	Closing WIP	1,600	136,960
Labour/overhead		350,060			
	8,250	828,560		8,250	828,560

(d)   A joint product is produced when two or more products arise simultaneously from the operation of a single process. Each joint product is of significant value to the producer.

A by-product arises in the same way as a joint product except that its value is small and NOT considered to be significant.

When accounting for joint products the common (or pre-separation) costs are apportioned between the products either on a value or output basis. Accounting for by-products requires that its realisable value be used to reduce the cost of the other product(s) from the same common process.

12.2   Process 21 and 22

(a)   Total cost

	£
Materials	194,550
Labour	140,000
Overheads (£140,000 × 50%)	70,000
	404,550

Equivalent units

	Actual units	Completion	Equivalent units
Finished goods stock	120,000	100%	120,000
Closing work in process	30,000	65%	19,500
	150,000		139,500

Cost per unit = $\dfrac{\text{Total input cost}}{\text{Equivalent units}}$

= $\dfrac{£404,550}{139,500 \text{ units}}$

= £2.90 per unit

Valuation

	£
Completed units (120,000 × £2.90)	348,000
Closing work in process (19,500 × £2.90)	56,550
	404,550

(b)   Total costs

	£
Materials costs	20,000
Conversion costs	19,900
	39,900

Expected output

	kg
Materials input	10,000
Normal loss (5% × 10,000 kg)	500
	9,500

(i)   Cost per kg

$\dfrac{\text{Cost of input}}{\text{Expected output}}$ = $\dfrac{£39,900}{9,500 \text{ kg}}$

= £4.20 per kg

Process account

	Kg	£		Kg	£
Materials	10,000	20,000	Process output	9,500	39,900
Conversion	-	19,900	Normal loss	500	-
	10,000	39,900		10,000	39,900

(*Tutorial note:* the process output is valued at the cost per kg of the process, 9,500 kg × £4.20 = £39,900.)

(ii)

Process account

	Kg	£		Kg	£
Materials	10,000	20,000	Process output	9,400	39,480
Conversion	-	19,900	Normal loss	500	-
			Abnormal loss	100	420
	10,000	39,900		10,000	39,900

(Tutorial note:

- The actual process output is valued at the cost per kg, 9,400 kg × £4.20 per kg = £39,480.

- The abnormal loss is also valued at the cost per kg, 100 kg × £4.20 per kg = £420.

- The abnormal loss will be debited to the profit and loss account as an expense via an abnormal loss account.)

(iii)

Process account

	Kg	£		Kg	£
Materials	10,000	20,000	Process output	9,700	40,740
Conversion	-	19,900	Normal loss	500	-
Abnormal gain	200	840			
	10,200	40,740		10,200	40,740

(Tutorial note:

- The actual process output is valued at the cost per kg, 9,700 kg × £4.20 per kg = £40,740.

- The abnormal gain is valued at the cost per kg, 200 kg × £4.20 per kg = £840.

- The abnormal gain will be credited to the profit and loss account via an abnormal gains account.)

Chapter 14

SERVICE COSTING

PATHFINDER INTRODUCTION

This chapter covers the following elements of the CAT Official Teaching Guide. At the end of this chapter you should have learned these teaching guide elements thoroughly.

Session 14
Service costing
Syllabus reference k

- Describe the practical problems relating to the costing of services
- Describe situations where the use of service costing is appropriate
- Illustrate suitable unit cost measures that may be used in a variety of different services

Putting the chapter in context

Service costing is the final type of costing in the syllabus. Many businesses provide a service not a product and need cost accountants to provide information. This chapter explains service costing.

1   PROBLEMS OF COSTING SERVICES

1.1   Introduction

In the chapters of this study text so far all of the costing has been within the context of a manufacturing organisation. This means that the costs of the organisation are gathered together and then spread over all the physical units of products that the organisation makes giving a cost per cost unit.

1.2   Service industries

However many organisations do not produce a physical cost unit or product. Instead, they provide a service.

This might be a restaurant that provides meals for customers, an accountant that provides a tax service for clients, a transport organisation transports goods for customers, or a service department such as a canteen within a manufacturer.

In exactly the same way as manufacturing organisations these service industries need to gather together their costs for information and control purposes.

1.3   Cost units for services

Although service industries do not produce physical cost units they can still have cost units being some suitable measure of the service provided.

Also, in just the same way as in manufacturing organisations many service industries will wish to spread the costs of the organisation over these cost units to determine a cost per cost unit.

1.4   Problems relating to costing of services

To cost the service provided, the service organisation must gather together all of its costs in the same way as a manufacturing organisation. However some costs may be more difficult to ascertain than in a manufacturing organisation.

Many service costs will be labour based, with all of the problems of overtime, holiday pay, bonuses etc. involved in such costs.

Also, many service industry costs are fixed costs rather than the typical variable costs of materials and labour that are found in manufacturing organisations. These fixed costs need to be apportioned to cost centres and absorbed into the service cost unit.

2   SERVICE COSTING METHODS

2.1   Application of service costing

The principle of service costing is that costs are charged to activities and averaged over the units of service provided.

The method is appropriate when the service can be expressed in a standardised unit of measurement e.g. an accountant provides a different service to each client, but all services can be measured in man-hour units.

2.2   Appropriate situations for service costing

Definition   **Service costing** is cost accounting for services or functions, e.g. canteens, maintenance, personnel. These may be referred to as service centres, departments or functions.

Therefore as well as service costing being applied to service industries it can also be applied to service functions within an organisation.

For example it might be possible within a manufacturing organisation to determine the total cost to the canteen of every person served in the canteen. Each manufacturing department could then be charged with a certain amount of canteen cost depending upon the number of employees in that manufacturing department.

3   COST UNITS FOR SERVICE INDUSTRIES

3.1   Introduction

A major problem in service industries is the selection of a suitable unit for measuring the service, i.e. in deciding what service is actually being provided and what measures of performance are most appropriate to the control of costs.

3.2   Examples of cost units

Service	Cost unit
Electricity generation	Kilowatt hours*
Canteens and restaurants	Meals served
Carriers	Miles travelled/ton-miles*
Hospitals	Patient-days*
Passenger transport	Passenger-miles/seat-miles*

* These are examples of composite cost-units, where the cost depends not only upon the time or distance over which the service is offered, but also on the level at which the service is operated.

3.3   Different types of service

A service undertaking may use several different units to measure the various kinds of service provided e.g. an hotel may use:

Service	*Cost unit*
Restaurant	Meals served
Hotel services	Guest-days
Function facilities	Hours

Once appropriate cost units have been determined, costing information must be collected. In a transport organisation this may involve the recording of mileages day-to-day for each vehicle in the fleet, with each driver completing a log sheet. Fuel usage per vehicle and loads or weight carried may also be recorded.

3.4   Collection, classification and ascertainment of costs

Costs will be classified under appropriate headings for the particular service. This will involve the issue of suitable cost codes for the recording and collection of costs. For a transport undertaking the main cost classification may be based on the following activities:

(a)   operating and running the fleet;
(b)   repairs and maintenance;
(c)   fixed charges;
(d)   administration.

Within each of these there would need to be a sub-classification of costs, each with its own code, so that under (c) fixed charges, there might appear the following breakdown:

(a)   road fund licences;
(b)   insurances;
(c)   depreciation;
(d)   vehicle testing fees; and
(e)   others.

In service costing it is often important to classify costs into their fixed and variable elements. Many service applications involve high fixed costs and the higher the number of cost units the lower the fixed costs per unit. The variable cost per unit will indicate to management the additional cost involved in the provision of one extra unit of service. In the context of a transport undertaking, fixed and variable costs are often referred to as standing and running costs respectively.

3.5   Cost sheets for service industries

At appropriate intervals (usually weekly or monthly) cost sheets are prepared by the costing department to provide information to management. A typical cost sheet for a service would incorporate the following for the current period and the cumulative year to date:

(a)   Cost information under the appropriate expense or activity headings.

(b)   Cost units statistics.

(c)   Cost per unit calculations using the data in (a) and dividing by the data in (b). Different cost units may be used for different elements of costs and the same cost or group of costs may be related to different cost unit bases to provide additional control information to management. In the transport organisation, for example, the operating and running costs may be expressed in per mile and per day terms.

(d)   Analyses based on the physical cost units.

On a transport cost sheet, the following non-cost statistics may be shown:

- average miles covered per day;
- average miles per gallon of fuel.

Conclusion   Service costing is the gathering together of all costs of a service organisation or department. These costs are then spread over the service cost units.

4   SELF TEST QUESTIONS

4.1   Give examples of service industries? (1.2)

4.2   Why might costing be more difficult in a service organisation? (1.4)

4.3   What is service costing? (2.2)

4.4   Give an example of a cost unit for a hospital (3.2)

4.5   Why is it important to separately identify fixed and variable costs? (3.4)

4.6   What information is recorded on a cost sheet? (3.5)

5   CHAPTER SUMMARY

In this chapter service costing and its application to service industries were considered.

6   PRACTICE QUESTIONS

6.1   Hotel rooms

(a)   Describe the benefits which cost accounting provides for an organisation.

Note: You may refer to your own experience in answering this question.

(7 marks)

(b)   The following information is provided for a 30 day period for the Rooms Department of a hotel:

	Rooms with twin beds	Single rooms
Number of rooms in hotel	260	70
Number of rooms available to let	240	40
Average number of rooms occupied daily	200	30
Number of guests in period	6,450	
Average length of stay	2 days	
Total revenue in period	£774,000	
Number of employees	200	
Payroll costs for period	£100,000	
Items laundered in period	15,000	
Cost of cleaning supplies in period	£5,000	
Total cost of laundering	£22,500	
Listed daily rate for twin-bedded room	£110	
Listed daily rate for single room	£70	

The hotel calculates a number of statistics, including the following:

| Room occupancy | Total number of rooms occupied as a percentage of rooms available to let. |

Room occupancy — Total number of rooms occupied as a percentage of rooms available to let.

Bed occupancy — Total number of beds occupied as a percentage of beds available.

Average guest rate — Total revenue divided by number of guests.

Revenue utilisation — Actual revenue as a percentage of maximum revenue from available rooms.

Average cost per occupied bed — Total cost divided by number of beds occupied.

You are required to:

Prepare a table which contains the following statistics, calculated to one decimal place:

Room occupancy (%)
Bed occupancy (%)
Average guest rate (£)
Revenue utilisation (%)
Cost of cleaning supplies per occupied room per day (£)
Average cost per occupied bed per day (£)

(c)   Explain what you understand by the following terms:

Cost unit
Cost centre

(d)   Identify **one cost centre** which might exist in a hotel, excluding the Rooms Department. For the cost centre identified give an appropriate **cost unit**.

6.2   Happy Returns Limited

Happy Returns Ltd operates a haulage business with three vehicles. The following estimated cost and performance data are available:

Petrol	£0.50 per kilometre on average
Repairs	£0.30 per kilometre
Depreciation	£1.00 per kilometre, plus £50 per week per vehicle
Drivers' wages	£300.00 per week per vehicle
Supervision and general expenses	£550.00 per week
Loading costs	£6.00 per tonne

During week 26 it is expected that all three vehicles will be used, 280 tonnes will be loaded and a total of 3,950 kilometres travelled (including return journeys when empty) as shown in the following table:

Journey	Tonnes carried (one way)	Kilometres (one way)
1	34	180
2	28	265
3	40	390
4	32	115
5	26	220
6	40	480
7	29	90
8	26	100
9	25	135
	280	1,975

Requirements:

(a)   Calculate the average cost per tonne-kilometre for week 26.

(b)   Briefly describe THREE ways a cost accounting system could aid cost control in a haulage business.

7   ANSWERS TO PRACTICE QUESTIONS

7.1   Hotel Rooms

(a)   The cost accounting systems will take basic cost data and, by following the basic costing principles, using one or more of the costing techniques in accordance with one or more of the costing methods, will produce information which can be used by management for planning, controlling and decision-making. The establishment of budgets, standard costs and actual costs will aid in the management of the organisation.

A specific example would be the establishment of standard costs and the reporting of actuals against these standards, the resulting variances being used for the control of operations, processes and departments.

(b)   Room occupancy $=\dfrac{\text{Total number of rooms occupied}}{\text{Rooms available to be let}}$

$=\dfrac{200+30}{240+40}$

$=82.1\%$

Bed occupancy $=\dfrac{\text{Total number of beds occupied}}{\text{Total number of beds available}}$

$=\dfrac{6{,}450 \text{ guests} \times 2 \text{ days per guest}}{((240 \times 2) + (40 \times 1)) \times 30 \text{ days}}$

$=\dfrac{12{,}900}{15{,}600}$

$=82.7\%$

Average guest rate $=\dfrac{\text{Total revenue}}{\text{Number of guests}}$

$=\dfrac{£774{,}000}{6{,}450}$

$=£120$

Revenue utilisation $=\dfrac{\text{Actual revenue}}{\text{Maximum revenue from available rooms}}$

$=\dfrac{£774{,}000}{((240 \times £110) + (40 \times £70)) \times 30 \text{ days}}$

$=\dfrac{£774{,}000}{876{,}000}$

$=88.4\%$

$$\text{Cost of cleaning supplies per occupied room per day} = \frac{£5,000}{(200 + 30) \times 30 \text{ days}}$$

$$= £0.7$$

$$\text{Average cost per occupied bed per day} = \frac{\text{Total cost}}{\text{Number of beds occupied}}$$

$$= \frac{£100,000 + £5,000 + £22,500}{6,450 \times 2}$$

$$= £9.9$$

(c)   **Cost unit**

A unit of product or service in relation to which costs are ascertained. They can be used to help build up the cost of a unit of output. In manufacturing firms the cost unit will often be the unit product, while for servicing firms (e.g. road haulage) it will relate to the type of service e.g. cost per tonne/mile.

Cost centre

This is a production or service location, function, activity or item of equipment for which costs are accumulated. They often enable production costs to be related to cost units in a structured manner.

(d)   **Note**:   Students should try to consider all the separate activities that take place in a hotel and select one where they are carried out in a separately identifiable department or area.

Cost centre:	Kitchen	**or**	Restaurant
Cost unit:	Meals produced	**or**	Meals served

7.2   Happy Returns Ltd

(a)   **Total costs week 26**

	£/km		£
Petrol	0.50		
Repairs	0.30		
Depreciation	1.00		
	1.80 × 3,950		7,110

	£/week		
Depreciation (£50 × 3)	150		
Wages (£300 × 3)	900		
Supervision and gen exp	550		1,600
Loading costs	(£6 × 280)		1,680
			10,390

Tonne-km week 26

$34 \times 180 + 28 \times 265 + 40 \times 390 + ...+ 25 \times 135$ 66,325 tonne-km

Average cost per tonne-kilometre   **0.157**

(Tutorial note: as the vehicles make their return journeys empty, it is assumed that the cost should only be averaged over the outward, freight carrying, journey.)

(b)   A cost accounting system could aid cost control in a haulage business in the following three ways:

(1)   It can help to identify vehicles with higher than average running costs (e.g. per kilometre). These are likely to be the older ones; they should then be considered for replacement. Those with the lowest costs should be allocated to jobs first.

(2)   Records of vehicle utilisation (by time and load) will aid more efficient future scheduling of jobs.

(3)   It will give a good cost basis for pricing purposes and for deciding whether to accept jobs at a fixed price (a split of fixed and variable costs will be needed).

Chapter 15

STANDARD COSTING - OVERVIEW

PATHFINDER INTRODUCTION

This chapter covers the following elements of the CAT Official Teaching Guide. At the end of this chapter you should have learned these teaching guide elements thoroughly.

Session 15
Standard costing - overview
Syllabus reference 1

- Compare and contrast budgets and standards
- Describe the features of a standard costing system and identify organisations where this system is likely to be appropriate
- Explain the methods of setting standards
- Describe the different types of standards which may be set and their relative advantages and limitations
- Explain the impact on employee motivation of the type of standard set
- Describe the process of reviewing standards
- Explain the meaning of variance analysis

Putting the chapter in context

One important technique for exercising control over costs is to establish standard costs (what the materials, labour, etc. are **expected** to cost) and then to compare these with the **actual** costs incurred. Any differences (variances) may suggest a need for corrective action to be taken. The process of setting standards, recording actual costs and comparing the two is referred to as standard costing.

1 RELATIONSHIP BETWEEN STANDARD COSTING AND BUDGETARY CONTROL

1.1 What is standard costing?

The current official definition of **standard costing** is:

Definition a control technique which compares standard costs and revenues with actual results to obtain variances which are used to stimulate improved performance.

In fact standard costing would normally be regarded as encompassing the determination of those standard costs (budgeted cost of a single unit of output). It would also be thought to have more objectives than merely stimulating improved performance e.g.: improving plans and budgets, assessing managerial performance, providing detailed profit reconciliation and supplying useful information for cost control.

1.2 Comparison

Historically, budgeting and standard costing developed as distinct techniques, though both were concerned with the same problems of financial control. Today, standard costing is normally thought of as a specific technique within the overall concept of budgetary control; often both standard costing and budgeting are used, as appropriate, for different types of cost within one entity.

Nevertheless, standard costing retains three distinct features which do not apply to other budget techniques:

(a)   Under standard costing, **all stocks are valued at standard**. This applies to raw materials, WIP, and finished goods, and is essential to the concept of standard costing. This is because at each stage variances are identified and segregated as they arise.

(b)   The **variance analysis can be carried out within the ledger accounting system**. This is in contrast to other forms of budgeting, where only actual data is recorded in the accounts, and variance analysis is carried out in separate memorandum records. However, the significance of this distinction is likely to diminish as accounting data is increasingly regarded as data base within a computer system, from which various reports are extracted.

(c)   Standard costs are **planned unit costs**. Budgets normally start as total costs estimates, though they may work down to unit costs.

These differences justify regarding standard costing as a distinct technique, though within the overall budget system.

In general, the term 'budget' is used when referring to a total cost and 'standard' when referring to unit cost, although they are interchanged.

1.3   Circumstances under which each technique may be applied

The circumstances under which each of the techniques may be used are, in general terms, as below:

(a)   **Standard costing**

This may be most effectively used where output or production is routine and regular and can, therefore, be easily and accurately measured. The principal advantage of standard costing is to enable a detailed comparison of individual inputs of materials, labour and other production costs to be made with the standard inputs which should be used for a given level of output. A superior variance analysis is, therefore, possible.

(b)   **Budgetary control**

This can be used for all activities within an organisation where costs and revenues can be predicted and actual results compared. Budgetary control is, therefore, of use in the control of overhead costs and service department costs, and also perhaps in the control of sales activity. The technique is broader in its application than standard costing, and budgets may be considered to be a more basic control tool generally.

The use of flexible budgets is suitable for cost centres where output or volume of activity has an effect on costs and in this situation there is a closer correlation with standard costing, although a broader measure of the level of output or activity will be used.

2   STANDARD COSTS

2.1   Standards

Definition   **Standards** are predetermined measurable quantities set in defined conditions.

A standard can be set for any activity. Suppose that a journey of 100 miles normally takes two hours. Then it could be said that the standard journey time was two hours. Equally it could be said that the standard speed on the journey was 50 miles per hour.

2.2   Standard cost

Definition   A **standard cost** is a predetermined cost for a future period of time.

The total standard cost of a product is built up from an assessment of the expected or standard value of each of the cost elements involved in making the product i.e. direct material, direct labour and production overheads.

2.3   Activity

Product PK is made up of two components, A and B. The standard cost of component A is £1 and the standard cost of component B is £2. The standard cost of the labour involved in working on these two components to make the product is £1.50.

What is the standard cost of product PK?

2.4   Activity solution

	£
Component A	1.00
Component B	2.00
Labour	1.50
Standard cost of product PK	4.50

2.5   Types of standard

There is a whole range of bases upon which standards may be set within a standard costing system. This choice will be affected by the use to which the standards will be put.

Most commentators identify four:
- basic standard
- ideal standard
- attainable standard
- current standard.

The definitions are as follows:

Definition   **Basic standard** - a standard established for use over a long period from which a current standard can be developed.

Definition   **Ideal standard** - a standard which can be attained under the most favourable conditions, with no allowance for normal losses, waste and machine downtime. Also known as potential standard.

Users believe that the resulting unfavourable variances will remind management of the need for improvement in all phases of operations. Ideal standards are not widely used in practice because they may influence employee motivation adversely.

Definition   **Attainable standard** - a standard which can be attained if a standard unit of work is carried out efficiently, a machine properly operated or material properly used. Allowances are made for normal losses, waste and machine downtime.

The standard represents future performance and objectives which are reasonably attainable. Beside having a desirable motivational impact on employees, attainable standards serve other purposes e.g. cash budgeting, inventory valuation and budgeting departmental performance.

Definition   **Current standard** - a standard established for use over a short period of time, related to current conditions.

Given the stated uses of standard costs, the first two types of standard will be rarely used unless a firm wants demotivated staff and information that provides little guidance for performance measurement or cost control. The third type of standard, attainable standards, will be used when operating a standard costing system and for two of the purposes previously mentioned, stock valuation and as a basis for pricing decisions. Whilst variance analysis will initially be carried out by reference to these attainable standards, more useful information comes by comparing with current standards as will be explained later.

2.6   Variance accounting

Definition   A method of accounting whereby cost variances are incorporated into ledger accounting records alongside the actual transactions.

2.7   Uses of standard costs

Standard costs may be used for stock valuation and as a basis for pricing decisions. They are implicit in the preparation of budgets and thus are part of the budgetary control/variance analysis activities of an organisation.

If standard costs are used they can minimise administration in the areas of stock valuation and promote the use of management by exception.

3   USING A STANDARD COSTING SYSTEM

3.1   Introduction

The operation of a standard costing system requires the accurate preparation of standard costs and their regular review.

3.2   Preparing standard costs

Standard costs are comprised of two estimates which are multiplied to produce the standard cost of the output unit. These two estimates are:

(a)   a physical measure of the resources required for each unit of output; and
(b)   the price expected to be paid for each unit of the resource.

The first step is to identify the resources required for each output unit. This includes:
- each type of different raw material or component;
- each grade and skill type of labour;
- each type of machine.

For each of these an estimate must then be made of the quantity of materials, number of components, number of hours etc., required for each output unit (allowing for normal losses, wastage, inefficiency).

For each of these resources an estimate must be made of the expected cost per unit of the resource (i.e. per kg, per unit, per hour). When making these estimates regard must be given towards the likely level of inflation and price changes expected in the budget period.

3.3   Measuring actual performance

Standard costing is part of the cost control system. Control is achieved by comparing actual performance with the standard that has been set, and explaining the cause of the difference.

The difference may be caused by a difference in the quantity of resources used, the cost per unit of the resource or a combination of both. These differences are known as variances and are explained in detail later in this chapter.

3.4   Revising standard costs

The calculation of variances referred to above may identify that the standard is unachievable or that it is out of date. In such circumstances the standard is not providing a realistic target and it should be revised.

Similarly, changes in the method of operation will invalidate the standard previously set; it should be reviewed on a regular basis and where appropriate revised using the same principles as are used to set new standards.

4   STANDARD COST OF MATERIALS

4.1   Introduction

In a previous paragraph (2.2) a standard cost was defined.

In order to determine the standard cost of the materials used in a product it will be necessary to identify two elements: the standard quantity of the material and the standard price of the material.

4.2   Standard quantity

It is, therefore, necessary to estimate the standard or expected amount of each material in lb, kg, litres, metres etc., that is to be input into the product.

There may be a number of different materials involved in the making of a product and the standard amount of each one must be determined.

4.3   Standard price

As well as determining the number of units of a material that is necessary to make a product the standard price of the material must also be determined. This will be the standard price of one unit i.e. lb, kg, litre, metre etc, of each of the materials input into the product.

4.4   Activity

It is estimated that 3 kg of material JG is to be used for each unit of a product. The standard cost of JG is £4.50 per kg.

What is the standard material cost for a unit of the product?

4.5   Activity solution

Standard material cost

	£
3 kg × £4.50 per kg	13.50

5   STANDARD USAGE OF MATERIALS

5.1   Introduction

When a product is designed or first made from a number of components, then the precise amount of each component required for the product will be recorded in the technical specification.

The standard or expected usage of a material or component for each unit of a product can thus be determined from the technical specification of the product.

Definition   The **standard usage** is the expected or standard quantity input into each product.

For example, suppose that a carpenter, Peter Chambers, has been making pine furniture for a number of years. The first time that he made a 1 metre single bed he had to calculate the amount of wood that he required.

His calculations showed that he required 6 metres of 1 metre wide pine in order to carve the two ends and sides of the bed. He also required 9 metres of 15 cm wide hardboard for the wooden slats of the bed. These quantities of pine and hardboard would be recorded as the standard amounts of material required per three foot bed.

5.2   Wastage

The standard material usage for a product is the amount of the material that is input into the product rather than the amount that can necessarily be found in the finished product. The reason for the difference between the amount of material input and the amount that is in the finished product is wastage, which is usually an expected and anticipated element of production.

To continue the example of Peter Chambers and the pine bed, suppose that Peter has to carve the two ends of the bed and the sides of the bed including the legs. This inevitably gives rise to an amount of the original 6 metres of pine being wasted and not included in the final product.

But the standard usage of pine is still 6 metres as this is the necessary amount of wood input into the bed even though the finished article is made up of less wood.

The amount of wood that is normally wasted each time a bed is carved is known as normal wastage (see later paragraph).

5.3   Activity

Super Soups makes a number of high quality soups for the delicatessen market. The recipe for one of its soups, carrot, requires 1 kg of carrots plus 2 litres of special vegetable stock for every 2.5 litre carton of soup.

Once the kg of carrots has been peeled and trimmed the usual weight that goes into the soup is 0.85 kg.

What is the standard material usage for each carton of carrot soup?

5.4   Activity solution

Standard material usage:

1 kg of carrots
2 litres of special vegetable stock

6   STANDARD PRICE OF MATERIALS

6.1   Introduction

The second piece of information required in order to determine the standard cost of materials is the standard price of each unit of each material used in the product.

6.2   Purchase cost

The standard price of a product will usually be taken from the most recent purchase price of the material. This can be discovered from the most recent purchase invoice for that product.

6.3   Discounts

It is common practice for suppliers of materials to grant discounts if larger amounts of a material are purchased at any one time in order to encourage larger orders rather than a number of smaller orders being placed. The price of the material should be based upon the price after such discounts - if those discounts are normally expected.

6.4   Example

Peter Chambers, the maker of pine furniture, has just looked out his latest purchase invoice from his supplier of pine.

INVOICE – FINE WOODS LTD

To: Peter Chambers

Date: 21 March 20X6

	£
For supply of high quality pine:	
60 metres of 1 metre wide pine @ £18 per metre	1,080.00
Less: Bulk discount of 10%	108.00
Invoice total	£972.00
Payment due in 30 days.	

What is the standard price per metre of pine?

6.5   Solution

	£
Invoice price of pine per metre	18.00
Less: Bulk discount of 10%	1.80
Standard price of pine per metre	£16.20

6.6   Activity

The latest invoice from Super Soups' vegetable supplier is shown below.

INVOICE – VG VEG	
To: Super Soups Date: 22 March 20X6	£
For supply of vegetables:	
12 kg parsnips @ £0.40 per kg	4.80
30 kg onions @ £0.12 per kg	3.60
80 kg carrots @ £0.20 per kg	16.00
	24.40
Less: bulk discount of 10% for orders of over 50 kg per vegetable	1.60
Total invoice price	£22.80
Payment due in 30 days	

What is the standard price of one kg of carrots?

6.7   Activity solution

Standard price of one kg of carrots

	£
Invoice price per kg	0.20
Less: Bulk discount 10%	0.02
Standard price	0.18

7   CALCULATION OF STANDARD COST OF MATERIALS

7.1   Introduction

The previous paragraphs have introduced the concepts of the standard usage of materials and the standard price. These are put together to establish the standard cost of the material input into a product.

7.2   Calculation

The standard cost of materials is arrived at as follows:

Standard usage of material × standard price per unit of material.

7.3   Example

Returning to the earlier example of Peter Chambers and his pine beds it was determined that the standard usage of pine was 6 metres of 1 metre wide pine per bed and the standard price of this pine is £16.20/metre.

What is the standard cost of the pine for the bed?

7.4   Solution

Standard cost of pine:

6 metres × £16.20/metre   £97.20

7.5   Activity

Super Soups, from an earlier activity (5.3), makes a number of high quality soups for the delicatessen market. The recipe for one of its soups, carrot, requires 1 kg of carrots plus 2 litres of special vegetable stock for every 2.5 litre carton of soup.

Once the kg of carrots has been peeled and trimmed the usual weight remaining is 0.85 kg. The carrots cost £0.18 per kg after discount.

What is the standard cost of the carrots that go into a 2.5 litre carton of soup?

7.6   Activity solution

Standard cost of carrots:

1 kg × £0.18   £0.18

Conclusion   The standard cost of materials is the standard usage multiplied by the standard price.

8   STANDARD COST CARD

8.1   Introduction

Most products or units of production are made up of a number of elements. There may be a number of different types of materials used in the product. The product will probably require a number of labour hours to be spent working on it and some other expenses or overheads might also be incurred whilst the product is being made.

8.2   Standard costs

For each of these elements that go into making a product a standard cost can be calculated (see later chapters). If the standard cost of the materials is added to the standard cost of any labour and overheads then the total standard cost of the product can be calculated.

8.3   Standard cost card

Definition   The standard cost of each of the elements of a product is brought together and totalled on a **standard cost card.**

8.4   Example of a standard cost card

STANDARD COST CARD FOR PRODUCT ABC	£	£
Standard selling price		X
Standard cost of material A	X	
Standard cost of material B	X	
Standard cost of material C	X	
Standard cost of labour	X	
Standard cost of variable production overhead	X	
Standard cost of fixed production overhead	X	
Total standard production cost		(X)
Standard gross profit		£X

Conclusion   A standard cost card records the details of all of the different costs of a product totalling in the total cost of that product.

9   STANDARD COST OF LABOUR

9.1   Introduction

The standard cost of labour is made up of two elements - the amount of time that it takes to produce the product and the wage rate that is paid to the worker or workers that produce it.

Definition   The **standard usage of labour** is the amount of time expressed in standard hours it takes to produce one unit of output.

In practice the time taken to produce a product will tend to vary. Different employees will work at different rates depending upon their experience, motivation, time of day or a combination of these and many other factors.

However a standard time for the operation or production will need to be established.

Definition   The **standard rate of labour** is the pre-determined wage rate that is paid to the employees that work on a particular product.

It will be necessary to establish what grade of employee works on the product and what hourly rate that grade of employee is paid.

9.2   Work study methods

The two main methods of determining a standard time are to use historical data or to start afresh with a work study.

One way of determining a standard time for the production of an item is to take an average of the times taken in the past to produce this product. This is historical data. This method tends to be widely used in practice.

There is little additional expense involved in this method and as the employees do not know that they are being timed then there is unlikely to be any distortion due to employees working faster or slower than usual. A more technical and theoretically sounder method of determining standard times is to use work study methods.

Definition   The function of **work study** is to analyse, measure and value operations and processes.

Work study results can be used in a number of different ways by organisations and just one of these is in setting standard times for the operation of processes or the production of products.

9.3   Elements of work study

There are three main elements of work study:

- Method study - observation and analysis of existing and suggested methods of operation to find the most efficient ways.

- Motion study - development or improvement in work by reducing effort and fatigue, and by relating human effort to the availability and use of mechanical data.

- Time study - using the results of method and motion study to determine a standard time for each operation.

9.4   Illustration of methods

Earlier in this chapter we used as an example Peter Chambers who was a maker of pine furniture. In particular we considered the materials involved in the making of a 1 metre wide single pine bed.

Suppose that when Peter first started making his furniture he called on the services of a friend of his who was a work study consultant. The consultant examined the way in which Peter made a pine bed.

He firstly considered the methods that Peter used to make the bed from the first cutting of the wood to the final sanding and polishing. He made a number of suggestions to improve the efficiency of the operation such as changing the order of the carving of the bed in order to reduce the amount of time spent storing away one portion in order to start work on another.

The consultant then considered the motion element and suggested rearrangement of Peter's tools in order to reduce the physical effort involved in moving from one section of the process to another.

9.5   Standard time

Continuing the example, when the consultant had finished his observations and commented on the methods used by Peter he was able to advise on a standard time for the production of a bed.

He took the revised method that Peter was using to make the bed and broke the whole process down into its constituent parts. For example:

Fetch piece of wood for ends of bed from storeroom	2.5 minutes
Mark out shape for cutting	1.5 minutes
Fetch saw for cutting	10 seconds

The time for each of the processes would then be totalled and this would be the standard time for the production of the bed.

10   STANDARD VARIABLE OVERHEAD COST

10.1   Variable overheads

Definition   **Variable overheads** are indirect materials, indirect labour and indirect expenses that tend to vary with the level of output.

Most indirect materials will tend to be variable, for example the amount of oil necessary for the machinery will depend upon the amount of production and the quantity of nuts and bolts used will depend upon the number of units produced.

Indirect labour costs that are variable will tend to include items such as the supervisor's wages as the hours worked by the supervisor will vary with the amount of production.

There are finally many examples of indirect expenses that are variable with the amount of production such as power, lighting and heating costs and insurance of the machinery.

10.2   Standard variable overhead cost

Definition   The **standard variable overhead cost** is the standard cost of the variable overheads for a production department.

As with all other standard costs the standards are set with regard to the expected usage and cost of the particular overhead item.

10.3   Establishing standard variable overhead costs

The standard variable overhead cost was considered above and will consist of indirect materials, indirect labour and indirect expenses. Therefore it is likely to be made up of many different items of cost. Some of these will be easier than others to establish standard costs for.

10.4   Activity

A production department in a factory has the following types of overhead.

Electricity - this is estimated at £500 per machine. The estimated number of machines for the next period is 14.

Small items such as nuts and bolts estimated at £4.50 per 100 units produced. The estimated production for the next period is 5,000 units.

What is the standard variable overhead expense for the next period?

10.5   Activity solution

Standard variable overhead expense

	£
Electricity (£500 × 14)	7,000
Indirect materials (5,000/100 × £4.50)	225
	£7,225

10.6   Treatment of the variable overhead

The total variable overhead expense for a production department has been incurred because it is impossible to run that department or produce those goods without those expenses. Therefore these are necessary costs of producing a particular product or a number of products. Without these costs being incurred the product itself could not have been produced. The variable overheads are therefore valid costs of the products themselves and as such should be included in the standard cost of the product.

The nature of the variable overhead is that it is a total figure for a particular production department.

By definition the variable overhead in total is made up of amounts that cannot be directly attributed to a unit of production. However they can often be attributed directly to a production department or cost centre.

The next task is therefore to attribute the total variable overhead for a production department to each unit produced in that department.

The total amount of the variable overhead depends upon the number of hours worked in the particular department, so the variable overhead is attributed to each product or cost unit in relation to the number of labour hours actually spent on that product or cost unit.

If one product takes twice as long to produce as another then twice the amount of variable overhead will be charged to its cost.

If the variable overhead is assumed to be generally related to time then an alternative basis would be to absorb the overhead into each product at a constant rate per labour hour.

10.7   Activity

A production department in a factory has the following overheads.

Electricity - this is estimated at £500 per machine. The estimated number of machines for the next period is 14.

Small items such as nuts and bolts estimated at £4.50 per 100 units produced. The estimated production for the next period is 5,000 units.

In this instance assume that the production department produces two different types of product. Product A requires 2 hours of labour time and product B requires 7 hours of labour time. 1,000 units of product A are due to be made in the period and 4,000 units of product B.

Attribute the variable overhead for the period to products A and B on the basis of the labour hour rate.

10.8   Activity solution

The labour hours are used to attribute the variable overhead cost to production. The results are as follows:

Total hours in department

	Hours
Product A (1,000 units × 2 hours)	2,000
Product B (4,000 units × 7 hours)	28,000
Total labour hours	30,000

Total variable overhead cost (from earlier example)	=	£7,225

$$\therefore \text{ Total variable overhead cost per hour} = \frac{£7,225}{30,000 \text{ hours}}$$

$$= £0.24 \text{ per hour}$$

Variable cost allocation:

	£
Product A (2,000 hours @ £0.24)	480
Product B (28,000 hours × £0.24)	6,720
	7,200
Rounding	25
Total variable cost	£7,225

Conclusion   The unit cost of a product depends not only on the direct costs of that product but also on the indirect costs or overheads. The overhead costs can be attributed to cost units in a variety of different ways: labour hours, machine hours and the other various absorption bases discussed in earlier chapters.

11   CHAPTER SUMMARY

The chapter has defined standard costing, standards and standard cost, comparing them with budgets and budgetary control. The features of a standard costing system have been explained together with when such a system is useful. The methods of setting standards and the various types of standards have been covered together with the effect these may have an employee motivation. Variance analysis has been reintroduced for further discussion and detailed explanation in the next few chapters.

12   SELF TEST QUESTIONS

12.1   What is standard costing? (1.1)

12.2   What is the difference between standard costing and budgeting? (1.2)

12.3   Under what circumstances is standard costing best applied? (1.3)

12.4   What are the four commonly described types of standard? (2.5)

12.5   What is variance accounting? (2.6)

12.6   How are standard costs prepared? (3.2)

12.7   Under what circumstances might a standard be revised? (3.4)

12.8   What is a standard cost card? (8.3)

12.9   What is work study? (9.2)

12.10   What are the main elements of work study? (9.3)

13   MULTIPLE CHOICE QUESTION

13.1   A standard hour is:

    A   always equivalent to a clock hour
    B   any hour during which no idle time occurs
    C   the quantity of work achievable at standard performance in an hour
    D   an hour throughout which the same units are made

14   ANSWER TO MULTIPLE CHOICE QUESTION

14.1   **C**   For example, if it is expected that 50 widgets will be produced in an hour, 200 widgets represents 4 standard hours (regardless of actual clock hours spent)

Chapter 16

MATERIAL AND LABOUR VARIANCES

PATHFINDER INTRODUCTION

This chapter covers the following elements of the CAT Official Teaching Guide. At the end of this chapter you should have learned these teaching guide elements thoroughly.

Session 16
Material and labour variances
Syllabus reference m

- Prepare and evaluate material (price and usage) and labour (rate and efficiency) variances
- Explain potential causes of material and labour variances
- Explain inter-relationships between material and labour variances

Note: Idle time variances and material mix variances will not be examined.

Putting the chapter in context

The topic of variances has been referred to in several earlier chapters and is now dealt with in detail over the next five chapters. Despite the amount of coverage given to variances it's worth remembering that a cost variance is just the difference between how much you actually spent and how much you should have spent.

1   STANDARD COSTING

1.1   Introduction

Standard costing is one method of cost control that can be adopted by an organisation. It is a specific approach to control that involves setting targets or standards for each cost element of each unit of production.

As we have seen in an earlier chapter these standards for each cost element are brought together in a standard cost card for each product.

1.2   Standard cost and actual results

A standard costing system involves the comparison of the actual costs of production with the standard costs. This comparison might take place hourly, daily, weekly, monthly or quarterly depending upon the business.

For each item of cost within the cost card there is a comparison made of the actual result with the standard set in the cost card. This comparison enables a detailed comparison of how materials, labour and expenses have varied from the budget or standard.

1.3   Variances

The differences between the actual costs and the standard costs are known as variances and are recorded within the cost accounting system. These differences are also reported to management in order that they can determine which variances (if any) require investigation and take appropriate action to rectify the situation (see later paragraph).

2   VARIANCES

2.1   Introduction

Definition   A **cost variance** is the difference between the actual cost incurred and the standard cost of actual production.

For materials, therefore, the total variance will be the difference between the actual cost of the materials used in production and the standard cost of the materials expected for that production taken from the standard cost card.

2.2   Reasons for direct materials variances

The actual cost of the materials used in production might differ from the standard cost for two reasons:

- the price paid for the materials might be different from the standard price used to set the standard cost for the materials. This would be a price variance.

- the amount of the material used in each product might be different from the standard usage used to set the standard cost. This would be a usage variance.

2.3   Favourable and unfavourable variances

Variances are not necessarily bad news. They can be either favourable or unfavourable.

A favourable variance is one where less of the material has been used than the standard usage or a lower price was paid than the standard price.

An unfavourable variance is where more of the material has been used than the standard usage or a higher price has been paid than the standard price.

Conclusion   The total material cost variance is the difference between the actual cost of the materials and the standard cost. This can be split into the **price variance** and the **usage variance.**

3   DIRECT MATERIAL PRICE VARIANCES

3.1   Introduction

A price variance is recognised when the price actually paid for the materials is different from the standard price used to set the standard cost.

Price variances can be either favourable or unfavourable.

3.2   Favourable price variance

Definition   A **favourable price variance** occurs where the price actually paid for the materials is less than the standard price.

3.3   Reasons for favourable price variances

Possible reasons for favourable price variances include the following:

- an unexpected change to a new and cheaper supplier of the material;
- an unexpected quantity discount offered by the current supplier of the material;
- use of lower quality and, therefore, cheaper grade of material than budgeted for.

3.4   Activity

In the recent past an organisation has always paid £5 per litre for a particular material. This is the standard price. The most recent invoice shows that the supplier has chosen to give a 2% discount due to the large quantities of the material purchased.

What type of price variance will this cause?

3.5   Activity solution

The standard price of the material is £5 per litre and the actual price paid is £4.90 (£5 × 98%). This will lead to a favourable price variance of 10 pence per litre.

3.6   Unfavourable price variance

Definition   An **unfavourable price variance** is where the price actually paid for the materials is more than the standard price.

3.7   Reasons for unfavourable price variances

Possible reasons for unfavourable price variances include the following:
- an unexpected price increase for that material;
- a reduction or withdrawal of a previously given quantity discount;
- use of a higher quality and, therefore, more expensive grade of material than budgeted for.

3.8   Activity

The latest purchase of a particular material shows that the price has increased from the previous price of £4.00 per metre to £4.25 per metre. The standard cost is based upon a standard price of £4.00 per metre.

What type of price variance will this cause?

3.9   Activity solution

The standard price was £4.00 and the actual price £4.25 per metre. Therefore, there will be an unfavourable price variance of 25 pence per metre.

3.10   Calculation of price variances

The materials price variance is the difference between the standard price and the actual price **for the actual quantity of material used**.

3.11   Activity

An extract from the standard cost card for a product is shown below

<table>
<tr><td colspan="2" align="center">STANDARD COST CARD</td></tr>
<tr><td></td><td align="right">£</td></tr>
<tr><td>Material A 4 kg @ £3.00 per kg</td><td align="right">12.00</td></tr>
</table>

The actual price of material A for the last period was £3.50 per kg.

100 units of the product were produced and 400 kg were purchased and used.

Calculate the price variance for the material.

3.12   Activity solution

(Standard price − actual price) actual usage

(£3.00 − £3.50) 400 kg = £200 A

A = adverse variance

That is what the materials should have cost, less what they did cost at actual usage.

4   MATERIAL USAGE VARIANCES

4.1   Introduction

A usage variance occurs when the amount of the material used is different from the standard usage specified for the actual level of production.

Usage variances can be either favourable or unfavourable.

4.2   Favourable usage variance

Definition   A **favourable usage variance** occurs when the amount of the material used is less than the standard usage specified.

4.3   Reasons for favourable usage variances

Possible reasons for **favourable usage** variances include the following:

- a change to the design or quality of the product since the standard was set which requires less material;

- a smaller amount of normal wastage than anticipated when the standard was set;

- use of a higher grade of material resulting in less being required.

4.4   Unfavourable usage variance

Definition   An **unfavourable usage variance** occurs when the amount of the material used is greater than the standard usage specified.

4.5   Reasons for unfavourable usage variances

Possible reasons for unfavourable usage variances include the following:
- a change to the design or quality of the product since the standard was set which requires more material;
- a higher amount of normal wastage than anticipated when the standard was set;
- use of a lower grade of material resulting in more being required;
- poorly trained staff;
- sub-standard production machinery.

4.6   Activity

A chemical company requires a particular liquid chemical for input into one of its products. The technical specification on which the standard usage is based states that 10 millilitres of this chemical is required for each batch of the product.

However, since the specification was drawn up the company policy has changed in that a lower grade of this liquid chemical is now used. This means, however, that in order to have the same effect on a batch of the product 15 millilitres must be used. This is the quantity that subsequently is actually used.

What type of usage variance is this?

4.7   Activity solution

This is an unfavourable usage variance. For each batch of the product 15 millilitres is now required compared to the standard usage of 10 millilitres. This will give an unfavourable usage variance of 5 millilitres per batch.

4.8   Calculation of usage variances

Introduction

Definition   The **materials usage variance** is calculated as the difference between the standard quantity for the actual amount of production, and the actual quantity used valued at the standard price.

In plain terms, this means that the actual production should have used a certain amount of material (the standard usage) but in fact actually used a different amount of material (the actual usage). This difference is valued at the standard price.

4.9   Activity

The standard cost card from an earlier example is used again.

STANDARD COST CARD	
	£
Material A 4 kg @ £3.00 per kg	12.00

Suppose that this time the price of material used equalled the standard price.

100 units of the product were produced and this actually required 380 kg of material A.

Calculate the usage variance for the material.

4.10   Activity solution

Material A:

Usage variance   =   (Standard quantity – Actual quantity used) × Standard price
                    =   (100 × 4kg – 380 kg) × £3/kg
                    =   (400 – 380) × £3 = 20 × £3 = £60

5   TOTAL DIRECT MATERIALS COST VARIANCE

5.1   Introduction

In the preceding paragraphs the calculation of a price variance and a usage variance for materials has been considered. If these two individual variances are added together then this may give the total materials cost variance. There can be complications if there is any change in raw material stock levels, but this will be ignored.

5.2   Activity

The following is the materials cost extract from the standard cost card for a unit of 'Chemex'..

STANDARD COST CARD – 'CHEMEX'	
	£
Material AC25 (2 metres @ £3.60 per metre)	7.20

The standard costs were based upon the expectation of 1,000 units being produced in the period but in fact only 940 were produced. The price actually paid for the AC25 was £3.20 per metre and 1,950 metres was bought and used.

Calculate the price variance, usage variance and total cost variance for the 'Chemex' production.

5.3   Activity solution

• Total direct material cost variance:

		Variance (A) = adverse F = favourable
Standard cost of actual production	*Actual cost*	
940 units × 2 metres = 1,880 metres	1,950 metres	
× £3.60/metre	£3.20/metre	
= £6,768	£6,240	528 F

• Direct material price variance
  (Standard price – actual price) actual usage
  (£3.60 – £3.20) 1,950 metres   780 F

- Direct material usage variance
  (Standard usage − actual usage) Standard price
  (1,880 − 1,950) £3.60/metre   £252

Summary

	£
Usage variance	252
Price variance	780 F
Total variance	£528 F

6   MATERIALS COST RECONCILIATION REPORT

6.1   Introduction

Chapter 19 looks at the various types of variance reconciliations and reports in detail, incorporating variances for materials, labour, overheads and sales. Looking just at materials at this stage, a report reconciling actual costs to standard costs might look something like this (using the data from Activity 5.2):

Materials
Variance report for the month ending 30 September 20X5

	£	£	Comment
Material costs			
Standard cost of actual production		6,768	
Materials price variance	780 F		
Materials usage variance	252 A		
		528	
Actual cost of production		£6,240	

The manager would be required to explain the variances in the comment column.

6.2   Activity

Below are the actual and standard costs for production of 'Agri-plus' for the week ended 7 June 20X2.

Standard materials per unit (2 kg × £6.50)	£13
Budgeted Production 4,000 units	
Actual results	
Materials purchased and used (8,000 kg × £6.40)	£51,200
Production 3,800 units of Agri-plus	

Using the reconciliation type variance report shown above reconcile the standard cost and actual cost of the materials for wodgits for this period.

6.3   Activity solution

Materials
Variance report for the production of wodgits for
the week ended 7 June 20X2

	£	£	Comment
Standard cost of actual production (3,800 units × £13)		49,400	
Price variance (W1)	800 F		
Usage variance (W2)	2,600 A		
		1,800 A	
Actual cost of production		£51,200	

(Tutorial note: the standard cost is the standard cost for the **actual** amount of production of 3,800 units.*)*

WORKINGS

(W1)   **Direct material price variance**

(Standard price − actual price) actual usage
(£6.50 − £6.40) 8,000 kg = £800 F

(W2)   **Direct material usage variance**

(Standard usage − actual usage) standard price
(£7,600 − 8,000) £6.50   £2,600 A

The price variance was favourable as there had been a reduction of £0.10 per kg in the purchase price from standard.

The usage variance was adverse as the actual usage of 8,000 kg was 400 kg greater than standard allowance for a production of 3,800 units of product.

Conclusion   The difference between what is spent on direct materials and what should have been is due to the price variance and/or the quantity variance.

7   RECORDING MATERIALS COST VARIANCES

7.1   Recording transactions

Transactions in a manufacturing organisation are recorded in ledger accounts in the same way as are those of other organisations. However, for a manufacturing organisation there may be some additional accounts such as a work-in-progress account.

If a manufacturing organisation operates a standard costing system there will also be accounts for variances.

However if the actual price paid for materials differs from the expected price this affects the entries made in the ledger accounts. This is illustrated by the following activity.

7.2   Activity

B Ltd bought 1,000 kg of material S on credit from its supplier at a cost of £2.90/kg. The standard price of the material was £3.00/kg. The standard usage of the material is 5 kg of S per finished product, but B Ltd used all of the 1,000 kg purchased to make only 195 units of its finished product.

7.3   Activity solution

Step 1   The first step is to calculate the material price and usage variances

Price variance

(Standard price – actual price) actual usage

(£3.00 – £2.90) 1,000   £100 F

Usage variance

(Standard usage – actual usage) standard price

(975 – 1,000) £3   £75 A

The transactions and variances are now recorded in the ledger accounts.

Step 2   Initially the purchase transaction is recorded at ACTUAL values to record the increase in stock and the liability to the supplier:

Materials

	kg	£		kg	£
Creditor	1,000	2,900			

Creditor

	£		£
		Materials	2,900

Step 3   Now we must amend the materials account so that the stock is valued at the standard price.

The price variance was £100 favourable, since the actual price paid was less than expected, the standard cost of the materials bought being 1,000 kg @ £3/kg = £3,000. An entry must be made in the materials account to increase its value to £3,000.

Materials

	kg	£		kg	£
Creditor	1,000	2,900			
Price variance		100			

The double-entry for the price variance is made to a separate ledger account, the material price variance account:

Material price variance

	£		£
		Materials	100

The balance on this variance account is eventually transferred to profit and loss.

Step 4   We now need to record the actual usage of the raw materials. The account used to collect the costs of production as they are incurred is the work-in-progress account.

In this example the quantity of materials used was 1,000 kg; these must be removed from stock (at standard price) and recorded as a cost of production:

Materials

	kg	£		kg	£
Creditor	1,000	2,900	Work-in-progress	1,000	3,000
Price variance		100			
	1,000	£3,000		1,000	£3,000

Work-in-progress

	kg	£		kg	£
Materials	1,000	3,000			

Note that there is no closing balance on the materials account; this is correct since all of the materials bought have been used.

Step 5   We must now consider the material usage variance; this is recorded in the work-in-progress account.

The usage variance was £75 adverse because the material which should have been used for the actual production was 975 kg but in fact 1,000 kg were used. The work in progress account must show this:

Work-in-progress

	kg	£		kg	£
Materials	1,000	3,000	Material usage variance	25	75
			Balance to finished goods	975	2,925
	1,000	£3,000		1,000	£3,000

Note that the balance on this account represents the standard material cost of the actual production (975 kg × £3/kg) = £3,000 − £75 = £2,925.

The double entry to the variance is entered in a variance account, the balance of which is eventually transferred to profit and loss:

Material usage variance

	£		£
Work-in-progress	75		

8   EXPLANATION OF MATERIALS VARIANCES

8.1   Introduction

It is not enough to calculate and report variances; they must also be explained to senior management.

The original explanation of how each variance came about must come from the line manager responsible for that particular cost.

The explanations for each individual cost variance will then be brought together by the management accountant when producing the variance report for senior management. It may be seen at this stage that one particular occurrence affects a number of different costs in different ways and can explain a number of different variances.

8.2   General reasons for variances

One management accounting author suggested four general causes for variances:

- bad budgeting
- bad measurement or recording
- random factors
- operational factors

Each of these can be illustrated in the case of materials.

Bad budgeting - If a new product was estimated to require 3kg of materials and this turned out to be totally impractical, (the original standard perhaps ignoring any allowance for normal losses), and 3.5kg was a more reasonable estimate, the difference of 0.5kg is attributable to bad budgeting.

Bad measurement recording - If 100 units requiring 2 kg of material per unit are produced in a period and 200kg of materials are actually used, this should not show a usage variance. If, however 250 kg of materials are purchased but the closing stock of 50 kg is recorded as 15 kg, this will suggest that actual usage was 250 – 15 = 235 kg giving rise to an adverse usage variance caused by bad recording of information.

Random factors - Any labour intensive manufacturing operation is likely give rise to random fluctuations in both time taken and material used. If decorative bricks are made from cement with a small allowance for spillage, one day the amount of spillage may be less than expected (hence a favourable usage variance) the next day it may be more than expected (an adverse variance). Both variances could be said to be of a random nature.

Operational factors

Several of these causes have already been mentioned. For materials price variances this may be due to: changing supplier, changing the type of material, changing to bulk buying, or delivery charges being imposed. The materials usage variance may be due to use of a different type of material, a different skill of production staff, or changes in the reliability of production machinery.

The specific cause of a variance needs to be investigated, (see a later chapter), and in the case of an adverse variance that cause may need to re remedied.

8.3   Interdependence of materials variances

Having said that calculating a variance is not enough, its cause must also be discovered. It was also suggested that one occurrence or event might be the cause of more than one variance. This is known as the interdependence of variances.

8.4   Example - quality of materials

If a lower grade or quality of material is used than envisaged in the standard then this may have more than one effect.

It will probably lead to a favourable materials price variance as the lower quality material will be cheaper. It may also give an adverse materials usage variance if the cheaper material causes more wastage than normal or more of the material has to be used in the product.

8.5 Example - improving productivity

If the work force attempts to improve its productivity then this could have an effect on both labour variances and materials variances.

An improvement in productivity should lead to a favourable labour efficiency variance. However, if the improvement in productivity has come about by rushed work and more waste being created then there could also be an adverse materials usage variance.

Conclusion   Variances can be caused by bad budgeting, bad recording, random factors or operational factors. The cause of one variance may well give rise to another variance. Variances need to be investigated to find their true cause.

The cause of some variances may have a corresponding or opposite effect on other variances. Therefore, it is important that variances should be considered as a whole rather than separately.

9 TOTAL DIRECT LABOUR COST VARIANCE

9.1 Introduction

Definition   The total direct labour cost variance is the difference between the standard labour cost for the production achieved and the actual direct labour cost incurred.

9.2 Calculation of total direct labour cost variance

The total labour cost variance is calculated as follows:

	£
Standard cost of direct labour for actual output	X
Actual cost of labour	(X)
Total labour cost variance	X

9.3 Activity

The standard cost card for product B includes the following information about direct labour:

	£
Standard cost of direct labour (5 hours @ £6 per hour)	30.00

During January 100 units of product B were produced. The total wage payment for the period for those workers involved with product B was £3,660 and this was for 600 hours of work.

Calculate the total labour cost variance.

9.4   Activity solution

Total labour cost variance

	£
Standard cost of direct labour for actual output (100 units × 5 hours × £6)	3,000
Actual cost	3,660
Total labour cost variance	£660 A

This is an adverse total cost variance as the actual cost of the labour was greater than the standard cost for production of 100 units of product B.

9.5   Breakdown of total direct labour cost variance

As with the direct materials cost variance the total labour cost variance can be split into the direct labour rate variance (similar to the materials price variance) and the direct labour efficiency variance (similar to the materials usage variance).

10   DIRECT LABOUR RATE VARIANCE

10.1   Introduction

A direct labour rate variance comes about because the wage rate paid for the actual labour hours paid for was different to the standard wage rate used in the standard labour cost calculation.
Labour rate variances can be either favourable or unfavourable.

Definition   A **favourable labour rate variance** occurs when the wage rate actually paid to the employees is lower than the wage rate used in the standard cost calculation.

Definition   An **unfavourable labour rate variance** occurs when the wage rate actually paid to the employees is greater than the rate used in the standard cost calculation.

10.2   Possible reasons for labour rate variances

Favourable labour rate variances might occur in two possible situations.

- If a cheaper grade of labour is used on a product than the standard grade then this will give a favourable labour rate variance.

- In some cases the standard hourly rate for labour has been based upon not only the basic labour rate per hour but also an estimate of possible bonuses to be earned by the employees. If the bonuses are less than expected this will also give a favourable labour rate variance.

Possible reasons for unfavourable labour rate variances include the following:

- an unexpected increase in wages due to, for example, a negotiated or national pay award;
- use of a more expensive grade of labour than expected;
- higher bonus payments than were anticipated when the standard labour rate was set.

10.3   Activity

The wage rate for a particular grade of labour has been £7.60 per hour for the last six months and was expected to remain at this level for some months to come. However, due to a threat of strike action by the employees the management decided to give a pay rate increase to all labour of 2.5%.

The standard rate of labour included in cost cards for this grade is £7.60. What type of labour rate variance will this increase cause?

10.4   Activity solution

The actual cost of the labour used will be £7.79 per hour (£7.60 × 1.025) and this will cause an unfavourable labour rate variance of £0.19 per hour.

10.5   Calculation of a direct labour rate variance

Definition   A direct **labour rate variance** is the difference between the standard and the actual labour rate per hour for the total hours paid for i.e. it is the difference between the amount that should have been paid for the labour paid for and the amount that was actually paid for the labour paid for.

10.6   Activity

An extract from a standard cost card for a product shows the standard labour cost:

	£
Standard cost of labour Grade A (2 hours × £4.60 per hour)	9.20

When 1,000 units of the product were actually produced it did indeed take two hours of Grade A labour per unit (2,000 hours in total). The wage rate paid however was £4.40 per hour to Grade A.

Calculate the labour rate variance.

10.7   Activity solution

Grade A

(Standard rate − actual rate) actual hours worked
(£4.60 − £4.40) 2,000   £400 F

This is a favourable labour rate variance as the price paid per hour of Grade A labour was £0.20 per hour less than the standard rate (£0.20 × 2,000 hours = £400).

11   DIRECT LABOUR EFFICIENCY VARIANCE

11.1   Introduction

Direct labour efficiency (or productivity) variances arise if the actual hours paid for to produce a given output are different from the standard hours allowed for the actual production.

The labour efficiency variance can be either favourable or unfavourable.

Definition   A **favourable labour efficiency variance** occurs when the hours worked on the product are less than the standard hours.

Definition   An **unfavourable labour efficiency** variance occurs when the hours actually worked for on a product are greater than the standard hours.

11.2   Possible reasons for labour efficiency variance

Possible causes of a favourable labour efficiency variance include the following:

- an improvement in working methods or conditions since the standard was set;
- use of a different grade of labour than was expected when the standard hours were set;
- introduction of a bonus or incentive scheme.

Possible causes of an unfavourable variance include the following:

- a change in working methods or a deterioration in working conditions;
- use of a different grade of labour than was expected when the standard was set.
- poor supervision.

11.3   Activity

When the standard labour for the production of one unit of 'Micro' was set it was expected that Grade II labour would be used and that production of one unit would take five minutes.

Due to unavoidable circumstances a less skilled grade of labour, Grade V, has had to be used and this has increased the time taken to produce a unit to six minutes.

What type of labour efficiency variance would this cause?

11.4   Activity solution

Each unit has actually taken six minutes to produce rather than the standard time of five minutes. Therefore, there will be an unfavourable efficiency variance of one minute per unit.

Conclusion   A labour efficiency variance can be either favourable or unfavourable. A favourable variance is when the actual hours paid for are less than the standard hours and an unfavourable variance is where the actual hours paid for are greater than the standard hours.

11.5   Calculation of labour efficiency variances

(Standard hours produced − actual hours worked) Standard rate of pay.

11.6   Activity

An extract from a standard cost card for a product shows the following standard labour cost:

	£
Standard cost of labour	
Grade I (4 hours × £5.00 per hour)	20.00

100 units of the product were produced and this took 430 hours of Grade I labour. The wage rates actually paid to labour were as in the standard cost card.

Calculate the labour efficiency variance.

11.7   Activity solution

(Standard hours produced – actual hours worked) Standard rate
(400 – 430) £5 = £150 A

This is an adverse or unfavourable labour efficiency variance as the actual hours paid are 30 (430 – 400) more than the standard hours allowed for production achieved. Valued at £5 per hour this gives the variance of £150 (30 hours × £5).

11.8   Interdependence of labour variances

It was mentioned earlier in the chapter that there might be some relationship between materials price and usage variances. For example if a cheaper material is used then this will give a favourable price variance but possibly also an adverse usage variance due to higher wastage.

A similar situation can arise for labour.

If a cheaper grade of labour is used to make a product than is anticipated when the standard is set then there will be a favourable labour rate variance. However, the cheaper and presumably less experienced workforce may well take longer to produce the product causing an unfavourable efficiency variance.

If a bonus scheme is introduced then the result may be that the time taken to produce the product is decreased but the material used in the production of that product is increased due to additional wastage or carelessness. This will produce a favourable labour efficiency variance but an unfavourable materials usage variance.

Conclusion   There may be a difference between how much we spent on direct labour and how much we should have spent for two reasons: worked a different number of hours, paid a different hourly rate.

In several text books you will seen an 'idle time variance' which arises if hours worked and hours paid differ. This is not examinable in Paper B2.

12   RECORDING LABOUR COST VARIANCES

12.1   Introduction

Having seen the recording of materials cost variances, the recording of labour cost variances is similar.

The gross wage cost for the period is recorded in the wages control account. In a standard costing system the standard cost of the actual labour hours for the actual production is then transferred to the work-in-progress account.

Any labour rate variance (the balancing figure in the wages control account) is recorded as a debit or credit to the profit and loss account at this stage.

The standard cost of labour for the actual completed production is then transferred to the finished goods account. Any labour efficiency variance is reported as a debit or credit to the profit and loss account.

12.2 Activity

An earlier example had relevant details as follows:

Actual number of units of product B made	100 units
Standard labour cost per B	
(5 hours per unit @ £6 per hour)	£30
Wages paid (600 hours)	£3,660

	£	
Labour rate variance (£6 − £6.10) 600	60	A
Labour efficiency variance (500 − 600) hrs @ £6	600	A
Total labour cost variance	£660	A

Standard cost of actual production:

100 units × 5 std hours
= 500 std hrs × £6 = £3,000

Actual cost

600 hrs × £6.10* = £3,660

Total variance £660 A

* i.e. £3,660 (given)/600 hours.

Write this up in the ledger accounts of the organisation.

12.3 Activity solution

Wages control

	hrs	£		hrs	£
Bank - actual payment	600	3,660	Work-in-progress - 600 hours at standard cost of £6	600	3,600
			Labour rate variance		36
	600	3,660		600	3,660

Work in progress

	Hrs	£		hrs	£
Wages control	600	3,600	Finished goods (100 units × £30)	500	3,000
			Labour efficiency variance	100	600
	600	3,600		600	3,600

Finished goods

	£		£
WIP account	3,000		

Labour rate variance

	£		£
Wages control	60	P&L account	60

Labour efficiency variance

	£		£
WIP account	600	P&L account	600

13   CHAPTER SUMMARY

The chapter has shown the calculation of total cost variances for direct materials, direct labour and other direct expenses. The materials variance has been analysed into price and usage, the labour into rate and efficiency. Some indication has been given of likely causes of variances - both general and specific - and the inter-relationship between variances has been discussed.

14   SELF-TEST QUESTIONS

14.1   How is any cost variance calculated? (2.1)

14.2   Give a possible cause of a favourable materials price variance. (3.3)

14.3   How are materials price and usage variances calculated? (5.3)

14.4   What is the double entry for initially recording a favourable materials price variance? (7.3)

14.5   What are the four general causes of variances? (8.2)

14.6   How is a total labour cost variance found? (9.1)

14.7   How are labour rate and efficiency variances calculated? (11.7)

14.8   How is an adverse labour efficiency variance initially recorded in a cost bookkeeping system? (12.3)

15   MULTIPLE CHOICE QUESTIONS

15.1   The following information relates to McGough's April production of Micks:

	Actual	Budget
Units produced	580	600
Input of material (kg)	1,566	1,500
Cost of material purchased and input	£77,517	£76,500

What is the materials usage variance?

A £5,916 A   **B** £5,742 A   **C** £3,366 A   **D** £2,349 F

15.2   Bueno's material price variance for the month of August was £1,000 F and the usage variance was £300 A. The standard material usage per unit is 3 kg, and the standard material price is £2 per kg. 500 units were produced in the period. Opening stocks of raw materials were 100 kg and closing stocks 400 kg.

Material purchases in the period were:

A 1,950 kg   **B** 1,650 kg   **C** 1,350 kg   **D** 1,050 kg

15.3   Evans Ltd's direct labour cost data relating to last month were:

Actual hours worked	28,000
Total direct labour cost	£117,600
Direct labour rate variance	£8,400 A
Direct labour efficiency variance	£3,900 F

To the nearest thousand, what were the standard labour hours last month?

A 31,000 hrs   **B** 29,000 hrs   **C** 27,000 hrs   **D** 25,000 hrs

15.4   In a period, 11,280 kilograms of material were used at a total standard cost of £46,248. The material usage variance was £492 adverse.

What was the standard allowed weight of material for the period?

A 11,520 kgs   **B** 11,280 kgs   **C** 11,394 kgs   **D** 11,160 kgs

15.5   During a period 17,500 labour hours were worked at a standard cost of £6.50 per hour. The labour efficiency variance was £7,800 favourable.

How many standard hours were produced?

A 1,200.   **B** 16,300.   **C** 17,500.   **D** 18,700.

16   PRACTICE QUESTION

16.1   Blyton Ltd

Blyton Ltd manufactures a range of distinctive garden gnomes from cement and sells them to large 'DIY' retailers. The standard production cost cards for the four models in the range are as follows:

	N	B	G	W
	£	£	£	£
Direct materials (£0.10/kg)	0.30	0.50	0.20	0.40
Direct labour (£6/hour)	0.40	0.60	0.40	0.50
Variable overheads	0.04	0.06	0.04	0.05
Fixed overheads	0.60	0.90	0.60	0.75
Total production cost	£1.34	£2.06	£1.24	£1.70

Production in February was:

Budget	2,000	1,000	500	500
Actual	2,200	1,500	600	200

Actual costs were:

Materials	16,500 kg for £1,584
Labour	330 hours for £2,120

Required:

(a)   Calculate the standard **direct** costs (materials and labour) of actual production

(b)   Calculate the materials variances (price, usage) and labour variances (rate, efficiency)

(c)   Using your answers to (a) and (b), reconcile the standard direct cost of actual production in February with actual total direct cost.

17   ANSWERS TO MULTIPLE CHOICE QUESTIONS

17.1   1,566 kg should cost ($\times$ £51) = £79,866. Did cost £77,517

Therefore **D.**

17.2   500 units should use 1,500 kg. Actual usage exceeded standard usage by (£300/£2) 150 kg.
Quantity used   = 1,500 + 150
= 1,650 kg

Quantity purchased = 1,650 + 400 – 100 = 1,950 kg

Therefore **A.**

17.3   Standard rate/hour = (117,600 – 8,400) ÷ 28,000 = £3.90
Standard hours = 28,000 + (3,900/3.90) = 29,000

Therefore **B.**

17.4   Standard price/kg $= \dfrac{\text{Standard cost}}{\text{Actual usage}}$

$= \dfrac{£46,248}{11,280}$

$= £4.10$

The usage variance is adverse so the actual usage exceeded the standard allowed weight. The excess usage is

$\dfrac{£492}{£4.10}$ = 120 kgs

Standard allowed weight   = Actual usage – Excess usage
= 11,280 kgs – 120 kgs
= 11,160 kgs

The correct answer is **D.**

17.5   **D**   An efficiency variance of £7,800 equates to 1,200 standard hours (1,200 $\times$ £6.50 = £7,800). Since the variance is favourable, this amount must be **added** to the actual hours worked: 17,500 + 1,200 = 18,700.

18   ANSWER TO PRACTICE QUESTION

18.1   Blyton Ltd

		£	£	£
(a)	Standard direct cost of actual production			
	N 2,200 $\times$ £0.70			1,540
	B 1,500 $\times$ £1.10			1,650
	G 600 $\times$ £0.60			360
	W 200 $\times$ £0.90			180
				3,730

(b)   Materials price variance

Actual price per kg = £1,584/16,500 = £0.096/kg

(Std price − actual price) actual usage
(£0.10 − £0.096) 16,500 = £665 F

Materials usage variance

Model	Std usage* kg/unit	Actual production (units)	Standard allowance kg
N	3	2,200	6,600
B	5	1,500	7,500
G	2	600	1,200
W	4	200	800

Standard usage	16,100
Actual usage	16,500
Difference	400 kg (adverse)

Variance = 400kg @ £0.10/kg = £40 A
    Labour rate variance

Actual labour rate per hour £2,120/330 = £6.42424

(Standard rate − actual rate) actual hours
(£6 − £6.42424) 330 = £140 A.

Labour efficiency variance

Model	Std time* min/unit	Actual prodn (units)	Standard allowance mins
N	4	2,200	8,800
B	6	1,500	9,000
G	4	600	2,400
W	5	200	1,000

Standard time	21,200
Actual time (330 × 60)	19,800
Difference	1,400 minutes (fav)

Variance = 1,400 minutes @ $\frac{£6.00}{60}$ /min = £140 F

* Standard cost ÷ £0.10/minute

i.e. (Standard hours − actual hours) standard rate
    (353.33 − 330) £6 = £140 F.

(c)   Variances

Materials		
	Price	66 (F)
	Usage	40 (A)
Total		26 (F)

Labour		
	Rate	140 (A)
	Efficiency	140 (F)
Total		-

Total direct cost variances		26 (F)
Actual direct cost		
Material	1,584	
Labour	2,120	
		£3,704
Standard direct cost		£3,730

◈ FOULKS*lynch*

Chapter 17

OVERHEAD VARIANCES

PATHFINDER INTRODUCTION

This chapter covers the following elements of the CAT Official Teaching Guide. At the end of this chapter you should have learned these teaching guide elements thoroughly.

Session 17
Overhead variances
Syllabus reference m

- Prepare and evaluate variable production overhead expenditure (sometimes called rate) and efficiency variances
- Prepare and evaluate fixed production overhead expenditure and volume variances
- Awareness of the sub-analysis of the fixed production overhead volume variance
- Explain the significance of overhead variances for control purposes
- Explain potential causes of overhead variances
- Explain the inter-relationships between material, labour and overhead variances

Putting the chapter in context

In the previous chapter we looked at the way in which direct cost variances were calculated and what they meant. In this chapter exactly the same principles are applied to calculating and interpreting variances for indirect costs.

1 TOTAL VARIABLE OVERHEAD COST VARIANCE

1.1 Introduction

The total variable overhead cost variance, as with all total cost variances, is the difference between the actual variable overhead cost incurred for the period and the standard variable overhead cost for the actual amount of production.

The total variable overhead variance is calculated as follows:

	£
Standard variable overhead cost for actual output	X
Actual variable overhead cost	(X)
Total variable overhead variance	X

1.2 Analysis of total variable overhead variance

Unlike variances for direct materials or labour, there is a question mark over whether the total variable overhead cost variance should be analysed at all. It could be argued that, if variable overhead cost varies with the number of units produced, then further analysis is impossible or irrelevant.

However, if variable overheads are thought to vary with labour (or possibly machine) hours, or bearing in mind that they are likely to be recovered in units of production on the basis of hours, a split of the total variance is possible. The total variable overhead cost variance can be split into two variances:

(a)   expenditure (sometimes referred to as rate)

(b)   efficiency.

The method of calculation is similar to that for labour variances as set out below.

2   VARIABLE OVERHEAD RATE VARIANCE

2.1   Variable overhead rate variance

We have seen that the total standard variable overhead cost can be divided by the standard number of labour hours to give the standard variable overhead cost per labour hour. The amount of variable overhead actually paid per hour may differ from this. This could lead to a variable overhead expenditure variance.

The variable overhead expenditure variance is calculated as follows:

(Std VORR* − actual VORR) actual hours

* VORR = variable overhead recovery rate.

2.2   Activity

The budgeted variable overhead cost for a period was £1,000 and the actual cost £1,200. The budgeted direct labour hours were 500 but only 400 were worked.

What is the variable overhead expenditure variance?

2.3   Activity solution

Step 1   Calculate the standard variable overhead rate per hour (this will usually be given to you):

The standard variable overhead rate for each direct labour hour is £2 (£1,000 ÷ 500).

Step 2   (Std VORR − actual VORR) actual hours
                (£2 − £3) 400 = £400 A

This is an adverse expenditure variance. We expected the overhead cost to be £2 per hour. It was actually £3 per hour (£1,200 ÷ 400 hours). Thus we spent £1 per hour more than expected for each of the 400 hours.

3   VARIABLE OVERHEAD EFFICIENCY VARIANCE

3.1   Introduction

The variable overhead efficiency variance is similar to the labour efficiency variance. It is calculated in the same way, but evaluated at a different hourly rate.

3.2   Calculation

The variable overhead efficiency variance is calculated as follows:

(Standard hours produced − actual hours worked) Std VORR

The variable overhead efficiency variance compares the hours that it should have taken to produce the number of units to the hours that actually were taken. The argument with the variable overhead is that the variable overhead tends to be incurred over time and therefore if more or less hours are spent working than the standard then more or less variable overhead will be incurred.

3.3   Example

Using the information from an earlier example the budgeted variable overhead cost for a period was £1,000 and the actual cost £1,200. The budgeted direct labour hours were 500 and the standard time for production actually achieved was also 500 hours, but only 400 were worked.

What is the variable overhead efficiency variance?

3.4   Solution

The standard variable overhead rate in this example is £2 per direct labour hour (£1,000 ÷ 500 hours).

Variable overhead efficiency variance

(Standard hours produced − actual hours worked) Std VORR
(500 − 400) £2 = £200 F

This is a favourable variance as the actual hours worked were less than the standard hours allowed for production achieved. This means that there were 100 hours less of the variable overhead being incurred at the standard rate of £2 per hour giving the favourable variance of £200.

3.5   Activity

Use the following information to calculate the total variable overhead cost variance and show how it can be analysed into the expenditure variance and efficiency variance.

The standard costs for a product show that the variable overhead cost is likely to be £12,000 for every 1,000 units produced. This is on the basis that it takes 4,000 direct labour hours to make these products.

The actual results for the latest period were that 1,200 units of the product were made and the variable overhead incurred was £12,400.

The number of direct labour hours worked were 5,000.

3.6   Activity solution

Standard variable overhead rate = £12,000 ÷ 4,000 hours = £3 per hour
Standard time per unit = 4,000 ÷ 1,000 = 4 hours per unit
Standard variable overhead cost per unit = 4 × £3 = £12 per unit
Standard hours achieved/produced = 4 × 1,200 = 4,800 std hrs.

Total variable overhead variance

	£
Standard variable overhead cost recovered in actual output achieved	
4,800 std hours × £3/hr	14,400
Actual variable overhead cost	12,400
Total variable overhead variance	£2,000 F

Variable overhead expenditure variance

> (Std VORR − actual VORR) actual hours
> (£3 − £2,148*) 5,000 = £2,600 F

> *actual variable overhead/hour
>   £12,400/5,000 hrs

Variable overhead efficiency variance

> (Std hours produced − actual hours worked) Std VORR
> (4,800 − 5,000) £3 = £600 A

Conclusion   The total variable overhead cost variance is found in the same way as all other total cost variances = standard variable overhead cost recovered in actual production − actual variable overhead cost. If an analysis is required it can be split into expenditure and efficiency. The expenditure variance is the result of an increase or decrease in the variable cost per hour. The efficiency variance is the result of a change in the efficiency level of the workforce.

4   TOTAL FIXED OVERHEAD VARIANCE

4.1   Introduction

The fixed overheads of an organisation are of a different nature from the materials costs, labour costs and variable overheads considered so far in this text. As they are fixed, by nature they are not expected to vary with the amount of production, however the actual amount of fixed overhead may differ from the standard or budgeted amount for one reason or another.

4.2   Product costs - absorption v marginal costing

In earlier paragraphs of this chapter it was seen how the variable overheads were included in the cost of each product usually on the basis of the number of direct labour hours used to make that product.
In marginal costing systems the fixed overhead costs are not included in the cost of each product, whilst in absorption costing systems they are. The way that fixed overhead variances are calculated depends upon whether an absorption or marginal costing system is used.   Initially we will assume **absorption costing**.

4.3   Activity

Budgeted fixed overheads for a period are £6,000 and this is based upon an estimate of 100 units to be produced and 4,000 hours to be worked.

Show how the standard fixed overhead of £6,000 could be included into the cost of each product on a per unit basis and on a direct labour hour basis.

4.4   Activity solution

Per unit basis

Standard fixed overhead		£6,000
Standard output		100 units
Standard fixed overhead per unit = £6,000 ÷ 100	=	£60 per unit

Direct labour hour basis

Standard fixed overhead		£6,000
Standard hours for production		4,000 hours
Standard fixed overhead rate per hour = £6,000 ÷ 4,000	=	£1.50 per hour
Standard hours for one unit of production = 4,000 ÷ 100	=	40 hours
Standard fixed overhead cost per unit of production		
(40 hours × £1.50 per hour)	=	£60 per unit

4.5   Total fixed overhead variance

Despite the different nature of fixed overheads from other costs, its total cost variance is calculated in exactly the same way as other total cost variances - if absorption costing is being used.

	£
Standard fixed overhead cost recovered in actual production achieved	X
Actual fixed overhead cost incurred	X
Total fixed overhead cost variance	X

Having highlighted the fact that this calculation is the same as previous total cost variances there are two important points to note:

(a)   this could be the same as the over or under absorption (recovery) of overheads discussed in an earlier chapter;

(b)   it is only relevant for an absorption costing system since, under a marginal costing system, the term 'standard fixed overhead cost of actual production' has no significance.

4.6   Example

The information from the previous example is reproduced below together with details of actual production.

Budgeted fixed overhead for a period is £6,000 and this is based upon an estimate of 100 units to be produced and 4,000 hours to be worked i.e. 40 std hours per unit.

The actual fixed overhead that was incurred for the period was £6,120, only 90 units were produced and 3,640 hours were worked.

Calculate the total fixed overhead cost variance.

4.7   Solution

Standard fixed overhead cost per standard hour = £6,000/4,000 = £1.50.

	£
Standard fixed overhead recovered in production achieved	
3,600 std hrs* × £1.50	5,400
Actual fixed overhead incurred	6,120
Total fixed overhead variance	720 A

* Standard hours produced = 90 × 40 std hrs/unit.
This represents an under-recovery of fixed overhead. The variance is adverse as the actual cost is greater than that recovered.

4.8   Activity

Calculate the total fixed overhead variance from the following information:

Budgeted fixed overhead cost	£50,000
Budgeted hours	10,000
Budgeted units	2,000
Actual units produced	2,100
Actual fixed overhead incurred	£49,750

4.9   Activity solution

Standard fixed overhead recovery rate per standard hour	$\dfrac{£50,000}{10,000 \text{ hrs}}$
	= £5/std hr

	£
Standard fixed overhead cost recovered in production achieved	
10,500 std hrs* × £5	52,500
Actual fixed overhead incurred	49,750
Total fixed overhead variance	2,750 F

* Standard hours produced 2,100 units × 5 std hrs = 10,500

5   ANALYSIS OF TOTAL FIXED OVERHEAD VARIANCE

5.1   Introduction

You are referred to an article on fixed overhead variances in the March 2001 copy of ACCA's Student Accountant by Dr Philip E. Dunn.

This paper looks at the fixed overhead variance, its analysis to expenditure and volume; and the sub-analysis of the volume variance.

There will be a difference between the standard fixed cost of actual production and actual fixed overhead cost for one of two reasons:

(a)   actual fixed overheads differ from budgeted fixed overheads;
(b)   actual production differs from budgeted production.

This can give rise to two possible variances, the expenditure variance and the volume variance.

This can be expressed diagrammatically:

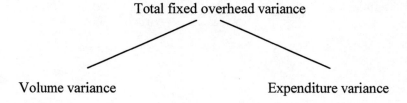

Total fixed overhead variance

Volume variance   Expenditure variance

These two variances could be said to quantify the extent to which the two figures used to calculate a predetermined standard fixed overhead cost per unit, budgeted fixed overheads and budgeted production, were inaccurate.

It is worth noting that, under standard marginal costing a volume variance has, as previously stated, no significance. The only fixed overhead cost variance calculated in an expenditure variance.

5.2   Fixed overhead expenditure variance

The expenditure variance measures the amount of the total variance that is due to the difference between what was budgeted to be spent on overheads and what was actually spent. It is calculated as follows:

	£
Total amount of fixed overhead budgeted	X
Total amount of fixed overheads incurred	(X)
Fixed overhead expenditure variance	X

5.3   Fixed overhead volume variance

The volume variance measures the amount of the total variance that is due to more or less units being produced, and therefore more or less overheads being absorbed than was planned. It is calculated as follows:

(Standard hours budgeted − standard hours produced) FORR*

* FORR = fixed overhead recovery rate

The volume variance in the difference between actual and budgeted production in standard hours multiplied by the standard fixed overhead per standard hour.

5.4   Example

An organisation has the following information regarding fixed overheads and production.

Budgeted fixed overhead cost	£50,000
Budgeted hours	10,000
Budgeted number of units to be produced	2,000
Actual number of units produced	2,100
Actual fixed overhead incurred	£49,750
Actual hours worked	11,000

Calculate the total fixed overhead variance and analyse it into the expenditure and volume variances.

5.5   Solution

The first step is to calculate the standard overhead absorption rate.

Budgeted overhead	£50,000
Budgeted number of hours	10,000
Standard overhead absorption rate =	$\dfrac{£50,000}{10,000 \text{ hours}}$
=	£5 per hour

Budgeted number of units is 2,000 and this is expected to take 10,000 hours therefore the standard time for one unit is 5 hours.

Standard fixed overhead cost per unit = £50,000 ÷ 2,000 = £25 per unit.
Standard hours produced = 2,100 units × 5 std hrs = 10,500 std hrs

Total overhead variance

	£
Amount of overhead absorbed into actual units of production (10,500 std hrs × £5)	52,500
Amount of overhead actually incurred	49,750
Total overhead variance	2,750 F

This is a favourable variance as the actual amount of overhead is less than would be anticipated for a production level of 2,100 units. This total variance can now be analysed into its expenditure and volume elements.

Expenditure variance

	£
Amount of overhead budgeted	50,000
Amount actually spent on overheads	49,750
Expenditure variance	250 F

The amount actually incurred on overhead was less than anticipated giving a favourable expenditure variance.

Volume variance

(Budgeted std hrs − std hours produced) FORR
(10,000 − 10,500) £5 = £2,500 F

This is a favourable variance as the volume of output is greater i.e. 500 std hours or 100 units. This represents an over-recovery due to increased volume of output.

5.6   Activity

The following information is available about an organisation and its products.

Budgeted fixed overhead	£150,000
Budgeted number of units of product A	4,000
Budgeted number of units of product B	7,000
Standard hours for production of a unit of A	2
Standard hours for production of a unit of B	1
Actual overhead	£154,000
Actual hours worked	14,000
Actual units produced A	3,600
B	7,500

(a)   Calculate the total overhead variance.
(b)   Calculate the expenditure and volume variances.

5.7   Activity solution

Budgeted overhead		£150,000

Budgeted hours:

Product A	4,000 units × 2 hours	8,000
Product B	7,000 units × 1 hour	7,000
		15,000 hours

$$\text{Standard overhead absorption rate (FORR)} = \frac{£150,000}{15,000 \text{ hours}}$$

$$= £10 \text{ per hour}$$

Standard fixed overhead cost per unit:

A 2 × £10 = £20
B 1 × £10 = £10

(a)   Total overhead variance

	£
Amount of overhead absorbed into actual production	
14,700 std hrs* × £10	147,000
Amount of overhead actually incurred	154,000
Total overhead variance	7,000 A

This is an adverse variance as the actual overhead incurred is greater than that recovered in the actual level of production.

* (36,000 × 2 std hrs) + (7,500 × 1 std hr)

(b)   Expenditure variance

	£
Amount of overhead budgeted	150,000
Amount actually incurred on overhead	154,000
Expenditure variance	4,000 A

This is an adverse variance as the amount actually incurred is greater than the amount budgeted for.

Volume variance

(Budgeted std hrs − std hours produced) FORR
(15,000 − 14,700) £10 = £3,000 A

This adverse variance is the result of a reduction in volume of output.

Conclusion   The total fixed overhead cost variance is found in the same way as any other total cost variance = standard fixed cost recovered in actual production − actual fixed overhead cost. In the first instance, this can be split into an expenditure and a volume variance. The fixed overhead expenditure variance = budgeted total fixed overheads − actual total fixed overheads. The fixed overhead volume variance = (budgeted std hrs − std hrs produced) FORR.

6   REASONS FOR OVERHEAD VARIANCES; SUB-ANALYSIS OF THE VOLUME VARIANCE

6.1   Introduction

It was explained in earlier chapters of this text that it is not enough to simply record variances, they must also be explained to management.

In the case of variable and fixed overheads this is more complex than perhaps with materials and labour as there are so many different elements that make up the overheads.

6.2   Examples - variable overhead variances

Possible reasons for variable overhead variances include:

*   unexpected price changes for overhead items;

*   changes in labour efficiency (remember that any labour efficiency variances are also reflected in any variable overhead efficiency variances).

6.3   Examples - fixed overhead variances

Possible reasons for fixed overhead variances include:

*   unexpected price changes for overhead items;
*   seasonal effects e.g. heat and light in winter and summer;
*   changes in production volume or productivity.

6.4   Analysis of fixed overhead volume variance

Some general reasons can be stated for a fixed overhead volume variance occurring. An adverse volume variance indicates that a firm hasn't produced as many units as its budget suggested it should.

There are two possible reasons for this and two variances that derive from those reasons:

(a)   not working **hard** enough → adverse **efficiency** variance.
(b)   not working **long** enough → adverse **capacity** variance.

Some authors argue that this analysis is unhelpful, but it does give some indication of a variation from expected performance.

6.5   Fixed overhead efficiency and capacity variances

The Official Teaching Guide talks of an 'awareness of the sub-analysis of the fixed production overhead volume variance'. This suggests that the paragraph above should be sufficient. The method of calculating the variances are shown below 'for completeness sake'.   The efficiency variance is similar to those for labour and variable overheads.

Fixed overhead efficiency variance = (Standard hours for actual production – actual hours worked) × standard fixed overhead rate per hour i.e. FORR.

(As with labour, ask: what did we make, how long should it have taken, how long did it take?)

Fixed overhead capacity variance = (actual hours worked – budgeted std hours) × standard fixed overhead rate per hour/FORR.

6.6   Activity

Budget
Production	4,000 units
Standard time per unit	3 hours
Standard fixed overhead rate per hour (FORR)	£8

(Budgeted total hours = 4,000 × 3 = 12,000 hours.   Budgeted total overhead = 12,000 × £8 = £96,000. Standard fixed overhead cost per unit = 3 × £8 = £24.)

Actual
Production	3,700 units
Hours worked	11,700 hours
Fixed overheads	£97,000

Produce a full analysis of the fixed overhead total cost variance.

6.7   Activity solution

The total fixed overhead variance

Fixed overhead recovered:

	£
3,700 units × 3 std hrs = 11,100 std hrs × £8 =	88,800
Actual incurred	97,000
	£8,200 A

The total variance is adverse and represents an under-recovery of fixed overhead. In that the actual incurred is greater than the amount recovered or absorbed in the actual output achieved.

The following diagram indicates how it can be analysed.

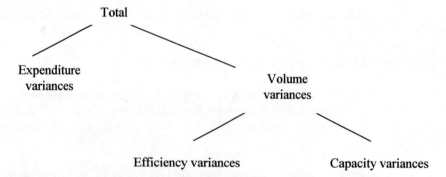

The initial split into expenditure and volume shows:

Expenditure variance

= Total budgeted fixed overheads − actual total fixed costs

= £96,000 − £97,000 = £1,000 (Adverse).

Volume variance

(Budget std hrs − std hrs produced) FORR
(12,000 − 11,100*) £8 = £7,200 A.

The volume variance can be split as previously suggested to show:

Efficiency variance

(Standard hours produced − actual hours worked) FORR
(11,100 − 11,700) £8 = £4,800 A.

Capacity variance

(Actual hours worked − budgeted std hours) FORR
(11,700 − 12,000) £8 = £2,400 A.

The full analysis, with all variances adverse, shows:

	£
Efficiency variance	4,800 A
Capacity variance	2,400 A
Volume variance	7,200 A
Expenditure variance	1,000 A
Total variance	8,200 A

7 INTERDEPENDENCE OF OVERHEAD VARIANCES

7.1 Introduction

In the earlier chapter on materials and labour variances it was noted that each variance could not necessarily be looked at in isolation. Very often an event on transaction or set of circumstances affected more than one cost element and therefore more than one variance.

7.2 Variable overhead variances

This is particularly true for overhead variances. In the previous paragraphs it has been shown how the variable overhead is included in the cost of products usually using the direct labour hour method. The assumption underlying this method is that if more labour hours are worked then more variable overhead is incurred or conversely if less labour hours are worked then less variable overhead is incurred.

Therefore the variable overhead efficiency variance will be directly related to the labour efficiency variance.

7.3 Fixed overhead variances

Perhaps the most obvious reason for a total fixed overhead variance will be if the actual amount of expenditure on fixed overheads is more or less than anticipated and this can often be due to items that affect other variances as well.

Examples of the interdependence of overhead variances with other variances might include the following:

- if a cheaper grade of material is used than has been budgeted for this will produce a favourable materials price variance but also possibly an unfavourable labour efficiency variance as the cheaper material takes longer to work on and therefore an unfavourable variable overhead efficiency variance as well;
- if a less experienced, and cheaper, grade of labour is used than the standard grade this will cause a favourable labour rate variance. However if the less experienced

labour force takes longer to produce the goods and also wastes more of the material then there will also be an unfavourable materials usage variance, an unfavourable labour efficiency variance and an unfavourable variable overhead efficiency variance.

- if a supplier of raw materials offers an organisation a quantity discount and this is accepted then this will lead to a favourable materials price variance. However if the quantity that must be purchased is such that additional warehouse space must be rented then this might also cause an unfavourable total fixed overhead variance.

8   RESPONSIBILITY FOR OVERHEAD VARIANCES

8.1   Introduction

In earlier chapters the importance of recognising any responsibility for variances was considered. Some variances are known as controllable and will be the direct responsibility of some manager in the organisation. Others are non-controllable and are caused by external events that are the direct responsibility of no one in the organisation.

8.2   Nature of overheads

The responsibility for overhead variances can be quite a complex matter due to the nature of the overheads themselves. As there are many cost elements that make up the variances so there are also many different managers that might be responsible. The variable overhead is made up of indirect materials, indirect labour and indirect expenses.

Indirect materials will probably be the responsibility of the purchasing and factory managers and indirect labour the responsibility of either the factory manager or the personnel manager. Indirect expenses can include a variety of different items such as machine insurance, heat, light and power. Some of these might be the responsibility of the production manager whilst others might fall within the responsibility of the administration manager.

8.3   Nature of overhead variances

Variable overhead variances are made up of a price variance and an efficiency variance. The price variance is the only one which is directly affected by the actual variable overhead expenses themselves.

In a system where the variable overhead expense is charged to cost units on the basis of direct labour hours then the efficiency variance will depend on the efficiency of direct labour rather than anything to do with the variable overheads themselves. This again complicates the matter of responsibility.

8.4   Examples

Examples of responsibility for overhead variances might include the following:

- an unfavourable variable overhead efficiency variance is recorded. It becomes clear that this was due to the fact that a cheaper grade of material had been purchased and this then took longer for the labour force to work on. This caused an unfavourable labour efficiency variance and the corresponding variable overhead variance. Responsibility for these variances should lie with the purchasing manager who was responsible for purchasing the cheaper materials.

- a favourable variance overhead variance is recorded. It is discovered that this was due to a more experienced grade of labour being used in production which resulted in the goods being produced more quickly. This gave not only a favourable labour efficiency variance but also a favourable variable overhead variance. The responsibility for these variances should lie with the manager responsible for scheduling the labour force.

- a favourable total fixed overhead variance is recorded and this is partly put down to the renegotiation of the rent for the premises by the administration manager. Due to the recession he has been able to negotiate a reduced rental for three years. This element of the variance is the responsibility of the administration manager.

9   CHAPTER SUMMARY

This chapter has explained the calculation and interpretation of variable and fixed overhead variances. The fixed overhead variances have been looked at in some detail to show a full analysis and the simpler approach required for standard marginal costing, as opposed to standard absorption costing, has been discussed.

10   SELF TEST QUESTIONS

10.1   Under what circumstances could it be argued that a total variable overhead cost variance need not be analysed? (1.2)

10.2   How are the labour and variable overhead efficiency variances linked? (3.1)

10.3   How is a variable overhead efficiency variance found? (3.6)

10.4   How is a variable overhead rate (sometimes called expenditure) variance calculated? (3.6)

10.5   How is a total fixed production overhead cost variance calculated? (4.5)

10.6   What other aspect of absorption costing does the total fixed production overhead cost variance resemble? (4.5)

10.7   How is a fixed production overhead expenditure variance calculated? (5.2)

10.8   How is a fixed production overhead volume variance calculated? (5.3)

10.9   What purpose does the analysis of a fixed production overhead volume variance specifically aim to achieve? (6.4)

11   MULTIPLE CHOICE QUESTIONS

11.1   F Ltd has the following budget and actual data:

Budget fixed overhead cost	£100,000
Budget production (units)	20,000
Actual fixed overhead cost	£110,000
Actual production (units)	19,500

The fixed overhead volume variance:

A   is £500 adverse.
B   is £2,500 adverse.
C   is £10,000 adverse.
D   is £17,500 adverse.

11.2   PQ Ltd operates a standard costing system for its only product. The standard cost card is as follows:

Direct materials	(4 kg @ £2/kg)	£8.00
Direct labour	(4 hours @ £4/hour)	£16.00
Variable overhead	(4 hours @ £3/hour)	£12.00

Fixed overhead   (4 hours @ £5/hour)   £20.00

Fixed overheads are absorbed on the basis of labour hours. Fixed overhead costs are budgeted at £120,000 per annum arising at a constant rate during the year.

Activity in period 3 of 20X5 is budgeted to be 10% of total activity for the year. Actual production during period 3 was 500 units, with actual fixed overhead costs incurred being £9,800 and actual hours worked being 1,970.

The fixed overhead expenditure variance for period 3 of 20X5 was:

A   £2,200 (F)   B   £200 (F)   C   £50 (F)   D   £200 (A)

11.2   The following details relate to product T, which has a selling price of £44.00:

	£/unit
Direct materials	15.00
Direct labour (3 hours)	12.00
Variable overhead	6.00
Fixed overhead	4.00
	37.00

During April 20X6, the actual production of T was 800 units, which was 100 units fewer than budgeted. The budget shows an annual production target of 10,800, with fixed costs accruing at a constant rate throughout the year. Actual overhead expenditure totalled £8,500 for April 20X6.

The overhead variances for April 20X6 were:

	Expenditure £	Volume £
A	367 A	1,000 A
B	500 A	400 A
C	100 A	1,000 A
D	100 A	400 A

11.3   QR Limited uses a standard absorption costing system. The following details have been extracted from its budget for April 20X7:

Fixed production overhead cost	£48,000
Production (units)	4,800

In April 20X7 the fixed production overhead cost was under-absorbed by £8,000 and the fixed production overhead expenditure variance was £2,000 adverse.

The actual number of units produced was:

A   3,800
B   4,000
C   4,200
D   5,400

11.4   F Ltd has the following budget and actual data:

Budget fixed overhead cost	£100,000
Budget production (units)	20,000
Actual fixed overhead cost	£110,000
Actual production (units)	19,500

The fixed overhead volume variance:

A   is £500 adverse.
B   is £2,500 adverse.
C   is £10,000 adverse.
D   is £17,500 adverse.

12   PRACTICE QUESTION

12.1   Labour-intensive product

A labour-intensive production unit operating a standard absorption cost accounting system provides the following information for period 10:

Normal capacity, in direct labour hours	9,600
Budgeted variable production overhead	£3 per direct labour hour
Budgeted fixed production overhead per four-week financial period	£120,000

To produce one unit of output takes two standard hours.

Actual figures produced for the four-week period 10 were:

Production, in units	5,000
Variable production overhead incurred	£28,900
Fixed production overhead incurred	£118,000
Actual direct labour hours worked	9,300

You are required to calculate:

(a)   variable production overhead expenditure variance,
(b)   variable production overhead efficiency variance,
(c)   fixed production overhead expenditure variance,
(d)   fixed production overhead volume variance.   **(8 marks)**

13   ANSWERS TO MULTIPLE CHOICE QUESTIONS

13.1   Absorption rate $= \dfrac{£100,000}{20,000} = £5/\text{unit}$

Difference in volume	=	20,000 – 19,500
	=	500 units

Volume variance	=	500 units $\times$ £5/unit
	=	£2,500 (A)

It is adverse because actual volume is less than that budgeted.

The correct answer is **B**.

13.2

Budget cost $= \dfrac{£120,000}{12} =$	£10,000
Actual cost =	£9,800
	£200 (F)

The correct answer is **B**.

Expenditure variance

Monthly budgeted production (10,800/12)	900 units
	£
Monthly budgeted expenditure	
900 × £4	3,600 Fixed
800 × £6	4,800 Variable
	8,400
Actual expenditure	8,500
Expenditure variance	100 A

Volume variance

This only applies to fixed overhead costs:

Difference in volume = 100 units
100 units × £4 per unit = £400 A

The answer is **D.**

13.3

$$\text{Absorption rate/unit} = \frac{£48,000}{4,800} = £10/\text{unit}$$

Under absorption	=	£8,000	
Expenditure variance	=	£2,000	Adverse
Volume variance	=	£6,000	Adverse

$$\text{Volume difference in units} = \frac{£6,000(A)}{£10/\text{unit}} = 600 \text{ units less than budget}$$

Budgeted units	=	4,800
Volume difference	=	600
Actual units	=	4,200

The correct answer is **C.**

13.4 $\text{Absorption rate} = \dfrac{£100,000}{20,000} = £5/\text{unit}$

Difference in volume	=	20,000 – 19,500
	=	500 units
Volume variance	=	500 units × £5/unit
	=	£2,500 (A)

It is adverse because actual volume is less than that budgeted.

The correct answer is **B.**

14   ANSWER TO PRACTICE QUESTION

14.1   Labour-intensive product

(a)   Variable production overhead expenditure variance

(Std VORR − actual VORR) actual hours worked
(£3 − £3.10753*) 9,300 = £1,000 A

* £28,900/9,300

(b)   Variable production overhead efficiency variance

	Hrs
Standard hours produced	
5,000 units × 2 hrs/unit	10,000
Actual hours	9,300
	700 F
× Std VORR	× £3
	£2,100 F

or:

(Standard hours produced − actual hours worked) VORR
(10,000 − 9,300) £3 = £2,100 F

(c)   Fixed production overhead expenditure variance

	£
Budgeted overheads	120,000
Actual overheads	118,000
	£2,000 F

(d)   Fixed overhead volume variance

(Budget std hrs − standard hrs produced) FORR
(9,600 − 10,000) £12.50 * = £5,000 F

WORKINGS
Fixed overhead recovery rate:

$$\frac{\text{*Fixed costs}}{\text{Budget standard hours}}$$

$$= \frac{£120,000}{9,600} = £12.50 \text{ per std hr}$$

Chapter 18

SALES VOLUME AND PRICE VARIANCES

PATHFINDER INTRODUCTION

This chapter covers the following elements of the CAT Official Teaching Guide. At the end of this chapter you should have learned these teaching guide elements thoroughly.

Session 18
Sales volume and price variances
Syllabus reference m

- Prepare sales price and volume variances in marginal and absorption costing systems
- Explain potential causes of sales variances
- Explain the inter-relationship between sales and cost variances

Putting the chapter in context

The previous two chapters dealt with costs variances, found by comparing how much a business spent with how much it should have spent. This chapter applies similar principles to assessing sales performance.

1 SALES VARIANCES

1.1 Introduction

The purpose of calculating sales variances is to show their effect on profit when reconciling budget and actual profit. There are two causes of sales variances, a difference in the selling price and a difference in the sales volume.

1.2 Sales price variance

This variance shows the effect on profit of selling at a different price from that expected. The following example is used to illustrate its calculation.

1.3 Example

TZ has the following data regarding its sales for March:

Budgeted sales	1,000 units
Standard selling price	£10/unit
Standard variable cost	£6/unit
Standard fixed cost	£2/unit*

* based upon budgeted annual fixed costs and activity levels

Actual sales	940 units
Actual selling price	£10.50/unit

If the actual sales volume had been sold at the standard selling price the sales revenue would have been:

	£
940 units × £10 =	9,400
But actual sales revenue was	
940 units × £10.50 =	9,870
Variance	£470 F

or (std selling price − actual selling price) actual units

The variance is favourable because the higher actual selling price causes an increase in revenue and a consequent increase in profit. This is clearly 940 units at an extra £0.50 per unit.

1.4   Sales volume variance

The purpose of this variance is to calculate the effect on profit of the actual sales volume being difference from that budgeted. The effect on profit will differ depending upon whether a marginal or absorption costing system is being used.

Under absorption costing all production costs are attributed to the cost unit, and the fixed production overhead volume variance accounts for the effects of actual volumes differing from those expected. Whereas under marginal costing contribution is emphasised (i.e. the difference between the selling price and the variable cost).

This affects the calculation of the sales volume variance. Under absorption costing any difference in units sold is valued at the standard profit per unit, whereas under marginal costing such a difference in units is valued at the standard contribution per unit.

In neither case is the standard selling price used. This is because when volumes change so do production costs and the purpose of calculating the variance is to find the effect on **profit** of the change in volume. (This statement will be reviewed when looking at profit reconciliations in a later chapter).

1.5   Sales volume variance - absorption costing (sometimes referred to as sales margin quantity variance)

Using the data from the example above:

Budgeted sales	1,000 units
Actual sales	940 units
Difference	60 units

These 60 units are valued at the standard profit of £2/unit (£10 - £6 - £2)

60 units × £2 = £120 A

The variance is adverse because actual sales volume was less than expected.

1.6   Sales volume variance - marginal costing

The difference of 60 units (as above) is valued at the standard contribution of £4/unit (£10 - £6):

60 units × £4 = £240 A

1.7   Reconciling the sales volume variances under absorption and marginal costing

Using the above example:

Variance under		
	- absorption costing	£120 A
	- marginal costing	£240 A

There is a difference between these variances of £120 (A).

In the previous chapter we learnt how to calculate fixed overhead variances. These too were affected by the choice of costing method. Absorption costing required the calculation of both an expenditure and a volume variance, whereas marginal costing only required an expenditure variance.

Continuing with the data from the above example there is a volume difference of 60 units. The fixed cost is absorbed at a rate equivalent to £2/unit.

Thus the fixed production overhead volume variance would be

60 units × £2/unit = £120 (A)

The variance would be adverse because actual volume was less than expected and, since the cost is fixed this would increase the cost per unit and so decrease profit.

Thus when reconciling the profits, the absorption and marginal systems would show:

	Absorption £	*Marginal* £
Variances:		
Sales volume	120 A	240 A
Fixed production overhead volume	120 A	Not applicable
	£240 A	£240 A

All other cost variances and the sales price variance would be identical under both systems.

The reconciliation of profits is covered in more depth in the next chapter.

1.8   Activity

Budgeted sales	500 units
Actual sales	480 units
Standard selling price	£100
Actual selling price	£110
Standard variable cost	£50/unit
Standard fixed cost	£15/unit

Calculate:

(i)   the sales price variance;
(ii)   the sales volume variance assuming an absorption costing system;
(iii)   the sales volume variance assuming a marginal costing system.

1.9   Activity solution

(i)   Sales price variance = 480 units × (£110 − £100) = £4,800 (F)
(ii)   Sales volume variance (TAC): 20 units × (£100 − £50 − £15) = £700 A
(iii)   Sales volume variance (MC): 20 units × (£100 − £50) = £1,000 A

Conclusion   The sales price variance looks at how many units were sold, what we should have received for them and what we did receive for them. This can be expressed in one of two ways (whichever is the more convenient in view of the way data is presented):

Sales price variance

=   Actual sales × (actual selling price − standard selling price)

The sales volume variance shows the effect on profit of a change in sales volume. This effect depends on whether absorption or marginal costing is used.

Sales volume variance

=   (Actual sales volume − budgeted sales) × standard margin/unit

The 'margin' used in the calculation is:

- absorption costing − standard profit per unit
- marginal costing − standard contribution per unit

2   SALES MIX VARIANCE

2.1   Introduction

Where more than one product is sold, it is likely that each will have a different unit profit. If they are sold in a mix different from that budgeted, a sales mix variance will result. Even though the products are not substitutes, a change of sales mix may indicate a change in emphasis of selling effort by sales staff or marketing resources. This sales mix variance and a sales quantity variance are the two variances into which the sales volume variance can be split.

Example

Note: The example assumes an absorption costing system.

The Omega company sets the following sales budgets for three products:

			Budgeted profit £
A	400	units at a standard profit of £8	3,200
B	600	units at a standard profit of £6	3,600
C	1,000	units at a standard profit of £4	4,000
	2,000	units	£10,800

The company expects to sell A, B and C in the proportion of 4 : 6 : 10 respectively. Actual sales are achieved at the standard profit:

			Actual profit £
A	300	units @ £8	2,400
B	700	units @ £6	4,200
C	1,200	units @ £4	4,800
	2,200	units	£11,400

There are many different ways of determining the effect of any change in the sales mix i.e. the proportion of the total sales each product represents. The methods compared here rely on taking the actual total quantity sold and determining the quantity of each product that would have been sold had the standard mix been achieved.

278   COST ACCOUNTING SYSTEMS

2.2   Method

In this example any differences in selling price have been ignored. If products are sold for anything other than their standard selling price this variance should be calculated **separately** first. Thereafter the calculation of the sales volume variance can be done at a standard margin (profit, as here, or contribution) per unit. A tabular approach is strongly recommended, although other approaches will be shown.

Step 1   Set up a table with the following 3 pairs of columns.

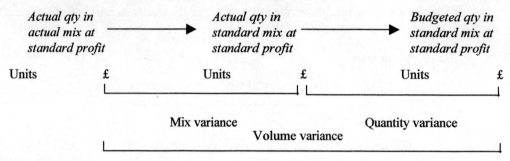

The previous figures show a favourable variance of £600 (£11,400 − £10,800) attributable to a change in sales volume which can be split into mix and quantity.

Step 2   Calculate the average standard profit per unit (which assumes standard mix and margins).

$$= \quad \frac{£10,800}{2,000} \quad = \quad £5.40$$

Step 3   Calculate the columns in the table

The table then shows:

	Actual qty in Actual mix at Standard profit		*Actual qty in standard mix at standard profit*		*Budgeted qty in standard mix at standard profit*	
	Units	£	Units	£	Units	£
A	300	2,400	440	3,520	400	3,200
B	700	4,200	660	3,960	600	3,600
C	1,200	4,800	1,100	4,400	1,000	4,000
	2,200	£11,400	2,200	£11,880	2,000	£10,800

at £5.40

The easiest way of finding the monetary amount in the middle pair of columns is to use the average standard profit per unit of £5.40 (beware of rounding errors - keep the average standard profit figure in the memory of your calculator).

Alternatively actual sales volume, 2,200 units, can be split in the standard mix (4:6:10) which would indicate sales of 440, 660 and 1,100. These sales volumes could then be evaluated using the three individual standard profit figures of £8, £6 and £4.

Step 4   Read off the variances.

				£	
Sales mix variance	=	£11,400 – £11,880	=	480	A
Sales quantity variance	=	£11,880 – £10,800	=	1,080	F
Sales volume variance	=	£11,400 – £10,800	=	£600	F

The mix variance will be favourable if more products with a higher profit per unit are sold in place of products with a lower profit per unit i.e. in this case the proportion of B and C, which have a lower profit per unit has been increased whereas A, which yields a higher profit per unit, has been reduced. Hence an overall adverse mix variance.

2.3   Other methods of calculation

There are many different methods of calculating the sales mix variance, including various methods of splitting it between products, bases for valuation (profit, contribution, sales value) etc.

You may expect to have to perform the above calculations for a firm using standard marginal costing (in which case you would use standard contribution per unit rather than standard profit). You may not be given any cost data about the products (in which case you could only carry out the calculations on the basis of standard revenue). Whether it is profit, contribution or revenue, the method of calculation remains the same.

Some authors suggest methods of calculation that attempt to split the mix variance between products. Some of these methods are illogical and misleading, all of them are confusing, and none are required by this particular examiner. The whole issue of splitting mix variances is pointless and, fortunately, your examiner has recognised that.

As if there weren't enough ways already of finding sales mix variances, other approaches are often discussed. Sales mix variances have been calculated by standardising the units sold. There may be circumstances where the prices are so different (e.g. transistor radios and colour TVs) that it would be inappropriate to base the comparison on units. Instead the sales mix may be found by standardising it in terms of £ value of sales, rather than unit sales. Profit per unit would then be replaced by profit to sales ratios.

2.4   Usefulness of the sales mix variance

Variances are calculated for the purpose of control. Managers are provided with a variance analysis of their areas of responsibility so that they can improve their decisions. The sales mix variance must be judged by this objective.

Two situations are possible:

(a)   The manager is responsible for two or more products which are to some extent substitutes for each other e.g. ranges of cheap and expensive cosmetics. Since the mix variance represents shifts in demand between the product ranges, it has significance. As stated before, it is even relevant for non-substitutes.

(b)   The manager is responsible for one line of products; other managers are responsible for other totally different product lines. In this situation, to provide a product manager with a mix variance when he can control only one product is meaningless.

2.5   Activity

From the following information provide a comprehensive sales variance analysis:

		Product X	Product Y	Product Z
Budget:				
	Sales price	£20	£20	£10
	Cost	£10	£15	£8
	Units	100	700	200
	Total profit	£1,000	£3,500	£400
Actual:				
	Sales price	£21	£24	£7
	Units sold	200	700	100

2.6   Activity solution

Sales price variance

((actual sales volume × standard selling price per unit) – actual sales revenue)

Product			£	
X	(200 × £20 – 200 × £21)	=	200	F
Y	(700 × £20 – 700 × £24)	=	2,800	F
Z	(100 × £10 – 100 × £7)	=	300	A
			£2,700	F

Sales volume variance - split into mix and quantity

	Actual qty in actual mix at standard margin			Actual qty in standard mix at standard margin			Budgeted qty in standard mix at standard margin	
	Units	£		Units	£		Units	£
X	200	2,000						
Y	700	3,500		at £4.90				
Z	100	200						
	1,000	£5,700		1,000	£4,900		1,000	£4,900

WORKINGS

Budgeted profit	=	£1,000 + £3,500 + £400	=	£4,900
Average standard profit/unit	=	£4,900 ÷ 1,000	=	£4.90

Analysis

				£	
Sales mix variance	=	£5,700 – £4,900	=	800	(F)
Sales quantity variance	=	£4,900 – £4,900	=	-	
Sales volume variance	=	£5,700 – £4,900	=	£800	(F)

2.7   Sales variance analysis - a summary

The size of each of the following variances will remain the same whichever method or approach is adopted:

(a)   selling price variance;
(b)   sales volume profit variance.

The volume variance can be sub-divided into quantity and mix variances where there is more than one product involved and products are to some extent interchangeable. If the concept of the standard mix is used to calculate these, it can be based on either:

(a)   the physical units in the budget; or
(b)   the sales value of products in the budget.

Each will lead to different mix and quantity variances, but in each case they will net to the same result (the volume profit variance).

The most efficient method of calculation expected in your exam is to **first** calculate the sales price variance, then produce a table with all quantities evaluated at standard margin:

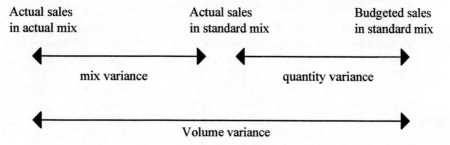

3   CAUSES AND INTER-RELATIONSHIPS

3.1   General causes of sales variance

Sales variances might be the results of the four general causes of variances mentioned in an earlier chapter:

(a)   bad budgeting;
(b)   bad measurement, recording;
(c)   random factors;
(d)   operational factors.

It is to be hoped that the second was not responsible for either sales volume or sales price - hopefully sales are properly recorded. Similarly the sales price variance is unlikely to be the result of random influences on a business, since selling price is controllable by the organisation making the sale.

3.2   Specific causes

The likely causes of sales volume variances include:

(a)   change in sales price;
(b)   additional advertising;
(c)   change in the nature of the competition for the product or service;
(d)   change in available production.

Typical reasons why a firm might wish to change a selling price from the budgeted figure include:

(a)   reducing price to stimulate demand;
(b)   increasing price since the market was thought to be buoyant (or costs rose)
(c)   responding to price challenges in a price war;
(d)   bulk discounts for unexpectedly large sales volumes.

3.3   Inter-relationships between sales price and volume

The specific causes of sales price and volume variances above are inevitably inter-linked. In most circumstances, if the price of goods or services is raised demand is likely to fall, and vice versa. There are exceptions to the rule, occasionally a firm will raise prices and demand will rise either because customers equate the higher price with better quality or, in general, customers in a different market (a different type of customer) are attracted to buy.

The topic of the link between price and demand, particularly as illustrated by 'demand curves', is discussed in a later chapter.

3.4   Inter-relationship between sales and cost variances

It was said earlier that a potential cause of a sales price variance was a change in the input costs. Some firms will use a pricing policy known as 'cost plus pricing', the price put on goods or services is what they cost plus a fixed mark-up. Thus if costs rise, the selling price rises. This may not always be possible and may not always be wise, but it does occur.

4   CHAPTER SUMMARY

This chapter has explained the calculation and interpretation of sales variances. The simple price and volume variances have been illustrated and the split of a volume variance into a sales mix and quantity shown.

5   SELF TEST QUESTIONS

5.1   How should a sales volume variance be calculated? (1.5)

5.2   What working enables a sales volume variance to be split between mix and quantity? (2.2)

5.3   When does a sales mix variance provide managers with useful information and when might it not? (2.4)

5.4   What might be a cause of an adverse sales volume variance? (3.2)

6   MULTIPLE CHOICE QUESTIONS

6.1   J Ltd operates a standard cost accounting system. The following information has been extracted from its standard cost card and budgets:

Budgeted sales volume	5,000 units
Budgeted selling price	£10.00 per unit
Standard variable cost	£5.60 per unit
Standard total cost	£7.50 per unit

If it used a standard marginal cost accounting system and its actual sales were 4,500 units at a selling price of £12.00, its sales volume variance would be:

A £1,250 adverse.
B £2,200 adverse.
C £2,250 adverse.
D £3,200 adverse.

6.2 P Ltd has the following data relating to its budgeted sales for October 20X7:

Budgeted sales	£100,000
Budgeted selling price per unit	£8.00
Budgeted contribution per unit	£4.00
Budgeted profit per unit	£2.50

During October 20X7, actual sales were 11,000 units for a sales revenue of £99,000.

P Ltd uses an absorption costing system.

The sales variances reported for October 20X7 were:

	Price £	Volume £
A	11,000 F	3,750 A
B	11,000 F	6,000 A
C	11,000 A	6,000 A
D	12,500 F	12,000 A

7 PRACTICE QUESTION

7.1 HS Buildings Ltd

HS Buildings Ltd fabricates, assembles and sells a range of wooden buildings for use as garden sheds, home offices, sun lounges, etc. After several years of successful sales at home, the company has now developed sufficient export business to merit two sales managers, UK and export, who report to the operations manager. Overall sales performance is the responsibility of the operations manager, individual UK or export sales are the responsibility of the two sales managers.

The budget for 20X8 showed the following:

	UK	Export	Total
Buildings sold	300	100	400
Average selling price	£7,500	£8,000	
Average cost	£5,000	£6,000	

Actual results were as follows:

Buildings sold	320	90	410
Average selling price	£7,400	£8,200	
Average cost	£5,100	£6,100	

An analysis of sales performance is needed for presentation to the board of HS Buildings Ltd.

Required:

(a)   Calculate the sales variances that assess the performance of the two individual sales managers.

(6 marks)

(b)   Calculate the sales variances that assess the sales performance of the operations manager.

(6 marks)

(c)   Comment on why you have produced different variances in (a) and (b) and on possible causes of the variances.   **(8 marks)**

(Total: 20 marks)

8   ANSWERS TO MULTIPLE CHOICE QUESTIONS

8.1   Standard contribution/unit = £10.00 − £5.60 = £4.40
Volume difference = 5,000 − 4,500 = 500 units.

Variance = 500 × £4.40 = £2,200 Adverse.

The correct answer is **B.**

8.2

	£
Actual sales revenue	99,000
Expected revenue from sales:	
11,000 units × £8.00	88,000
Selling price variance	11,000 (F)

Since an absorption costing system is used any sales volume difference will be valued using budgeted (i.e. standard) profit per unit.

	Units
Budgeted sales £100,000/£8.00 =	12,500
Actual sales	11,000
Shortfall	1,500

1,500 units shortfall × £2.50/unit = £3,750 (A)

Answer is **A.**

9   ANSWER TO PRACTICE QUESTION

9.1   HS Buildings Ltd

(a)   Sales price and volume variances

(i)   UK sales

Sales price variance = 320 × (£7,400 − £7,500) = £32,000 A
Sales volume variance = (320 − 300) × (£7,500 − £5,000) = £50,000 F

(ii)   Export sales

Sales price variance = 90 × (£8,200 − £8,000) = £18,000 F
Sales volume variance = (£90 − 100) × (£8,000 − £6,000) = £20,000 A

(b)   Sales price, mix and quantity

Sales price variance = £32,000 (Adverse) + £18,000 (Favourable) = £14,000 A
Sales volume variance = £50,000 (Favourable) + £20,000 (Adverse) = £30,000 F

Analysis

Budgeted profit

=	$300 \times (£7,500 - £5,000) + 100 \times (£8,000 - £6,000)$	
=	$(300 \times £2,500) + (100 \times £2,000)$	= £950,000

Average standard profit

=	£950,000 ÷ 400
=	£2,375

	Actual sales in actual mix at standard profit		Actual sales in standard mix at standard profit		Budgeted sales in standard mix at standard profit	
	Units	£'000	Units	£'000	Units	£'000
UK	320	800				
Exp	90	180	@ £2,375			
	410	980	410	973.75	400	950

Mix variance
£6,250 (Fav)

Quantity variance
£23,750 (Fav)

Volume
£30,000 (Fav)

(c)   **Comment**

The sales manager's variances had to be those related to their market alone. Given the information available that would be just price and volume variances. It is worth noting that the question talks of a range of buildings sold and average standard selling prices. It would be useful to calculate mix and quantity variances for the sales managers to see whether they were selling the correct mix from their range of buildings.

The operational manager is responsible for controlling both of the two sales managers and their performance. He may also be responsible for the fabrication of sheds and therefore controls the supply to the two markets. In these circumstances a volume variance for total sales and an analysis that shows the split of these sales between the two markets would be useful. Again, an alternative mix variance between the various products in the range could be calculated for overall sales.

The possible causes of the variances are:

Sales price

(i)   Pressure on margins due to competition in the UK market.

(ii)   Increases in costs being passed on to export customers.

(iii)   Change in marketing policy to cut prices to stimulate growth in sales overall.

Sales volume

(i)   Original UK budget understated so as to show subsequent excellent sales effort.
(ii)   Original export budget overstated so as to justify appointment of sales manager.
(iii)   General difficulty in making any sales forecasts.

Sales mix

(i)   Additional effort made to sell in the UK due to the higher margins there.
(ii)   Extra effort given to producing for the UK market to earn higher profits.
(iii)   Lack of understanding of the export market and lack of interest because of its lower margins.

Chapter 19

RECONCILIATION

PATHFINDER INTRODUCTION

This chapter covers the following elements of the CAT Official Teaching Guide. At the end of this chapter you should have learned these teaching guide elements thoroughly.

Session 19
Reconciliation
Syllabus reference l

- Produce statements reconciling budgeted and actual profit in absorption and marginal costing systems
- Produce reports explaining the key features of variances and making recommendations for management action.

Putting the chapter in context

Having spent three chapters showing the variances that are calculated to explain the difference between budgeted and actual costs and revenues, we now put them all together to produce a formal statement reconciling budgeted and actual profit. It may be worth reviewing that approach to the presentation of variances before studying this chapter which sets out the reconciliation of budgeted and actual profits using 'operating statements'.

As with much of management accounting, where the same ideas is often given several names and the same name used to describe several different ideas, there is potential for confusion here. However if asked to produce an operating statement, the most likely format would start with budgeted profit and reach actual profit by means of variances. If asked to produce such a statement, the most likely description would be an operating statement.

1 RECONCILIATION OF BUDGET AND ACTUAL PROFITS - ABSORPTION COSTING

1.1 Absorption costing pro-forma operating statement

The purpose of calculating variances is to identify the different effects of each item of cost/income on expected profit. These variances are summarised in a reconciliation statement, an **'operating statement'**.

The format of the operating statement for a firm using absorption costing will have budgeted profit at the top, then sales variances (split volume and price) then cost variances (split into the various variances for materials, labour, variable and fixed overheads) and finally actual profit. In summarised form it will show:

	£
Budgeted profit (1)	X
Sales volume variance (2)	X
Standard profit on actual sales (3)	X
Sales price variance	X
Profit before cost variances	X

Cost variances (4)			Adv £	Fav £	
Materials	-	price	X		
		usage		X	
Labour	-	rate		X	
		efficiency	X		
Variable overheads	-	rate	X		
		efficiency	X		
Fixed overheads	-	expenditure		X	
		volume	X		
			£X	£X	X
Actual profit					£X

Notes

(1)   Budgeted profit = budgeted sales × standard profit

(2)   Sales volume variance = (actual sales – budgeted sales) × standard profit

(3)   Standard profit on sales = actual sales × standard profit (this third line is a very useful subtotal to produce)

(4)   It is useful to split cost variances between favourable and adverse (done at random here) since it makes it clearer where performance has been satisfactory and where it has not. It also makes the addition easier.

1.2   Activity

The following example illustrates the variances covered in the previous chapters.

Chapel ELF Ltd manufactures a chemical protective called Rustnot. The following standard costs apply for the production of 100 cylinders:

		£
Materials	500 kgs @ 80p per kg	400
Labour	5 hours @ £6 per hour	30
Fixed overheads	5 hours @ £4 per hour	20
Total cost per 100 cylinders (£4.50 per cylinder)		£450

The monthly production/sales budget is 10,000 cylinders. Selling price = £6 per cylinder.

For the month of November the following production and sales information is available:

Produced/sold	10,600 cylinders
Sales value	£63,000
Material purchased and used 53,200 kgs	£42,500
Labour 510 hours	£3,100
Fixed overheads	£2,200

You are required to prepare an operating statement for November detailing all the variances.

1.3   Activity solution

	£
Budgeted profit (10,000 cylinders) (a)	15,000
Add: Sales volume variance (f) (Favourable)	900
Standard profit on actual sales (10,600 cylinders) (c)	15,900
Sales price variance (f) (Adverse)	(600)
	15,300

Less: cost variances (g) – (i)

			Adv. £	Fav. £	
Materials	-	price		60	
		usage	160		
Labour	-	rate	40		
		efficiency		120	
Fixed overhead	-	expenditure	200		
		volume		120	
			£400	£300	
					100
Actual profit (b)					£15,200

WORKINGS

		£	£
(a)	**Budgeted profit**		
	10,000 cylinders @ (£6 - £4.50 = £1.50)		15,000
(b)	**Actual profit**		
	Sales		63,000
	Less: Materials	42,500	
	Labour	3,100	
	Fixed overheads	2,200	
			47,800
			15,200
(c)	**Actual units/standard profit**		
	10,600 × £1.50		15,900
(d)	**Standard hours**		
	10,600 cylinders × 0.05 hours = 530 hours		
(e)	**Budgeted hours**		
	10,000 × 0.05.= 500 hours		

Variances

(f)   **Sales**

The standard selling price is £6 per cylinder. Actual sales were 10,600 cylinders for £63,000. If the actual cylinders sold had been sold at the budgeted selling price of £6 then sales would have been

$$10,600 \times £6 = £63,600.$$

Thus the difference in selling price resulted in a lower sales value by £600. This is an adverse sales price variance.

The budgeted volume was 10,000 cylinders costing £4.50 each. At the budgeted selling price of £6 each this is a budgeted profit of £1.50 per cylinder.

Actual sales volume was 10,600 cylinders, 600 more than budget. These extra 600 cylinders will increase profit by

$$600 \times £1.50 = £900.$$

This is a favourable sales volume variance.

(g)   **Raw materials**

The standard price of the raw material is £0.80 per kg the actual price per kg was £42,500/53,200 = £0.79887.

The price variance was:

(Std price – actual price) actual usage
(£0.80 – £0.79887) 53,200 = £60 F

Each 100 cylinders should use 500 kgs of material. Therefore the 10,600 cylinders produced should use:

$$10,600 \times 500 \text{ kg}/100 = 53,000 \text{ kgs}$$

The actual usage was 53,200 kgs. These additional 200 kgs of material have a value (using standard prices) of

$$200 \text{ kgs} \times £0.80 = £160 \text{ A}.$$

Thus (std usage – actual usage) std price = (53,000 – 53,200) £0.80.

This is an adverse material usage variance.

(h)   **Labour**

The standard labour rate is £6 per hour. The actual labour hours were 510 and cost £3,100 or £6.07843 per hr.

Rate variance

(Std rate – actual rate) actual hrs = (£6 – £6.07843) 510 = £40 A.

Each 100 cylinders should take 5 hours to produce. The actual production was 10,600 cylinders so these should have taken

$$10,600 \times 5/100 = 530 \text{ hours}$$

Actual hours were 510, a saving of 20 hours. These hours (valued at the standard rate) are worth

$$20 \times £6 = £120.$$

Thus (standard hrs produced − actual worked) standard rate
(530 − 510) £6 = £120 F.

This is a favourable labour efficiency variance.

(i) **Fixed overheads**

The standard fixed overhead cost is £20 per 100 cylinders. Monthly production is budgeted at 10,000 cylinders. Therefore the budgeted fixed overhead cost is

$$10,000 \times £20/100 = £2,000.$$

The actual cost was £2,200. The extra cost of £200 is an adverse fixed overhead expenditure variance.

But the actual production was 10,600 cylinders, 600 more than budgeted. This extra volume of 600 units (valued at the standard absorption rate of £20/100 units) is

$$600 \times £20/100 = £120 \text{ or (budget std hrs − standard hrs produced) FORR}$$
$$= (500 − 530) £4 = £120 \text{ F}$$

This is a favourable fixed overhead volume variance.

2 RECONCILIATIONS UNDER STANDARD MARGINAL COSTING

2.1 Two formats

The previous example was based on a standard absorption costing system and the operating statement drawn up along standard absorption costing lines. If a firm uses standard marginal costing alternative presentations are required of which there are two:

(a) Starting from budgeted contribution
(showing variances to reconcile to actual contribution and then actual profit - this is probably the most logical and easy to understand).

(b) Starting from budgeted profit
(you may have to produce one of these statements - it requires a little more thought).

2.2 Comparison of standard absorption and marginal costing

The principle of variance calculation is very similar, however there are a few differences.

(a) The sales volume variance must now be in terms of standard **contribution** per unit rather than standard profit.

(b) The **only** fixed overhead variance now is the expenditure variance.

There is also the possibility that profit figures will differ.

2.3 Activity

In the example of Chapel ELF Ltd, actual profit using absorption costing was £15,200.

What would be the reported profit using marginal costing?

2.4   Activity solution

Production and sales levels were the same, since stock levels didn't change, so the profit using marginal costing would also be £15,200.

2.5   Marginal costing pro-forma operating statement

If starting from budgeted contribution, the operating statement would show:

	£
Budgeted contribution (1)	X
Sales volume variance (2)	X
Standard contribution on actual sales (3)	X
Sales price variance	X
Contribution before cost variances	X

Variable cost variances

		Adv	Fav	
		£	£	
Materials, labour, variable overheads				
(analysed as before)	X	X	X	
Actual contribution (4)				X
Fixed costs				
Budgeted (5)			X	
Expenditure variance			X	
Actual				(X)
Actual profit				£X

Notes

(1)   Budgeted contribution = Budgeted sales × standard contribution/unit.

(2)   Sales volume variance = (Budgeted sales – actual sales) × standard contribution/unit

(3)   Contribution on actual sales = actual sales × standard contribution/unit.

(4)   The difference between actual contribution and actual profit is actual fixed overheads; these have been shown in three lines (budgeted, difference between budgeted and actual - the expenditure variance – and actual).

(5)   The alternative format deducts budgeted fixed overheads at the top of the statement (budgeted contribution – budgeted fixed costs = budgeted profit).

2.6   Activity

Produce a reconciliation of budgeted contribution and actual profit for Chapel ELF in November using the data supplied earlier.

2.7   Activity solution

		£
Budgeted contribution (10,000 × [£6 − £4.30])		17,000
Sales volume variance ([10,600 − 10,000] × £1.70)		1,020
Standard contribution on actual sales (10,600 × £1.70)		18,020
Sales price variance (as before)		(600)
Contribution before cost variances		17,420

Variable cost variances (as before)			Adv £	Fav £	
Materials	-	price		60	
		usage	160		
Labour	-	rate	40		
		efficiency		120	
			£200	£180	(20)

		£
Actual contribution (a)		17,400
Fixed costs		
Budgeted	2,000	
Expenditure variance (as before)	200	
Actual		2,200
Actual profit (as before)		£15,200

WORKINGS

(a)   Actual contribution = £63,000 − (£42,500 + £3,100) = £17,400

(b)   Standard contribution/unit = £6 − (£4 + £0.3) = £1.70

2.8   Alternative presentation

As indicated earlier, the only difference is that the statement starts with budgeted (marginal costing) profit. This means that fixed overheads are deducted at the top rather than the bottom of the statement. You may wish to try for yourself before checking with the statement below.

		£
Budgeted profit (£17,000 − £2,000)		15,000
Sales volume variance (600 × £1.70)		1,020
		16,020
Sales price variance		(600)
Profit before cost variances		15,420

Cost variances			Adv £	Fav £	
Materials	-	price		60	
		usage	160		
Labour	-	rate	40		
		efficiency		120	
Fixed overheads	-	expenditure	200		
			£400	£180	(220)

	£
Actual profit	£15,200

Conclusion   Operating statements are used to show the difference between budgeted and actual profit using variances.

The statements can be produced according to marginal or absorption costing conventions.

Under standard marginal costing there will be no fixed overhead volume variance and the sales volume variance is different from that calculated for absorption costing.

The conventional way of setting out a marginal costing operating statement is to start with budgeted contribution, although it is possible to start with budgeted profit.

At this stage it might be worth attempting the second of the two 'Practice Questions' at the end of the chapter.

3   CAUSES OF VARIANCES

3.1   Introduction

The calculation of variances is only the first stage. Management wants information to plan and control operations. It is not sufficient to know that a variance has arisen: we must try to establish why. The figures themselves do not provide the answers, but they point to some of the questions that should be asked.

Having discussed causes of variances in earlier chapters, you may wish to test yourself now.

3.2   Activity

Provide a short list of ideas for possible causes of each of the cost and sales (price and volume) variances studied so far.

3.3   Activity solution

Four general causes of variances are:

- bad budgeting;
- bad measurement or recording
- random factors
- operational factors.

Specific causes, most of which come under the fourth heading above, include:

(a)   Material price variance

This could be due to:

- different source of supply
- unexpected general price increase;
- alteration in quantity discounts;
- substitution of a different grade of material;
- standard set at mid-year price so one would expect a favourable price variance in the early months and an adverse variance in the later months of the year.

(b)   Material usage variance

This could be due to:

- higher/lower incidence of scrap;
- alteration to product design;
- substitution of a different grade of material.

(c)   **Wages rate variance**

Possible causes:

- unexpected national wage award;
- overtime/bonus payments different from plan;
- substitution of a different grade of labour.

(d)   **Labour efficiency variance**

Possible causes:

- improvement in methods or working conditions;
- introduction of incentive scheme;
- substitution of a different grade of labour.

(e)   **Variable overhead variance**

Possible causes:

- unexpected price changes for overhead items;
- labour efficiency variances, (see above).

(f)   **Fixed overhead expenditure variance**

Possible causes:

- changes in prices relating to fixed overhead items e.g. rent increase;

- seasonal effects e.g. heat/light in winter. (This arises where the annual budget is divided into four equal quarters of thirteen equal four-weekly periods without allowances for seasonal factors. Over a whole year the seasonal effects would cancel out.)

(g)   **Fixed overhead volume**

Possible causes:

- change in production volume due to change in demand or alterations to stockholding policy;

- changes in productivity of labour or machinery;

- production lost through strikes, etc.

(h)   **Sales price variance**

Possible causes:

- unplanned price increase;
- unplanned price reduction e.g. to try and attract additional business.

(i)   **Sales volume variance**

This is obviously caused by a change in sales volume, which may be due to:

- unexpected fall in demand due to recession;
- additional demand attracted by reduced prices;
- failure to satisfy demand due to production difficulties.

3.4   Interdependence of variances

We have said that the cause of a particular variance may affect another variance in a corresponding or opposite way.

(a)   If supplies of a specified material are not available, this may lead to a favourable price variance (cheaper material used), an adverse usage variance (cheaper material caused more wastage), an adverse fixed overhead volume variance (production delayed while material was unavailable) and an adverse sales volume variance (unable to meet demand due to production difficulties).

(b)   A new improved machine becomes available which causes an adverse fixed overhead expenditure variance (because this machine is more expensive and depreciation is higher) offset by favourable wages efficiency and fixed overhead volume variances (higher productivity).

(c)   Workers trying to improve productivity (favourable labour efficiency variance) might become careless and waste more material (adverse material usage variance).

4   STANDARD COSTING AND INTERNAL REPORTING

4.1   Reporting back to managers

The control information reported back to managers at regular intervals is an important aspect of standard costing. This is the stage where managers are made aware of the effect of any deviations between the actual results and the pre-determined standards. Normally, variances should not come as a surprise to a manager as they only represent the monetary quantification of the effect on profits of any deviations that have occurred. A conscientious manager would have a number of his own sub-systems monitoring what is happening within his area of responsibility day-by-day or even hour-by-hour. These controls would normally be in terms of physical units (kg used, amount wasted, hours worked, hours idle etc.). The manager would have to make decisions on matters arising, all the time.

In reporting variances, the concept of **responsibility accounting** would normally be followed so a variance report to an individual manager should only include figures relating to his own area of responsibility i.e. within his area of control. If more figures are given, then they are usually reported in the form of 'for information only' as a help to a manager in seeing the total picture or context in which his figures arise.

Variance reporting associated with a standard costing system complies with the principle of **management by exception**. Variances represent deviations (or exceptions) between actuals and standards. By drawing the attention of management to the variances, the management accountant is concentrating on what is not going according to plan (standard) and highlighting the fact rather than producing masses of information about what is in line with what was expected. It is the former that is more likely to require management action than the latter.

The reporting frequency must be related to the particular needs of management. Monthly, weekly, daily or any other time period for variance reporting may be appropriate.

The amount of detail included in reports will vary according to the needs of management. As a guide, they should be in sufficient detail to motivate the individual manager to take the most appropriate action in all the circumstances. If a report lacks the required amount of detail, then an individual manager should request this from the management accountant.

4.2   Example of a report

Since most middle managers are only responsible for a small proportion of total costs and revenues, a full operating statement would be in appropriate.

A smaller report such as the following would suffice:

Machining department
Performance report for week ended 7 July 20X4

	Actual £	Standard £	Variance £	Comments
Controllable costs:				
Direct labour time	220	175	45 A	Idle time due to machine failure
Raw materials usage	120	110	10 A	No explanation
Repairs	50	20	30 A	Machine failure
Power consumption	40	50	10 F	Idle time due to machine failure
	£430	£355	£75 A	

The report may also show year to date figures.

4.3 Periodic reporting to top management

Since most middle managers are only responsible for a small proportion of total costs and revenues, a fully operating statement would be inappropriate. A smaller report such as the following would suffice.

(a) Top management is likely to be concerned only with significant variances. A form of exception reporting can be used, only specifying significant variances (the question of what is significant is considered later).

(b) It is not enough merely to report variances without some attempt to investigate their causes.

4.4 Example

The report might follow the lines shown previously or further explanations could be given as follows:

X Ltd – Profit and loss account for November 20X4

Ref. to notes		£	£
	Budgeted profit		17,500
	Loss of profit due to:		
(1)	Failure to achieve budgeted volume	2,100	
(2)	Wage rate variance	450	
(3)	Raw materials price variance	800	
	Sundry adverse variances not reported individually	700	
			4,050
			13,450
	Improved profit due to:		
(4)	Sales price increase	1,500	
(5)	Favourable labour efficiency variance	400	
	Sundry favourable variances not reported individually	300	
			2,200
	Actual profit for period		15,650

Comments on variances

(1)   Primarily due to credit restrictions imposed during October. See marketing department report dated 21 October 20X4.

(2)   Negotiated national pay increase.

(3)   Failure to anticipate effects of inflation when setting standards.

(4)   Agreed price increase due to higher raw material cost.

(5)   Badly set standard under review.

Note: the above comments are indications of the type of points that might be raised. In a real situation these would be enlarged and might well include recommendations for action.

5   STANDARD COSTING AND EXTERNAL REPORTING

5.1   Use of standard costs in ledger accounts

It was noted earlier that a special feature of standard costing was the use of standard cost figures in the ledger accounts. This procedure has the result that stocks and work in progress are generally carried at standard cost (depending on the treatment of material price variances). This poses two questions:
(a)   Are standard costs a proper basis for valuing stocks for external reporting?
(b)   If not, is their use in the ledgers still justified?

5.2   Example

The entries which would appear in the following ledger accounts of Chapel ELF Ltd (from the example earlier in this chapter) show how standard cost book-keeping applies in an integrated accounting system:

Raw material control a/c

	£		£
Creditors	42,500	Work-in-progress	42,560
Raw material price variance	60		
	£42,560		£42,560

Wages control a/c

	£		£
Cash	3,100	Wages rate variance	40
		Work in progress	3,060
	£3,100		£3,100

Work-in-progress control a/c

	£		£
Raw material control	42,560	Raw material usage variance	160
Wages control	3,060	Finished goods/Cost of sales	47,700
Labour efficiency variance	120		
Production overhead control	2,120		
	£47,860		£47,860

Production overhead control a/c

	£		£
Creditor	2,200	Expenditure variance	200
Fixed overhead volume		Work-in-progress	2,120
variance	120		
	£2,320		£2,320

Profit & Loss

	£		£
Cost of sales	47,700	Sales	63,000
Material usage variance	160	Material price variance	60
Wage rate variance	40	Labour efficiency variance	120
Overhead expenditure variance	200	Fixed overhead volume variance	120
Net profit	15,200		
	£63,300		£63,300

Alternative treatments of sales are possible, but a simplified approach has been used here.

5.3   Advantages of using standard costs in ledgers

There are three major advantages:

(a)   Bookkeeping is made simpler – the problems of similar stock items having different values is avoided.

(b)   Variances are automatically segregated without further work and without the possibility of discrepancies between financial and cost statements.

(c)   Experience shows that managers take variances more seriously if they are included in the financial accounts.

5.4   Importance of the types of standard used

Amongst the types of standard, **high but attainable** is the most generally useful (see below). From the point of view of stock valuation, the **attainable** suggests acceptability. However, the term 'high but attainable' obviously allows a degree of variation between the tight and loose standards. From a valuation point of view loose standards are preferable in that they represent the most realistic estimates. On the other hand, from a control point of view, tight standards, making only the minimum allowance for inefficiency, may be desirable.

5.5   Variances and stock valuations

Consider again the implications of raw materials price variance on raw materials stock value when the variance is calculated at purchase.

(a)   Adverse variance – standard cost lower than actual. Raw materials stocks carried at below actual cost, and difference written off as price variance in reporting period.

(b)   Favourable variance – standard cost higher than actual. Raw materials carried at above actual cost, and difference taken as a credit in current reporting period.

Similar analysis could be applied to all variances (remembering that work in progress and finished goods valuations must include conversion cost): adverse variances indicate conservative valuations, favourable variances inflated valuations.

Since one of the fundamental accounting concepts specified in SSAP 2 is prudence, the usual treatment is to make no adjustments for favourable variances, but to write off adverse variances so as to reduce stock values.

Conclusion   It is common, and generally accepted, to use standard costs for stock valuation (see, for example, paras 11 & 12 of SSAP 9). This is based on the view that all methods of stock valuation are to some extent arbitrary and, provided standard costs are realistic, they represent a reasonable valuation basis. The key word, however, is **realistic**: the test lies in the variances that arise. The usual approach to variances has been indicated above. However, any large variances suggest inadequacies in the standards as a basis for valuation and will require further investigation.

6   CHAPTER SUMMARY

This chapter has shown how budgeted and actual profit can be reconciled using both absorption and marginal costing.

The causes of variances have then been revised and the importance of including the causes as part of the reporting process discussed.

7   SELF TEST QUESTIONS

7.1   What figure is produced if you adjust budgeted profit by the sales volume variance? (1.1)

7.2   Would an adverse variance increase or decrease profit? (1.3)

7.3   How is a fixed overhead volume variance found? (1.3)

7.4   In what ways are absorption and marginal costing operating statements similar, and in what ways are they different? (2.2)

7.5   How, apart from the initial figure, does a standard marginal costing operating statement beginning with budgeted profit differ from one beginning with budgeted contribution? (2.8)

8   PRACTICE QUESTIONS

8.1   Department 7

Shown below is the previous month's overhead expenditure and activity, both budget and actual, for department 7 in a manufacturing company:

	Month's budget	Month's actual
Production (units)	8,000	8,400
	£	£
Fixed overheads:		
Salaries	6,750	6,400
Maintenance	3,250	3,315
	10,000	9,715

Variable overheads:		
Power	17,600	20,140
Consumable materials	6,000	5,960
Indirect labour	4,400	4,480
Total overheads	£38,000	£40,295

The budgeted overheads shown above are based upon the anticipated activity of 8,000 units and it should be assumed that the department's budgeted overhead expenditure and activity occur evenly throughout the year. Variable overheads vary with units produced. Each unit takes two standard hours to produce.

Required:

(a)   Calculate the following variances incurred by the department during the previous month assuming the firm uses an absorption costing system:

(i)   Fixed overhead volume variance;
(ii)   Fixed overhead expenditure variance; and
(iii)   Variable overhead total cost variance.

(9 marks)

(b)   Draft a marginal costing statement which will assist management in controlling the department's overheads - tabulating, for each element of cost, budget, actual and variance.

(7 marks)

(c)   Explain carefully why the difference between budgeted and actual activity will cause a change in the anticipated profit by the amount of the volume variance calculated in (a) above.

(4 marks)
(Total: 20 marks)

8.2   Gunge

The standard cost per gallon of Gunge, the only product manufactured by Chemit plc, is shown below:

	£
Direct material (4kg @ £3/kg)	12
Direct labour (5 hours @ £4/hour)	20
Variable overhead	5
Fixed overhead	15
Standard cost per gallon	£52

The standard selling price of Gunge is £60/gallon and the budgeted quantity to be produced and sold in each period is 10,000 gallons. It may be assumed that variable overheads vary directly with the number of gallons produced.

The actual results achieved during period 4 were:

	£	£
Sales (9,500 gallons)		588,500
Cost of sales:		
Direct material (37,000 kg)	120,000	
Direct labour (49,000 hours)	200,000	
Variable overhead	47,000	
Fixed overhead	145,000	
		512,000
Profit		£76,500

There were no stocks of raw materials, work-in-progress or finished goods stocks at the beginning or end of the period.

Required:

(a)   Calculate the relevant manufacturing cost variances for period 4; and   **(12 marks)**

(b)   Calculate the appropriate sales variances for period 4, showing the effect on budgeted profit of actual sales being different from those specified, and prepare a statement reconciling the budgeted and the actual profit for the period showing total variances only for costs.   **(8 marks)**
(Total: 20 marks)

9   ANSWERS TO PRACTICE QUESTIONS

9.1   Department 7

(a)   **Calculation of variances**

(F = Favourable; A = Adverse)

Fixed overhead volume variance

	Budget		*Actual*	*Variance*
	8,000	-	8,400	$= 400 \text{ units} \times \dfrac{(£6,750 + £3,250)}{8,000}$

$$= 400 \times £1.25 = £500 \text{ (F)}$$

or (budget std hrs − standard hours produced) FORR
$(16,000 - 16,800)$ £0.625/hr = £500 F

Fixed overhead expenditure variance

Budget	*Actual*	*Variance*
£	£	
6,750	6,400	
3,250	3,315	
£10,000	£9,715 =	£285 (F)

Variable overhead total cost variance

Flexed budget	*Actual*	*Variance*
£	£	
17,600	20,140	
6,000	5,960	
4,400	4,480	
$28,000 \times \dfrac{8,400}{8,000} = 29,400$	30,580	£1,180 (A)

(***Tutorial note:*** Total overhead cost variance = standard overhead cost of actual production − actual overhead cost = £38,000 × (8,400/8,000) − £40,295 = £395(A), i.e. £785 − £1,180).

(b)   **Marginal costing statement for control of department overheads**

	Budget £	Actual £	Variance £
Fixed overhead:			
Salaries	6,750	6,400	350 (F)
Maintenance	3,250	3,315	65 (A)
Total	£10,000	£9,715	£285 (F)
Variable overhead:			
Power $17,600 \times \dfrac{8,400}{8,000} = 18,480$		20,140	1,660 (A)
Consumable materials $6,000 \times \dfrac{8,400}{8,000} = 6,300$		5,960	340 (F)
Indirect labour $4,400 \times \dfrac{8,400}{8,000} = 4,620$		4,480	140 (F)
Total	£29,400	£30,580	£1,180 (A)
Overall total	£39,400	£40,295	£895 (A)

(c)   **Explanation of the volume variance**

In this case the business initially uses a standard absorption costing system which involves absorbing fixed as well as variable overhead to production and therefore stock is valued inclusive of fixed production overhead.

As fixed overheads are, by definition, unaffected by changes in volume of output, an over-recovery will arise where volume increases above budget - called here a fixed overhead volume variance.

The way in which profit is affected depends on the relationship between production and sales. Firstly, if production increases but sales volume remains in line with budget, there will be an increase in the amount of fixed overhead included in stock equal to the amount of the fixed overhead volume variance. Hence profit would be higher by that amount.

Secondly, if sales and production increase by the same amount, then the overall effect of the increase will be an increase in contribution amounting to the increase in sales volume multiplied by the contribution per unit. In an absorption costing system this contribution is shown as two separate items i.e.

(1)   sales volume variance valued at the standard profit per unit; and
(2)   fixed overhead volume variance valued at the standard fixed overhead per unit.

Hence in this second situation where sales volume increases, profit increases by more than the amount of the fixed overhead volume variance.

9.2   Gunge

(a)   Direct material:

Price variance

(Std price − actual price) actual usage
(£3 − £3.24324) 37,000 = £9,000 A.

Usage variance

(Std usage − actual usage) std price
(38,000 − 37,000) £3 = £3,000 F.

Direct labour

Rate variance

(Std rate − actual rate) actual hours
(£4 − £4.08163) 49,000 = £4,000 A.

Efficiency variance

(Std hours produced − actual hours) std rate
(47,500 − 49,000) £4 = £6,000 A.

Variable overhead variance

Standard hours produced × standard VORR

	£
47,500 × £1 per std hr =	47,500
Actual incurred	47,000
Variance	£500 F

Fixed overhead variance

Standard hours produced × FORR

	£
47,500 × £3 per std hr	142,500
Actual fixed cost	145,000
Variance	£2,500 A

(b)   Sales and profit performance

(i)   **Sales variances**

(Std selling price − actual selling price) actual volume
(£60 − £61.94738) 9,500   }   =   Price variance £18,500 F

(Budget volume − actual volume) std margin =
(10,000 − 9,500) £8   }   =   Volume variance £4,000 A

(ii)   **Profit reconciliation statement - Period 4**

	£	£
Budgeted profit		80,000
Sales volume variance		4,000 A
Standard profit on actual volume sold		76,000
Sales price variance		18,500 F
		94,500
Cost variances: Materials	6,000 A	
Labour	10,000 A	
Variable overhead	500 F	
Fixed overhead	2,500 A	
		18,000 A
Actual profit		£76,500

◈ FOULKS*lynch*

Chapter 20

DATA COLLECTION AND INTERPRETATION

PATHFINDER INTRODUCTION

This chapter covers the following elements of the CAT Official Teaching Guide. At the end of this chapter you should have learned these teaching guide elements thoroughly.

Session 20
Data collection and interpretation
Syllabus reference n, o

- Describe quantitative and qualitative data and information
- Describe internal and external sources of data
- Describe the relevance and limitations of data sources and collection techniques
- Extract and interpret key information from tables and charts

Putting the chapter in context

The first 19 chapters have shown how cost information is recorded or analysed by cost accounting systems. The final 6 chapters explain how information is collected and how it could be presented and analysed to maximise its use to the business. This chapter covers obtaining data and how it can be displayed in tables.

1 DATA AND INFORMATION

1.1 Quantitative and qualitative data

Not all data can be numerically measured.

Definition   **Quantitative** data is capable of being measured numerically e.g. the time taken to complete a journey.

Definition   **Qualitative** data is not capable of being measured numerically but reflects a distinguishing characteristic e.g. male or female, was a service satisfactory or not.

1.2 Discrete and continuous data

Definition   Data is said to be **discrete** if it can only take on specific, fixed values e.g. the number of people in a room can be 60 but you cannot have 60.3 people.

Definition   **Continuous** data can however take on any numerical value e.g. a person's height or weight can be measured to any degree of accuracy.

1.3 Primary and secondary data

Data has to be collected and summarised in the form required by the persons requesting the data; however not all data will be specifically collected for the purpose for which it is being used.

Definition   **Primary** data is expressly collected for a particular enquiry, for example by observation or interviews.

Definition   **Secondary** data is collected for some enquiry other than the one of immediate interest. For example, data collected by a government department for national statistics becomes secondary data when used by a company for an enquiry of its own.

Primary data is usually more difficult, more costly and more time consuming to collect; but secondary data should be used with caution as it may not really be appropriate to the enquiry, for example, it may not cover the exact time period required.

1.4   Raw and aggregated data

The terms primary and secondary data are also used to distinguish between raw data that has not been analysed and that data after it has been sorted, categorised, grouped, in the ways that will be described later in this chapter.

Definition   **Raw data** is in its most original form as collected and before being processed, hence any analysis based on this data should be more accurate than that based on data which has been aggregated.

Definition   **Aggregated data** is formed by separate units of information being collected together as a whole i.e. data which has been summarised in some way.

1.5   Information

Data is often difficult to use or interpret in its raw form, if must be turned into useful information.

Definition   **Information** is data that has been classified aggregated and summarised.

2   SOURCES OF DATA

2.1   Internal sources of data

If a business requires data about its own operations then this data must come from internal sources. For example the number of defective products per batch of production can only be discovered from samples of the organisations batches.

2.2   External sources of data

There is a wealth of published statistical data covering many aspects of the nation's economy: population, manpower, trade, agriculture, price levels, capital issues, and similar matters.

The primary purpose of this data is to provide information for economic planning at the national level. The data serves the secondary purpose of providing industry with useful background information for deciding on future policies such as raising new finance or recruiting specialised labour. The data is only published in general terms, e.g. for a particular industry or geographical area.

The following list shows some of the main sources.

Title	Frequency of publication	Main topics covered
Employment Gazette	Monthly	Earnings, basic wage rates, unemployment, indices of wholesale and retail prices.
British Business	Weekly	Wholesale and retail prices, production for specific sectors of industry, capital expenditure.
National Income and Expenditure Blue Book	Annually	Personal income and expenditure, gross national product.
Financial Statistics	Monthly	Money supply, interest rates, hire purchase liabilities, building societies.
Bank of England Quarterly Bulletin	Quarterly	} Both summarise many of the above statistics.
Monthly Digest of Statistics	Monthly	
Economic Trends	Monthly	} Similar coverage to Monthly Digest, but given information stretching back over a long period.
Annual Abstract of Statistics	Annually	
Price Indices for Current Cost Accounting	Annually, but updated by monthly supplement	Retail price index, also industry specific and asset specific price indices.

All the above publications relate to the UK. Publications concerned with statistics relating to the EEC include *European Economy Annual Statistical Yearbook*, *Eurostat* (monthly) and *OECD Main Economic Indicators* (monthly). Information on the World Economy is available from the United Nations (*Demographic Yearbook* and *Statistical Yearbook*), the International Labour Organisation (*Yearbook of Labour Statistics*) and UNESCO (*Statistical Yearbook*).

Conclusion   Internal data is collected by the organisation. External sources are readily available outside the organisation.

3   POPULATION AND SAMPLE

3.1   Introduction

The purpose of sampling is to gain as much information as possible about the population by observing only a small proportion of that population, i.e. by observing the sample.

Definition   The term **population** means all the items under consideration in a particular enquiry. A **sample** is a group of items drawn from that population. The population may consist of items such as metal bars, invoices, packets of tea, etc.; it need not be people.

Definition   A **sampling frame** is a list of all the members of the population. It is used to select the sample. For example, if the population is electors, the sampling frame is the electoral register.

For example, to ascertain which television programmes are most popular, a sample of the total viewing public is interviewed and, based on their replies, programmes are listed in order of popularity with all viewers.

3.2   Reasons for sampling

There are three main reasons why sampling is necessary:

(a)   The whole population may not be known.

(b)   Even if the population is known the process of testing every item can be extremely costly in time and money.

For example, checking the weight of every packet of tea coming off a production line would be a lengthy process.

(c)   The items being tested may be completely destroyed in the process.

In order to check the lifetime of an electric light bulb it is necessary to leave the bulb burning until it breaks and is of no further use.

There are a variety of different methods of sampling.

3.3   Random sampling

A simple random sample is defined as a sample taken in such a way that every member of the population has an equal chance of being selected. To achieve this, every item in the population must be numbered in order. If a sample of, say 20, items is required then 20 numbers from a table of random numbers are taken and the corresponding items are extracted from the population to form the sample, e.g. in selecting a sample of invoices for an audit. Since the invoices are already numbered this method can be applied with the minimum of difficulty.

This method has obvious limitations when either the population is extremely large or, in fact, not known. The following methods are more applicable in these cases.

3.4   Systematic sampling

If the population is known to contain 50,000 items and a sample of size 500 is required, then 1 in every 100 items is selected. The first item is determined by choosing randomly a number between 1 and 100, e.g. 67, then the second item will be the 167th, the third will be the 267th . . . up to the 49,967th item.

Strictly speaking, systematic sampling (also called quasi-random) is not truly random as only the first item is so selected. However, it gives a very close approximation to random sampling and it is very widely used, e.g. in selecting a sample of bags of sugar coming off a conveyor belt.

There is danger of bias if the population has a repetitive structure. For example, if a street has five types of house arranged in the order, A B C D E A B C D E . . . etc., an interviewer visiting every fifth home would only visit one type of house.

3.5   Stratified sampling

If the population under consideration contains several well defined groups (called strata), e.g. men and women, smokers and non-smokers, different sizes of metal bars, etc., then a random sample is taken from each group. This is done in such a way that the number in each sample is proportional to the size of that group in the population and is known as sampling with **probability proportional to size** (pps).

For example, in selecting a sample of people in order to ascertain their leisure habits, age could be an important factor. So if 20% of the population are over 60 years of age, 65% between 18 and 60 and 15% are under 18, then a sample of 200 people should contain 40 who are over 60 years old, 130 people between 18 and 60 and 30 under 18 years of age, i.e. the subsample should have sizes in the ratio 20 : 65 : 15.

This method ensures that a representative cross-section of the strata in the population is obtained, which may not be the case with a simple random sample of the whole population.

The method is often used by auditors to chose a sample to confirm debtors' balances. In this case a greater proportion of larger balances is selected.

3.6   Multi-stage sampling

If a nationwide survey is to be carried out, then this method is often applied.

Step 1	The country is divided into areas (counties) and a random sample of areas is taken.
Step 2	Each area chosen in Step 1 is then subdivided into towns and cities or boroughs and a random sample of these is taken.
Step 3	Each town or city chosen in Step 2 is further divided into roads and a random sample of roads is then taken.
Step 4	From each road chosen in Step 3 a random sample of houses is taken and the occupiers interviewed.

This method is used for example, in selecting a sample for a national opinion poll of the type carried out prior to a general election.

3.7   Cluster sampling

This method is similar to the previous one in that the country is split into areas and a random sample taken. Further sub-divisions can be made until the required number of small areas have been determined. Then every house in each area will be visited instead of just a random sample of houses. In many ways this is a simpler and less costly procedure as no time is wasted finding particular houses and the amount of travelling by interviewers is much reduced.

3.8   Quota sampling

With quota sampling the interviewer will be given a list comprising the different types of people to be questioned and the number or quota of each type, e.g. 20 males, aged 20 - 30 years, manual workers. 15 females, 25 - 35, housewives (not working). 10 males, 55 - 60, professional men . . . etc. The interviewer can use any method to obtain such people until the various quota are filled. This is very similar to stratified sampling, but no attempt is made to select respondents by a proper random method, consequently the sample may be very biased.

3.9   Sampling methods compared

Alternatives to truly random sampling have been outlined above. They are all concerned with minimising costs whilst maintaining the representative nature of the sample compared to the population.

To use these alternatives it is often necessary to have some knowledge of the population. Systematic sampling should not be used if the population follows a repetitive pattern. Quota sampling must be used with caution because the data collector may introduce bias because they choose how to fill the quota.

Conclusion	The objective of a sample is to collect data upon which an opinion can be formed, and a conclusion drawn in respect of the population of which the sample is representative.

Ideally the sample would be chosen at random, and be large enough to be representative of the population. Unfortunately both of these aspects introduce costs which are often unacceptably high.

4   DATA SOURCES AND COLLECTION TECHNIQUES

4.1   Introduction

There are many ways of collecting data - censuses, questionnaires, postal inquiries, personal interviews, random samples, public opinion polls etc. It is obviously very important to use a method that is suitable for the purposes of the inquiry, so that time and hence money is not wasted.

4.2   Postal questionnaire

This allows respondents to remain anonymous if desired. The main disadvantage is that many people will not bother to return the questionnaire, resulting in a low response rate. Those who do respond may do so because they have a special interest in the subject, resulting in bias.

4.3   Personal interview

Questions are asked by a team of interviewers. A set questionnaire is still used to ensure that all interviewers ask the same questions in the same way, to minimise interviewer bias. The response rate is usually higher than in a postal questionnaire but employment of trained interviewers is costly.

4.4   Telephone interview

Similar to personal interview, but only suitable where all members of the population have a telephone (e.g. business surveys). It is cheap and produces results quickly.

4.5   Observation

Only suitable for obtaining data by counting (e.g. number of cars passing a traffic census point) or measuring (e.g. time taken to perform a task in work study).

4.6   Questionnaires

Questionnaires consist of a series of questions which the recipient may answer without being under any pressure. As a consequence the answers may be more informed than those obtained by interview but will be less spontaneous. Difficulties arise if the question is misread or misunderstood. This is because the answers do not match with any of those expected.

Conclusion   There are a variety of different data sources and collection techniques each being relevant to specific types of situation.

5   TABLES

5.1   Introduction

Very often raw data is in a form that is not easy to understand or form a clear opinion on. Often, presenting the data in a table shows the information much more clearly.

The purpose of writing any type of report is to present the necessary information clearly. Tabulation is a common method of achieving this aim of clarity.

5.2   Tabulation

Definition   **Tabulation** is the systematic arrangement of numerical data to provide a logical account of the results of analysis.

There are a number of basic rules of tabulation to ensure clarity.

5.3   Rules of tabulation

The following rules or principles of tabulation should always be borne in mind.

(a)   **Title:** the table must have a comprehensive and self explanatory title. This should indicate the relationships to be demonstrated, not just a general title.

(b)   **Source:** the source of the material used in drawing up the table should always be stated (usually by way of a footnote).

(c)   **Units:** the units of measurement that have been used must be stated e.g. 000s means that the units are in thousands. This can be done in the title, to keep the number of figures to a minimum. Alternatively this can be done in the column headings.

(d)   **Headings:** all column and row headings should be concise and unambiguous.

(e)   **Totals:** these should be shown where appropriate, and also any subtotals that may be useful. These need only be shown where they are meaningful for making comparisons.

(f)   **Percentages and ratios:** these are sometimes called **derived statistics** and should be shown if meaningful, with an indication of how they were calculated.

(g)   **Column layout:** for ease of comparison columns containing related information should be adjacent and derived figures should be adjacent to the column to which they refer.

(h)   **Simplicity:** the material used should be classified and detail kept to a minimum. The table should be as concise as possible.

(i)   **Layout:** wherever possible ensure that the table is set up so that there is no need to turn the page. This will affect the choice of columns and rows (see later in this chapter).

5.4   Layout of a table

The purpose of tabulation of data is to provide a clearer picture of the figures involved. In order to do this, the layout that is chosen for the table is obviously of very great importance.

5.5   Columns and rows

A table is set up in the form of a number of columns headed up across the page and then a number of rows of information moving down the page. A typical table would be set up as follows:

	Column 1	Column 2	Column 3
Row 1			
Row 2			
Row 3			
etc.			

This table can show only two variables, one in the columns and one in the rows.

A key element of setting up a good table is to decide upon the optimal arrangement of columns and rows.

Three general rules apply here:

- try to ensure that the page does not need to be turned onto its side. This will generally be done by choosing the minimum number of columns.

- the columns should be arranged so that related information is adjacent.

- the information shown in the rows should be arranged so that there is a logical progression through the information and any meaningful totals or subtotals can be made clearly.

5.6   Activity

Suppose that a table is drawn up showing the actual and percentage change in number of employees from year to year for the years 20X0 to 20X9. How would this be set up?

5.7   Activity solution

Changes in labour force 20X0 to 20X9

	Actual number of employees	Increase/ decrease	Percentage change
20X0			
20X1			
20X2			
20X3			
20X4			
20X5			
20X6			
20X7			
20X8			
20X9			

Source: Company records

5.8   Conversion of narrative data into tabular form

Numerical data may be given in narrative form. Such data is often difficult to assess and analyse and it is necessary to convert this narrative into a table of some sort.

5.9   Activity

Alpha Products plc has two departments, A and B. The total wage bill in 20X7 was £513,000, of which £218,000 was for department A and the rest for department B. The corresponding figures for 20X8 were £537,000 and £224,000. The number employed in department A was 30 in 20X7 and decreased by 5 for the next year. The number employed in department B was 42 in 19X7 and increased by 1 for the year 20X8. Tabulate this data to bring out the changes over the two year period for each department and the company as a whole.

5.10   Activity solution

Alpha Products plc
Changes in Labour Force 20X7 to 20X8

	Dept A			Dept B			Total		
	20X7	20X8	Change %	20X7	20X8	Change %	20X7	20X8	Change %
Wage Bill (£'000s)	218	224	+2.8	295	313	+6.1	513	537	+4.7
Number employed	30	25	−16.7	42	43	+2.4	72	68	−5.6

Source *Company records*

(Tutorial note: the aim of the table is to show clearly the changes over the two year period. The most effective method of doing this is to show the two annual figures and the percentage changes in the column. Therefore the rows are made up of wages and numbers employed. Try it the other way around and you will see that it is not so effective.*)*

Conclusion   Tabulation can frequently be used as part of the process of turning raw data into useful information.

6   CHAPTER SUMMARY

In this chapter we have looked at a key area of accounting the collection and interpretation of data. We shall continue with this in the next chapter.

7   SELF TEST QUESTIONS

7.1   What is quantitative data? (1.1)

7.2   What is qualitative data? (1.1)

7.3   Distinguish between discrete and continuous data. (1.2)

7.4   What is primary data? (2.2)

7.5   What is secondary data? (2.2)

7.6   What is a sample? (3.1)

7.7   What is random sampling? (3.3)

7.8   What is stratified sampling? (3.5)

7.9   What is cluster sampling? (3.7)

7.10   What are the main rules for successful tabulation of data? (5.3)

8   PRACTICE QUESTIONS

8.1   Minute sampling

Briefly describe the following types of sampling AND indicate the circumstances under which they may be of value to management:

- simple random sampling,
- stratified sampling,
- quota sampling.

8.2   Weekly newspaper

A local weekly newspaper sells about half a million copies a week in a region of about 100 square miles. Market research indicates that the readership profile is as follows:

	%	Age (£'000)	Annual income %	Sex	%
Under 25	10	Under 10	10	Male	50
25 - 34	15	10 - 15	10	Female	50
35 - 44	20	15 - 20	25		
45 - 54	20	20 - 25	25	Region	%
55 - 64	20	25 - 30	20		
65+	15	Over 30	10	Rural	10
				Suburban	30
Total	100	Total	100	Town	60

You are working with a marketing colleague on the design of a sample survey to find out (i) current strengths and weaknesses of the paper and (ii) whether the introduction of colour, leisure and/or business supplements etc. would increase sales and by how much.

You are required:

(a)   considering the information requirements, to recommend a method for collecting the data (e.g. by post, telephone, personal interviews etc.), giving reasons;

(b)   to design and explain a suitable practical sampling scheme that would achieve the objectives.

DO NOT ATTEMPT TO WRITE A QUESTIONNAIRE.

9   ANSWERS TO PRACTICE QUESTIONS

9.1   Minute sampling

Simple random sampling

A simple random sample is defined as a sample taken in such a way that every member of the population has an equal chance of selection. For a reasonably small population, items may be mixed up and drawn by random physical selection (as in the UK National Lottery); for larger populations, items will be numbered, and can be chosen using a random number table. It is therefore a reasonably straightforward method that can be quick and cheap to use for management purposes. The method cannot be used when the population's limits are unknown (e.g. if a sample of cats in the UK were required). However, statistical sampling theory assumes this method of sampling.

Stratified sampling

If the population under consideration contains several well-defined groups (strata) - e.g. people in different age-groups, invoices in different value ranges, components manufactured on different machines - the sample is stratified by taking a random sample from each group. The proportion of the total sample represented by each stratum sample will imitate the structure of the population.

This method ensures that a representative cross-section of the strata in the population is obtained, particularly where it is thought that the characteristic being tested may be affected by the stratum to which the sample item belongs. For example, if the average weekly spending on, say, the Lottery and other forms of gambling was to be estimated from a sample, the results would probably be biased if all the sample members came from one age group.

Quota sampling

This is similar to stratified sampling, in that the population is initially defined into several categories, possibly by more than one factor - e.g. by age-group and income group - and the sample is made up of a pre-determined number (quota) of items from each category. For example, an interviewer may be told to interview 10 people aged between 20 and 30, with income over £50,000; 50 people between 30 and 40, income between £20,000 and £50,000 etc. The difference is that the sample from each category is not necessarily drawn at random - so the market researcher may take the first ten 20 to 30 year-olds earning over £50,000 that they come across. This may result in a biased sample, if they all come from one location, or all happen to be male etc. However, it gives management some control over the composition of the sample without making the task of sampling too complex.

9.2 Weekly Newspaper

(a) (i)   When determining the method to be used to collect data as part of survey the key considerations are the cost of collecting the data and the sensitivity of the accuracy of the results.

(ii)   The newspaper is described as being local, covering an area of 100 square mile, this indicates that its budget for surveys and data collection is likely to be small and consequently cost considerations are highly important.

(iii) The use of personal interviews requires much labour time together with travelling expenses which is costly, this method is rejected because of its high cost. The use of telephone interviews introduce bias by restricting respondents to those who have a telephone. However, the survey is concerned with the use of supplements which are of most interest to groups who tend to have a telephone. This bias is therefore considered to be irrelevant, and this method is significantly cheaper than the use of personal interviews. The cheapest option is the use of postal services but these are likely to have the lowest response rate, and the reliability of the results collected by this method is questionable.

(iv)   In conclusion, the use of telephone interviews is recommended because it represents a balance between cost and the likelihood of reliable results.

(b) (i)   When using telephone interviews as the means of collecting data, the source of information (or sampling frame) is the telephone directories for the area. This introduces bias by the exclusion of ex-directory numbers, but to include these would be too costly.

(ii)   The respondents selected should be stratified according to the criterion set out by the market research. Some of these are easier to achieve than others, particularly when using telephone interviewing to collect the data. Regions may be identified from the telephone directory and gender may be satisfied by the use of a quota system. Age is more difficult because people will tend not to wish to divulge their age, but this problem can be solved by careful interviewing. Stratification by annual income will be the most difficult, and is likely to be the least reliable of the criteria and for these reasons is probably best ignored.

(iii)   The overall sample size will depend on the newspaper's budget for this exercise, but, using 1% of the market (i.e. 5,000) as a sample size, the quotas for the suburban area (30%) would be:

Under 25	150
25 - 34	225
25 - 44	300
45 - 54	300
55 - 64	300
65 plus	225
Total	1,500

These would be divided equally between male and female respondents for each age range.

Chapter 21

DATA PRESENTATION

PATHFINDER INTRODUCTION

This chapter covers the following elements of the CAT Official Teaching Guide. At the end of this chapter you should have learned these teaching guide elements thoroughly.

Session 21
Data presentation
Syllabus reference o

- Present and evaluate the use of charts and graphs
- Present data in diagrammatic form, simple bar charts and graphs

Note: the following methods of data presentation are not examinable: histograms, frequency curves, ogives, Lorenz curves and pie charts.

Putting the chapter in context

Having considered the collection of data and use of tables, this chapter covers alternative methods of presentation which make information easy to assimilate.

1   DIAGRAMMATIC PRESENTATION OF DATA

1.1   Introduction

In an earlier chapter the tabulation of data was considered. Data is tabulated to present a clearer picture of the message the data is trying to convey. In some cases, a clearer picture still is given if diagrammatic or pictorial representation of the data is made.

1.2   Tables and diagrams

The choice as to whether a table or a diagram is the most appropriate method to illustrate data will depend upon three main factors:

- the nature and complexity of the data itself;
- the audience that the data is designed for;
- the method of presentation of the data.

1.3   Nature of the data

A diagram is often most suitable if only a few particular points about a set of data are to be made. A diagram can make these points or relationships very clearly. However if a large number of relationships or points are to be made by a set of data then a table is more appropriate.

For example if the breakdown of sales into the four products that an organisation produces is required then this might well be shown clearly in a diagram. However if the purpose of the data was to indicate the detailed make up of the profit or loss on each of the four types of product then a table would probably be more useful.

1.4 Nature of the audience

When determining the method of presenting data it is important to consider exactly who the data is aimed at. For example in some circumstances the data might be for a board of a company or alternatively the purpose might be to inform the workforce of the company as a whole.

It is difficult to generalise about this area but some individuals might find diagrammatic data more easily digestible than tabulated data. Equally the level of detail of data required at board level might be higher than that required to inform the workforce of the relevant information.

1.5 Method of presentation

The method of eventual presentation of the data will often affect the choice of the most appropriate form of presentation.

For example if the data is to be presented in the form of a written report to management which the management team will have time to study and digest then tabulated data might be most appropriate. However if the data is to be presented as part of an oral presentation then a diagram might be most useful in order to highlight the salient points quickly and clearly.

1.6 Rules for preparation of diagrams

If it is determined that a diagram is the most appropriate method of presenting the data, it is important that the diagram is as clear and unambiguous as possible. To achieve this a number of rules should be followed:

- give each diagram a name or a title;
- state the source of any data that has been used;
- state the units of measurement that have been used;
- give a scale so that the diagram can be properly interpreted;
- ensure that the presentation is neat.

For this syllabus students will need to be able to present graphs and bar charts.

1.7 Pictograms

These are, as the name implies, pictures (or symbols) which can readily be associated with the data under consideration. One picture or symbol is used to represent a unit of the variable.

The following pictogram represent the car sales of International Cars for the three consecutive years 20X1 to 20X3:

Car sales International Cars, 20X1 to 20X3

A higher value should be shown by a greater number of pictorial units , (as in this example) not be increasing the size of the pictorial units, as this can be deceptive.

If the latter approach, increasing the size, is used, bear in mind that if both the width and the height of a picture double, its area increases by a factor of 4. (In general the method should be avoided).

2   GRAPHICAL PRESENTATION OF DATA

2.1   Introduction

In many instances data can be more clearly and intelligibly presented in the form of a diagram called a graph than it can in either a table or any other diagrammatic form. As graphs must be clear and neat and also drawn up correctly. There are a number of rules concerning the construction of a graph that will now be considered.

2.2   Graph paper

The first rule is that whenever possible students should use graph paper to draw a graph. The graph paper makes both drawing and interpretating the graph easier.

2.3   Title

The purpose of a graph is to provide information therefore it is important that all graphs have a title to explain what it is that they are showing. If the source of the information is also known then this should be shown.

2.4   Axes of a graph

A graph has two axes known as the x axis and the y axis. The x axis is always the horizontal axis and the y axis the vertical axis.

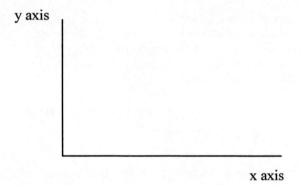

It is important that the correct variable is plotted on each axis.

Definition   **Dependent** variables are those that are dependent upon the value of the other variable.

Definition   **Independent** variables are those that are not dependent upon another variable.

The dependent variable must always be plotted on the vertical (y) axis and the independent variable on the horizontal (x) axis.

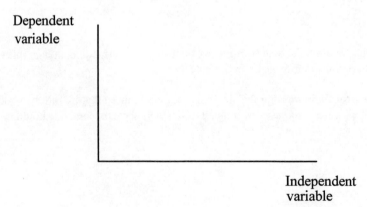

Each axis must be labelled and the units used must be stated e.g., £'000, years, hours, miles etc.

2.5   Activity

(a)   How would a graph be drawn to show the annual sales of an organisation from 2004 to 2014?

(b)   How would a graph be drawn to show the total cost of production for a number of different levels of production?

2.6   Activity solution

Annual sales 2004/2014

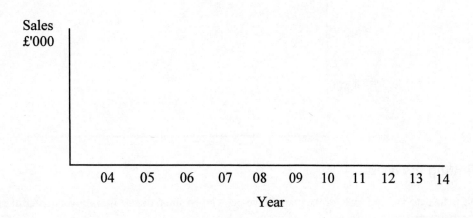

Sales £'000

04   05   06   07   08   09   10   11   12   13   14

Year

Tutorial note: whenever time is one of the variables then this will always be plotted on the x axis.

Total production costs

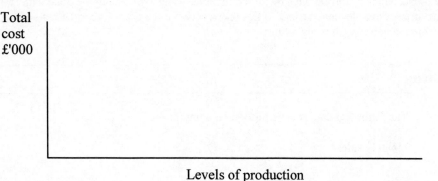

Total cost £'000

Levels of production

In this instance the cost of production will be dependent upon the level of production. Therefore the cost is the dependent variable and is plotted on the y axis and the level of production is the independent variable plotted on the x axis.

2.7   Scales of the axes

Once the variables that are to be plotted on the x and y axis have been determined, the next step is to decide the scale to be used on each axis. There are four rules to remember here:

- try to fill as much of the page of graph paper as possible. A tiny graph on an A4 sheet not only looks ridiculous but is difficult to draw and interpret.

- use sensible numbers for the scale such as 1cm = 1, 2, 5 or 10 rather than 3 or 7. Again this makes the graph easier to draw and interpret.

- there is no necessity for the same scale to be used on each axis. Even if the units on the x and y axis are the same a different scale is quite permissible.

- the scale must be continuous. For example if the scale on the x axis starts at 1 cm = £100 then it must not change to 1 cm = £1,000 part way along the axis.

2.8   Starting point of axis

In most cases the scales on both axes should start at zero. However in some circumstances this is just not practical. For example if the items to be plotted on the y axis are £4,600, £4,900 and £5,000 then it would not be practical to start the scale at zero. In such a case it is permissible to show a break in the scale with a zig zag line as follows:

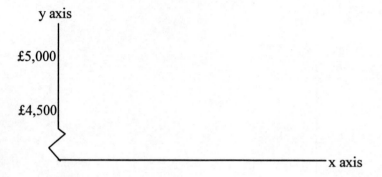

2.9   Plotting the graph

Once the axes and the scale of the graph have been determined then it is simply a matter of plotting the points accurately on the graph.

This is done by taking each pair of variables in turn and reading along to the x variable and up to the y variable. A cross is marked on the graph where the two lines intersect.

The points on the graph can then be joined together. This will usually be done with straight lines although in some instances curves may be used if figures in between the points are to be read off. However as a general rule join the points with straight lines.

2.10   Activity

The following data is to be plotted on a graph:

Monthly sales

Month	£
January	6,800
February	7,200
March	5,600
April	6,900
May	7,500
June	8,000

Draw a graph to illustrate this information.

2.11 Activity solution

Monthly sales

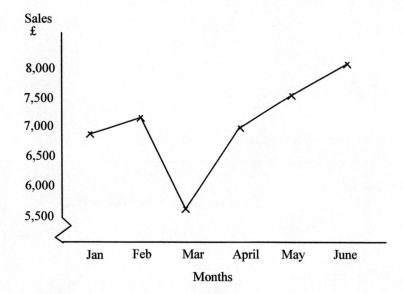

Tutorial note: do not draw a line from the point of intersection of the two axes to the first plotted point since no variables have been given for that point.

Conclusion   If a graph is the most appropriate method of presenting data then it should be drawn accurately and neatly to an appropriate scale or each axis. The horizontal or x axis will always be the independent variable.

3 BAR CHARTS

3.1 Introduction

A bar chart is a common method of illustrating quantitative data. A bar chart is drawn up in the form of a graph with two axes and the actual amounts of the data are represented by bars drawn along, usually, the horizontal axis.

There are a number of different types of bar chart but the only one to be considered for this syllabus is a simple bar chart.

3.2 Simple bar charts

A simple bar chart is where one variable only is being illustrated. The bar chart is drawn using the following steps:

Step 1   draw up the two axes and clearly label them with the scale to be used. Ensure that the scale on the vertical axis starts at zero as if it does not the visual effect of the chart will be incorrect.

Step 2   give the bar chart a title and note the source of any data.

Step 3   draw bars with equal widths with their heights representing the relevant amount of the variable. The bars can be either separated by a space or they can be drawn side by side with no space between them.

3.3   Activity

The production of grain in the UK for the years 20X1 to 20X3 was as follows:

Year	Production m tonnes
20X1	150
20X2	375
20X3	600

Illustrate this data using a simple bar chart.

3.4   Activity solution

Grain production UK, 20X1 to 20X3

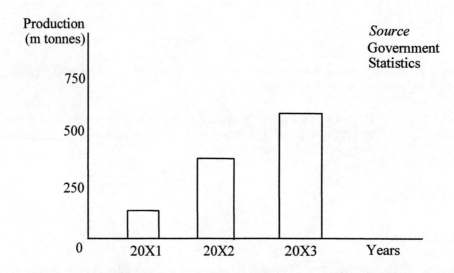

Conclusion   A simple bar chart shows not only the actual amount of the data which can be read off from the vertical axis but also the relationship between the data.

In the example the actual amount of wheat production each year can be determined by reading off the amounts on the vertical axis. It is also possible to see at a glance that wheat production increased by significant amounts over the three year period.

4   CHAPTER SUMMARY

This chapter has continued our look at data presentation, looking at diagrammatic and graphical presentation methods as well as bar charts.

5   SELF TEST QUESTIONS

5.1   What factors will effect the choice of presentation method for data? (1.2)

5.2   What is the vertical axis of a graph called? (2.4)

5.3   What is the independent variable on a graph? (2.4)

5.4   On which axis is the dependent variable plotted on a graph? (2.4)

5.5   How is a simple bar chart constructed? (3.2)

5.6   What information does a simple bar chart present? (3.4)

6   PRACTICE QUESTIONS

6.1   Families

The following data shows a breakdown of two families' monthly expenditure:

	Expenditure	
Item	*Family 1*	*Family 2*
	£	£
Food and drink	540	180
Housing	730	370
Fuel and light	125	84
Transport	600	124
Other	315	32
Net monthly income	2,310	790

You are required:

(a)   to draw simple bar charts to represent the above data to enable a comparison between the two families' expenditure;

(b)   to briefly compare each family's expenditure.

7   ANSWERS TO PRACTICE QUESTIONS

7.1   Families

(a)   Family 1

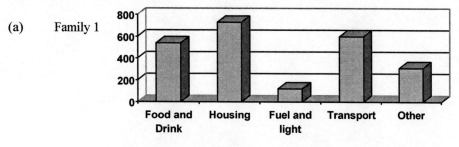

Family 2

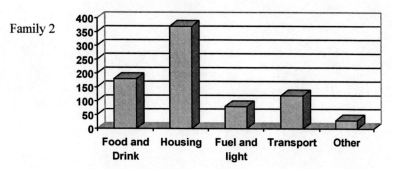

(b)   The first point to note is that Family 1's expenditure is generally higher than that of Family 2, due to their higher net monthly income. What the charts help us to compare are the relative levels (or proportions) of expenditure between the two categories. There are more sophisticated forms of bar charts – e.g. percentage component bar charts – that can particularly highlight proportions; however, we can still get quite a lot of information from the simple bar charts shown here, including:

- Both families spend the greatest absolute amount on housing, with Family 2's representing a far greater proportion of their total expenditure than Family 1's.

- Family 1 spends a significantly higher part of their income on transport than Family 2.

- Whereas in Family 1 'other' expenditure is more than twice as much as 'fuel and light', this position is reversed for Family 2.

Chapter 22

INDEX NUMBERS

PATHFINDER INTRODUCTION

This chapter covers the following elements of the CAT Official Teaching Guide. At the end of this chapter you should have learned these teaching guide elements thoroughly.

Session 22
Index numbers
Syllabus reference n

- Define the nature of an index number
- Calculate simple price and quantity indices for a single product
- Describe the nature of a weighted index and the limitations of their use
- Use price indices for adjusting for changing price levels
- Use indices for comparing performance between cost units and cost/profit centres

Putting the chapter in context

This chapter explains another way of making data easier to assimilate, by calculating index numbers to show how values have changed over time.

1 NATURE OF INDEX NUMBERS

1.1 Introduction

Often a series of numbers will be produced for a number of accounting periods or years. For example, sales volumes from year to year, sales values from year to year or a variety of cost information over a period of time.

If a manager or user of such information is presented with simply a list of numbers or values for a number of years then at first sight only very limited information can be gained.

1.2 Problems with a series of values

For example suppose that the following information is available regarding the selling price of a product over:

Year	Selling price £
20X1	200
20X2	232
20X3	256
20X4	250
20X5	280

If the information is given in this form it is immediately possible to see that the selling price has increased nearly every year but without further information or calculations it is not possible to tell by how much the price has increased each year, whether the increase is constant year by year or indeed whether the selling price increases have kept in line with changing price levels or inflation.

Most managers, if given such basic information, would probably be tempted to calculate some sort of percentage increases or decreases for each year.

1.3   What is an index?

In the example given above the calculation of percentage increases or decreases in comparison to say the 20X1 selling price is a simple index.

Definition	An **index** is a technique for comparing, over time, changes in some property of a group of items (e.g. price, quantity consumed etc.,) by expressing the property each year as a percentage of some earlier year.
Definition	The year that is used as the initial year for comparison of price, quantity etc. is known as the **base year**.

1.4   Activity

If 20X1 is the chosen base year, the index for the 20X1 price is 100.

Year	Selling price £	Index
20X1	200	100
20X2	232	
20X3	256	
20X4	250	
20X5	280	

Calculate the index for each subsequent year comparing that year's price to the price in 20X1.

1.5   Activity solution

The calculation of the index for each year is as follows:

20X2 $\dfrac{232}{200} \times 100$ =   116

20X3 $\dfrac{256}{200} \times 100$ =   128

20X4 $\dfrac{250}{200} \times 100$ =   125

20X5 $\dfrac{280}{200} \times 100$ =   140

The completed table will appear as follows:

Year	Selling price £	Index
20X1	200	100
20X2	232	116
20X3	256	128
20X4	250	125
20X5	280	140

This now shows that in 20X2 the increase in selling price over the 20X1 price was 16%. The 20X3 price shows an increase of 28% over the 20X1 price, the 20X4 price an increase of only 25% over 20X1 and finally the 20X5 price an increase of 40% over 20X1.

Conclusion   This simple calculation immediately provides more information for management. There are many other uses of indices in more complex examples and these will be considered later in the chapter. The purpose of this simple example is merely to indicate what it is that an index measures.

1.6 Interpretation of an index

Care must be taken when interpreting an index. When comparing the 20X4 and 20X5 selling prices it would be incorrect to state that there had been a 15% (140 - 125) increase in selling price over that year.

The way that this should be expressed is that there has been a 15 point increase over the period or alternatively a 12% (15/125 × 100%) increase.

2 SIMPLE INDICES

2.1 Introduction

Definition   a **simple index** is one that measures the changes in either price or quantity of a single item.

There are two types of simple index:

- a price index;
- a quantity index.

These simple indices are also known as relatives giving either a price relative or a quantity relative.

2.2 Simple index measurement

As in the example above, a simple index measures the percentage change in a single item in comparison to the base year. The index can measure either the price of the item or the quantity of the item that was sold or made.

A price index shows the percentage increase in price of the item since the base year. A quantity index shows the increase in quantity or volume sold or made since the base year.

2.3 Calculation of a simple index

The formulae for calculating simple indices are:

$$\text{Simple price index} \quad = \quad \frac{p_1}{p_0} \times 100$$

$$\text{Simple quantity index} \quad = \quad \frac{q_1}{q_0} \times 100$$

Where p_0 is the price at time 0
p_1 is the price at time 1
q_0 is the quantity at time 0
q_1 is the quantity at time 1

(***Tutorial note:*** the concept of time 0, time 1 and so on is simply a scale counting from any given point in time. Thus, for example, if the scale started on 1 January 20X0 it would be as follows:

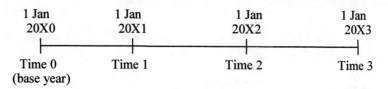

The starting point is chosen to be most convenient for the problem under consideration.**)**

2.4   Activity - price index

If a commodity costs £2.60 in 20X4 and £3.68 in 20X5, calculate the simple price index for 20X5, using 20X4 as base year (i.e. time 0).

2.5   Activity solution

Simple price index $\quad = \quad \dfrac{p_1}{p_0} \times 100$

$$= \quad \dfrac{3.68}{2.60} \times 100$$

$$= \quad 141.5$$

This means that the price has increased by 41.5% of its base year value i.e. its 20X4 value.

2.6   Activity - quantity index

6,500 items were sold in 20X8 compared with 6,000 in 20X7. Calculate the simple quantity index for 20X8 using 20X7 as base year.

2.7   Activity solution

Simple quantity index $\quad = \quad \dfrac{q_1}{q_0} \times 100$

$$= \quad \dfrac{6,500}{6,000} \times 100$$

$$= \quad 108.3$$

This means that the quantity sold has increased by 8.3% of its 20X7 figure.

Conclusion   A simple price or quantity index measures the increase or decrease in a price or an amount compared to a particular earlier year known as the base year.

3   WEIGHTED INDICES

3.1   Introduction

In the previous paragraphs simple indices were discussed. A simple index measures changes either in price or quantity of a single item. What is perhaps more practical and useful is the calculation of an index that measures overall changes in either price or quantity of a number of different items.

3.2   Weighted index measurement

Definition   A **weighted index** measures the change in overall price or overall quantity of a number of different items compared to the base year.

To be able to do this for a price index there are two steps:

Step 1   calculate the price relative (simple price index) for each of the items.

Step 2   these price relatives must then be weighted in some suitable manner in order to produce an overall price index.

Similarly if a quantity index is to be calculated:

Step 1   calculate the quantity relative (simple quantity index) for each of the items.

Step 2   these quantity relatives must then be weighted in some suitable manner in order to produce an overall quantity index.

3.3   Activity

An organisation produces three products. Information about the selling prices of these three products for the last two years are as follows:

	Selling price 20X1 £	Selling price 20X2 £
Product A	2	3
Product B	9	10
Product C	25	30

In order to produce a weighted index of the overall price increase over the period, weightings are to be assigned to each of the three products as follows:

	Weighting
Product A	4
Product B	5
Product C	1

Calculate a weighted price index for 20X2 for these three products with 20X1 as the base year.

3.4   Activity solution

Step 1   Calculate the price relative or simple price index for each of the products.

Product A $\dfrac{3}{2} \times 100 = 150$

Product B $\dfrac{10}{9} \times 100 = 111$

Product C $\dfrac{30}{25} \times 100 = 120$

Step 2   Weight the price relatives on the weighting basis given.

	Price relative $\dfrac{P1}{P0} \times 100$	Weighting W	Total $W \times \dfrac{P1}{P0} \times 100$
A	150	4	600
B	111	5	555
C	120	1	120
		10	1,275

$$\text{Weighted price index} \quad = \quad \frac{1,275}{10}$$

$$= \quad 127.5$$

The selling price of the three products together has therefore increased by 27.5% from 20X1 to 20X2.

3.5   Selection of weightings

In the example in the previous paragraph weightings for each of the items to be included in the index were given. This will not always be the case. Students may be required to calculate the weightings to apply to the price or quantity relatives.

3.6   Weightings for price indices

The most common weightings for a price index are either the physical quantity of each item in the index or the total value of each item. The total value of each item is the quantity multiplied by the price.

3.7   Weightings for a quantity index

If a quantity index is to be calculated then the weightings will either be the price of each item or more usually the total value of each item in the index.

The method of calculating a quantity index is exactly the same as for a price index and the same steps are used.

3.8   Problems with weighted indices

The problem with weighted indices is that over a period of time not only will the prices change but the weights will also change. If one considers a price index weighted according to quantities sold then it is likely that over time the proportion of each product sold may change.

How then is the index to be constructed? Should the weights used be the original weights from the base year or should they be the weights from the current year representing current patterns of expenditure?

In fact indices can be constructed using either method but both have limits.

If the base year quantities are used for the index it will fail to take account of the changing pattern of consumption. As a result, this index tends to overstate the real impact of inflation on individuals.

On the other hand, if an index uses current year quantities this involves recalculating data for all preceding years each year. With a large number of indices to maintain, this is not practicable. Also, this type of index based on current consumption patterns tends to understate the overall effect of inflation on consumers.

4   PRICE INDICES AND CHANGING PRICE LEVELS

4.1   Introduction

In the previous paragraphs the construction and interpretation of different types of indices have been considered. In this paragraph a common practical use (and commonly examined use) for indices will be discussed.

The indices, that have been constructed in the earlier paragraphs, provide additional information to management regarding the price or volume of its sales or production. However one question that has not yet been addressed is how to assess whether selling prices have kept pace with inflation.

4.2   Measurement of inflation

In the UK the generally accepted measurement of general price inflation is the Retail Price Index, an index constructed using the price of a variety of household goods and services.

Organisations however not only face general inflation but also specific price changes in their inputs (raw materials and wages) and their outputs (sales). There are a number of published statistics from the Central Statistical Office showing specific price indices for different sectors of industry.

4.3   Use of indices to account for inflation

An organisation can choose to compare its results and costs to a general inflation index such as the RPI or a specific price index for its inputs or outputs. This is done by stripping out the effects of inflation leaving only the 'real terms' increase or decrease in sales or costs.

Which type of index to use is a management decision and will help to provide a more realistic comparison between the results of different periods. If the general or specific increases in prices are taken out of an organisation's results then this will leave only the real or genuine increase (or decrease) due to selling price, sales volume and costs.

4.4   Method

A series of costs or revenues over a period of time can be adjusted for inflation in one of two ways:

- all figures can be reduced to base year figures by stripping out the effects of inflation.

- all figures can be inflated to current year prices.

4.5   Activity

Suppose that an organisation has the following sales over a number of years. The specific index that relates to those sales is also given:

	Sales £'000	Specific price index
20X1	140	112
20X2	150	118
20X3	154	128
20X4	160	135
20X5	170	140

Remove from these sales figures the effect of the specific price changes for this product to give the real increase or decrease in sales for the period.

4.6   Activity solution

To remove the effects of inflation two different methods can be used:
(a)   all figures can be reduced to base year figures by stripping out the effects of inflation.
(b)   all figures can be inflated to current year prices.

(a)   Reduction or deflation of sales figures

The sales figures for each year are deflated or reduced by dividing by the price index for the year being considered and multiplying by the index for the earliest year.

20X1 $£140,000 \times \dfrac{112}{112}$ =   £140,000

20X2 $£150,000 \times \dfrac{112}{118}$ =   £142,373

20X3 $£154,000 \times \dfrac{112}{128}$ =   £134,750

20X4 $£160,000 \times \dfrac{112}{135}$ =   £132,741

20X5 $£170,000 \times \dfrac{112}{140}$ =   £136,000

(b)   Inflation to current year prices

This is done by dividing each year's figures by the index for that year and then multiplying by the current year, 20X5, index.

20X1 $£140,000 \times \dfrac{140}{112}$ =   £175,000

20X2 $£150,000 \times \dfrac{140}{118}$ =   £177,966

20X3 $£154,000 \times \dfrac{140}{128}$ =   £168,438

20X4 $£160,000 \times \dfrac{140}{135}$ =   £165,926

20X5 $£170,000 \times \dfrac{140}{140}$ =   £170,000

Conclusion   Each set of calculations tells the same story. The actual sales figures appear to be increasing each year. However when the specific price changes of those products are taken into account using the price index the picture is different.

Whether the prices are deflated by stripping out the effects of inflation or inflated to current prices the resulting information is the same:

- 20X2 sales have increased in real terms. Even after taking price inflation into account the real sales figure is greater.

- sales in 20X3 and 20X4 have both reduced in real terms. Despite the appearance of increases from £150,000 to £154,000 for 20X3, and then from £154,000 to £160,000 for 20X4, when inflation is taken into account the real sales figures have in fact decreased.

- finally the sales for 20X5 have increased not only on paper from £160,000 to £170,000 but also in real terms as the amount of increase in sales has been greater than the specific price increases over the same period.

5   INDICES USED FOR COMPARING PERFORMANCE

5.1   Introduction

Now that the construction of various indices has been considered it is finally possible to summarise the uses of indices for comparing performance of individual cost units and cost/profit centres.

5.2   Cost units

If an organisation produces a number of different products then it may wish to have a clear picture of the relative price increases or quantity increases of each of these products or cost units.

5.3   Activity

An organisation produces two products, A and B, and their selling prices for the last two years have been as follows:

	Product A	Product B
20X6	£4.50	£21.60
20X7	£4.95	£22.90

Use indices with a base year of 20X6 to determine which product has had the highest relative price increase.

5.4   Activity solution

Product A	Price index	=	$4.95/4.50 \times 100$	=	110
Product B	Price index	=	$22.90/21.60 \times 100$	=	106

Product A has had the highest relative price increase over the two year period.

5.6   Cost/profit centres

Similarly, indices could be used to compare the performance of cost or profit centres in an organisation. This could be by producing indices to compare cost, profit or quantity of output.

5.7   Activity

Two production departments of a factory had the following units of output for the past two years:

	Department I	Department II
20X6	24,000 units	112,000 units
20X7	25,600 units	115,000 units

Use indices with 20X6 as the base year to determine which of the two production departments has had the faster growth rate over the period.

5.8   Activity solution

Department I	Quantity index	$25,600/24,000 \times 100$	=	107
Department II	Quantity index	$115,000/112,000 \times 100$	=	103

Department I has the higher growth rate of output over the period.

Conclusion   Either simple price indices or quantity indices can be used to compare the performance of cost units or cost/profit centres. It would also be possible to use general or specific price indices to adjust the results of cost units or cost/profit centres for changing prices.

6   CHAPTER SUMMARY

In this chapter we have looked at how index numbers can be used to assimilate data and show how it is changed over time.

7   SELF TEST QUESTIONS

7.1   What is an index? (1.3)

7.2   What is a base year? (1.3)

7.3   What is a simple index? (2.1)

7.4   How is a simple quantity index calculated? (2.3)

7.5   What is a weighted index? (3.2)

7.6   How are price indices normally weighted? (3.6)

7.7   What is the main problem with a weighted index? (3.8)

7.8   What are the two methods of adjusting costs for inflation over a period of time? (4.4)

8   MULTIPLE CHOICE QUESTION

8.1   The price index for a commodity in the current year is 135 (base year = 100). The current price for the commodity is £55.35 per kg.

What was the price per kg in the base year?

A   £35
B   £41
C   £74.72
D   £100

9   PRACTICE QUESTIONS

9.1   Salaries of systems analysts

You have been requested by a UK based client to research into the area of salaries paid to their systems analysis team, to prepare a report in order that a pay review may be carried out.

The following table shows the salaries, together with the retail price index (or consumer price index) for the years 20X0 to 20X8.

Year	Average Salary £	Retail Price index* (2087 = 100)
20X0	9,500	89.2
20X1	10,850	94.6
20X2	13,140	97.8
20X3	14,300	101.9
20X4	14,930	106.9
20X5	15,580	115.2
20X6	16,200	126.1
20X7	16,800	133.5
20X8	17,500	138.5

Required:

(i) What is the purpose of an index number?

(ii) Tabulate the percentage increases on a year earlier for the average salary and the retail price index;

(iii) Revalue the average salary each year to its equivalent 20X8 value using the retail price index;

(iv) Using the results of (ii) and (iii) above, comment on the average salary of the systems analysts of your client.

9.2 Constructing an index number

What are the main considerations to be borne in mind when constructing an index number?

10 ANSWER TO MULTIPLE CHOICE QUESTION

10.1 B

$$£55.35 \times \frac{100}{135} = £41$$

9 ANSWERS TO PRACTICE QUESTIONS

9.1 Salaries of systems analysts

(i) The purpose of an index number is to show the changes in prices, quantities, wages, etc., over a period of time. Many items can be included in the index, combining them as a weighted average. By expressing this as a percentage of the weighted average in the base year, the index becomes independent of units, so that different items with different units can be compared. For example, prices (£) can be compared with quantities which are not in monetary units.

| | Comparison with Previous Years | | | |
| | Average salary | | Index of Retail Prices | |
Year	Increase	%	Increase	%
20X0	–	–	–	–
20X1	1,350	14.2	5.4	6.1
20X2	2,290	21.1	3.2	3.4
20X3	1,160	8.8	4.1	4.2
20X4	630	4.4	5.0	4.9
20X5	650	4.4	8.3	7.8
20X6	620	4.0	10.9	9.5
20X7	600	3.7	7.4	5.9
20X8	700	4.2	5.0	3.7

(iii)   To convert the salary for year n into the equivalent salary in year 20X8, multiply by I_{20X8}/I_n.

(iv)

Year	Average salary At 20X8 values
20X0	14,751
20X1	15,885
20X2	18,608
20X3	19,436
20X4	19,343
20X5	18,731
20X6	17,793
20X7	17,429
20X8	17,500

Note:

The value for 20X0 is $\dfrac{9,500 \times 138.5}{89.2}$

The value for 20X1 is $\dfrac{10,850 \times 138.5}{94.6}$ and so on.

(iv)   In real terms, based on 20X8 prices, the average salary has steadily decreased from a maximum of £19,436 in 20X3 to £17,500 in 20X8. Comparison of the % increase columns in section (ii) shows that this effective decrease is because in every year since 20X4, the index of retail prices has increased at a greater rate than the average wage. In the first three years, from 20X0 to 20X3, the reverse was the case, and salaries increased in real terms.

9.2   Constructing an index number

There are four main considerations to be borne in mind when constructing an index number:

(a)   **The purpose of the index number**

Unless the purpose is defined clearly, the eventual usefulness of the final index will be suspect. In other words it must be designed to show **something in particular**.

(b)   **Selection of items for inclusion in an index**

The main principles to be followed here are that the items selected must be unambiguous, relevant to the purpose, and of ascertainable value.

Since index numbers are concerned largely with making comparisons over time periods, an item selected one year must be clearly identified (i.e. in terms of size, weight, capacity, quantity, etc.) so that the same items can be selected the following year for comparison.

(c)   **Selection of appropriate weights**

Deciding on the level of importance to attach to each change from one year to the next, or the relative importance of each item to the whole list.

(d)   **Selection of a base year**

Care must be exercised so that an 'abnormal' year is not chosen in relation to the characteristic being measured. If an abnormally 'high' year is chosen, all subsequent changes will be understated; whereas if an abnormally 'low' year is chosen, all subsequent changes will be overstated in percentage terms.

Chapter 23

TIME SERIES ANALYSIS

PATHFINDER INTRODUCTION

This chapter covers the following elements of the CAT Official Teaching Guide. At the end of this chapter you should have learned these teaching guide elements thoroughly.

Session 23
Time series analysis
Syllabus reference n

- Describe the components of a time series
- Use moving averages to isolate the trend
- Chart time series data
- Comment on the use of time series analysis for forecasting

(**Note:** Calculations of average seasonal variations or seasonally adjusted data will not be required)

Putting the chapter in context

This is another chapter concerned with the presentation and use of data. This chapter explains how trends can be identified from historical data and used to forecast future values.

1   COMPONENTS OF A TIME SERIES

1.1   Introduction

Time series analysis is a method of analysing data produced over a period of time.

Definition   A **time series** is a set of observations taken at equal time intervals.

The observations might be taken hourly, daily, weekly, monthly, quarterly or annually.

The observations may be monetary such as sales figures or costs totals, or non-monetary such as temperature measurements or numbers of people.

1.2   Examples of time series

Examples of time series might include the following:

- quarterly sales totals;
- annual profit figures;
- weekly payroll totals;
- hourly temperature readings;
- daily production output;
- monthly number of employees;
- quarterly totals for unemployment.

1.3   Basic aims of time series analysis

A time series shows how the value of a particular variable (sales, unemployment etc.) has changed over time. The aim of time series analysis is to use this historical data to form a model from which *future* values may be predicted. This is useful to businesses and the government in planning future strategy and budgets.

Initial analysis breaks the time series down into components, each of which is easier to project into the future than the original time series. These projections can then be combined into an overall forecast.

1.4   Components of a time series

There are a variety of different factors that cause a variable to change over time. Some of these factors are long term and some short term. Some factors are due to the economy as a whole whereas others are specific to a particular business.

The four main factors that are of interest when analysing a time series are:

(a)   long-term trends;
(b)   cyclical variations;
(c)   seasonal variations;
(d)   residual or random variations.

1.5   Long-term trends

Definition   The **long term trend** is the way in which a time series appears to be moving over a long interval of time when the short-term fluctuations have been smoothed out.

The rise or fall is due to factors which change slowly e.g.

(i)   increase or decrease in population;
(ii)   technological improvements;
(iii)   competition from abroad;
(iv)   inflation.

1.6   Cyclical variations

Definition   **Cyclical variations** are the causes of the wave-like appearance of a time series when taken over a number of years.

Generally, it is due to the influence of booms and slumps in industry. The distance in time from one peak to the next is often approximately 5 to 7 years. The cyclical variations represent long-term economic changes and are only noticeable if a time series spans a considerable number of years.

1.7   Seasonal variations

Definition   **Seasonal variations** are the regular rises and falls over specified intervals of time.

The interval of time can be any length - hours, days, weeks etc., and the variations are of a periodic type with a fairly definite period e.g.

(i)   rises in the number of goods sold before Christmas and at sale times;
(ii)   rises in the demand for gas and electricity at certain times during the day;
(iii)   rises in the number of customers using a restaurant at lunch-time and dinner time.

These are referred to under the general heading of 'seasonal' variations as a common example is the steady rise and fall of, for example, sales over the four seasons of the year.

However, as can be seen from the examples, the term is also used to cover regular variations over other short periods of time.

They should not be confused with cyclical variations (see above) which are long-term fluctuations with an interval between successive peaks greater than one year.

1.8   Residual or random variations

Definition   **Random variations** are any other variations which cannot be ascribed to the three factors discussed above.

This is taken as happening entirely at random due to unpredictable causes e.g.:

(i)   strikes;
(ii)   fires;
(iii)   sudden changes in taxes;
(iv)   loss of goodwill

Not all time series will contain all four elements. For example, not all sales figures show seasonal variations.

Conclusion   The four components of a time series are the trend, cyclical variation, seasonal variation and random variation.

2   TREND OF A TIME SERIES

2.1   Introduction

Definition   The **trend** of a time series is the way that the time series tends to move overall.

The trend is a rough estimate of how the time series increases or decreases over time.

2.2   Types of trend

If the figures in a time series are on the whole increasing as time progresses then such a time series will have an upwards trend.

If alternatively the figures are generally falling over a period of time then the trend will be downwards.

Finally, it is not necessarily the case that the figures will be either increasing or decreasing as they may appear to be reasonably similar for each of the periods under review. In this case the trend is said to be static.

2.3   Moving averages

The simplest method of determining the trend is that of moving averages, which shows, on average, how the time series increases and decreases.

The best way to illustrate the calculation of a moving average is to use a simple example.

2.4   Activity

The number of employees in a manufacturing concern for each of six months were:

	Number of employees
Month 1	50
Month 2	54
Month 3	65
Month 4	58
Month 5	70
Month 6	68

Calculate the trend of these figures using a three figure moving average.

2.5   Activity solution

The steps in the calculation are as follows:

Step 1   Calculate a three month total for each successive three month period (the choice of averaging period - here three months - is discussed after illustration of the technique).

The first moving total will therefore be months 1 to 3 employees:

$$50 + 54 + 65 \qquad = \qquad 169$$

Then months 2 to 4:

$$54 + 65 + 58 \qquad = \qquad 177$$

Then months 3 to 5 etc.

Step 2   Produce an average for each three month period by dividing by 3.

Thus months 1 to 3:

$$\frac{169}{3} \quad = \quad 56$$

months 2 to 4:

$$\frac{177}{3} \quad = \quad 59$$

This can be laid out in the form of a table.

(*Tutorial note:* the three month moving total and the three month moving average are shown in the middle of the time period, i.e. on the line of, or against, the middle figure for the three years. Therefore the month 1 to month 3 moving figures are shown in the month 2 line and the month 2 to month 4 figures in the month 3 line. There will therefore be no moving totals or moving averages for month 1 or month 6.)

Month	Number of employees	3 month moving total Step 1	Trend 3 month moving average Step 2
Month 1	50	-	-
Month 2	54	169	56
Month 3	65	177	59
Month 4	58	193	64
Month 5	70	196	65
Month 6	68	-	-

Conclusion   The trend indicates the general direction in which the time series figures are moving.

2.6   Choice of moving average figure

In this example, a three figure moving average was chosen. The figure taken for the moving average period should be the most appropriate for the circumstances of the particular time series.

If it is known that there is a cycle for a time series over which seasonal variations tend to occur, the moving average period chosen is the length of the cycle.

2.7   Examples of moving average periods

- A time series covers a number of years and it is apparent from the time series that there is in general a six year cycle. A six year moving average would be the most appropriate in this case as this would cover the entire six year cycle.

- Figures are given for monthly sales for four years and those sales vary throughout the year. A twelve month moving average might be chosen as this would cover the entire annual cycle of sales variations.

- Figures are given for daily numbers of customers in a restaurant for a two month period and the number of customers varies significantly for each day of the week. A seven day moving average might be most appropriate in order to cover the whole week.

- Figures are given for quarterly sales and there appears to be four distinct quarterly seasons to the sales. A four period moving average to cover the entire year might be chosen as the most appropriate.

2.8   Moving averages and even number periods

Earlier it was noted that the moving total and moving average are recorded at the mid-point of the time period chosen. If the moving average period is an odd number then the mid-point will be a specific time period. However if an even number is chosen for a moving average then the mid-point of that period will be between specific time periods.

For example the following four years of sales figures are given:

	£'000
20X1	100
20X2	120
20X3	160
20X4	180

The total for these four periods is 560 and therefore the 4 year average is 140 (560/4).

This average of 140 relates to the middle of the four year period therefore somewhere between 20X2 and 20X3. This would be shown in the averaging table between the lines for 20X2 and 20X3 as follows:

Year	Sales	Moving total	Moving average/trend
20X1	100		
20X2	120		
		560	140
20X3	160		
20X4	180		

The problem with this is that the trend line must relate to specific time periods to be plotted on the graph of the time series (see later in this chapter).

This problem is solved by taking a moving average of the moving average. This is known as centring the moving average.

2.9   Activity

The sales figures for Barb Ltd, a retailer of barbecue equipment and accessories, for three years are given below:

Year	Quarter 1 £'000	Quarter 2 £'000	Quarter 3 £'000	Quarter 4 £'000
20X1	121	188	290	88
20X2	125	201	301	102
20X3	146	227	318	103

Using a four period moving average calculate the trend of these figures. Work to the nearest £1,000.

2.10   Activity solution

Step 1   calculate each four period moving total and position this figure in the middle of the four quarter time period.

Step 2   calculate each four period moving average by dividing the total by four and also position this figure in the middle of the four quarter time period.

Step 3   calculate a two period moving average of each of the four period moving averages. This will give the trend at specific time periods.

This example would therefore be tackled as follows:

Step 1   calculate the four period moving totals:

20X1: Quarter 1 to quarter 4: $121 + 188 + 290 + 88 = 687$

X1 Quarter 2 to X2 quarter 1: $188 + 290 + 88 + 125 = 691$

X1 Quarter 3 to X2 quarter 2: $290 + 88 + 125 + 201 = 704$, etc.

Step 2   calculate the four period moving averages:

20X1: Quarter 1 to quarter 4: $\dfrac{687}{4} = 172$

X1 Quarter 2 to X2 quarter 1: $\dfrac{691}{4} = 173$

X1 Quarter 3 to X2 quarter 2: $\dfrac{704}{4} = 176$, etc.

Step 3   calculate two period moving averages of the four period moving averages in order to give the trend. These figures will now relate to a specific time period.

Trend for quarter 3: $\dfrac{172 + 173}{2} = 173$

Trend for quarter 4: $\dfrac{173 + 176}{2} = 175$, etc.

The completed table is now shown:

Quarter		Sales	Four period moving total Step 1	Four period moving average Step 2	Trend Step 3
20X1 -	1	121			
	2	188			
			687	172	
	3	290			173
			691	173	
	4	88			175
			704	176	
20X2 -	1	125			178
			715	179	
	2	201			181
			729	182	
	3	301			185
			750	188	
	4	102			191
			776	194	
20X3 -	1	146			196
			793	198	
	2	227			199
			794	199	
	3	318			
	4	103			

(*Tutorial note:* when calculating the trend all of the numbers have been rounded to the nearest £'000.)

Conclusion   When an even number of periods is used for the moving average trend calculation then a further centred average must be calculated.

3   GRAPH OF TIME SERIES DATA

3.1   Introduction

Time series are often shown on a graph. The observations are plotted against time to give an overall picture of what is happening. Time is always plotted on the horizontal axis and the observations on the vertical axis.

3.2   Activity

The following data are the quarterly sales figures for Barb Ltd, a retailer of barbecue equipment and accessories, for three years.

	Quarter 1 £'000	Quarter 2 £'000	Quarter 3 £'000	Quarter 4 £'000
20X1	121	188	290	88
20X2	125	201	301	102
20X3	146	227	318	103

Plot this data on a graph, together with the trend figures calculated in the previous paragraph and given again below.

Barb Ltd - trend figures:

Quarter		Trend
20X1	- 1	-
	- 2	-
	- 3	173
	- 4	175
20X2	- 1	178
	- 2	181
	- 3	185
	- 4	191
20X3	- 1	196
	- 2	199
	- 3	-
	- 4	-

3.3   Activity solution

Sales

£'000

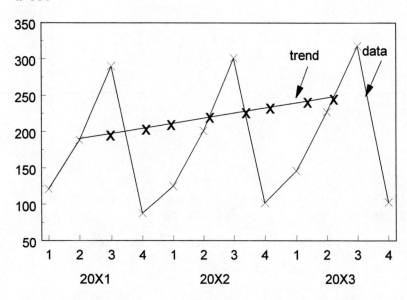

(*Tutorial note:* each point is plotted at the end of the relevant quarter.)

4   FORECASTING USING TIME SERIES ANALYSIS

4.1   Introduction

The principal use of the time series analysis that has been studied in this chapter is as an aid to forecasting results for future periods.

This can involve some quite complex calculations but for the purposes of this syllabus only an understanding of the technique used is required.

4.2   Technique

The technique for forecasting future results involves the following steps:

Step 1   estimate the trend for the future period.

This can be done by extending the trend line on the time series graph and reading off the figure at the future point in time that is being used in the forecast.

Step 2   apply the appropriate seasonal adjustment (or cyclical adjustment) in order to determine the forecast figure. (no calculations required for this syllabus)

It is not possible to forecast residual or random variations as they are unforeseeable by their very nature.

4.3   Activity

Given below is the time series graph for Barb Ltd showing the original time series and the trend.

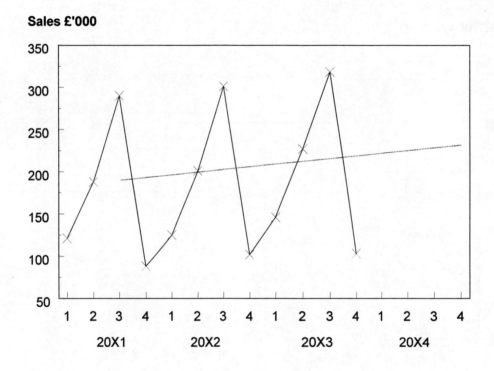

Sales £'000

How could this be used to estimate sales in each quarter of 20X4?

4.4   Activity solution

Step 1   estimate the trend figure for each of the quarters of 20X4.

This can be done by extending the trend line on the graph and reading off the relevant figures. This is also known as extrapolation.

Sales £'000

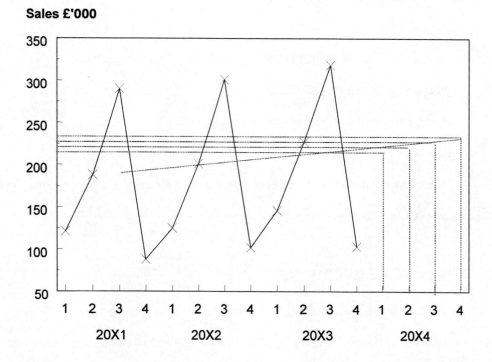

The estimated sales for each quarter of 20X4 will then be above or below this trend line depending upon the various seasonal variations.

4.5   Problems with forecasting

There are a number of problems with using time series analysis to estimate or forecast future results.

- the main problem is the inherent weakness of extrapolation. To estimate the trend for the future the trend line is extended on the graph and the figures read off. However although the time series has moved in that particular manner in the past it does not necessarily mean that it will continue to do so in the future.

- the seasonal adjustments used to find the forecast for the future are again based upon historic figures that may well already be out of date. There is no guarantee that the seasonal variations will remain the same in the future.

- if the time series has a large residual or random variation element this will make any forecasts even less reliable.

Conclusion   Time series analysis is a useful forecasting tool. However it does have a number of theoretical and practical problems.

5   CHAPTER SUMMARY

In this chapter we have considered time series analysis, its purpose and its use in forecasting and trend determination.

6   SELF TEST QUESTIONS

6.1   What is a time series? (1.1)

6.2   What is the basic aim of time series analysis? (1.3)

6.3   What is meant by the long term trend of a time series? (1.5)

6.4   What are cyclical variations? (1.6)

6.5   What are seasonal variations? (1.7)

6.6   What are random variations? (1.8)

6.7   How can the trend of a time series be calculated? (2.3)

6.8   How is the moving average period chosen for trend calculations? (2.6)

6.9   What is the effect of choosing an even number period for calculation of the moving average? (2.8)

6.10   How is time series analysis used for forecasting? (4.2)

7   MULTIPLE CHOICE QUESTIONS

7.1   Based on 20 past quarters, the underlying trend equation for forecasting is $y = 23.87 + 2.4x$.

If quarter 21 has a seasonal factor of times 1.08, using a multiplicative model, then the forecast for the quarter, in whole units, is

A   75
B   80
C   83
D   85

7.2   The following data represents a time series for the last seven days:

2   6   10   6   10   14   10

Which ONE of the following moving averages would result in a straight-line graph?

A   2-point   B   3-point   C   4-point   D   none of these

8   PRACTICE QUESTIONS

8.1   Brand Y

Annual sales of Brand Y over a period of eleven years were as follows:

Unit sales of Brand Y, 20X0 –20Y0 (thousands)

20X0	20X1	20X2	20X3	20X4	20X5	20X6	20X7	20X8	20X9	20Y0
50	59	46	54	65	51	60	70	56	66	76

You are required:

(a)   to calculate a **three-year** moving average trend;

(b)   to plot the series and the trend on the same graph.

8.2   Yelesol ice cream

The sales of Yelesol ice cream for the last twelve quarters are as follows:

		Sales (thousand units)	Moving annual total (thousand units)
20X1	Q$_4$	14	-
20X2	Q$_1$	16	-
			100
	Q$_2$	30	
			104
	Q$_3$	40	
			104
	Q$_4$	18	
			108
20X3	Q$_1$	16	
			112
	Q$_2$	34	
			108
	Q$_3$	44	
			108
	Q$_4$	14	
20X4			112
	Q$_1$	16	
			120
	Q$_2$	38	-
	Q$_3$	52	-
	Q$_4$		

You are required:

(a)   to calculate a centred moving average;

(b)   to plot a graph of the data and the centred moving average.

9   ANSWERS TO MULTIPLE CHOICE QUESTIONS

9.1   B

Trend = y = 23.87 + 2.4x
Trend = 23.87 + 2.4 (21) = 74.27

Forecast = trend × seasonal variation
⇒ forecast = 74.27 × 1.08 = 80.21

9.2   3 point moving totals are 18,22,26,30,34, i.e. they are increasing by constant amount, hence the moving average would also increase by constant amount and therefore would follow a straight line.

Answer **B**

10   ANSWERS TO PRACTICE QUESTIONS

10.1   Brand Y

(a)

Year	Sales ('000)	Moving Sums in 3's	average trend
X0	50		
X1	59	155	51.7
X2	46	159	53.0
X3	54	165	55.0
X4	65	170	56.7
X5	51	176	58.7
X6	60	181	60.3
X7	70	186	62.0
X8	56	192	64.0
X9	66	198	66.0
Y0	76		

(b)   **Brand Y**

Annual sales of Brand Y and trend
20X0-20Y0

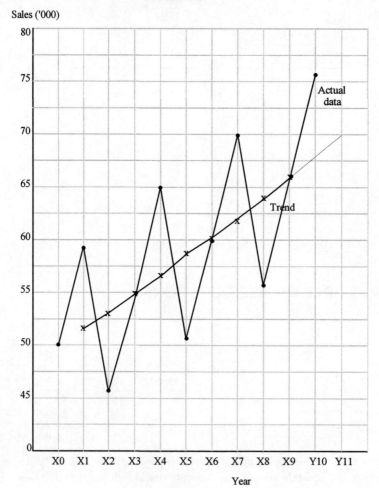

8.2   Yelesol ice cream

(a)

Year	Quarter	(000s) Sales	Moving total	Moving average (W1)	(a) Centred average (W2)
20X1	4	14			
20X2	1	16			
			100	25	
	2	30			25.5
			104	26	
	3	40			26.0
			104	26	
	4	18			26.5
			108	27	
20X3	1	16			27.5
			112	28	
	2	34			27.5
			108	27	
	3	44			27.0
			108	27	
	4	14			27.5
			112	28	
20X4	1	16			29.0
			120	30	
	2	38			
	3	52			
	4				

WORKINGS

(W1)   The moving average is found by dividing each four period total by 4.

e.g. $100 \div 4 = 25$
$104 \div 4 = 26$
etc.

(W2)   The centred moving average is calculated by taking pairs of data and finding their average.

e.g. $(25 + 26)/2 = 25.5$
$(26 + 26)/2 = 26.0$
$(26 + 27)/2 = 26.5$
$(27 + 28)/2 = 27.5$
etc.

(b)   **Graph showing sales of ice cream**

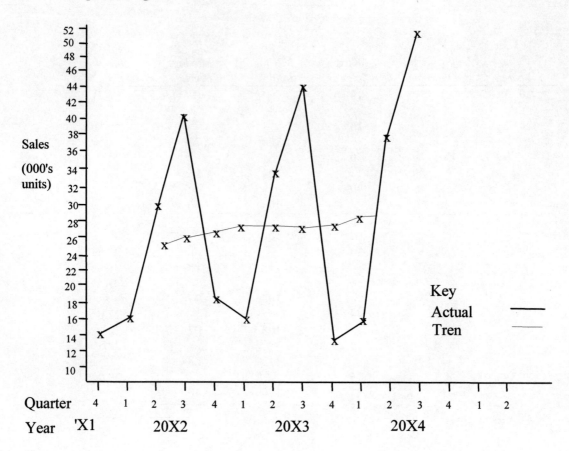

Chapter 24

RATIOS

PATHFINDER INTRODUCTION

This chapter covers the following elements of the CAT Official Teaching Guide. At the end of this chapter you should have learned these teaching guide elements thoroughly.

Session 24
Ratios
Syllabus reference n

- Calculate and explain gross profit margin, net profit margin, return on capital employed and asset turnover ratios
- Explain the significance of movements in these ratios over time

Putting the chapter in context

The last four chapters have been concerned with the collection, presentation and analysis of data to assist management in their planning and control functions. The next two chapters continue this theme, looking at the calculation of various ratios and other measures from data to help in the assessment of the performance of the business. This chapter concentrates on general profitability measures, whilst Chapter 25 looks at more specific indicators for separate parts of the business.

1   PROFITABILITY PERFORMANCE MEASURES

1.1   Introduction

In assessing the performance of a business, a major concern of management is, of course, whether or not the organisation is profitable and if so how profitable.

The following general types of profitability indicators will be considered in the final paragraphs of this chapter:

- gross profit and net profit measures;
- return on capital employed and its constituent elements.

1.2   Importance of profitability measures

The most obvious indicators of profit for an organisation are the gross profit and net profit figures. However these figures on their own do not give much information.

Suppose that an organisation has a net profit of £200,000. This would probably be an admirable figure for a small family business but disappointing for British Telecom.

Therefore the profit figure should be linked in some way to other figures in the profit and loss account or balance sheet in order to give some idea of the size of the business. Thus a £200,000 profit compared to sales of £400,000 would appear to be excellent whereas if sales were £4,000,000 one might not be so impressed.

Therefore one way of expressing the profit figures is as percentages of the sales or turnover of the business – the resulting measures being known as 'margins'.

1.3   Gross profit

Gross profit is made up as follows:

	£
Sales	x
Less: cost of sales	(x)
Gross profit	x

1.4   Gross profit margin

Definition   The **gross profit margin** is the gross profit figure expressed as a percentage of the sales for the period.

This is calculated as follows:

$$\frac{\text{Gross profit}}{\text{Sales}} \times 100$$

1.5   Activity

A profit and loss account is given for an organisation for the year ended 31 December 20X4.

	£	£
Sales		340,000
Cost of sales		226,000
		114,000
Less: Expenses		
Rent and rates	11,000	
Power, heat and light	6,000	
Wages	44,000	
Depreciation	10,000	
		71,000
Net profit		43,000

Calculate the gross profit margin.

1.6   Activity solution

Gross profit margin $= \dfrac{\text{Gross profit}}{\text{Sales}} \times 100$

$= \dfrac{114,000}{340,000} \times 100$

$= 33.5\%$

Conclusion   A gross profit margin measures the profit made on buying, making and then selling the products of the organisation.

A gross profit margin might change due to either a change in selling price or a change in the cost of these sales.

1.7 Net profit

Net profit is made up as follows:

	£
Sales	x
Less: Cost of sales	(x)
Gross profit	x
Less: Expenses	(x)
Net profit	x

1.8 Net profit margin

Definition The **net profit margin** is the net profit figure expressed as a percentage of sales.

The calculation is as follows:

$$\frac{\text{Net profit}}{\text{Sales}} \times 100$$

1.9 Activity

Using the profit and loss account from the previous example, printed below, what is the net profit margin?

	£	£
Sales		340,000
Cost of sales		226,000
		114,000
Less: Expenses		
Rent and rates	11,000	
Power, heat and light	6,000	
Wages	44,000	
Depreciation	10,000	
		71,000
Net profit		43,000

1.10 Activity solution

Net profit margin = $\dfrac{\text{Net profit}}{\text{Sales}} \times 100$

= $\dfrac{43,000}{340,000} \times 100$

= 12.6%

Conclusion The net profit margin measures the overall profitability of the organisation after deducting all expenses.

The net profit margin might change over a period due to a change in either the gross profit margin or expenses.

1.11 Return on capital employed

So far, when considering profitability indicators, profit has been compared to total sales or turnover to give a profitability margin, or percentage. Return on capital employed compares profit to the capital that has been used to earn that profit.

Definition   The **return on capital employed (ROCE)** is the net profit as a percentage of the capital of the business.

ROCE is calculated as:

$$\frac{\text{Profit}}{\text{Capital employed}} \times 100$$

1.12 Activity

The net profit of a business for a year is £10,000 and the total capital, or net assets, of the business are £80,000 at the end of the year. What is the return on capital employed?

1.13 Solution

ROCE $= \dfrac{\text{Profit}}{\text{Capital employed}} \times 100$

$= \dfrac{£10,000}{£80,000} \times 100$

$= 12.5\%$

1.14 Where does return on capital employed come from?

We shall see that the return on capital employed can be analysed as the product of two 'sub-ratios':

- net profit margin
- net asset turnover.

Where the net profit margin is, as before:

Net profit margin $= \dfrac{\text{Net profit}}{\text{Sales}} \times 100$

Asset turnover discussed in more detail in the next chapter, is calculated as:

Net asset turnover $= \dfrac{\text{Sales}}{\text{Net assets}}$

(*Tutorial note:* remember from the previous paragraph that net assets are equal to share capital plus reserves, or capital employed.)

The net asset turnover shows the amount of revenue generated from each £1 of net assets.

These two calculations can be combined:

$$\frac{\text{Net profit}}{\text{Sales}} \times \frac{\text{Sales}}{\text{Net assets}} \times 100$$

and simplified:

$$\frac{\text{Net profit}}{\text{Sales}} \times \frac{\text{Sales}}{\text{Net assets}} \times 100$$

to give return on capital employed:

$$\frac{\text{Net profit}}{\text{Net assets}} \times 100 \qquad \text{OR} \qquad \frac{\text{Net profit}}{\text{Capital employed}} \times 100$$

(*Tutorial note:* care must be taken to ensure that the same profit and capital employed figures are used throughout the calculation depending upon whether the return is for shareholders only or all long term capital providers.)

1.15   Activity

Given below is a profit and loss account and balance sheet:

Profit and loss account for the year ended 30 June 20X6

	£'000	£'000
Turnover		1,200
Cost of sales		680
Gross profit		520
Selling expenses	160	
Administrative expenses	170	
		330
		190
Interest paid and payable		30
Profit before tax		160
Tax		70
Profit after tax		90
Dividend		40
Retained profit		50

Balance sheet as at 30 June 20X6

	£'000	£'000
Fixed assets		650
Current assets	140	
Current liabilities	100	
Net current assets		40
		690
Long term liabilities:		
Bank loan		300
		390

Financed by:

Ordinary share capital	200
Reserves	190
	390

Show the return as capital employed figures and how it is made up.

1.16 Activity solution

Return on capital employed

$$= \frac{\text{Profit after tax}}{\text{Net assets(share capital plus reserves)}} \times 100$$

$$= \frac{90}{390} \times 100$$

$$= 23.08\%$$

Net profit margin $= \dfrac{\text{Profit after tax}}{\text{Turnover}} \times 100$

$$= \frac{90}{1,200} \times 100$$

$$= 7.5\%$$

Asset turnover $= \dfrac{\text{Turnover}}{\text{Net assets (share capital plus reserves)}}$

$$= \frac{1,200}{390} = 3.08$$

ROCE $= $ Net profit margin $\times$ Asset turnover $\times 100$

$$= 7.5\% \times 3.08 \times 100$$

$$= 23.10\% \text{ (difference is due to rounding)}$$

Conclusion   The use of the profit figures and capital employed figures must be consistent for net profit margin asset turnover and ROCE for the relationship to work.

Any changes in ROCE will therefore be investigated by firstly considering the profit margin and asset turnover. The change in ROCE may be explained by a change in profit margins or more or less effective use of assets, or indeed by a combination of the two.

2   SIGNIFICANCE OF MOVEMENTS IN PROFITABILITY RATIOS OVER TIME

2.1   Introduction

As with all ratios, a single figure in isolation is of little use in performance assessment. It must be **compared** with similar ratios reflecting:

- the performance of the business in previous years;
- the budgeted performance for the current year; and/or
- the performances of similar businesses.

As the syllabus implies, we shall concentrate here on the first of these, looking at changes in the profitability ratios over time. This will be illustrated by reference to the following summarised financial data.

2.2   Data for illustration

Summarised balance sheets at 30 June

	20X7		20X6	
	£'000	£'000	£'000	£'000
Fixed assets (net book value)		130		139
Current assets:				
Stock	42		37	
Debtors	29		23	
Bank	3		5	
	74		65	
Creditors: amounts falling due within one year:				
Trade creditors	36		55	
Taxation	10		10	
	46		65	
Net current assets		28		-
Total assets less current liabilities		158		139
Creditors: amounts falling due beyond one year:				
5% secured loan stock		40		40
		118		99
Share capital		60		60
Share premium account		17		17
Revaluation reserve		10		-
Profit and loss account		31		22
		118		99

Summarised profit and loss account for the year ended 30 June

	20X7		20X6	
	£'000	£'000	£'000	£'000
Sales		209		196
Opening stock	37		29	
Purchases	162		159	
	199		188	
Closing stock	42		37	
		157		151
Gross profit		52		45
Interest	2		2	
Depreciation	9		9	
Sundry expenses	14		11	
		25		22
Net profit		27		23
Taxation		10		10
Net profit after taxation		17		13
Dividends		8		7
Retained profit		9		6

2.3 Gross profit margin

In the illustration the ratios for the two years are as follows:

$$20X7 \qquad\qquad 20X6$$

$$\frac{52}{209} \times 100 = 24.9\% \qquad\qquad \frac{45}{196} \times 100 = 23.0\%$$

What can be learned from these figures? Clearly, the gross profit percentage has improved, a higher figure means a better return for investors, but it is not known why. Nor is it obvious whether these figures are better or worse than those which would be expected in a similar type of business. Before coming to definite conclusions one would need further information. For example, most businesses sell a wide range of products, usually with different gross profit margins. It may be that in 20X7 the **sales mix** changed and that a larger proportion of items with a high profit percentage were sold, thus increasing the overall gross profit percentage of the business.

Percentage change in sales

It is relevant to consider the change in sales at this point. The percentage growth in sales is:

$$\frac{209 - 196}{196} \times 100 = 6.6\%$$

This is not a significant increase. A larger increase might have given some evidence of the type of changes in trading conditions that may have occurred. An increase could be due to a larger quantity being sold, or to price increases.

2.4   Net profit margin

$$\frac{20X7}{209} \times 100 = 12.9\% \qquad\qquad \frac{20X6}{196} \times 100 = 11.7\%$$

What conclusions can be drawn from this apparent improvement? Very few! Since net profit equals gross profit less expenses, it would be useful to tabulate, for each of the two years, the various expenses and express them as a percentage of sales. A suitable tabulation might be:

	20X7		20X6	
	£'000	%	£'000	%
Sales	209	100.0	196	100.0
Cost of sales	157	75.1	151	77.0
Gross profit	52	24.9	45	23.0
Interest	(2)	(1.0)	(2)	(1.1)
Depreciation	(9)	(4.3)	(9)	(4.6)
Sundry expenses	(14)	(6.7)	(11)	(5.6)
Net profit	27	12.9	23	11.7

Given a detailed trading and profit and loss account, the above type of summary could be very useful. Care must be taken in interpreting the results, particularly since sales (£) are used as the denominator and an increase in sales (£) could be due to a combination of price and quantity effects.

Gross profit margin and net profit margin levels and how they change give an indication of how well an organisation is controlling its costs or increasing selling prices or quantities. If the two measures move in parallel, it may indicate stable efficiency but divergence suggests that cost structures are changing.

2.5   Return on capital employed (ROCE)

This is an important ratio as it relates profit to the capital invested in a business. Finance for a business is only available at a cost – loan stock finance requires interest payments and further finance from shareholders requires either the immediate payment of dividends or the expectation of higher dividends in the future. Therefore a business needs to maximise the profits per £ of capital employed.

Due to its importance the ROCE is sometimes referred to as the **primary ratio**.

There are several ways of measuring ROCE, but the essential point is to relate the profit figure used to its capital base e.g.

Total capital employed in the business

$$\frac{\text{Profit before interest and tax}}{\text{Share capital} + \text{reserves} + \text{long term liabilities}} \times 100$$

The denominator could alternatively be calculated as total assets less current liabilities.

Equity shareholders' capital employed

$$\frac{\text{Profit after interest but before tax}}{\text{Share capital} + \text{reserves}} \times 100$$

The denominator could alternatively be calculated as net assets.

Although it is better to base the calculation on average capital employed during the year, the calculation is often based on year-end capital employed (because there is insufficient data for all years to compute an average).

An increase in ROCE is considered good for shareholders, since the more profit is generated by the capital in a business the more is available each year either to distribute to investors (as dividend or interest) or to invest in making the business even more profitable.

2.6   Activity

Calculate ROCE for 20X6 and 20X7 using each of these alternatives.

2.7   Activity solution

Total capital employed

20X7	20X6
$\dfrac{(27+2)}{158} \times 100 = 18.4\%$	$\dfrac{(23+2)}{139} \times 100 = 18.0\%$

Equity capital employed

20X7	20X6
$\dfrac{27}{118} \times 100 = 22.9\%$	$\dfrac{23}{99} \times 100 = 23.2\%$

There is a slight improvement in total ROCE and a falling off in equity ROCE.

A reason for the variation is the revaluation of fixed assets during the year. This has the effect of increasing the denominator in 20X7 relative to 20X6 and creates an unfair comparison as it is likely that the fixed assets were worth more than their book value last year as well. It is not common, however, for UK companies to revalue their assets every year so that comparisons from year to year can be difficult.

The differences in returns for equity compared to total capital employed are significant. It means that equity shareholders have had a significant increase in their return because of the company's using fixed interest finance to enlarge the capital employed in the business.

3   CHAPTER SUMMARY

In this chapter we have considered how the calculation of financial ratios helps assess business performance. We shall now consider this in more detail in chapter 25.

4   SELF TEST QUESTIONS

4.1   What does the gross profit margin measure, and how might it change? (1.6)

4.2   What does the net profit margin measure, and how might it change? (1.10)

4.3   How is the return on capital employed measured? (1.11)

4.4   Into which ratios can the ROCE be sub-analysed? (1.14)

4.5   How should a ratio be used in assessing the performance of a business? (2.1)

5   MULTIPLE CHOICE QUESTION

5.1   A retailer buys in a product for £50 per unit and wishes to achieve 40% gross profit on sales. The selling price per unit must be

A	£70.00
B	£83.33
C	£90.00
D	£125.00

6   PRACTICE QUESTION

6.1   PQR plc

The following details have been extracted from the accounts of PQR plc for three years of recession. The company's year ends on 31 March.

	20X2 £m	20X3 £m	20X4 £m
Turnover (sales)	100	103	108
Gross profit	33.0	34.0	35.6
Net profit	15	15	15
Fixed assets	64	72	68
Stock	4	4	4
Debtors	8	11	15
Creditors	(5)	(6)	(6)
Cash at bank	5	-	-
Bank overdraft	-	6	5

Required:

(a)   Calculate, for each of the three years:

- gross profit percentage;
- net profit percentage.

(b)   Comment briefly on the ratios you have calculated.

7   ANSWER TO MULTIPLE CHOICE QUESTION

7.1   **B**

	£	%
Selling price		100
– Cost	50	(60)
= Gross profit		40

$\Rightarrow$ selling price is $\dfrac{£50}{60} \times 100 = £83.33$.

8   ANSWER TO PRACTICE QUESTION

8.1   PQR plc

(a)

		20X4	20X2	20X3
•	$\dfrac{\text{Gross profit}}{\text{Sales}} \times 100$	33%	33%	33%
•	$\dfrac{\text{Net profit}}{\text{Sales}} \times 100$	15%	14.6%	13.9%

(b)   These ratios indicate that PQR plc has been able to maintain its gross profit margin throughout the three year period, but has seen a slight decrease in its net profit percentage.

The overdraft would result in an interest charge which would affect profitability without changing the gross margin. This interest could be one of the causes of the reduction in the net profit percentage.

Chapter 25

PERFORMANCE INDICATORS

PATHFINDER INTRODUCTION

This chapter covers the following elements of the CAT Official Teaching Guide. At the end of this chapter you should have learned these teaching guide elements thoroughly.

Session 25
Performance indicators
Syllabus reference n

- Calculate and explain productivity, cost per unit, resource utilisation and profitability performance indicators for cost units, cost centres and profit centres
- Prepare and evaluate control ratios: efficiency, capacity and activity (also called volume)

Putting the chapter in context

This is the final chapter concerned with making data easy to assimilate. It explains the calculation of ratios and statistics used to indicate how a business is performing.

1 PRODUCTIVITY MEASURES

1.1 Introduction

In this chapter a variety of performance indicators will be examined. Performance indicators provide information to management as to how the business is operating. There is a huge range of such indicators, made up of financial information, non-financial information or a mixture of the two. This chapter will consider many types of performance indicators including productivity measures.

1.2 What is a productivity measure?

Definition   a **productivity measure** is a measure of the efficiency of an operation.

It relates the goods or services produced to the resources used to produce them. The most productive or efficient operation produces the maximum output from given resource inputs or alternatively, uses the minimum inputs for any given quantity or quality of output.

1.3 Production and productivity

It is important to be able to distinguish between production and productivity.

Production is the quantity of goods or services that are produced. Productivity is a measure of how efficiently those goods or services have been produced.

Production levels are reasonably straightforward for management to control as they can be increased by working more hours or taking on more employees, or decreased by cutting overtime or laying off employees. Production levels can also be increased by increasing productivity and vice versa.

Productivity however, is perhaps more difficult for management to control as it can only be increased by producing more goods or services in a set period of time, or alternatively, reaching set production targets in a shorter period of time.

1.4   Productivity ratios

Productivity is often analysed using three labour control ratios:

- production-volume ratio;
- capacity ratio; and
- productivity or efficiency ratio.

1.5   Activity

The budgeted output for a period is 2,000 units and the budgeted time for the production of these units is 200 hours.

The actual output in the period is 2,300 units and the actual time worked by the labour force is 180 hours.

1.6   Production/volume ratio

Definition   The **production/volume ratio** assesses the overall production. Over 100% indicates that overall production is above planned levels and below 100% indicates a shortfall compared to plans.

The production/volume ratio is calculated as:

$$\frac{\text{Actual output measured in standard hours}}{\text{Budgeted production hours}} \times 100$$

1.7   Solution - production/volume ratio

Standard hour	=	$\dfrac{2,000 \text{ units}}{200 \text{ hours}}$
	=	10 units
Actual output measured in standard hours	=	$\dfrac{2,300 \text{ units}}{10 \text{ units}}$
	=	230 standard hours
Production/volume ratio	=	$\dfrac{230}{200}$
	=	115%

This shows that production is 15% up on planned production levels.

1.8   Capacity ratio

Definition   The **capacity ratio** indicates worker capacity, in terms of the hours of working time that have been possible in a period.

The capacity ratio is calculated as:

$$\text{Capacity ratio} = \frac{\text{Actual hours worked}}{\text{Budgeted hours}} \times 100$$

1.9   Solution - capacity ratio

$$\text{Capacity ratio} = \frac{180 \text{ hours}}{200 \text{ hours}} = 90\%$$

Therefore this organisation had only 90% of the production hours anticipated available for production.

1.10   Efficiency ratio

Definition   The **efficiency ratio** is an indicator of productivity with the benchmark being 100%.

The efficiency ratio is calculated as follows:

$$\frac{\text{Actual output measured in standard hours}}{\text{Actual production hours}}$$

The efficiency ratio is often referred to as the productivity ratio.

1.11   Solution - efficiency ratio

$$\text{Efficiency ratio} \quad = \quad \frac{230}{180} \times 100\%$$

$$= \quad 127.78\%$$

This can be proved. The workers were expected to produce 10 units per hour, the standard hour. Therefore, in the 180 hours worked it would be expected that 1,800 units would be produced. In fact 2,300 units were produced. This is 27.78% more than anticipated (500/1,800).

1.12   Ratio relationships

The three ratios calculated above can be summarised diagrammatically as follows:

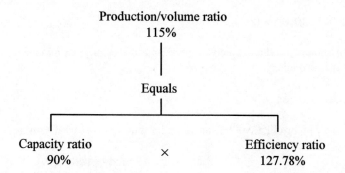

Conclusion   Note the difference between production and productivity. Production is output in terms of units e.g., 1,000 units per month. Productivity is this output expressed relative to a vital resource e.g., 10 cars per man per year or 12 tons of steel per man per month.

The efficiency or productivity ratio measures the productivity of the labour force in comparison to 100%. If the productivity ratio is higher than 100% then this indicates higher than anticipated productivity and if it is lower than 100% lower than anticipated productivity.

2   COST PER UNIT

2.1   Introduction

If management are to control the operations of an organisation, they must be well informed. One vital piece of information is the cost of the products produced. Indeed, a large part of this textbook has been devoted to just this.

This cost per product or cost per unit is needed to make a large number of management decisions, such as the selling price of the product, assessing the profitability of the product and comparing the actual cost of the product to the standard or budgeted cost.

Cost per unit is therefore a vital piece of management information and a very important performance indicator.

2.2   Types of cost per unit

A cost per unit can either be expressed as:

*   a direct cost per unit; or
*   a total cost per unit (including overhead or indirect costs).

The cost per unit can also be based upon either:

*   standard or budgeted costs; or
*   actual costs.

These types of unit cost can be combined to give four possible options:

*   direct standard cost;
*   direct actual cost;
*   total standard cost;
*   total actual cost.

2.3   Direct cost per unit

The simplest method of producing a cost figure for a unit of production is to show the cost as the total of the direct costs of that product.

2.4   Direct standard cost

The standard cost of a product will be shown on its standard cost card. An example of a standard cost card is given below.

Standard cost card - product X

	£
Direct materials (4 kg @ £2 per kg)	8.00
Direct labour (6 hours @ £3 per hour)	18.00
Direct expenses	1.00
Standard direct cost	27.00

The standard direct cost per unit can therefore be taken directly from the standard cost card as £27 for one unit of product X.

2.5   Direct actual cost

The actual costs of producing a product can be determined in different ways depending upon the type of product.

If the product is large and individual, generally known as a job, then all of the actual costs incurred will be recorded on a job card for that product and then totalled when the job is completed in order to give the cost per unit.

However in the majority of production situations the costs for producing a large number of the product over a period of time will be known in total. In order to determine the cost per unit the total of actual direct costs must be divided by the number of units produced.

2.6   Activity

During week 25 2,000 units of product x were produced. The actual direct costs incurred in the production of product X were as follows:

	£
Direct materials	17,500
Direct labour	38,500
Direct expenses	1,000
	57,000

What is the actual direct cost per unit of product X?

2.7   Activity solution

$$\text{Actual direct cost per unit} = \frac{\text{Actual direct costs}}{\text{Number of units produced}}$$

$$= \frac{£57,000}{2,000 \text{ units}}$$

$$= £28.50 \text{ per unit}$$

2.8   Total cost per unit

An alternative way of showing cost per unit is to show a total cost per unit. This total cost includes the direct costs already considered plus the indirect costs or overheads applicable to a unit of the product.

2.9   Total production cost

Production cost is made up of the following elements:

	£
Direct materials	x
Direct labour	x
Direct expenses	x
Total direct cost	x
Production overheads	x
Total production cost	x

Note that this includes only the overheads that are related to the production activity i.e. only factory overheads. This total production cost figure is sometimes also known as factory cost.

As with the direct costs, the production cost per unit can be expressed as a standard cost per unit or an actual cost per unit.

2.10   Standard production cost

In order to find the standard production cost per unit an estimate must be made for the amount of production overheads to be incurred in total in the period and also the amount of production for the period. The estimated production overhead is apportioned and absorbed into each unit of production on some pre-agreed basis.

This was covered in depth earlier on in the book.

2.11   Actual total production cost

The actual cost of a product will not of course be known until the end of the manufacturing or accounting period. At this point figures would be available for total direct costs, total production overhead and the number of units of a product produced. From this information the actual total production cost can be calculated.

2.12   Activity

During month 6 12,000 units of an organisation's only product were produced. The costs incurred in the production of that product were as follows.

	£
Direct materials	68,000
Direct labour	72,000
Direct expenses	15,000
Production overheads	54,000

Calculate the actual direct cost and actual total production cost for one unit of the organisation's product.

2.13   Activity solution

	£
Direct costs:	
Direct materials	68,000
Direct labour	72,000
Direct expenses	15,000
Total direct cost	155,000

$$\text{Direct cost per unit} = \frac{£155,000}{12,000 \text{ units}}$$

$$= £12.92 \text{ per unit}$$

	£
Total production costs:	
Direct costs	155,000
Production overhead	54,000
Total production costs	209,000

$$\text{Total production cost per unit} = \frac{£209,000}{12,000 \text{ units}}$$

$$= £17.42 \text{ per unit}$$

3   RESOURCE UTILISATION MEASURES

3.1   Introduction

Closely allied to productivity measures are measures of resource utilisation. Productivity looks at the amount of output for a particular input, be it labour hours or machine hours. Resource utilisation measures look more generally at how an organisation uses its inputs or resources.

The types of resource utilisation measures considered are:

- current ratio
- acid test or quick ratio
- stock turnover
- debtors turnover
- creditors turnover
- net asset turnover
- fixed asset turnover.

3.2   Current ratio

If an organisation is to succeed in the medium to long term it must be not only profitable but also liquid. This means that it has enough cash at any point in time to pay off its creditors as they fall due. Therefore indicators of the liquidity of a business are important factors as without liquidity an organisation cannot survive.

Definition   The **current ratio**, sometimes also called the working capital ratio gives some measure of the immediate liquidity position of a business. The current ratio answers the question has the business enough current assets to cover its current liabilities?

The current ratio is calculated as:

$$\frac{\text{Current assets}}{\text{Current liabilities}}$$

The current ratio determines how many times larger the current assets are than the current liabilities.

3.3   Activity

An organisation has current assets and current liabilities as follows at the end of June and July 20X8:

	June £'000	July £'000
Current assets:		
Stock	230	260
Debtors	338	252
Cash	6	12
	574	524
Current liabilities:		
Bank overdraft	12	16
Trade creditors	200	210
	212	226

Calculate the current ratio at the end of each of these months.

3.4   Activity solution

	June	July
Current assets	574	524
Current liabilities	212	226
	2.7	2.3

(*Tutorial note:* an overdraft is viewed to be technically a liability that is due on demand.)

Conclusion   The current ratio measures in general terms how safe an organisation is in terms of liquidity. If it were able to turn all of its current assets into cash would it be able to pay off all of its current liabilities?

3.5   Acid test ratio

In the previous paragraph an indication of the liquidity of an organisation was given by calculating the current ratio. This determined how much larger the current assets were than the current liabilities. However, whereas most of the current liabilities are likely to be trade creditors for whom payment will be due reasonably soon, one of the current assets is an item that it may take much longer to turn into cash. The asset concerned is stock.

For the stock to be turned into cash, firstly a buyer has to be found and the stock sold and then the money has to be collected from the buyer. All of this may take a considerable amount of time.

In order to overcome this problem a further liquidity ratio, the acid test or quick ratio, is calculated which excludes stock from the current assets figure.

Definition   The **acid test ratio** is calculated as:

$$\frac{\text{Current assets - stock}}{\text{Current liabilities}}$$

3.6   Activity

The previous activity is given again below.

An organisation has current assets and current liabilities as follows at the end of June and July 20X8.

	June £'000	July £'000
Current assets:		
Stock	230	260
Debtors	338	252
Cash	6	12
	574	524
Current liabilities:		
Bank overdraft	12	16
Trade creditors	200	210
	212	226

Calculate the acid test ratio at the end of each of these months.

3.7 Activity solution

	June X8 £'000	July X8 £'000
Current assets	574	524
Less: Stock	230	260
	344	264
Current liabilities	212	226
Acid test ratio	$\dfrac{344}{212}$	$\dfrac{264}{226}$
	= 1.6	= 1.2

Conclusion   The acid test ratio measures, perhaps more genuinely, how liquid an organisation is. If the bank were to call in the overdraft and the trade creditors require immediate payment then would the organisation be able to call upon enough cash to satisfy these demands?

3.8 Stock turnover ratio

Stock is necessary for most organisations to satisfy customer demand. However a balance has to be found between holding enough stock to satisfy demand and the cost of having too much capital tied up in stock. The stock turnover ratio can help management in its control of stock levels.

Definition   The **stock turnover ratio** can be calculated in one of two ways:

(1) $\dfrac{\text{Cost of sales}}{\text{Average stock level during the period}}$

This gives a measure of the number of times that stock turns over during the period.

(2) $\dfrac{\text{Average stock level during the period}}{\text{Cost of sales}} \times 365$

This gives the number of days that stock is held on average.

3.9 Activity

The stock level of an organisation on 1 January 20X5 was £10,200 and on 31 December 20X5 had risen to £11,200. The cost of sales figure for the period was £107,000.

Calculate stock turnover using both methods shown above.

3.10 Activity solution

The average stock level for the period is determined by adding together the opening and closing stock and dividing by two.

Average stock   = $\dfrac{10,200+11,200}{2}$

=   £10,700

Stock turnover:

(1)

$$\frac{\text{Cost of sales}}{\text{Average stock level during the period}}$$

$$\frac{£107,000}{£10,700} = 10 \text{ times}$$

This indicates that stock turns over on average 10 times during the year.

(2)

$$\frac{\text{Average stock level during the period}}{\text{Cost of sales}} \times 365$$

$$\frac{£10,700}{£107,000} \times 365 = 36.5 \text{ days}$$

This indicates that stock turns over every 36.5 days.

Conclusion   The stock turnover measure gives an indication of the speed at which an organisation uses up and replaces its stock. Different types of business will have different stock turnover periods. For example, a jeweller is likely to have a low stock turnover whereas a seller of fresh fish would hopefully have a very high stock turnover.

3.11   Debtors turnover

If a business makes sales on credit then it will specify its credit terms on the invoice. However not all debtors will pay up within the specified time scale.

The debtors turnover indicator is also known as the debt collection period and it measures the average collection period for the organisation's debts.

Definition   **Debtors turnover** is calculated as:

$$\frac{\text{Average or closing trade debtors}}{\text{Credit sales for the year}} \times 365$$

3.12   Activity

The debtors at 1 January 20X5 for an organisation were £12,000 and at 31 December 20X5 were £10,000. Credit sales for the year totalled £80,000.

Calculate the debtors turnover figure.

3.13   Solution

As both the opening and closing debtors figure is given, average trade debtors can be calculated:

Average trade debtors $= \dfrac{£12,000 + £10,000}{2}$

$= £11,000$

Debtors turnover $= \dfrac{£11,000}{£80,000} \times 365$

$= 50$ days

Conclusion   The debtor turnover period measures the amount of time on average that it takes for the debtors to pay up. The actual debtor turnover can be compared to the credit terms of the organisation to assess the effectiveness of credit control procedures.

3.14   Creditors turnover

Just as debtors turnover gives an indication of the average amount of credit being allowed to credit customers, so the creditors turnover indicates the average amount of credit being taken from suppliers. Credit from suppliers is effectively a form of short term finance as it allows goods to be purchased and used before payment has to be made. The effective utilisation of this resource will therefore need to be monitored by management.

Definition   **Creditors turnover** is calculated as:

$$\frac{\text{Average or closing trade creditors}}{\text{Credit purchases for the year}} \times 365$$

Again, as with debtors turnover, it is also acceptable to calculate creditors turnover as:

$$\frac{\text{Closing trade creditors}}{\text{Credit purchases for the year}} \times 365$$

3.15   Activity

The following is a balance sheet extract for an organisation:

	20X7 £	20X8 £
Current liabilities:		
Trade creditors	9,800	12,300

Of the total purchases for the year of £94,000 only £79,000 were on credit terms.

Calculate the creditors turnover.

3.16   Activity solution

Average trade creditors $= \dfrac{£9,800 + £12,300}{2}$

$= £11,050$

Creditors turnover $= \dfrac{£11,050}{£79,000} \times 365$

$= 51$ days

(*Tutorial note:* if only the closing creditors figure had been given then it would have been quite acceptable to have calculated the creditors turnover using closing creditors rather than average creditors.)

Conclusion   The creditor turnover measures how long on average an organisation takes to pay off its creditors. The higher the creditor turnover figure the greater is the time being taken between receipt of goods and payment for them. This is advantageous in purely financial terms but an organisation does run the risk of the loss of supplier goodwill or quantity discounts.

3.17   Net asset turnover

The resource utilisation indicators considered so far have concentrated on the amounts of assets and liabilities in relation to each other. Asset turnover compares the turnover or sales from the profit and loss account with the assets of the business.

Definition   Net asset turnover is calculated as:

$$\frac{\text{Turnover or sales}}{\text{Net assets}}$$

The resultant figure shows the amount of turnover or sales revenue for every pound of net assets.

3.18   Activity

The summarised balance sheet of an organisation at 31 December 20X4 is given below. If the turnover for 20X4 is £250,000 then what is the net asset turnover?

Balance sheet summary extract as at 31 December 20X4

	£	£
Fixed assets		340,000
Current assets	58,000	
Current liabilities	38,000	
		20,000
		360,000
Long term liabilities		120,000
		240,000

3.19   Activity solution

Net asset turnover $= \dfrac{\text{Turnover or sales}}{\text{Net assets}}$

$= \dfrac{£250,000}{£240,000}$

$= 1.04$

(*Tutorial note:* remember net assets are not only fixed assets plus net current assets but any long term liabilities must also be subtracted.)

Conclusion   The **net asset turnover** indicator shows how well, or effectively, the net assets of the organisation have been used. It shows how much revenue has been earned for each £1 of net assets.

In the example above this means therefore that for every £1 of net assets £1.04 of turnover has been earned. If management were able to increase the turnover using the same net assets then the profit of the organisation would be likely to increase.

3.20 Fixed asset turnover

In a similar manner to net asset turnover the fixed asset turnover measures the amount of revenue earned for every £1 of fixed assets. It is therefore a measure of the efficient utilisation of the fixed assets.

Definition   **Fixed asset turnover** is calculated as:

$$\frac{\text{Turnover or sales}}{\text{Fixed assets}}$$

3.21 Activity

The summarised balance sheet from the previous activity is given below. The turnover for the year was £250,000.

Balance sheet as at 31 December 20X4

	£	£
Fixed assets		340,000
Current assets	58,000	
Current liabilities	38,000	
		20,000
		360,000
Long term liabilities		120,000
		240,000

What is the fixed asset turnover and what does this figure mean?

3.22 Activity solution

$$\text{Fixed asset turnover} = \frac{\text{Turnover or sales}}{\text{Fixed assets}}$$

$$= \frac{£250,000}{£340,000}$$

$$= 0.74$$

This indicates that for every £1 of fixed assets that the organisation has £0.74 is earned in revenue.

Conclusion   Different types of organisation will have different levels of fixed asset turnover.

Some organisations such as computer software businesses might have high fixed asset turnover figures as they tend to have fairly low fixed assets as most of their assets are the people that work for them. In contrast a manufacturing organisation that owns its factory and a great deal of plant and machinery is likely to have a much lower fixed asset turnover figure.

4 CHAPTER SUMMARY

In this chapter the use of ratios and statistics to measure performance has been considered, as well as the importance of interpreting figures calculated.

5 SELF TEST QUESTIONS

5.1   What is a productivity measure? (1.2)

5.2   How is the production/volume ratio calculated? (1.6)

5.3   How is the efficiency or productivity ratio calculated? (1.10)

5.4   Name four different ways to calculate a cost per unit? (2.2)

5.5   How is the current ratio calculated? (3.2)

5.6   Why might an acid test ratio be of more use than a current ratio? (3.5)

5.7   What are the two methods of calculating stock turnover? (3.8)

5.8   What does net asset turnover measure? (3.17)

6   PRACTICE QUESTIONS

6.1   Ratios

(a)   X, Y and Z are the members of a team making metal brackets. The expected output of the team is 6,000 brackets per week. The basic working week is 40 hours per employee. During week 2 of the year X worked for 40 hours, Y 39 and Z 38 hours. The output of brackets for the week was 6,786.

Calculate the team's production/volume ratio, capacity ratio and efficiency ratio.

(b)   In the context of the output from a factory or group of workers, define and distinguish 'production' and 'productivity'.

6.2   Extracts

Below is an extract from a company's balance sheet

	31 May 20X4 £	31 May 20X5 £
Current assets:		
Stock	8,600	9,200
Debtors	5,100	5,000
Bank	1,500	-
Cash	800	200
Current liabilities:		
Bank overdraft	-	2,300
Trade creditors	6,100	7,500

Calculate the current ratio and the acid test ratio for the two years. Then comment on what these ratios reveal.

7   ANSWERS TO PRACTICE QUESTIONS

7.1   Ratios

(a)   Standard hour $= \dfrac{6,000 \text{ units}}{40 \times 3 \text{ hours}}$

$= 50 \text{ units}$

The production/volume ratio is calculated as:

$$\frac{\text{Actual output measured in standard hours}}{\text{Budgeted production hours}} \times 100$$

Actual output in standard hours $\qquad = \dfrac{6,786}{50}$

$= 135.72$

Production/volume ratio $\dfrac{135.72}{40 \times 3} \times 100 \qquad = 113.1\%$

The capacity ratio is calculated as follows:

$$\text{Capacity ratio} = \frac{\text{Actual hours worked}}{\text{Budgeted hours}} \times 100$$

$$= \frac{40 + 39 + 38}{120} \times 100 = \uparrow 97.5\%$$

The efficiency ratio is calculated as follows:

$$\frac{\text{Actual output measured in standard hours}}{\text{Actual production hours}}$$

$$= \frac{135.72}{40 + 39 + 38} \times 100$$

$$= 116\%$$

Summary

The relationship between the ratios is as follows:

$$\text{Capacity} \times \text{efficiency} = \text{production volume}$$

$$0.975 \times 1.16 = 1.131$$

(b)   The term *production* usually refers to the quantity of output produced, whereas *productivity* is the measure of the relationship between production output and specific units of input (in terms of human or physical resources) in a specific time, e.g.:

	Factory 1	*Factory 2*
Production output	10,000 units of X	12,000 units of X
Time taken	400 man-hours	500 man-hours
Productivity per man-hour	25 units	24 units

Thus, production is higher in factory 2, but productivity is lower.

Note: production may also be used to denote the general manufacturing activity of a business.

7.2   Extracts

31 May 20X4

Current assets $\qquad = £8,600 + £5,100 + £1,500 + £800$

$= £16,000$

Current liabilities $\qquad = £6,100$

Current ratio $= \dfrac{£16,000}{£6,100}$

$= 2.6$

31 May 20X5

Current assets $= £9,200 + £5,000 + £200$

$= £14,400$

Current liabilities $= £2,300 + 7,500$

$= £9,800$

Current ratio $= \dfrac{£14,400}{£9,800}$

$= 1.5$

The current ratio has decreased dramatically over the year and reflects in particular the change from a balance at the bank to a bank overdraft.

31 May 20X4

Current assets - stock $= £5,100 + £1,500 + £800$

$= £7,400$

Current liabilities $= £6,100$

Acid test ratio $= \dfrac{£7,400}{£6,100}$

$= 1.2$

31 May 20X5

Current assets - stock $= £5,000 + £200$

$= £5,200$

Current liabilities $= £2,300 + £7,500$

$= £9,800$

Acid test ratio $= \dfrac{£5,200}{£9,800}$

$= 0.5$

The acid test ratio has fallen dramatically and this may indicate a liquidity problem.

◆ FOULKS*lynch*

CAT Order Form

4 The Griffin Centre, Staines Road, Feltham, Middlesex, TW14 0HS, UK.
Tel: +44 (0) 20 8831 9990 Fax: + 44 (0) 20 8831 9991
Order online: www.foulkslynch.com Email: info@foulkslynch.com

New Syllabus Examination Dates: Dec 02 and Jun 03

		Textbooks 8/02 editions		Examination Kits Dec 02 only	
Level A					
A1	Transaction Accounting	£16.95	☐		
A2	Office Practice and Procedures	£16.95	☐		
A1 & A2	Transaction Accounting, Office Practice and Procedures			£8.95	☐
Level B					
B1	Financial Records and Accounting	£16.95	☐	£8.95	☐
B2	Cost Accounting Systems	£16.95	☐	£8.95	☐
B3	Information Technology	£16.95	☐	£8.95	☐
Level C					
C1	Financial Statements (Industry and Commerce)	£16.95	☐	£8.95	☐
C2	Information for Management	£16.95	☐	£8.95	☐
C3	Audit Practice and Procedure	£16.95	☐	£8.95	☐
C4	Preparing Taxation Computations and Returns FA 2001 (Dec 02)	£15.95	☐	£8.50	☐
C4	Preparing Taxation Computations and Returns FA 2002 (June 03)	£16.95	☐	£8.95	☐
C5	Managing Finances	£16.95	☐	£8.95	☐
C6	Managing People	£16.95	☐	£8.95	☐

Postage, Packaging and Delivery:

Study Text	First	Each Extra	Exam Kit	First	Each Extra
UK	£5.00	£2.00	UK	£5.00	£2.00
Europe (incl ROI and CI)	£7.00	£4.00	Europe (incl ROI and CI)	£7.00	£4.00
Rest of World	£22.00	£8.00	Rest of World	£22.00	£8.00

Postage, Packing and Delivery

Product Sub Total £..................	Post&Packing £.......................	Order Total £....................	(Payments in UK £ Sterling)

Customer Details

☐ Mr ☐ Mrs ☐ Ms ☐ Miss Other ....

Initials:................................. Surname: ....

Address: ....

....

....

Postcode: ....

Telephone: ....

Delivery Address – if different from above

Address: ....

....

Postcode: ....

Telephone: ....

Fax: ....

Payment

1. I enclose Cheque/PO/Bankers Draft for £......................................
   Please make cheques payable to **'Foulks Lynch'**.
2. Charge MasterCard/Visa/Switch A/C No:

Valid from: ☐☐☐ Expiry date: ☐☐☐

Issue No: (Switch only) ☐☐

Signature: .... Date: ....

Declaration

I agree to pay as indicated on this form and understand that Foulks Lynch Terms and Conditions apply (available on request).

Signature: .... Date: ....

Delivery please allow:
United Kingdom – 5 working days
Eire & EU Countries – 10 working days
Rest of World – 10 working days

Notes: All orders over 1kg will be fully tracked & insured. Signature required on receipt of order. Delivery times subject to stock availability.

Notes: Prices are correct at time of going to print but are subject to change

◈ **FOULKS** *lynch*